Rover 3500 Owners Workshop Manual

J H Haynes
Member of the Guild of Motoring Writers

and C D Barge
T Eng (CEI), AMIMI, AIRTE

Models covered
Rover 3500; 3500 SE, V8S, Vanden Plas, Vitesse
and Vanden Plas EFi; 3528 cc

(365-7S8)

ABCDE
FGHIJ
KLMNO
PQ

2

Haynes Publishing Group
Sparkford Nr Yeovil
Somerset BA22 7JJ England

Haynes Publications, Inc
861 Lawrence Drive
Newbury Park
California 91320 USA

Acknowledgements

Thanks are due to the Champion Sparking Plug Company Limited who supplied the illustrations showing spark plug conditions, to Holt Lloyd Limited who supplied the illustrations showing bodywork repair, and to Duckhams Oils who provided lubrication data.

Thanks are due to BL Cars UK Limited (now the Austin Rover Group Ltd) for the supply of technical information and certain illustrations. A special mention must go to Wincanton Garages and to Lucas Services, both of Yeovil, Somerset, who were particularly helpful in supplying information. Vincents of Yeovil Limited kindly lent a Vitesse model for research and photographic purposes during the preparation of the updated edition of the manual.

Lastly, special thanks are due to all those people at Sparkford who helped in the production of this manual.

British Library Cataloguing in Publication Data
Barge, C.D.
   Rover 3500 owners workshop manual.–
   (Owners Workshop Manuals).
   1. Rover automobile
   I. Title   II. Series
   629.28'722   TL215.R64
   ISBN 1-85010-363-1

Whilst every care is taken to ensure that the information in this manual is correct, no liability can be accepted by the authors or publishers for loss, damage or injury caused by any errors in, or omissions from, the information given.

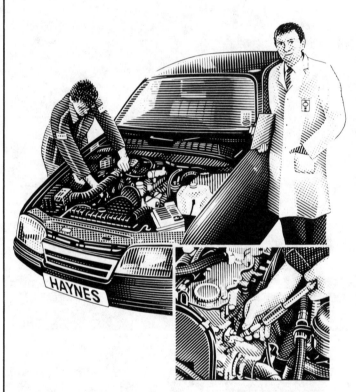

Contents

About this manual

Its aim

The aim of this manual is to help you get the best value from your vehicle. It can do so in several ways. It can help you decide what work must be done (even should you choose to get it done by a garage), provide information on routine maintenance and servicing, and give a logical course of action and diagnosis when random faults occur. However, it is hoped that you will use the manual by tackling the work yourself. On simpler jobs it may even be quicker than booking the car into a garage and going there twice, to leave and collect it. Perhaps most important, a lot of money can be saved by avoiding the costs a garage must charge to cover its labour and overheads.

The manual has drawings and descriptions to show the function of the various components so that their layout can be understood. Then the tasks are described and photographed in a step-by-step sequence so that even a novice can do the work.

Its arrangement

The manual is divided into thirteen Chapters, each covering a logical sub-division of the vehicle. The Chapters are each divided into Sections, numbered with single figures, eg 5; and the Sections into paragraphs (or sub-sections), with decimal numbers following on from the Section they are in, eg 5.1, 5.2, 5.3 etc.

It is freely illustrated, especially in those parts where there is a detailed sequence of operations to be carried out. There are two forms of illustration: figures and photographs. The figures are numbered in sequence with decimal numbers, according to their position in the Chapter – eg Fig. 6.4 is the fourth drawing/illustration in Chapter 6. Photographs carry the same number (either individually or in related groups) as the Section or sub-section to which they relate.

There is an alphabetical index at the back of the manual as well as a contents list at the front. Each Chapter is also preceded by its own individual contents list.

References to the 'left' or 'right' of the vehicle are in the sense of a person in the driver's seat facing forwards.

Unless otherwise stated, nuts and bolts are removed by turning anti-clockwise, and tightened by turning clockwise.

Vehicle manufacturers continually make changes to specifications and recommendations, and these, when notified, are incorporated into our manuals at the earliest opportunity.

Whilst every care is taken to ensure that the information in this manual is correct, no liability can be accepted by the authors or publishers for loss, damage or injury caused by any errors in, or omissions from, the information given.

Introduction to the Rover 3500

The Rover 3500 SDI model was introduced in June 1976 and took the place of the 'old' Rover 3500 which utilized the Rover 2000 type bodyshell.

The V8 engine fitted to the SDI was inherited from its predecessor but has undergone various modifications to achieve both improved performance and fuel economy.

The bodyshell of the SDI is of the five-door type, the fifth door taking the form of an opening hatchback. Its striking shape was evolved as a result of extensive wind tunnel tests and the result is an aerodynamically near-perfect body producing very little drag.

In basic form the SDI is very well appointed, but optional extras such as alloy road wheels, electric windows and Dunlop Denovo tyres can be specified.

Comfort, safety, economy and performance were all prime considerations during the design and manufacturing stages, and the application of all these qualities makes the Rover 3500 SDI an exceptional car.

All references to 'BL Cars' or 'BL dealers' should now read 'Austin Rover' and 'Rover dealers'.

Buying spare parts
and vehicle identification numbers

Buying spare parts

Spare parts are available from many sources. BL Cars have many dealers throughout the UK, and other dealers, accessory stores and motor factors will also stock Rover spare parts. Our advice regarding spare part sources is as follows:

Officially appointed vehicle main dealers – This is the best source of parts which are peculiar to your vehicle and are otherwise not generally available (eg complete cylinder heads, internal transmission components, badges, interior trim etc). It is also the only place at which you should buy parts if your vehicle is still under warranty. To be sure of obtaining the correct parts it will always be necessary to give the storeman your vehicle's engine and chassis number, and if possible, to take the 'old' part along for positive identification. Remember that many parts are available on a factory exchange scheme – any parts returned should always be clean! It obviously makes good sense to go straight to the specialists on your vehicle for this type of part, for they are best equipped to supply you.

Other dealers and auto accessory shops – These are often very good places to buy materials and components needed for the maintenance of your vehicle (eg oil filters, spark plugs, bulbs, fan belts, oils and greases, touch-up paint, filler paste etc). They also sell general accessories, usually have convenient opening hours, charge lower prices and can often be found not far from home.

Motor factors – Good factors will stock all of the more important components which wear out relatively quickly (eg clutch components, piston, valves, exhaust systems, brake cylinders/pipes/hoses/seals/shoes and pads etc). Motor factors will often provide new or reconditioned components on a part exchange basis – this can save a considerable amount of money.

Vehicle identification numbers

Modifications are a continuing and unpublicised process in vehicle manufacture. Spare parts manuals and lists are compiled on a numerical basis, the individual vehicle numbers being essential to identify correctly the component required.

The vehicle identification number is the number used for registration purposes; this is stamped on the right-hand side of the bulkhead panel (photo) on early models, or on a plate fixed to the driver's side centre door pillar on later models.

The engine number is stamped on the top face of the cylinder block on the oil filler side of the engine. The number is just visible and can be viewed by looking between the exhaust manifold branches. On later models, the engine number may be located on the left-hand side of the cylinder block, adjacent to the dipstick tube.

The vehicle identification number

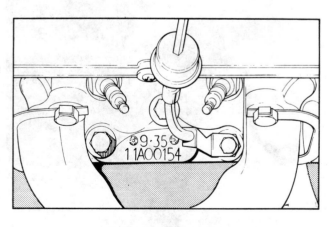

Location of engine number

Rover 3500 (SDI)

Jacking and towing

Jacking

The jack supplied with the car should be used whenever it is necessary to raise the car for changing a roadwheel (photo). Jacking points are provided at the front and rear of the car at both sides. When jacking the car up, the chock supplied in the car's tool kit (photo) should be placed in front of or behind the roadwheel diagonally opposite the wheel being raised, in addition to applying the handbrake.

If the car is to be raised for maintenance/repair operations it is permissible to jack up on the suspension subframe, rear axle or bodyframe sidemembers. Place a suitable wooden packing piece on the jack head to prevent damage to the car metalwork.

Towing precautions

Towing eyes are provided at the front and rear of the bodyframe sidemembers, just behind the bumpers. No other points should be used for towing.

Certain precautions must be observed before towing a Rover 3500 if damage is to be avoided.

Manual gearbox models **must not** be towed with the rear wheels on the ground unless the propeller shaft has been disconnected at the rear axle (and properly secured) or removed completely.

Automatic transmission models may be towed without disconnecting the propeller shaft, provided that:

(a) Transmission failure is not the reason for seeking a tow
(b) An extra quart (1.2 litres) of ATF is added to the transmission
(c) The towing distance does not exceed 30 miles (50 km)
(d) The towing speed does not exceed 30 mph (50 kph)

On all models, make sure that the front spoiler (when fitted) is not damaged by towing attachments or by contact with trailer ramps. Make sure that the steering is unlocked and remember that power steering and brake servo assistance will not be available if the engine is not running.

Using the vehicle jack to raise the rear right-hand roadwheel

The vehicle tool kit: wheel chock, wheel brace and spark plug spanner

Tools and working facilities

Introduction

A selection of good tools is a fundamental requirement for anyone contemplating the maintenance and repair of a motor vehicle. For the owner who does not possess any, their purchase will prove a considerable expense, offsetting some of the savings made by doing-it-yourself. However, provided that the tools purchased meet the relevant national safety standards and are of good quality, they will last for many years and prove an extremely worthwhile investment.

To help the average owner to decide which tools are needed to carry out the various tasks detailed in this manual, we have compiled three lists of tools under the following headings: *Maintenance and minor repair, Repair and overhaul,* and *Special.* The newcomer to practical mechanics should start off with the *Maintenance and minor repair* tool kit and confine himself to the simpler jobs around the vehicle. Then, as his confidence and experience grows, he can undertake more difficult tasks, buying extra tools as, and when, they are needed. In this way, a *Maintenance and minor repair* tool kit can be built up into a *Repair and overhaul* tool kit over a considerable period of time without any major cash outlays. The experienced do-it-yourselfer will have a tool kit good enough for most repair and overhaul procedures and will add tools from the *Special* category when he feels the expense is justified by the amount of use to which these tools will be put.

It is obviously not possible to cover the subject of tools fully here. For those who wish to learn more about tools and their use there is a book entitled *How to Choose and Use Car Tools* available from the publishers of this manual.

Maintenance and minor repair tool kit

The tools given in this list should be considered as a minimum requirement if routine maintenance, servicing and minor repair operations are to be undertaken. We recommend the purchase of combination spanners (ring one end, open-ended the other); although more expensive than open-ended ones, they do give the advantages of both types of spanner.

Combination spanners – $\frac{7}{16}$, $\frac{1}{2}$, $\frac{9}{16}$, $\frac{5}{8}$, $\frac{11}{16}$, $\frac{3}{4}$, $\frac{13}{16}$, $\frac{15}{16}$, in
Combination spanners - 10, 13, 17, 19, 22 mm
Adjustable spanner - 9 inch
Engine sump/gearbox/rear axle drain plug key (where applicable)
Spark plug spanner (with rubber insert)
Spark plug gap adjustment tool
Set of feeler gauges
Brake adjuster spanner (where applicable)
Brake bleed nipple spanner
Screwdriver - 4 in long x $\frac{1}{4}$ in dia (flat blade)
Screwdriver - 4 in long x $\frac{1}{4}$ in dia (cross blade)
Combination pliers - 6 inch
Hacksaw, junior
Tyre pump
Tyre pressure gauge
Grease gun (where applicable)
Oil can
Fine emery cloth (1 sheet)
Wire brush (small)
Funnel (medium size)

Repair and overhaul tool kit

These tools are virtually essential for anyone undertaking any major repairs to a motor vehicle, and are additional to those given in the *Maintenance and minor repair* list. Included in this list is a comprehensive set of sockets. Although these are expensive they will be found invaluable as they are so versatile - particularly if various drives are included in the set. We recommend the $\frac{1}{2}$ in square-drive type, as this can be used with most proprietary torque wrenches. If you cannot afford a socket set, even bought piecemeal, then inexpensive tubular box spanners are a useful alternative.

The tools in this list will occasionally need to be supplemented by tools from the *Special* list.

Sockets (or box spanners) to cover range in previous list
Reversible ratchet drive (for use with sockets)
Extension piece, 10 inch (for use with sockets)
Universal joint (for use with sockets)
Torque wrench (for use with sockets)
'Mole' wrench - 8 inch
Ball pein hammer
Soft-faced hammer, plastic or rubber
Screwdriver - 6 in long x $\frac{5}{16}$ in dia (flat blade)
Screwdriver - 2 in long x $\frac{5}{16}$ in square (flat blade)
Screwdriver - 1$\frac{1}{2}$ in long x $\frac{1}{4}$ in dia (cross blade)
Screwdriver - 3 in long x $\frac{1}{8}$ in dia (electricians)
Pliers - electricians side cutters
Pliers - needle nosed
Pliers - circlip (internal and external)
Cold chisel - $\frac{1}{2}$ inch
Scriber (this can be made by grinding the end of a broken hacksaw blade)
Scraper (this can be made by flattening and sharpening one end of a piece of copper pipe)
Centre punch
Pin punch
Hacksaw
Valve grinding tool
Steel rule/straight edge
Allen keys
Selection of files
Wire brush (large)
Axle-stands
Jack (strong scissor or hydraulic type)

Special tools

The tools in this list are those which are not used regularly, are expensive to buy, or which need to be used in accordance with their manufacturers' instructions. Unless relatively difficult mechanical jobs are undertaken frequently, it will not be economic to buy many of these tools. Where this is the case, you could consider clubbing together with friends (or a motorists' club) to make a joint purchase, or borrowing the tools against a deposit from a local garage or tool hire specialist.

The following list contains only those tools and instruments freely available to the public, and not those special tools produced by the vehicle manufacturer specifically for its dealer network. You will find occasional references to these manufacturers' special tools in the text of this manual. Generally, an alternative method of doing the job without the vehicle manufacturer's special tool is given. However, sometimes, there is no alternative to using them. Where this is the case and the relevant tool cannot be bought or borrowed you will have to entrust the work to a franchised garage.

> Valve spring compressor
> Piston ring compressor
> Balljoint separator
> Universal hub/bearing puller
> Impact screwdriver
> Micrometer and/or vernier gauge
> Carburettor flow balancing device (where applicable)
> Dial gauge
> Stroboscopic timing light
> Dwell angle meter/tachometer
> Universal electrical multi-meter
> Cylinder compression gauge
> Lifting tackle
> Trolley jack
> Light with extension lead

Buying tools

For practically all tools, a tool factor is the best source since he will have a very comprehensive range compared with the average garage or accessory shop. Having said that, accessory shops often offer excellent quality tools at discount prices, so it pays to shop around.

There are plenty of good tools around at reasonable prices, but always aim to purchase items which meet the relevant national safety standards. If in doubt, ask the proprietor or manager of the shop for advice before making a purchase.

Care and maintenance of tools

Having purchased a reasonable tool kit, it is necessary to keep the tools in a clean serviceable condition. After use, always wipe off any dirt, grease and metal particles using a clean, dry cloth, before putting the tools away. Never leave them lying around after they have been used. A simple tool rack on the garage or workshop wall, for items such as screwdrivers and pliers is a good idea. Store all normal spanners and sockets in a metal box. Any measuring instruments, gauges, meters, etc, must be carefully stored where they cannot be damaged or become rusty.

Take a little care when tools are used. Hammer heads inevitably become marked and screwdrivers lose the keen edge on their blades fom time to time. A little timely attention with emery cloth or a file will soon restore items like this to a good serviceable finish.

Working facilities

Not to be forgotten when discussing tools, is the workshop itself. If anything more than routine maintenance is to be carried out, some form of suitable working area becomes essential.

It is appreciated that many an owner mechanic is forced by circumstances to remove an engine or similar item, without the benefit of a garage or workshop. Having done this, any repairs should always be done under the cover of a roof.

Wherever possible, any dismantling should be done on a clean flat workbench or table at a suitable working height.

Any workbench needs a vice: one with a jaw opening of 4 in (100 mm) is suitable for most jobs. As mentioned previously, some clean dry storage space is also required for tools, as well as the lubricants, cleaning fluids, touch-up paints and so on which become necessary.

Another item which may be required, and which has a much more general usage, is an electric drill with a chuck capacity of at least ⅜ in (8 mm). This, together with a good range of twist drills, is virtually essential for fitting accessories such as wing mirrors and reversing lights.

Last, but not least, always keep a supply of old newspapers and clean, lint-free rags available, and try to keep any working area as clean as possible.

Spanner jaw gap comparison table

Jaw gap (in)	Spanner size
0·250	¼ in AF
0·275	7 mm AF
0·312	5/16 in AF
0·315	8 mm AF
0·340	11/32 in AF; ⅛ in Whitworth
0·354	9 mm AF
0·375	⅜ in AF
0·393	10 mm AF
0·433	11 mm AF
0·437	7/16 in AF
0·445	3/16 in Whitworth; ¼ in BSF
0·472	12 mm AF
0·500	½ in AF
0·512	13 mm AF
0·525	¼ in Whitworth; 5/16 in BSF
0·551	14 mm AF
0·562	9/16 in AF
0·590	15 mm AF
0·600	5/16 in Whitworth; ⅜ in BSF
0·625	⅝ in AF
0·629	16 mm AF
0·669	17 mm AF
0·687	11/16 in AF
0·708	18 mm AF
0·710	⅜ in Whitworth; 7/16 in BSF
0·748	19 mm AF
0·750	¾ in AF
0·812	13/16 in AF
0·820	7/16 in Whitworth; ½ in BSF
0·866	22 mm AF
0·875	⅞ in AF
0·920	½ in Whitworth; 9/16 in BSF
0·937	15/16 in AF
0·944	24 mm AF
1·000	1 in AF
1·010	9/16 in Whitworth; ⅝ in BSF
1·023	26 mm AF
1·062	1 1/16 in AF; 27 mm AF
1·100	⅝ in Whitworth; 11/16 in BSF
1·125	1⅛ in AF
1·181	30 mm AF
1·200	11/16 in Whitworth; ¾ in BSF
1·250	1¼ in AF
1·259	32 mm AF
1·300	¾ in Whitworth; ⅞ in BSF
1·312	1 5/16 in AF
1·390	13/16 in Whitworth; 15/16 in BSF
1·417	36 mm AF
1·437	1 7/16 in AF
1·480	⅞ in Whitworth; 1 in BSF
1·500	1½ in AF
1·574	40 mm AF; 15/16 in Whitworth
1·614	41 mm AF
1·625	1⅝ in AF
1·670	1 in Whitworth; 1⅛ in BSF
1·687	1 11/16 in AF
1·811	46 mm AF
1·812	1 13/16 in AF
1·860	1⅛ in Whitworth; 1¼ in BSF
1·875	1⅞ in AF
1·968	50 mm AF
2·000	2 in AF
2·050	1¼ in Whitworth; 1⅜ in BSF
2·165	55 mm AF
2·362	60 mm AF

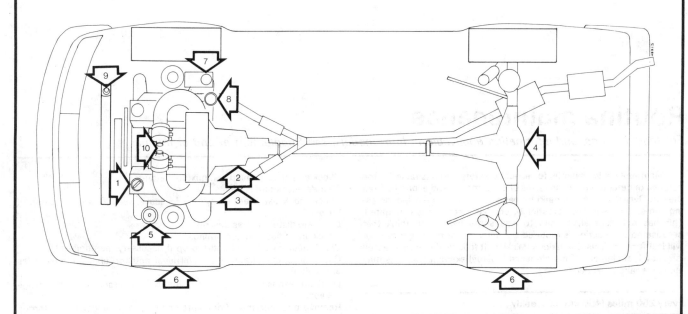

Recommended lubricants and fluids

Component or system	Lubricant type/specification	Duckhams recommendation
1 Engine*	Multigrade engine oil, viscosity SAE 10W/30, or 10W/40, 10W/50, or 15W/50 to BLS 22-OL-02 or API SE or SF	Duckhams QXR, Hypergrade, or 10W/40 Motor Oil
2 Manual gearbox Up to VIN 133000	Hypoid gear oil, viscosity SAE 75W EP (refill), or SAE 80EP (top-up only) to API-GL5 or MIL-L-2105B	Duckhams Hypoid 75 (refill) or Hypoid 80S (top-up only)
Later models	Type 'G' ATF to M2C 33F or M2C 33G	Duckhams Q-Matic
3 Automatic transmission Borg Warner GM 180	Type 'G' ATF to M2C 33F or M2C 33G Dexron IID type ATF	Duckhams Q-Matic Duckhams D-Matic
4 Rear axle	Hypoid gear oil, viscosity SAE 90EP to BLS 22-OL-03 or MIL-L-2105B	Duckhams Hypoid 90S
5 Power steering	Type 'G' ATF to M2C 33F or M2C 33G	Duckhams Q-Matic
6 Wheel bearings	Multi-purpose lithium based grease to NLGI 2	Duckhams LB10
7 and 8 Brake and clutch hydraulic reservoirs	Hydraulic fluid to FMVSS 116 DOT 3 or SAE J1703	Duckhams Universal Brake and Clutch Fluid
9 Cooling system	Ethylene glycol based antifreeze suitable for mixed metal engines	Duckhams Universal Antifreeze and Summer Coolant
10 Carburettor dashpots	Clean engine oil	Duckhams QXR, Hypergrade, or 10W/40 Motor Oil

***Note**: *Austin Rover specify a 10W/40 oil to meet warranty requirements for models produced after August 1983. Duckhams QXR and 10W/40 Motor Oil are available to meet these requirements*

Routine maintenance

For modifications, and information applicable to later models, see Supplement at end of manual

Maintenance is essential for ensuring safety and desirable for the purpose of getting the best in terms of performance and economy from the car. Over the years the need for periodic lubrication – oiling, greasing and so on – has been drastically reduced if not totally eliminated. This has unfortunately tended to lead some owners to think that because no such action is required the items either no longer exist or will last for ever. This is a serious delusion. It follows therefore that the largest initial element of maintenance is visual examination. This may lead to repairs or renewals.

Every 250 miles (400 km) or weekly

Check tyre pressures and inflate if necessary.
Check engine oil level and top-up if necessary (photo).
Check battery electrolyte level and top-up if necessary.
Check. and if necessary, top up water reservoir adding a screen wash such as Turtle Wax High Tech Screen Wash.
Check coolant level in reservoir and top-up if necessary (photo).
Check brake fluid level and top-up if necessary (photo).
Check clutch fluid level and top-up if necessary.
Check operation of all lights, instruments and controls.

Every 3000 miles (5000 km) or 3 months, whichever occurs first

Check for oil leaks from engine, transmission, steering rack and rear axle.
Check condition of cooling system hoses.
Check condition and tension of all drivebelts.
Check condition of clutch system hydraulic pipes.
Check power steering reservoir fluid level; top-up if necessary (photo).
Check power steering system for leaks, chafed or corroded pipes.
Check shock absorbers for fluid leaks.
Check condition of steering/suspension joints and gaiters.
Check condition of brake system hydraulic pipes and hoses.
Check condition of brake discs and pads.
Check condition of brake servo hose.
Check headlamp alignment and adjust if necessary.
Check windscreen wiper blades and renew if necessary.
Check condition of pipes and hoses in fuel system.
Check exhaust system for leaks and security.
Check condition of tyre treads and sidewalls.
Check roadwheel nuts for tightness.
Check condition and security of seats, seatbelts and anchorage points.
Check operation of seatbelt warning system.
Check operation of footbrake and handbrake.

Every 6000 miles (10 000 km) or 6 months, whichever occurs first

Renew engine oil filter.
Renew engine oil
Unscrew the carburettor piston dampers and top-up the oil level.
Lubricate carburettor linkages and pivots with engine oil or light lubricating oil.

Check engine idle speed and mixture settings.
Clean/adjust spark plugs.
Check crankcase breather system for leaks, security and condition of hoses.
Lubricate distributor, as described in Chapter 4.
Check and adjust ignition timing.
Check gearbox oil level and top-up if necessary (as applicable).
Check automatic transmission oil level and top-up if necessary (as applicable).
Lubricate exposed linkage of automatic transmission selector linkage (as applicable).
Remove dust and mud from slots and screen on underside of torque converter housing (as applicable).
Check rear axle oil level and top-up if necessary.
Check front wheel alignment (toe-in).
Check handbrake operation and adjust if necessary.
Check condition of brake linings and drums.
Clean battery terminals and smear with petroleum jelly.
Lubricate all locks, hinges and pivots (except steering lock).

Every 12 000 miles (20 000 km), whichever occurs first

Renew carburettor air cleaner elements.
Renew fuel filter(s).
Renew engine breather filter.
Check air intake temperature control system.
Clean engine flametrap.
Check operation of distributor vacuum unit.
Renew spark plugs.
Check tightness of propeller shaft coupling bolts.
Lubricate clutch pedal pivots (as applicable).
Check security of suspension fixings.
Adjust front hub bearing endfloat.
Lubricate brake pedal pivots.

Every 18 000 miles (30 000 km) or 18 months, whichever occurs first

Renew brake fluid.

Every 24 000 miles (40 000 km) or 2 years, whichever occurs first

Drain, flush and refill cooling system with new antifreeze solution.

Every 36 000 miles (60 000 km) or 3 years, whichever occurs first

Renew brake servo filter.
Renew all rubber seals and hoses in the braking system.
Renew brake pressure reducing valve.

Topping up the engine oil

Topping up brake fluid level

Topping up coolant level

Checking power steering fluid reservoir level

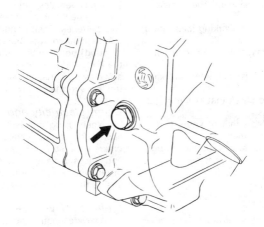

Location of gearbox oil level/filler plug

(on left-hand side of rear extension)

Safety first!

Professional motor mechanics are trained in safe working procedures. However enthusiastic you may be about getting on with the job in hand, do take the time to ensure that your safety is not put at risk. A moment's lack of attention can result in an accident, as can failure to observe certain elementary precautions.

There will always be new ways of having accidents, and the following points do not pretend to be a comprehensive list of all dangers; they are intended rather to make you aware of the risks and to encourage a safety-conscious approach to all work you carry out on your vehicle.

Essential DOs and DON'Ts

DON'T rely on a single jack when working underneath the vehicle. Always use reliable additional means of support, such as axle stands, securely placed under a part of the vehicle that you know will not give way.

DON'T attempt to loosen or tighten high-torque nuts (e.g. wheel hub nuts) while the vehicle is on a jack; it may be pulled off.

DON'T start the engine without first ascertaining that the transmission is in neutral (or 'Park' where applicable) and the parking brake applied.

DON'T suddenly remove the filler cap from a hot cooling system – cover it with a cloth and release the pressure gradually first, or you may get scalded by escaping coolant.

DON'T attempt to drain oil until you are sure it has cooled sufficiently to avoid scalding you.

DON'T grasp any part of the engine, exhaust or catalytic converter without first ascertaining that it is sufficiently cool to avoid burning you.

DON'T allow brake fluid or antifreeze to contact vehicle paintwork.

DON'T syphon toxic liquids such as fuel, brake fluid or antifreeze by mouth, or allow them to remain on your skin.

DON'T inhale dust – it may be injurious to health (see *Asbestos* below).

DON'T allow any spilt oil or grease to remain on the floor – wipe it up straight away, before someone slips on it.

DON'T use ill-fitting spanners or other tools which may slip and cause injury.

DON'T attempt to lift a heavy component which may be beyond your capability – get assistance.

DON'T rush to finish a job, or take unverified short cuts.

DON'T allow children or animals in or around an unattended vehicle.

DO wear eye protection when using power tools such as drill, sander, bench grinder etc, and when working under the vehicle.

DO use a barrier cream on your hands prior to undertaking dirty jobs – it will protect your skin from infection as well as making the dirt easier to remove afterwards; but make sure your hands aren't left slippery. Note that long-term contact with used engine oil can be a health hazard.

DO keep loose clothing (cuffs, tie etc) and long hair well out of the way of moving mechanical parts.

DO remove rings, wristwatch etc, before working on the vehicle – especially the electrical system.

DO ensure that any lifting tackle used has a safe working load rating adequate for the job.

DO keep your work area tidy – it is only too easy to fall over articles left lying around.

DO get someone to check periodically that all is well, when working alone on the vehicle.

DO carry out work in a logical sequence and check that everything is correctly assembled and tightened afterwards.

DO remember that your vehicle's safety affects that of yourself and others. If in doubt on any point, get specialist advice.

IF, in spite of following these precautions, you are unfortunate enough to injure yourself, seek medical attention as soon as possible.

Asbestos

Certain friction, insulating, sealing, and other products – such as brake linings, brake bands, clutch linings, torque converters, gaskets, etc – contain asbestos. *Extreme care must be taken to avoid inhalation of dust from such products since it is hazardous to health.* If in doubt, assume that they *do* contain asbestos.

Fire

Remember at all times that petrol (gasoline) is highly flammable. Never smoke, or have any kind of naked flame around, when working on the vehicle. But the risk does not end there – a spark caused by an electrical short-circuit, by two metal surfaces contacting each other, by careless use of tools, or even by static electricity built up in your body under certain conditions, can ignite petrol vapour, which in a confined space is highly explosive.

Always disconnect the battery earth (ground) terminal before working on any part of the fuel or electrical system, and never risk spilling fuel on to a hot engine or exhaust.

It is recommended that a fire extinguisher of a type suitable for fuel and electrical fires is kept handy in the garage or workplace at all times. Never try to extinguish a fuel or electrical fire with water.

Note: *Any reference to a 'torch' appearing in this manual should always be taken to mean a hand-held battery-operated electric lamp or flashlight. It does NOT mean a welding/gas torch or blowlamp.*

Fumes

Certain fumes are highly toxic and can quickly cause unconsciousness and even death if inhaled to any extent. Petrol (gasoline) vapour comes into this category, as do the vapours from certain solvents such as trichloroethylene. Any draining or pouring of such volatile fluids should be done in a well ventilated area.

When using cleaning fluids and solvents, read the instructions carefully. Never use materials from unmarked containers – they may give off poisonous vapours.

Never run the engine of a motor vehicle in an enclosed space such as a garage. Exhaust fumes contain carbon monoxide which is extremely poisonous; if you need to run the engine, always do so in the open air or at least have the rear of the vehicle outside the workplace.

If you are fortunate enough to have the use of an inspection pit, never drain or pour petrol, and never run the engine, while the vehicle is standing over it; the fumes, being heavier than air, will concentrate in the pit with possibly lethal results.

The battery

Never cause a spark, or allow a naked light, near the vehicle's battery. It will normally be giving off a certain amount of hydrogen gas, which is highly explosive.

Always disconnect the battery earth (ground) terminal before working on the fuel or electrical systems.

If possible, loosen the filler plugs or cover when charging the battery from an external source. Do not charge at an excessive rate or the battery may burst.

Take care when topping up and when carrying the battery. The acid electrolyte, even when diluted, is very corrosive and should not be allowed to contact the eyes or skin.

If you ever need to prepare electrolyte yourself, always add the acid slowly to the water, and never the other way round. Protect against splashes by wearing rubber gloves and goggles.

When jump starting a car using a booster battery, for negative earth (ground) vehicles, connect the jump leads in the following sequence: First connect one jump lead between the positive (+) terminals of the two batteries. Then connect the other jump lead first to the negative (–) terminal of the booster battery, and then to a good earthing (ground) point on the vehicle to be started, at least 18 in (45 cm) from the battery if possible. Ensure that hands and jump leads are clear of any moving parts, and that the two vehicles do not touch. Disconnect the leads in the reverse order.

Mains electricity and electrical equipment

When using an electric power tool, inspection light etc, always ensure that the appliance is correctly connected to its plug and that, where necessary, it is properly earthed (grounded). Do not use such appliances in damp conditions and, again, beware of creating a spark or applying excessive heat in the vicinity of fuel or fuel vapour. Also ensure that the appliances meet the relevant national safety standards.

Ignition HT voltage

A severe electric shock can result from touching certain parts of the ignition system, such as the HT leads, when the engine is running or being cranked, particularly if components are damp or the insulation is defective. Where an electronic ignition system is fitted, the HT voltage is much higher and could prove fatal.

Chapter 1 Engine

For modifications, and information applicable to later models, see Supplement at end of manual

Contents

Specifications

General

Type	8 cylinder, V-formation
Bore	3.50 in (89.90 mm)
Stroke	2.80 in (71.12 mm)
Cylinder capacity	3528 cc (215 cu in)
Compression ratio	9.35 : 1
BHP	155 at 5250 rpm
Maximum torque	198 lbf ft at 2500 rpm
Firing order	1,8,4,3,6,5,7,2 (No. 1 front, left cylinders odd numbers, right cylinders even numbers)

Cylinder block

Material	Aluminium alloy
Cylinder liner type	Dry
Liner material	Cast iron

Cylinder heads

Material	Aluminium alloy
Type	Two heads with separate alloy inlet manifold
Inlet and exhaust valve seat material	Brico alloy 318
Inlet and exhaust valve seat angle	$46 + \frac{1}{4}$ degrees

Crankshaft

Main journal diameter	2.2992 to 2.2997 in (58.400 to 58.413 mm)
Minimum regrind diameter	2.2592 to 2.2597 in (57.384 to 57.396 mm)
Crankpin journal diameter	2.0000 to 2.0005 in (50.800 to 50.812 mm)
Minimum regrind diameter	1.9600 to 1.9605 in (49.784 to 49.797 mm)
Crankshaft end thrust	Taken on thrust faces of centre main bearing
Crankshaft endfloat	0.004 to 0.008 in (0.10 to 0.20 mm)

Main bearings

Number and type	5 Vandervell shells
Material	Lead indium
Diametrical clearance	0.0009 to 0.0025 in (0.023 to 0.065 mm)
Undersizes	0.010 in (0.254 mm), 0.020 in (0.508 mm), 0.030 in (0.762), 0.040 in (1.016 mm)

Connecting rods

Type	Horizontally split big-end, plain small end
Length between centres	5.662 to 5.658 in (143.81 to 143.71 mm)
Big-end bearings:	
Type and material	Vandervell VP lead indium
Diametrical clearance	0.0006 to 0.0022 in (0.015 to 0.055 mm)
Endfloat on crankpin	0.006 to 0.014 in (0.15 to 0.37 mm)
Undersizes	0.010 in (0.254 mm), 0.020 in (0.508 mm), 0.030 in (0.762), 0.040 in (1.016 mm)

Gudgeon pins

Length	2.861 to 2.866 in (72.67 to 72.79 mm)
Diameter	0.8746 to 0.8749 in (22.215 to 22.220 mm)
Fit-in con rod	Press fit
Clearance in piston	0.0001 to 0.0003 in (0.002 to 0.007 mm)

Pistons

Type	Aluminium alloy with W slot skirt
Clearance:	
Top land	0.003 to 0.005 in (0.08 to 0.13 mm)
Skirt top	0.0016 to 0.0028 in (0.040 to 0.071 mm)
Skirt bottom	0.0007 to 0.0013 in (0.018 to 0.033 mm)

Pistons are available in standard service oversize 0.001 in (0.0254 mm) for honed standard size bores, and 0.010 in (0.25 mm) or 0.020 in (0.50 mm) oversizes for rebored cylinders. The clearance limits with new pistons and a new or rebored cylinder are 0.018 to 0.033 mm (0.0007 to 0.0013 in)

Piston rings

Number one compression ring type	Chrome parallel faced
Number two compression ring type	Stepped L shape and marked T or Top
Compression ring gap in bore	0.017 to 0.022 in (0.44 to 0.57 mm)
Compression ring clearance in groove	0.003 to 0.005 in (0.08 to 0.13 mm)
Oil control ring type	Perfect circle, type 98-6
Oil control ring gap in bore	0.0155 to 0.055 in (0.38 to 1.40 mm)

Camshaft

Location	Central
Bearings	Five non-serviceable
Timing chain	0.375 in (9.52 mm) pitch x 54 pitches

Valves

Inlet:

Overall length	4.590 to 4.620 in (116.58 to 117.34 mm)
Head diameter	1.565 to 1.575 in (39.75 to 40.00 mm)
Angle of face	45 degrees
Stem diameter	0.3402 to 0.3412 in (8.640 to 8.666 mm) at the head and increasing to 0.3407 to 0.3417 in (8.653 to 8.679 mm)
Stem to guide clearance	Top 0.001 to 0.003 in (0.02 to 0.07 mm); Bottom 0.0005 to 0.0025 in (0.013 to 0.0635 mm)

Exhaust:

Overall length	4.590 to 4.620 in (116.58 to 117.34 mm)
Head diameter	1.3475 to 1.3575 in (34.226 to 34.480 mm)
Angle of face	45 degrees
Stem diameter	0.3397 to 0.3407 in (8.628 to 8.654 mm) at the head and increasing to 0.3402 to 0.3412 in (8.640 to 8.666 mm)
Stem to guide clearance	Top 0.0015 to 0.0035 in (0.038 to 0.088 mm); Bottom 0.002 to 0.004 in (0.05 to 0.10 mm)

Valve spring length

1.577 in (40.05 mm) under load of 66.5 to 73.5 lbs (147.15 to 164.55 kg)

Valve timing

Inlet opens	30° BTDC
Inlet closes	75° ABDC
Inlet duration	285°
Inlet peak	112.5° ATDC
Exhaust opens	68° BBDC
Exhaust closes	37° ATDC
Exhaust duration	285°
Exhaust peak	105.5° BTDC

Engine lubrication

Oil capacity (with filter change)	9.7 pints (5.5 litres)
*Oil type/specification.	Multigrade engine oil, viscosity SAE 10W/30, 10W/40, 10W/50, or 15W/50 to BLS 22-OL-02 or API SE or SF (Duckhams QXR, Hypergrade or 10W/40 Motor Oil)
Oil filter	Champion C105

*Note: *Austin Rover specify a 10W/40 oil to meet warranty requirements for models produced after August 1983. Duckhams QXR and 10W/40 Motor Oil are available to meet these requirements*

Torque wrench settings

	lbf ft	Nm
Cylinder head bolts:		
Long and medium length	65 to 70	88.14 to 94.92
Short length	40 to 50	54.24 to 67.8
Main bearing cap bolts (one to four)	55	75
Rear main bearing cap bolts	70	95
Big-end bearing cap bolts	35	47
Rocker shaft bolts	30	40
Flywheel bolts	60	81
Oil pump cover bolts	9	11.5
Oil pressure relief valve cap	30	40
Timing cover bolts	20	27.5
Crankshaft pulley	140 to 160	190 to 217
Distributor drive gear to camshaft	40 to 45	54 to 61
Inlet manifold bolts	30	40
Exhaust manifold bolts	16	22
Automatic transmission driveplate to crankshaft mounting flange . . .	50 to 60	68 to 81
Starter motor mounting bolts	35	47
Power steering pump bolts	20 to 25	27 to 34
Water pump to timing cover	20	27.5
Torque converter housing to engine bolts:		
10 mm diameter	20 to 30	27 to 41
12 mm diameter	30 to 50	41 to 68
Driveplate to torque converter bolts	25 to 30	34 to 41

1 General description

Two banks of four cylinders form the main cylinder block. The material used is cast aluminium and the cylinder banks are set at a 90° angle. Each bore is fitted with a cylinder liner which may be rebored within certain tolerances.

The cylinder heads are also aluminium castings into which iron valve inserts and valve guides are fitted. The valves themselves are arranged in line and operate at a 10° angle above the bore centre line.

The camshaft lies between the two banks of cylinders above the crankshaft, it is driven by a single chain and is supported by five bearings. There is no chain tensioner.

To ensure quiet operation the tappets are hydraulically operated and valve clearance is automatically maintained without any adjustment being required.

The engine lubrication is conventional, the oil pressure pump being located within the timing chain cover and fitted with a normal full flow external oil filter.

IMPORTANT: Because the engine block is of aluminium construction, it is vital when tightening bolts related to the engine, that the correct torque settings specified should be strictly observed. It is also of equal importance that bolt lengths are noted and bolts replaced in the same location from which they were removed. Where specified, always use thread lubricant and sealer.

Because of the weight and bulk of this unit it is essential that substantial lifting tackle is available otherwise the removal of the engine is undesirable and impracticable for the average home mechanic. It is fully realised that any major overhaul tasks could be greatly facilitated if the unit were out of the frame and supported on an engine stand or strong workbench. For those who are determined, or find it really necessary to remove the unit, the procedure is outlined in the following text. In the following section all the items that can be tackled with the engine in position are progressively listed, and the owner must fully assess the amount of work entailed before starting the task.

2 Major operations which can be performed with the engine in the car

1 *Removal and refitting of radiator*
2 *Removal and refitting of carburettors and ancillaries*
3 *Removal and refitting of alternator*
4 *Removal and refitting of starter motor/solenoid*
5 *Removal and refitting of distributor*
6 *Removal and refitting of the cylinder heads and valve assembly*
7 *Removal and refitting of the water pump*
8 *Removal and refitting of the cooling fan*
9 *Removal and refitting of the inlet manifold*
10 *Removal and refitting of pistons and connecting rods*
11 *Removal and refitting of timing chain and wheels*
12 *Removal and refitting of sump and big-end bearings*
13 *Removal and refitting of oil pump*
15 *Removal and refitting of thermostat and water temperature transmitter*
16 *Removal and refitting of gearbox unit (manual and automatic) (types)*
17 *Removal and refitting of torque converter (automatic)*
18 *Removal and refitting of exhaust system*

3 Operations which require removal of the engine from the car

Any internal engine work (other than listed previously) such as refitting of crankshaft and main bearings, will require removal of the engine from the car.

4 Engine removal - general

Rover recommend that the engine is lifted complete with the gearbox or automatic transmission unit.

From a safety angle, the operator is advised to use adequate lifting tackle. He will need tackle that will give him at least three feet of lift.

At no time during the lifting operation should the operator be directly beneath the suspended weight of this large heavy engine.

5 Engine removal – with manual gearbox

1   Before commencing this task it is advisable to cover the wings with protective sheets.

2   Now disconnect both battery terminal connections and in the case of the positive (+) terminal remove the nut and pull out the bolt together with the attached wiring cables. This will save disconnecting any cables at the starter motor solenoid (photo).

3   Mark around the bonnet hinge plates with a soft pencil, pull out the wires to the under bonnet lights at the wiring connector and switch situated at the forward right-hand side of the engine compartment. Separate also the screen washer hose at the Y connector.

4   At this stage it will be necessary to enlist some assistance to support the bonnet before removing the hinge bolts and disconnecting the stay rod. The stay rod, at its lower end, slides along a slotted guide which is sandwiched between two nylon spacers, the whole assembly being retained by a single split pin.

5   After removing the bonnet store it in a safe place, preferably lying down.

6   To drain the radiator. Remove the expansion tank pressurised filler cap, open the radiator drain tap and drain off the coolant into a suitable container.

7   Drain the cylinder block. Drain taps are provided on each cylinder bank directly beneath the exhaust manifolds. When draining the cylinder block ensure that the car heater controls are set at Hot otherwise water will be trapped in the heater radiator and may cause air locks when refilling.

8   Should the coolant flow be very slow or non-existent, despite the fact that the drain tap(s) are opened fully, then it will be necessary to remove the drain tap(s) and clear the obstruction using a short length of stiff wire.

9   Whilst the cylinder block is draining move to the car interior and remove the gear change lever.

10 Slide the seats fully back and cover them to prevent grease on the fabric.

11 Unscrew the gear lever knob, and pull out the upper shroud, foam insulator and rubber grommet.

12 Remove the single bolt and lift off the ball cap. Remove the countersunk screw and the bolt which retain the hairpin bias screw clamp, then remove the clamp. Carefully prise the ends of the spring

aside and lift out the gear lever, taking care not to lose the strong anti-rattle spring and nylon plunger.

13 Now drain off the engine oil by removing the sump drain plug and allowing the oil to flow into a suitable container. After draining the sump refit the plug (photo).

14 Slacken the hose clips and disconnect the hoses at the radiator connections, including the two small bore hoses at the right-hand side.

15 Undo the two bolts securing the radiator upper mounting to the front body panel. Now lift the radiator straight up and out, taking care to prevent the cooling fan blades from damaging the matrix.

16 Pull off the emission control hoses at the carburettor connections and disconnect the large emission control hose from the left-hand rocker cover connection point. This larger hose is retained by a spring clip which can be released using a pair of pliers to squeeze together the clip ends.

17 Loosen the clips retaining the flexible trunking to the forward section of the air cleaner housing. Pull the trunking from the air cleaner and its other connection.

18 Snap open the spring retaining clips of the air cleaner housing and extract the air cleaner elements together with the curved elbows which are a push fit on the carburettor intakes.

19 The remainder of the air cleaner assembly can now be lifted away from its locating posts, two at either end, together with the engine breather filter which is attached by a hose to the rear of the left-hand rocker cover.

20 At the ignition coil pull out the main HT lead and after identifying the LT cables pull them out also (photo).

21 Disconnect the multi-plug from the heat sink at the inner wing panel (photo).

22 Slacken the fuel inlet pipe union at the forward end of the fuel filter, undo the nut and bolt at the carburettor air intake flange and pull back the fuel inlet pipe and support bracket. Plug the end of the filter to prevent the fuel escaping and tie the pipe back out of the way.

23 Pull the vacuum servo unit supply hose off at the inlet manifold connection.

24 Disconnect the braided earth strap at the point where it is bolted to the alternator mounting bracket (photo).

25 Adjacent to the battery is a multi-plug which can be separated simply by pulling the two parts away from one another (photo).

26 At the rear of the alternator is a further multi-plug which can be pulled off after releasing the special locking device which is an integral part of the multi-plug. The alternator harness can now be released from the engine retaining clip (photo).

27 Identify and pull off the leads from the oil pressure switch, and the oil pressure and coolant temperature transmitter units (photo).

28 Pull off the HT leads at the spark plugs and separate the leads from the plastic retainers attached to the rocker covers. Spring back the distributor cap retainers and lift away the distributor cap and leads.

29 Loosen the hose clips which retain the heater hoses to the inlet manifold connection pipes. Pull the hoses off and tie them back against the bulkhead.

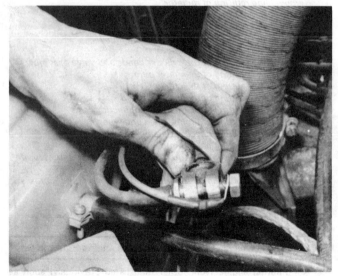

5.2 Removing the battery positive terminal. Note the cable joined to the clamp bolt

5.13 The sump drain plug

5.20 The main HT lead removed from the ignition coil

5.21 The multi-plug connector of the heat sink unit

5.24 The braided earth strap connected to the alternator mounting bracket

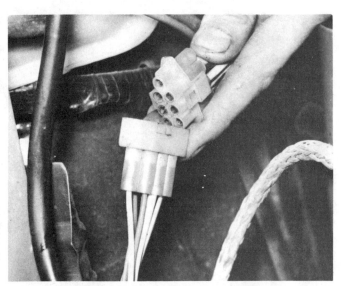

5.25 Separating the two parts of the engine multi-plug

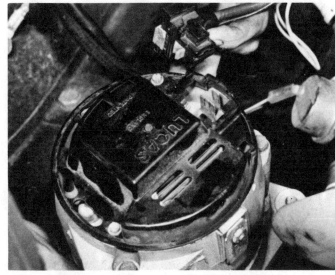

5.26 Disconnecting the alternator multi-plug

5.27 The oil pressure switch and pressure transmitter unit

5.30 Loosen the trunnion pinchbolt to release the choke inner cable

5.31 The throttle cable angled-fork retainer bracket

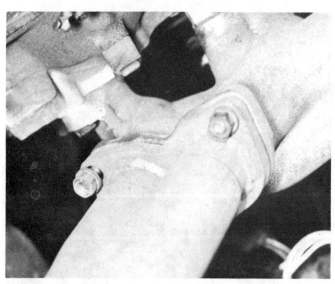
5.37A Remove the forward section of the exhaust system after disconnecting the manifold flange end and ...

5.37B ... the intermediate pipe connection flange joint

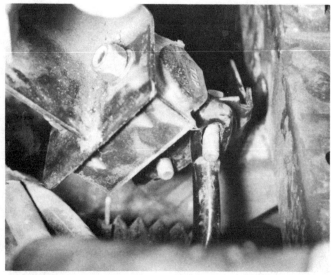
5.47A The right-hand engine mounting

5.47B The left-hand engine mounting

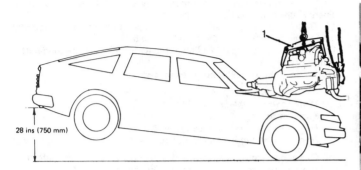

Fig. 1.1 Lifting the engine out by making use of the lifting eyes provided. Raise the rear of the car by approximately 28 in (75 cm)

1 *Engine sling*

28 ins (750 mm)

5.50 Lifting the engine clear of the car. Note the positioning of the lifting chains and the protective wooden block (arrowed)

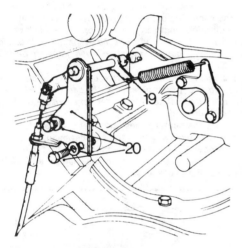

Fig. 1.2 Disconnecting the kickdown linkage (automatic transmission models)

19 *Return spring*
20 *Bracket and retaining bolts*

30 Slacken the trunnion pinchbolt, remove the cable retaining clip and pull out the choke cable from the right-hand carburettor (photo).
31 Slide the throttle cable upwards out of the angled fork retainer bracket and release the inner cable end nipple from the throttle quadrant (photo).
32 Disconnect the brown cable to the diagnostic socket at the connector.
33 Undo the power steering pump mounting bolts and move the pump to one side leaving the flexible hydraulic pipes still attached.
34 Undo the alternator mounting bolts and remove the alternator. This measure creates better access to the left-hand engine mounting.
35 Raise the car and support it on axle stands to gain access to the underside.
36 Mark the relative positions of the propeller shaft flanges in relation to the gearbox and rear axle flanges. Support the propeller shaft and remove the retaining bolts and nuts.
37 Remove the forward section of the exhaust system by disconnecting the manifold flange nuts, the support bracket bolts at the rear of the gearbox housing and the flange coupling bolts and nuts at the intermediate pipe flange joint (photo).
38 Pull off the reversing light switch wires and release the wiring harness from the retaining clip at the top of the gearbox.
39 Remove the two bolts securing the clutch slave cylinder to the bellhousing. Support the slave cylinder from a convenient point to prevent straining the pipe.

40 Undo the bolt, remove the retainer plate and pull out the speedometer cable.
41 Place a jack under the rear of the gearbox extension housing. Raise the jack until it is just in contact with the casing then remove the four bolts securing the gearbox crossmember to the body frame.
42 Remove the nuts and washers securing the engine mountings to the crossmember, but leave the bolts in position.
43 Arrange the lifting tackle and attach the slings or chains.
44 If the lifting brackets, provided at the forward and rear ends of the engine, are being utilised then it will be necessary to have the front roadwheels resting on the ground and the rear of the car raised by approximately 28 inches (75 cm) (Fig. 1.1). This measure will ensure that there will be adequate ground clearance. Remember to chock the front wheels if you use this method.
45 The method we used was to attach the lifting chains around the rear two exhaust manifold brackets at either side. This ensured that the engine was tipped at an angle which made removal a simple operation and did not necessitate raising the car at either end. If you choose to attach the lifting tackle in this manner insert wooden packing pieces between the outer faces of the rocker covers and the chains or slings to prevent damage.
46 Having arranged the lifting tackle as described in paragraphs 44 or 45, raise the hoist until the weight of the engine unit is just taken by the chains or slings.
47 Now remove the four bolts which are retaining the engine mountings to the crossmember (photos).
48 Having removed the bolts slowly raise the hoist and lower the jack which has been temporarily supporting the gearbox.
49 Check now before lifting the engine/gearbox assembly further that everything has been disconnected from the engine which would otherwise prevent it from being removed.
50 The procedure for removing the engine is to raise the hoist in stages at the same time drawing the hoist away from the car (photo). Alternatively the car can be pushed slowly away from the hoist if space permits.
51 When lifting the engine/gearbox assembly out from the car take care to avoid damaging any components. The reversing light control switch is, for example, very vulnerable and extremely fragile.
52 The gearbox can now be separated from the engine. Details of this procedure are given in Chapter 6.

6 Engine removal – with automatic transmission

1 The procedure for removing an engine fitted with automatic transmission is basically identical to that for cars fitted with a manual gearbox, and will present no problems, provided care is taken. The additional information covering the automatic transmission models is given in the following paragraphs.

2   When removing the radiator of automatic transmission models, two additional hoses will be found. These are flow and return hoses or the transmission oil cooler. The oil cooler is incorporated as an integral part of the engine cooling radiator. When disconnected the ends of the hoses and their connection points at the oil cooler should be plugged to prevent the loss of fluid and the ingress of dirt.

3   Automatic transmission models are fitted with a kickdown facility which is connected to the throttle linkage as shown in Fig. 1.2. In order to disconnect the kickdown cable first remove the return spring and then undo the two kickdown bracket bolts. The bracket, spindle and cable can now be separated from the assembly and placed to one side.

4   Disconnect the wires from the inhibitor/reverse lamp switch.

5   Move the speed selector lever to the P (park) position, then from beneath the car pull out the split pins, extract the washers and clevis pins securing the selector rod in position. Remove the selector rod from the gearbox and hand lever.

7   Ancillary engine components – removal prior to top overhaul (engine in car)

1   Drain the radiator and cylinder block as outlined in Section 5.

2   Disconnect the battery at the negative terminal.

3   Remove the air cleaner assembly as detailed in Section 5.

4   Pull off the HT leads at the spark plugs and ignition coil. Spring back the distributor cap clips, separate the HT leads from the rocker cover retainers and remove the distributor cap and leads.

5   Disconnect the water feed hose from the inlet manifold connection.

6   Disconnect the throttle and cable control cables – see Section 5.

7   Remove the emission control hoses from the carburettors and rocker cover box.

8   Undo the bolt securing the engine oil dipstick tube to the left-hand cylinder head.

9   Pull off the brake servo vacuum hose from the inlet manifold connection.

10   On automatic transmission models disconnect the transmission oil dipstick tube from the left-hand cylinder head.

11   Disconnect the kickdown cable and bracket on automatic transmission models as detailed in Section 5.

12   Pull off the wiring connection at the water temperature transmitter unit.

13   Remove the six water hoses as follows:

Radiator top hose
Water pump to inlet manifold
Pump to heater return pipe (front end)
Heater to inlet manifold feed pipe
Heater to inlet manifold return pipe

14   Disconnect the advance/retard vacuum pipe from the left-hand carburettor. Also detach the retaining clip on the manifold.

15   Pull off the carburettor vent pipes.

16   Pull off the block connector at the rear of the alternator. Undo the pivot and clamp bolts and remove the alternator.

8   Inlet manifold – removal and refitting

1   There are twelve bolts securing the inlet manifold to the cylinder heads. These should be eased off progressively and then removed. The bolts are of differing length so take note of their exact locations.

2   **Note**: *Any bolts removed from the cylinder heads or block should have their threads cleaned with a wire brush dipped in paraffin or clean petrol.*

   If this cleaning cannot be carried out immediately, it is vital that they are stored in petrol or paraffin as the sealant used when the bolts were originally fitted will tend to harden on exposure to the air making its removal difficult.

3   Move aside the heater hoses and the hose from the water pump, and ease the manifold away from the cylinder head.

4   Before removing the gasket clamps ensure that there is no coolant lying on top of the gasket. Remove the clamps and lift the gasket followed by the rubber gasket seals.

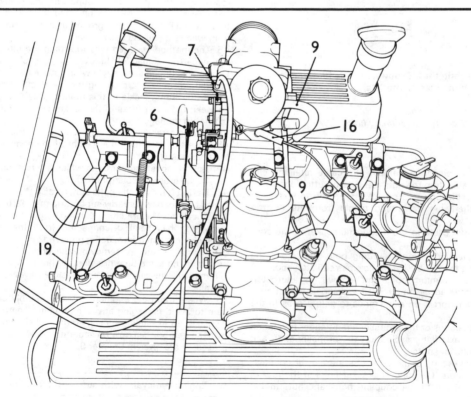

Fig. 1.3 The inlet manifold (with ancillaries) showing the locations of the retaining bolts

6 Throttle cable end connection	*9 Carburettor vent pipes*	*19 Two of the twelve manifold retaining bolts*
7 Choke cable	*16 Distributor vacuum pipe*	

9.1 The right-hand rocker gear shown with the rocker cover removed

9.2 Removing the rocker shaft assembly

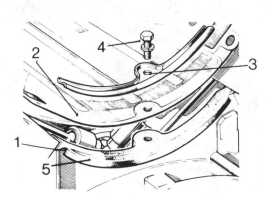

Fig. 1.4 Inlet manifold gasket detail

1 Notch for locating ends
2 Manifold gasket
3 Gasket clamp
4 Fixing bolt for clamp
5 Rubber gasket seals

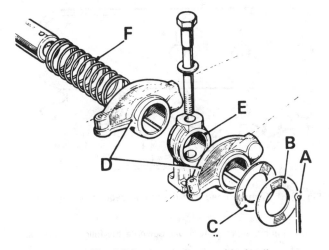

Fig. 1.5 Rocker shaft assembly detail

A Split pin
B Plain washer
C Wave washer
D Rocker arms
E Brackets
F Springs

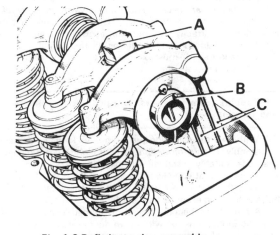

Fig. 1.6 Refitting rocker assembly

A Retaining bolt
B Notch to ensure correct alignment of oilways (Shafts are right and left-handed, care must be taken in reassembly)
C Pushrods

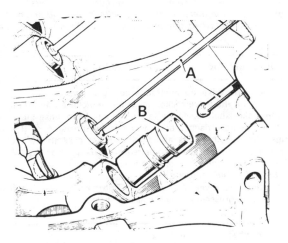

Fig. 1.7 Pushrods and hydraulic tappets

A Pushrod
B Tappet block

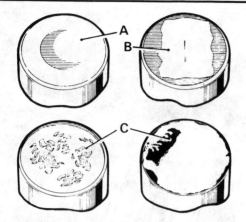

Fig. 1.8 Typical wear patterns on tappet block faces

A   Normal wear, tappet rotating correctly
B   Oblong pattern denoting faulty tappet rotation
C   Excessive wear patterns, pitting or soft spot

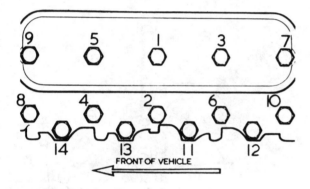

Fig. 1.10 Cylinder head bolt tightening sequence diagram

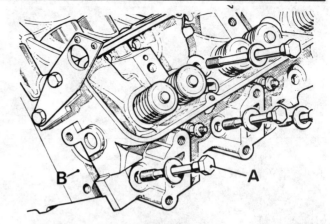

Fig. 1.9 Cylinder head bolt A and cylinder head B

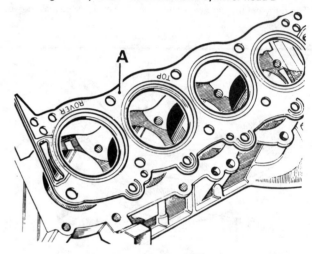

Fig. 1.11 Correct fitting of cylinder head gasket A

5   Refitting is a reversal of removal, but note the following points:

(a) Always use new seals and a new gasket. Coat the seals with
     silicone grease before fitting
(b) Apply sealing compound to the gasket, the manifold, the
     corners of the cylinder head and around the water passage
     joints
(c) Observe the 'FRONT' marking on the gasket
(d) Use thread lubricant/sealant on the securing bolts
(e) Tighten the manifold securing bolts evenly and progressively
     to the specified torque before tightening the gasket clamp
     bolts

9 Rocker assembly – removal and refitting

1   Remove the rocker covers (four securing screws) (photo).
2   To remove the valve rocker assembly, remove the four bolts that
hold the rocker shaft assembly to the cylinder head. Ease them off so
that the assembly rises gradually under the pressure of the valve
springs. Remove the bolts and lift the rocker assembly off (photo).
Note: If only the valve gear is to be removed, then it is advised that the
pushrods are left undisturbed; to remove them may result in displace-
ment of the hydraulic tappets.
3   Refitting is a reversal of removal. Tighten the rocker shaft bolts
evenly and progressively to the specified torque.

10 Rocker shafts – dismantling

1   If dismantling of the rocker shaft assembly is intended, then it
must be noted that the shafts are left and right-handed and must be
correctly refitted to align the oilways.
2   Remove the split pin from one end of the rocker shaft and slide off

the components carefully retaining them in the correct order of
sequence for reassembly, as follows: (A) split pin; (B) plain washer; (C)
wave washer; (D) rocker arm; (E) brackets; (F) springs (Fig. 1.10)
3   If new rocker arms are being fitted ensure that the protective
coating material used in storage is removed from the oil holes, and the
new rocker given a smearing of clean oil before fitting to the shaft.
4   Note: Two different types of rocker arm are used; they must be
fitted ensuring that the valve ends slope away from the brackets.
5   The rocker shafts are notched. This is to ensure that the oil feed
holes line up correctly. The notch in each case should be uppermost.
On the right-hand bank it should be located facing forwards, and on
the left-hand bank it must be located to the rear of the engine. (Fig.
1.11). Use a new split pin.

11 Tappets (cam followers) and pushrods – removal, inspection and refitting

1   Withdraw the pushrods and store them in the correct sequence for
reassembly. A strip of cardboard with eight holes punched to accept
the rods suitably inscribed RH or LH and the holes marked 1-8,
remembering that you always work from the front of the engine, numbering to the rear. Now carefully withdraw each tappet (cam follower),
block in turn and examine for wear (Fig. 1.7 and 1.8).
2   A tappet can become belled or rimmed at its lower end. In this
case the tappet must be withdrawn downwards entailing the removal
of the camshaft. A prominent wear pattern just above the lower end of
the body does not indicate the need for renewal, unless it is decidedly
grooved or scored. This condition is caused by the side thrust of the
cam against the body whilst the tappet is moving vertically.
3   Retain the tappet blocks in their correct sequence of removal.
4   Examine all the surfaces of the tappet blocks for blow holes or
scoring. If in doubt replace with new components.

5   Notes on tappet wear patterns (see Fig 1.8). The tappet block *must* rotate and the circular pattern (A) is normal. If a tappet does not rotate then it will be shown by an oblong wear pattern (B) and it is advisable to replace with new parts.

6   In the case of any other sort of uneven wear, eg, pitting or scoring, (C) being apparent, then replace with a new part.

7   Examine the area where the pushrod engages with the tappet for roughness or damage. Replace if necessary.

8   Similarly replace any pushrod so affected. Check each pushrod for straightness. A bent or distorted rod must be renewed.

9   Refitting is a reversal of removal.

12 Cylinder heads – removal and refitting

1   Proceed as previously outlined in Sections 7 to 11.

2   Disconnect the exhaust down pipe at the manifold flange on both sides.

3   If both cylinder heads are being removed then they should be marked left or right respectively.

4   Slacken the cylinder head retaining bolts evenly and progressively reversing the tightening sequence as shown in Fig. 1.10.

5   Remember that all bolts removed from any part of the aluminium engine must be cleaned immediately.

6   Lift off the cylinder heads and discard the head gaskets (photo).

7   For easier working it may be desirable to remove the exhaust manifolds. If this is done then the manifold gaskets will have to be renewed.

8   After four repetitive cylinder head removals, then it is strongly advised that all head bolts be replaced by new items.

9   During any servicing operations, renew any bolts which show signs of stretching (elongation) or thread damage.

10 Refitting is a reversal of removal, but note the following points:

   (a) *Do not use any jointing compound on the head gasket, and observe the 'TOP' marking (Fig. 1.11)*

   (b) *Coat the threads of the cylinder head bolts with thread lubricant/sealant*

   (c) *Tighten the bolts progressively, in the sequence shown in Fig. 1.10, to the specified torque. Note that two torques are specified, according to the length of the bolt. Long bolts are Nos. 1, 3 and 5; short bolts are Nos. 11, 12, 13 and 14; the remainder are of medium length*

13 Top overhaul (engine in car) – general

1   Having removed the cylinder heads it is now assumed that a top overhaul will follow.

2   For a straightforward decoke (decarbonisation) which includes the regrinding of the valves, the replacement of valve springs and/or perhaps the odd suspect valve, no special tools or equipment are required, and the procedures are common knowledge to the majority of home mechanics.

3   More ambitious work to the order of replacement of the valve guides or valve seats can be tackled by the amateur possessing the necessary facilities. However, it is always found less frustrating to go to the local motor engineering works, with the cylinder heads and new valve guides. Cylinder heads of this type are expensive items easily damaged by inexperienced hands, and the comparative cost of pressing out the old guides – or valve seats and refitting new ones, using professional equipment and knowledge is worth the effort and extra outlay.

14 Valves – removal

1   Though it is recommended that the service tool spring compressor is used, many standard universal valve lifting tools will do the job adequately.

2   Lay the cylinder head on its side and arrange the valve lifting tool so that the valve spring is sufficiently compressed allowing the split cotters to be removed (photo).

3   Release the valve lifting tool and withdraw the valve cap and

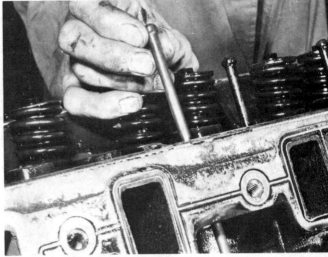
11.1A Withdrawing a pushrod followed ...

11.1B ... by the hydraulic tappet (cam follower)

12.6 Lifting off the right-hand cylinder head

14.2 Compressing the valve spring with a valve lifting tool

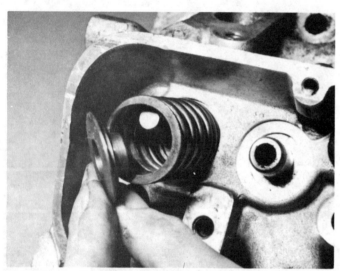

14.3 Removing the valve cup and spring

14.4 Withdrawing an exhaust valve

spring (photo).

4   The valve can now be withdrawn (photo). Should a burr exist on the end of the valve stem then this should be 'dressed off' with a file before withdrawing the valve otherwise the valve guide can be easily damaged.

5   Retain the valves in correct sequence of removal. Numbering from the front of the engine, use the same method of storing as for pushrods – see Section 11, paragraph 1.

15 Valves – servicing

1   Examine the heads of the valves for pitting and burning especially the heads of the exhaust valves. The valve seating should be examined at the same time. If the pitting on valve and seat is very slight, the marks can be removed by grinding the seats and valves together with coarse, and then fine grading paste. Where bad pitting has occurred to the valve seats it will be necessary to recut them and fit new valves. If the valve seats are so worn that they cannot be recut then it will be necessary to fit new valve seat inserts. These latter two jobs should be entrusted to the local Rover agent. In practice it is seldom that the seats are so badly worn that they require renewal. Normally, it is the exhaust valve that is too badly worn, and the owner can easily purchase a new set of valves and match them to the seats by valve grinding.

2   Clean the valves. Remove all the hard carbon deposit from the tops and underside using a blunt knife blade. Care should be taken not to mark or score the valve seating faces. Finish off the valve cleaning with a soft wire brush, again exercising care not to touch the seat face or valve stems.

16 Cylinder heads – servicing

1   Thoroughly clean the cylinder heads using paraffin, or, a mixture of paraffin and petrol, and dry off.

2   Clean the combustion chambers and ports using a brass wire brush. Draw clean rag through each valve guide bore.

3   Wash or, using a tyre pump, blow away all loose carbon particles.

17 Valves – grinding-in and refitting

1   Support the head on wooden blocks and start with No 1 valve.

2   Smear a trace of coarse or medium carborundum paste on the seat face and apply a suction grinder tool to the valve head. With a semi-rotary motion, grind the valve head to its seat, lifting the valve occasionally to redistribute the grinding paste. When a dull matt even surface finish is produced on both the valve seat and the valve, then wipe off the paste and repeat the porcess with fine carborundum paste, lifting and turning the valve to redistribute the paste as before. A light spring placed under the valve head will greatly ease this operation. When a smooth unbroken ring of light grey matt finish is produced, on both valve and valve seat faces, the grinding operation is completed.Scrape away all carbon from the valve head and the valve stem. Carefully clean away every trace of grinding compound, taking great care to leave none in the ports or in the valve guides. Clean the valves and valve seats with a paraffin soaked rag then with a clean rag. If an air line is available, blow the valves, valve guides and valve parts clean.

3   Finally give the cylinder head a rinse in clean paraffin to remove any remaining traces of valve grinding paste. Discard this paraffin, and dry the head with a clean non-fluffy rag.

4   Draw clean rag through each guide bore.

5   Refit the valves into their correct positions, oiling the stems as each valve is replaced in its respective guide.

6   Refit the valve springs; compress them, and secure the collets.

7   When all the valves and springs have been replaced, place the head face down on the bench and give each valve stem end a light tap with the butt end of a hammer handle or with a plastic headed mallet to ensure that the collets are well seated into their respective caps.

18 Cylinder heads – additional servicing hints

1   Take special care to protect the gasket faces from scoring or

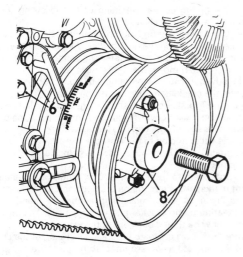

Fig. 1.12 Removing the crankshaft pulley assembly

6   Fixed timing pointer bracket retaining bolts
8   Crankshaft pulley bolt and spacer washer

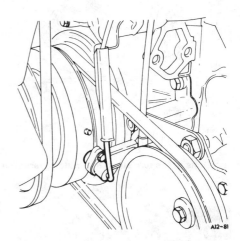

Fig. 1.13 The transducer unit(s)

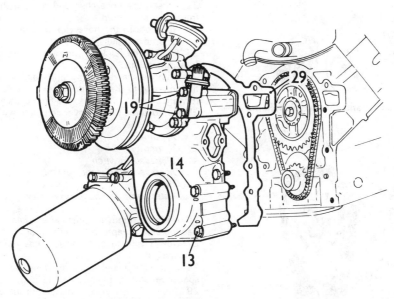

Fig. 1.14 The timing cover assembly

13   Transducer retaining bolt
14   Power steering pump bracket and vent pipe clip bolt
19   Diagnostic socket bracket bolts
29   Timing cover gasket

scratching, so after cleaning, work with the head placed on a clear bench with several layers of newspaper beneath it. Remove the top sheet as it gets dirty.

2   Destroy any rags that have been used to clean off carborundum grinding paste.

3   Have plenty of clean rag available. Do not attempt to grind-in any valves that are worn and possess sharp edges; instead, scrap and replace. It is advisable to have at least one or two spare (new or serviceable) exhaust and inlet valves to hand just in case.

4   Do not attempt work for which you do not possess adequate tools or equipment.

5   If the car has completed more than 30 000 miles (48 000 km) fit new valve springs.

6   Obtain all the aids and spares required for the job before starting. Do not try to 'make-do', especially with gaskets, seals and washers.

19   Timing cover, chain and gears – removal

1   Disconnect the battery at the negative terminal.

2   Remove the bonnet as detailed in Section 5.3.

3   Drain the cooling system and remove the radiator (Section 5).

4   Remove the alternator adjuster bolt and loosen the mounting bolts. Tip the alternator towards the engine and remove the drivebelt.

5   Undo the four nuts and bolts securing the cooling fan blades to the viscous coupling. Remove the fan blades.

6   Undo the crankshaft front pulley securing bolt.

7   Set the engine so that No. 1 piston (one nearest the radiator on the left -hand bank) is at TDC (on firing stroke). This may be observed by removing the spark plug and feeling the compression being generated as the piston travels up the cylinder bore or by removing the

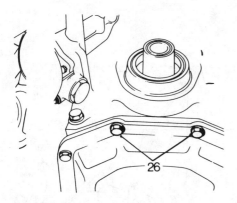

Fig. 1.15 Locations of the two sump to timing cover retaining bolts

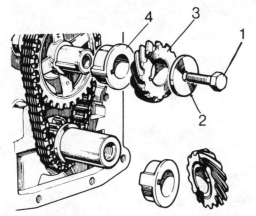

Fig. 1.16 Distributor drive gear and spacer components

| 1 | Retaining bolt | 3 | Distributor drive gear |
| 2 | Washer | 4 | Spacer |

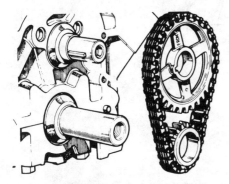

Fig. 1.17 Withdrawing the timing gears and chain

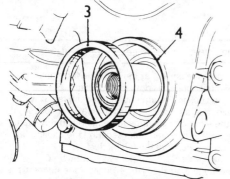

Fig. 1.18 The timing cover and oil seal

| 3 | Oil seal | 4 | Timing cover |

rocker cover and checking that the valves for No. 1 cylinder are closed and in balance.

8   Loosen the timing pointer retaining bolts and swing the pointer away from the crankshaft pulley.

9   Loosen the power steering pump mounting bolts, tip the pump towards the engine and slip the drivebelt off the pump pulley.

10 In order to remove the power steering pump drivebelt it will be found necessary to remove the transducer unit from its mounting bracket. The drivebelt can now be removed (Fig. 1.13).

11 Withdraw the crankshaft pulley assembly.

12 Pull off the HT leads from the spark plugs and ignition coil, release the leads from the rocker cover fixing clips, spring back the distributor cap retaining clips and lift the cap and leads away.

13 Pull off the vacuum pipe to the distributor vacuum capsule.

14 Make a mark on the distributor body to coincide with a centre line drawn along the rotor arm.

15 If it is intended to remove the distributor body, then similar realignment marks must be made on the body and the timing cover.

16 Refer to Fig. 1.14 and remove bolt number 14 thereby releasing the power steering pump bracket and vent pipe clip. The power steering pump can now be tipped back out of the way.

17 Separate the brown cable, to the transducer unit, at the connector.

18 Pull off the wire at the water temperature transmitter unit.

19 Undo the timing cover bolts which retain the diagnostic socket in position. Move the socket to one side and pull off its connection leads at the ignition coil.

20 Disconnect the electronic ignition system leads at the distributor and ignition coil and pull out the connector plug at the heat-sink unit.

21 Loosen the hose clips and remove the thermostat by-pass hose from the water pump.

22 Now loosen the hose clip securing the heater return pipe at the water pump and pull the pipe off.

23 Pull off the leads at the oil pressure switch and the oil pressure transmitter unit.

24 Remove the remaining bolts and a single nut, which retain the timing cover to the cylinder block, followed by two bolts securing the forward end of the sump to the timing cover.

25 Remove the timing cover complete with the following:

> Oil pump
> Distributor
> Oil pressure switch
> Oil pressure indicator transmitter
> Oil filter
> Water pump and pulley assembly

26 All bolts removed must be cleaned immediately as described in Section 8 paragraph 2 of this Chapter.

27 Now check that the engine has remained at TDC; if not, then reposition it.

28 Remove the centre bolt retaining the distributor skew gear and the spacer beneath it, and remove the components.

29 The chain wheels complete with the chain can now be slid away from their respective shafts.

30 If the rocker shafts are to remain in position do not, on any account, rotate the engine, otherwise damage will be caused by the valves and pistons coming into contact with one another.

20 Timing cover oil seal – renewal

1   The timing cover casing need not be removed in order to remove and insert the oil seal.

2   If the seal is to be renewed with the cover in situ then take care to prevent damaging the cover when extracting the old seal.

3   Where the timing cover has to be removed then drive the seal out from the cover squarely.

4   After extracting the old seal clean the housing and remove any burrs on the front edge.

5   Lubricate the new seal and fit it squarely with the lip face leading.

6   Drive the seal carefully into position with a suitable drift. A flat block of wood and a hammer are ideal if the cover has been removed. Otherwise a large socket or similar object can be used.

7   Check that the seal is seated to the correct depth and is square with the casing using a straight-edge as a guide.

21.4 Fitting the timing gears and chain

21.5 Close-up of the timing gear alignment marks

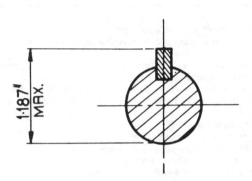

Fig. 1.19 Measuring the overall dimension of the shaft and keyway
The dimension shown must not be exceeded

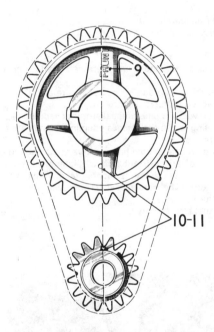

Fig. 1.20 Correct alignment of timing marks and keyways

9 'Front' marking (camshaft gear)   10-11 Alignment marks

21 Timing chain and gears – refitting

1   Assuming that great care has been taken and that neither the camshaft or crankshaft has been disturbed, proceed as follows.
2   First check the locating keys for signs of wear or looseness in their fixing grooves (keyway). If the keys have been removed or renewed then it is essential to ensure that the key is located to its full depth in the keyway. Measure the overall dimension of the shaft and key, and if this dimension exceeds 1.187 in (30.15 mm) it will be necessary to reduce the effective height of the key. This measure is important as the space between the key and the mating keyway of the timing wheel acts as an oilway for lubricating the drivegear.
3   Line up the timing marks on the timing wheels and carefully wrap the chain around both wheels keeping the timing marks aligned. **Note:** *the camshaft wheel is marked 'front'.* (Fig. 1.20).
4   Carefully pick up the whole assembly and offer it up to the shafts until you can just engage the keys in their respective locations (photo).
5   Recheck that the timing marks are still in line (photo).
6   If all is well, push the timing wheels fully home.
7   Slide on the spacer so that the larger diameter boss is facing away from the camshaft wheel.
8   Now refit the distributor skew drivegear and secure it in position with the larger washer and bolt. Tighten the bolt to the recommended torque setting.

22 Timing cover – refitting

1   Ensure that the mating faces of the timing cover and cylinder block are clean and free from all traces of old gasket residue. Fit a new oil seal as detailed in Section 20.
2   Apply jointing compound to both sides of the new timing cover gasket and position the gasket on the cylinder block face. Apply a little jointing compound to the forward end of the sump gasket which is exposed.
3   Inject engine oil through the suction port of the oil pump to prime the pump.
4   Reset the distributor rotor arm to a new position approximately 30° in advance of the final positioning mark. (This will compensate for the movement that will take place as the distributor engages the skew gear on replacement).

5   Offer up the timing cover and locate in position on the crankcase.

6   Make sure the alignment marks previously placed on the distributor, coincide correctly.

7   The threads of the fixing bolts should be cleaned already. Coat these with Thread Lubricant Sealant 3M EC776, (Rover part No 605764).

8   Locate and screw in the five bolts and one nut which retain the timing cover and the sump.

9   Place the power steering pump drive in position and refit the power steering pump, bracket and vent pipe clamp.

10 Slide the crankshaft front pulley assembly into position, taking care to relocate the power steering pump drivebelt in its respective groove.

11 Screw in the crankshaft pulley retaining bolt and tighten it to the recommended torque setting.

12 Refit the transducer unit taking care to locate it on the two dowels.

13 Refit the diagnostic socket.

14 Reconnect the wires and plug at the ignition coil and heat-sink unit.

15 Lever the power steering pump away from the engine and retension the drivebelt. With the pump so held tighten the mounting and adjuster bolts.

16 Reposition the timing pointer and tighten the securing bolts.

17 Slide the alternator towards the adjuster link and relocate the adjuster bolt; fit the drivebelt and retension it.

18 Reconnect the wires to the following components:

Oil pressure switch
Oil pressure transmitter unit
Water temperature transmitter
Transducer

19 Reconnect the heater return and thermostat bypass hoses to the water pump.

20 Refit the distributor cap and HT leads. Secure the HT leads to the retainer clips attached to the rocker box covers.

21 Reconnect the vacuum pipe to the distributor vacuum capsule.

22 Refit the cooling fan to the viscous coupling taking care to tighten the nuts and bolts evenly.

23 Fit the radiator, reconnect the hoses and refill the cooling system.

24 With the help of an assistant refit the bonnet remembering to realign it and to reconnect the under-bonnet lamp wires at the switch and block connector. The screenwasher hose will also have to be reconnected at the Y piece.

25 Finally reconnect the battery.

23 Timing chain assembly – refitting (after disturbance)

1   Dismantle the engine top end to remove the rocker shaft assemblies detailed in Section 9.

2   Set the engine, so that No. 1 piston is at TDC on the compression stroke.

3   Using the camshaft chain wheel as a temporary tool to rotate the camshaft fit it with the word 'front' facing away from the engine.

4   Slowly turn the camshaft until the timing mark, on the camshaft chain wheel, is exactly at the six o'clock position. **Note**: *these instructions are assuming that the engine is standing in its normal fitted position.*

5   Now the timing wheel can be removed and reassembled with the chain and crankshaft timing wheel as described previously in Section 21.3.

6   Proceed from Section 21, paragraph 3.

24 Timing chain and gears (automatic transmission) – removal

1   The procedures are the same as for manual gearbox cars. However, to facilitate the removal of the crankshaft pulley fixings, it is possible to lock the engine by placing a suitable bar between the lower engine face and a convenient bolt head within the bellhousing, accessible by removing the bellhousing cover plate. Do not use the starter ring gear for this purpose.

25 Camshaft – removal

1   Disconnect the battery at the negative terminal

2   Remove the bonnet as described in Section 5.3.

3   Drain the cooling system and remove the radiator as described in Section 5.

4   Remove the entire air cleaner and air temperature control assembly (Section 5, paragraphs 17 to 19).

5   Loosen the alternator mounting pivot bolts and remove the adjuster link bolt. Lift away the drivebelt and tip the alternator away from the engine.

6   Remove the inlet manifold (see Section 8).

7   Remove the valve gear (see Section 9).

8   Remove the timing chain cover (see Section 19).

9   Now remove the timing chain and gears (see Section 19).

10 The camshaft can now be withdrawn (photo).

25.10 Withdrawing the camshaft

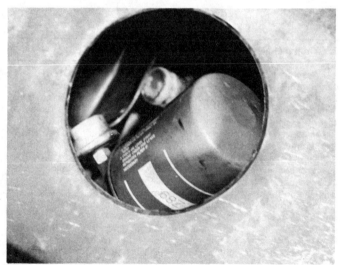

28.1 The external oil filter as viewed through the aperture in the underbelly panel

11 Exercise extreme care when withdrawing the camshaft as any damage caused to the bearings cannot be rectified by servicing in situ.

26 Camshaft – inspection

1   Thoroughly clean the camshaft and dry off, handling with care.
2   Examine all the bearing surfaces for obvious defects, wear, score marks etc.
3   Similarly inspect the cam lobes for excessive wear.
4   Ensure that key or key way is not damaged or burred and that the key is a tight fit in its key way.
5   If in doubt seek professional advice and/or replace with a new component.

27 Camshaft – refitting

1   Reverse the order of dismantling.
2   Extreme care should be taken when inserting the camshaft into the bearings for the reasons given in Section 25.11.

28 Oil pump – removal

1   Unscrew the external oil filter. If it is intended to refit the same filter, do not allow it to drain (photo).
2   Disconnect the electrical connector from the pressure switch.
3   Release the bolts securing the pump cover using a multi-splined socket. Place an oil tray underneath. Remove the bolts and cover.
4   Remove and discard the old cover gasket.
5   Slide out the pump gears (See Fig. 1.21).

29 Oil pump – refitting

1   Use a new gasket, placing it on the pump cover.
2   Pack the pump housing with petroleum jelly (no other type of grease will do).
3   Locate the pump gears into their correct positions ensuring that the petroleum jelly is filling every visible cavity. If the pump is not completely packed with jelly then the pump may not prime itself when the engine is restarted.
4   Offer up the pump cover to the body and locate it in position. Have the special fixing bolts handy, refit them and finger tighten.
5   Finally tighten up all the securing bolts evenly, working in alternate sequence to a final torque figure as given in the Specifications Section.

6   Replace the external oil filter and reconnect the pressure switch lead.

30 Oil pump – inspection and overhaul

If the car has covered a high mileage then be prepared to renew all the working parts contained in the oil pump.
1   First clean all the components as they are dismantled.
2   Visually check the gears for obvious scoring or chipping of the teeth. Renew if they are in poor condition.
3   Now work on the components contained within the cover.
4   Dismantle the pressure relief valve and inspect it for excessive wear and/or scoring (Fig. 1.22).
5   Pay special attention to the relief valve pressure spring. Note whether it shows signs of wear on its sides or whether it is on the point of collapse, if not collapsed.
6   Thoroughly clean the gauze filter housed within the relief valve bore.
7   Test the valve in its bore in the cover; it should have no more clearance than to make it an easy sliding fit. If any side movement is obviously apparent, then the valve and/or the cover will have to be renewed.
8   Wash the stripped casting in clean paraffin or petrol. Dry with a clean rag. Smear parts with clean engine oil before reassembly.
9   With the gears replaced in the pump cover, check the pump gear end float (Fig. 1.23). Lay a straight edge across the two gear wheels and with a feeler gauge, measure the clearance between the straight edge and the surface of the front cover. The clearance should be between 0.0018 in and 0.0058 in (0.05 mm to 0.15 mm). If the measurement shows less than 0.0018 in (0.05 mm) then inspect the front cover recess for signs of wear.

31 Oil pump – reassembly after overhaul

1   Use clean engine oil to lubricate the oil pressure relief valve. Fit the valve into its bore.
2   Fit the relief valve spring.
3   Fit the sealing washer to the relief valve plug then locate and screw up the plug. Tighten it to the recommended torque setting.

32 Sump – removal (engine in car)

1   Drive the car onto ramps or alternatively jack up the front of the

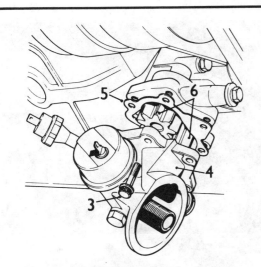

Fig. 1.21 Oil pump detail

3   *Special fixing screws*   5   *Gasket*
4   *Pump cover plate*   6   *Pump gears*

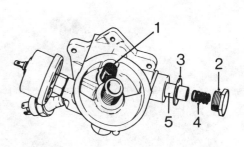

Fig. 1.22 Oil pump cover detail

1   *Gauze filter*   4   *Relief valve spring*
2   *Relief valve plug*   5   *Relief valve*
3   *Sealing washer*

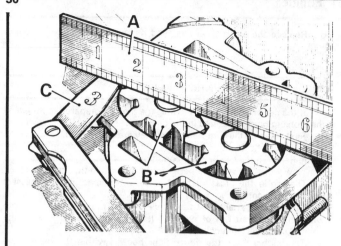

Fig. 1.23 Checking the oil pump gears for wear

A Straight edge   C Feeler gauge
B Pump gears

Fig. 1.24 Raise the engine until a dimension of 1.5 in (38 mm) exists between the centres of the inner mounting holes

32.10 Access to the sump reinforcing plate is gained by making use of the holes provided in the coupling plate (engine removed for clarity)

35.3A Offering up the sump

35.3B The sump reinforcing plate is positioned at the rear of the sump

36.4 The sump removed, revealing the oil pick-up strainer and the baffle plate

car and support it on axle stands or wooden packing blocks.

2   Disconnect the battery.

3   Remove the sump drain plug and drain the engine oil into a suitable container.

4   Undo the underbelly panel retaining screws and lower the panel in order to gain access to the crankshaft front pulley.

5   Place a jack under the crankshaft pulley taking care to ensure that the sensing pip attached to the periphery of the pulley is clear of the jack lifting pad.

6   Raise the jack until it is just in contact with the pulley and then undo and remove the two left-hand front mounting bolts.

7   Raise the jack until a dimension of 1.5 in (38 mm) exists between the centres of the inner engine mounting hole and its corresponding hole of the crossmember bracket (refer to Fig. 1.24). When raising the jack take care to ensure that the air cleaner does not foul the bulkhead.

8   Having raised the engine remove the power steering hose clamp bolt.

9   Proceed to remove the fourteen sump retaining bolts from both sides and the front.

10 Now remove the two rear retaining bolts and the reinforcing plate. Access to these bolts can be gained by making use of the holes provided in the coupling plate (photo).

11 The coupling plate bolts can now be removed and the sump lifted away.

12 It may be necessary to give the sump a few gentle taps with a mallet to free it from its gasket. *Never try prising it off* by inserting a blade or chisel between the faces, damage will most certainly occur.

13 Clean all the fixing bolts in a paraffin bath.

33 Sump – removal (engine out of car)

1   The procedure is identical to that covered in Section 32, paragraphs 9 to 13.

34 Sump – overhaul

1   Thoroughly clean off the exterior removing all traces of encrusted road dirt.

2   Wash the sump interior with paraffin brushing out any sludge which may be there.

3   With the sump now perfectly clean, carefully scrape off the remains of the sump gasket.

4   Similarly clean up the mating surface of the crankcase paying particular attention to the joints between the timing cover and cylinder block.

35 Sump – refitting (general)

1   Always use a new sump gasket.

2   Apply a coating of gasket jointing compound to both sides of the sump gasket and locate the gasket. If the engine is out of the car, place it on the crankcase. But where the engine is still in the car it will be found far simpler to locate the gasket on the sump.

3   Offer up the sump, having the fixing bolts and spring washers available. Fit all the fixing bolts and tighten them evenly, working in a diagonal sequence. Remember that the reinforcing plate goes at the rear of the sump and its retaining bolts are slightly longer than the side ones (photo).

4   If the engine is still fitted in the car reverse the instructions given in Section 32 paragraphs 1 to 8.

5   Finally refill the sump in the normal manner.

6   Allow time for the oil to drain through the engine into the sump and take a reading from the engine oil level dipstick. *Do not overfill.*

7   Run the engine and check for leaks. Recheck that you have properly tightened the sump drain plug.

36 Connecting rods and pistons – removal

1   Strip the engine as for a top end overhaul Sections 7, 8, 9, 11 and 12.

2   The pistons complete with their connecting rods are pushed out, through the tops of the cylinder bores.

3   If working on an automatic model, remove the torque converter cover plate. This gives access to the sump rear fixing and will also enable the engine to be turned over, using the drive plate as a crank.

4   Remove the engine oil sump Sections 32 or 33 (photo).

5   Remove the oil pick-up strainer which is retained by a central retaining nut and two bolts at the pick-up pipe flange at the crankcase. If required remove the two nuts and bolts securing the strainer to the bracket as shown in Fig. 1.25.

6   Remove the baffle plate (six bolts) (photo). Have an oil drain pan handy as the baffle will retain a quantity of engine oil. Note the positions of the spacers which are a loose fit on the mounting stud between the baffle plate and the main bearing cap (photo).

7   Rotate the crankshaft to gain easy access to the connecting rod (big-end) cap fixing nuts.

8   Detach the cap (big-end) from each of the connecting rods. Push the connecting rod/piston partially down the bore to clear the crankshaft; then remove the bearing shells from the caps and connecting rods. Push the connecting rod/piston upwards out of each bore taking care to prevent the connecting rod from scratching the bore. Ensure

36.6A Remove the sump baffle plate

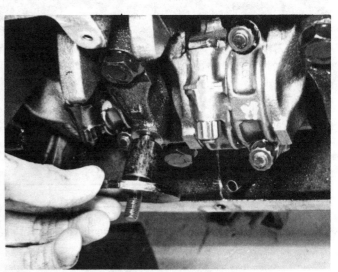

36.6B The position of the spacers which are located between the baffle plate and the main bearing cap

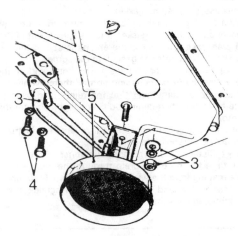

Fig. 1.25 The oil pick-up strainer and pipe assembly

3   *Strainer bracket to mounting stud retaining nut and washers*
4   *Strainer pick-up pipe flange retaining bolts*
5   *Strainer assembly*
8   *Pick-up pipe*

Fig. 1.26 Withdraw connecting rod (piston assembly through top of block)

37.4 Piston location mark FRONT stamped on the crown

39.2 Fitting the piston ring clamp

that the caps are returned to, and kept with the connecting rods from which they came (Fig. 1.26).
9   Retain the connecting rods, pistons, and bearing caps in their correct order.

37 Pistons and connecting rods – overhaul

1   The condition of the pistons, rings, and the big-end bearings and small end bushes will be governed by many factors, but principally:

(a) The total mileage covered by the car
(b) The maintenance of oil level and regular oil and filter changes and usage to which the car has been subjected

2   The home mechanic is advised that to assess the true condition of these components, he must be in possession of, or have access to, certain professional equipment and tools. For instance, the gudgeon

pin has to be removed by means of an hydraulic press or ram that will exert a pressure of not less than 8 tons (8128 kg); a micrometer especially constructed for measurement of cylinder bore wear and ovality; a normal micrometer capable of encircling a piston to assess the degree of piston wear.
3   Special standard bore (oversize service pistons are available as 0.001 in (0.0254 mm) oversize, but these can only be fitted to a standard size bore which has been honed to achieve the necessary piston to cylinder clearance dimensions.
4   When fitting pistons to the connecting rods it should be noted that the pistons are marked *Front* on their crowns (photo). It should also be remembered that the connecting rods will have to be fitted the correct way round and identified by a domed boss (see Section 39, paragraph 3 for further details).
5   Where the same pistons are to be refitted, then they must be marked to correspond with their respective connecting rods, and cylinder bore positions.
6   If new rings are to be fitted, this can be achieved without removing

the pistons from their connecting rods.

7 Carefully remove the piston rings and retain in sequence.

8 Clean all the carbon deposits from the piston head, and clean out the ring grooves and remove any gummy deposits that have accumulated, using a suitable solvent.

9 Examine the piston carefully for any scoring of the bearing surfaces, cracking or chipping particularly at the skirt. Examine the crown for dents or marks caused by foreign objects in the combustion chamber or broken rings, plug electrodes etc. Rings that have been broken in the bore during running will have caused damage to the grooves in the piston making the rings sloppy through having excessive clearance in the grooves. Damaged or faulty pistons of this nature should be renewed. It is also possible that broken rings will have scratched the cylinder wall – in bad cases this will necessitate a rebore.

10 If the engine has been rebored then oversize pistons of 0.010 in (0.25 mm) and 0.020 in (0.50 mm) are available.

38 Fitting new piston rings

1 When fitting new rings it is advisable to remove the glaze from the cylinder bores. It is strongly advised that the deglazed bore should have a cross hatch finish (diamond pattern) and should be carried out in such a way as not to increase the bore size in any way. This cross hatch finish provides the cylinder walls with good oil retention properties.

2 The top compression ring is surfaced with a chrome material and must only be fitted in the top piston ring groove. The second compression ring is of the stepped type and must only be fitted ring groove from the top of the piston. The second compression ring is marked *T* or *Top* and it is this side of the ring which must face uppermost.

3 The special oil control ring needs no gapping, but care must be taken to ensure that the ends of the expander, (fitted first), do not overlap but just abut each other. Fit the rails, one at a time, making sure that they locate snugly within the piston groove.

4 Fit the rings by holding them open, using both hands, thumbs at the gaps with fingers around the outer edges, easing them open enough to slip over the piston top and straight to the groove in which they belong. Use feeler gauges or strips of tin as guides to prevent the rings dropping into the wrong groove. Do not twist the rings whilst doing this or they will snap.

5 Before fitting however, a word on gapping. Push a compression ring down the cylinder bore using a piston to position it squarely at about 1 in (25 mm) below the top of the block and measure the piston ring gap with a feeler gauge (Fig. 1.27). The gap should be between 0.017 in and 0.022 in (0.44 and 0.57 mm). If required, file the gap using a flat 'fine cut' file. Exercise care and judgement not to overdo it. Refit the ring, square off the piston as before and re-measure. Repeat the process until correct.

6 Once the rings have been fitted to the piston, then the vertical clearance in the groove should be checked. This will be in the region of between 0.003 and 0.005 in (0.08 to 0.13 mm) (Fig. 1.28).

7 Fit the compression rings so that the gaps in each ring are diametrically opposite, and the oil control ring so that its gap appear on same side between gudgeon pin and the piston thrust face but staggered. Locate the rail ring gaps approximately 1 in (25 mm) either side of the expander join (Fig. 1.29). This will ensure good compression.

39 Pistons and connecting rods – refitting

1 Make sure that all parts are scrupulously clean and smeared with clean engine oil.

2 Fit the ring compression tool, adjusting the compression rings so that their gaps are positioned as described in the preceding Section (photo).

3 Ensure that the connecting rod/piston assembly enters the bore facing the correct way round. The identifying boss (photo) must face forwards on the right-hand cylinder bank, and to the rear on the left-hand bank. This means that on each crankshaft journal the two projections or bosses on the connecting rods will face each other.

4 Rotate the crankshaft until the journal being fitted is at BDC.

5 Liberally lubricate the cylinder walls and big-end journals and bearings with clean engine oil.

6 Insert the pistons and connecting rods with the ring compressor

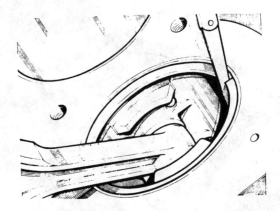

Fig. 1.27 Gapping the piston rings, using a feeler gauge

Fig. 1.28 Checking the ring clearance in groove

A Compression rings
B Expander (oil control ring)
C Ring rails of oil control ring
D Feeler gauge

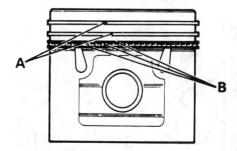

Fig. 1.29 Correct location of piston ring gaps

A Compression ring gaps on opposite sides of piston
B Oil control ring gaps staggered on same side of piston

attached. Use a hammer handle to gently drive the assembly into the bore.

7 Lubricate the bearing shells in both the connecting rods and cap using clean engine oil. Locate the big-end bearing on to its crankshaft journal.

8 Fit the bearing shells and caps. **Note**: *Details of inspection and renewal of bearing will be found in Section 45 and 46. The identifying rib on the bearing cap must face the same way as the boss on the web of the connecting rod*

9 Tighten the bearing cap retaining nuts evenly to the recommended torque setting (see Specifications).

39.3 The identifying boss on the connecting rod

42.1 Removing the driveplate (automatic transmission model shown)

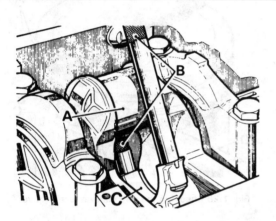

Fig. 1.30 Fitting connecting rod to crankshaft

A   Crankshaft journal   C   Connecting rod bearing
B   Special guide bolts

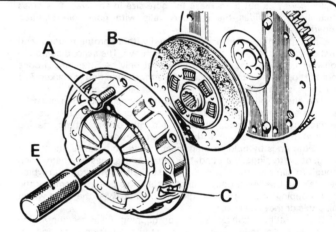

Fig. 1.31 Clutch components

A   Cover and bolts   D   Flywheel
B   Driven plate   E   Aligning tool for refitting
C   Recessed bolts (do not   (see Chapter 5)
    remove)

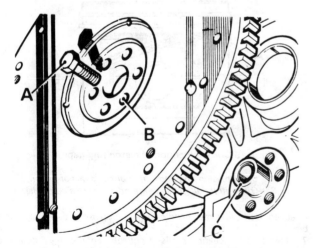

Fig. 1.32 Flywheel removal

A   Fixing bolts
B   Offset hole
C   Crankshaft flange

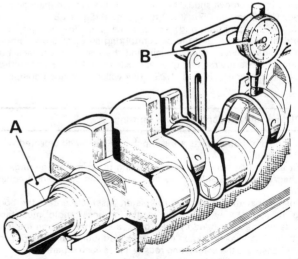

Fig. 1.33 Testing crankshaft for straightness

A   V-blocks   B   Dial gauge indicator

40 Crankshaft – reasons and preparation for removal

1   Work on the crankshaft is not normally practicable with the engine in the car.
2   The need for removal of the crankshaft from the engine could be due to:

(a) *High mileage and the engine is to be completely renovated.*
(b) *Obvious knocking noises emitted from the crankcase or sump region, indicating either a big-end failure or in the case of a knocking accompanied by rumbling noises, a failed main bearing.*

3   Removal of the engine has already been covered in Sections 4, 5 and 6 of this Chapter.
4   With the engine out of the car and preferably resting on a suitable engine stand proceed as for top overhaul. (Sections 7, 8, 9, 10 and 12 of this Chapter).
5   Drain the oil from the engine sump; remove the sump, the baffle and the sump oil strainer. (See Section 33 of this Chapter).
6   Turn the engine over and remove the pistons and connecting rods. (See Section 36 of this Chapter).
7   Keep all bearings, connecting rods and pistons in correct order of removal for subsequent replacement.
8   Remove the timing gear chain and wheels, but not the camshaft. See Section 19 (or Section 24 automatic transmission).
9   Remove the clutch assembly (See Section 41).
10 Remove the flywheel (See Section 42).
11 The crankshaft will then be ready for removal (See Section 43).

41 Clutch – removal and refitting

1   With the engine out of the car this operation is comparatively simple. It can be achieved with the engine in situ after removing the gearbox (see Chapter 6).
2   Mark the clutch cover in relation to its position on the flywheel (Fig. 1.31).
3   First progressively slacken the ring of bolts securing the clutch cover to the flywheel and remove them and the clutch assembly. **Warning**: *Do not remove the three bolts located in the recesses of the clutch cover.*
4   Slide out the driven plate which is sandwiched between the pressure plate and the flywheel.
5   When refitting, centralise the driven plate (Chapter 5) and align the pressure plate with the marks previously made on the cover and flywheel.

42 Flywheel – removal and refitting

1   There are six bolts securing the flywheel (or drive plate – automatic transmission) to the crankshaft flange. Slacken and remove these bolts – the flywheel can then be removed (photo).
2   When refitting, it will be noticed that the securing bolt positions are offset, so that incorrect fitting is impossible.
3   When refitting these bolts, fit all the bolts before final tightening. Rotate the flywheel or driveplate against the direction of engine rotation and against the leverage of the spanner used. Finally tightening to the recommended torque setting (see Specifications).

43 Crankshaft – removal

1   With the engine stripped and out of the car as outlined in the foregoing sections, remove all the main bearing cap bolts, bearing caps and shells – retaining them in the correct sequence for refitting.
2   Carefully lift out the crankshaft.

44 Crankshaft – inspection

1   With the crankshaft suitably mounted on V blocks at No 1 and 5 journals, give a thorough visual check for scoring of, or white metal sticking to, the journals. Heavy scoring indicates that the crankshaft

should be reground.
2   Check for straightness using a dial test indicator (Fig. 1.33) as follows:

(a) *The run out at main journals 2,3 and 4.*
(b) *Note the relatively eccentricity of each journal to the others.*
(c) *The maximum indication should come at nearly the same angular location on all journals.*

3   With an engineer's micrometer check each journal for ovality. If this proves to be more than 0.0015 in (0.04 mm), the crankshaft must be reground.

45 Crankshaft bearings – general information and checking clearances

Crankshaft bearings (big-end and main) should only be used if they are known to have done a very low mileage only (less than 15 000 miles). As replacement bearings are relatively cheap it is false economy to replace the old ones. Where the condition of the bearings and journals was so bad that the crankshaft has to be reground, new bearings of the correct undersize will be provided by the firm which carried out the regrinding.
If replacement bearings of standard size are being fitted, or if for some reason you do not know which undersize bearings should be used – the following paragraphs detail a method of establishing bearing clearance, and therefore correct bearing size.
1   Use Plastigage to measure the bearing clearances.
2   Before using Plastigage, all the parts to be measured must be clean, dry and free from oil.
3   With a piece of the Plastigage laid on the top of each main bearing journal, (Fig. 1.34), refit the bearing caps as though reassembling.
4   The main bearing oil seals should not be fitted during this operation.
5   Tighten all bolts to correct torque as listed in Specification.
6   Remove the main bearing caps – the Plastigage will be found sticking to either the journal or the shell face: *Do not remove it.*
7   With the scale provided, measure the compressed piece of Plastigage on each bearing at its widest point.
8   The graduation number that most closely corresponds to this width indicates the bearing clearance in thousandths of an inch.
9   The specified clearance of a new main bearing is 0.0009 in (0.023 mm) to 0.0025 in (0.065 mm). A reading of between 0.001 in (0.025 mm) and 0.0025 in (0.065 mm) is acceptable.

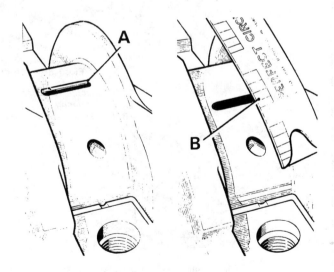

Fig. 1.34 Using Plastigage to check bearing clearance

A   *Plastigage placed on journal*
B   *Pressed Plastigage and microscale*

46.2 The crankshaft centre main bearing installed. Note the integral thrust washer

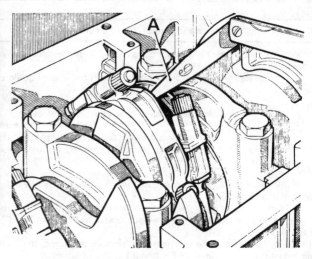

Fig. 1.35 Checking connecting rod end-float

A   Feeler gauge

Fig. 1.36 Bottom end engine detail

11   Connecting rod caps
12   Main bearing caps
13   Crankshaft rear boss and

oil seal
27   Cruciform side seals

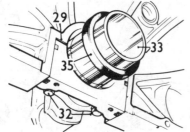

Fig. 1.37 Installing the crankshaft rear oil seal

29   Jointing compound application point
32   Rear main bearing cap retaining bolts
33   Seal guide/protector (Service tool RO.1014)
35   Crankshaft rear oil seal

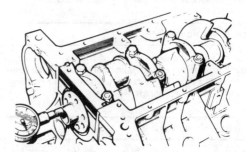

Fig. 1.38 Checking the crankshaft end-float with a dial gauge

10 *Do not* rotate the crankshaft whilst Plastigage is in position.

11 The same procedures are adopted for checking the connecting rod big-end bearing clearances but tighten the bolts to the correct torque as specified.

12 Crankshaft bearings for the main journals and the connecting rod journals (big-ends) are available in the following undersizes:

    0.010 in (0.25 mm)
    0.020 in (0.50 mm)
    0.030 in (0.76 mm)
    0.040 in (1.01 mm)

13 Specified clearance for new big-end bearings is 0.0006 to 0.0022 in (0.015 to 0.055 mm).

14 A Plastigage reading of between 0.001 in and 0.0025 in (0.025 mm and 0.065 mm) is acceptable.

15 If a bearing has seen long service, and a reading in excess of 0.003 in (0.08 mm) is shown then it is advisable to renew it.

16 If new bearing shells are being fitted to a crankshaft with journals of unknown size it will be a matter of selective assembly, trial and error until the nearest correct assembly is achieved.

17 **Never** grind or file bearing caps to make a fitting.

18 Having found the correct clearance, clean off all trace of the Plastigage material, and oil all surfaces to be refitted.

19 With the bearings refitted and tightened, it should be possible to freely move the connecting rods on the crank journal as allowed by the end clearance.

20 Check the endfloat (side-to-side movement) of the connecting rod big-end bearings on each crank journal (Fig. 1.35). This should be between 0.006 and 0.014 in (0.15 and 0.37 mm).

46 Crankshaft refitting and engine reassembly

1 Fit all the main bearing upper shells into position in the cylinder block. These are the ones with the drilled oil holes.

2 The flanged upper main bearing shells locate in the centre position. They act as the crankshaft main thrust bearing (photo).

3 Place wooden blocks of about half an inch (12.5 mm) thick to fit over the upper bearing housing. These are to rest the crankshaft on, before the final fitting.

4 Place the crankshaft into position allowing it to rest on the wooden blocks (photo).

5 Lubricate all the bearing surfaces liberally with clean engine oil (photo).

6 Draw the connecting rod bearings up into position on their crankshaft journals. Remove first one wooden block and lower the crankshaft into its upper bearing. Repeat the process for the other end.

7 Fit the connecting rod bearing caps as detailed in Section 39 of this Chapter.

8 Refit the main bearing caps 1 to 4, having applied clean engine oil first (photo). Tighten the bolts only finger tight at this stage.

46.4 Fitting the crankshaft

46.5 Lubricating the bearing surfaces

46.8 Fitting a main bearing cap

46.9 Tightening a main bearing cap bolt to the recommended torque setting

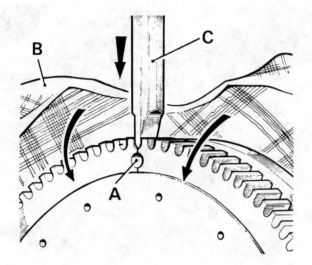

Fig. 1.39 Removing damaged starter ring gear from flywheel

A   Hole drilled in ring gear to weaken it
B   Rag to protect operator
C   Chisel

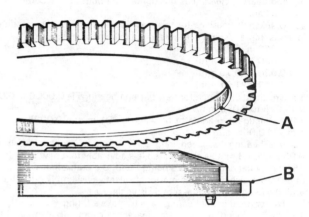

Fig. 1.40 Installing a new starter ring gear

A   Chamfered inner edge
B   Flywheel flange

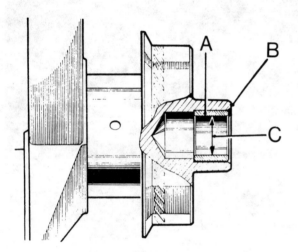

Fig. 1.41 Refitting spigot bearing

A   Spigot bearing
B   Crankshaft end face
C   Internal diameter of bearing

9   In order to align the thrust faces of the centre main bearing tap the end of the crankshaft with a mallet, forward and rearward. The securing bolts of the main bearing caps can now be tightened down evenly to the recommended torque setting (see Specifications) (photo).
10   Fit the new 'cruciform' side seals to the grooves at the sides of the rear main bearing cap.
11   Do not cut the 'cruciform' seals at this stage as they must project above the bearing cap mating facing approximately 0.062 in (1.5 mm). Trim the ends of the seals, after pressing home, but only if necessary.
12   Apply a coating of jointing compound to the rear half of the rear main bearing cap mating face or alternatively apply the jointing compound to the equivalent area on the cylinder block.
13   Lubricate the bearing shelld and the 'cruciform' side seals with clean engine oil and refit the bearing cap.
14   Do not fully tighten the two retaining bolts at this stage, but make sure that the cap is both fully home and squarely seated on the cylinder block.

15   Tighten the retaining bolts equally by one quarter of a turn from finger tight to settle the cap. Now back off the bolts by one complete turn.
16   The crankshaft rear oil seal can now be fitted, but it is strongly recommended that the Rover service tool (RO 1014), which is a seal guide, be used when fitting the oil seal (Fig. 1.37).
17   First make sure that the oil seal guide and the crankshaft journal are scrupulously clean and then coat the seal guide and crankshaft journal with clean engine oil. **Note** *The lubricant must totally coat the outer surface of the oil seal guide to prevent the possibility of turning back the lip of the oil seal when fitting it.*
18   In respect of handling the oil seal avoid touching the seal lip at any time. Visually inspect the seal for damage and make sure that the outer diameter of the seal remains both clean and dry at all times.
19   Position the oil seal, onto the seal guide tool, with the lip of the oil seal facing towards the engine.
20   Position the seal guide tool on the end of the crankshaft and push the seal, by hand, into the recess formed in the main bearing cap and cylinder block. The seal must fit squarely and abut the machined step in the recess.
21   With the seal so held in position, carefully withdraw the guide tool.
22   Tighten the rear main bearing cap bolts to the recommended torque setting (see Specifications).
23   With a dial gauge or a set of feeler gauges, check the crankshaft endfloat. This should be in the limits of 0.004 in and 0.008 in (0.10 mm to 0.20 mm). If incorrect, then examine for faulty components and/or faulty reassembly (Fig. 1.38).
24   Reassemble the rest of the engine by reference to the appropriate Section, and reversing the dismantling procedure.

47 Starter ring gear – removal

1   Where automatic transmission is fitted the starter ring gear is attached to the drive plate and cannot be removed separately. The drive plate must be renewed as an assembly. With the flywheel removed from the engine, drill a small hole approximately 0.375 in (10 mm) laterally across the starter ring gear. Take care not to allow the drill to enter or score the flywheel or flange. The hole should be made between the root of any gear teeth. This will weaken the ring gear and facilitate removal by breaking with a cold chisel (Fig. 1.39).
2   Hold the flywheel in a soft jawed vice.
3   **Warning** *Beware of flying fragments. A piece of cloth draped over the whole assembly will protect the operator from possible injury.*
4   Split the starter ring gear with a hammer and chisel.

48 Starter ring gear – refitting

1 The new starter ring gear must be heated uniformly. The expansion of the metal permits it to fit over the flywheel and against the flange. Heat to between 338 degrees and 347 degrees Farenheit (170 to 175 degrees Centigrade). **Do not exceed the specified temperature.**
2 Place the flywheel on a flat surface with the flanged side downwards.
3 Offer up the heated ring to the flywheel with the chamfered inner diameter downwards (Fig. 1.40), pressing it firmly against the flange until the ring contracts sufficiently to grip the flywheel. Allow cooling to take place naturally and do not attempt to hasten cooling in any way as this could cause weakening by setting up internal stresses in the ring gear leading to later break up. Where the ring gear is chamfered on both sides it may be fitted either way round.

49 Crankshaft spigot bearing – renewal

1 The spigot bearing can be renewed with the engine in the car. First remove the gearbox (Chapter 6) and clutch assembly (Chapter 5).
2 If the engine is undergoing complete workshop overhaul and is out of the car the job is much facilitated and should be considered at this time.
3 Remove the old bearing which is a push fit into the crankshaft end flange. Do this by screwing in a thread tap and then a bolt. Alternatively, fill the bearing with grease and then drive in a close-fitting rod. Hydraulic pressure will push out the bearing.
4 Push in the new bearing A which should finish flush with the end face of the crankshaft B. Below this level is acceptable provided it does not recess more than 0.063 in (1.6 mm). (See Fig. 1. 41).
5 It may be necessary to have the inside of the spigot bearing reamed to accept the gearbox input shaft. Seek advice on this point when purchasing the new bearing.

50 Engine/gearbox – refitting

1 The splined end of the gearbox input shaft, the clutch centre and the withdrawal unit abutment faces should be smeared with approved grease (high melting-point type).
2 Line up the gearbox with the engine locating the gearbox input shaft into the clutch, ease forward until the bellhousing dowels engage. (See Chapter 5 for clutch driven plate alignment).

3 Secure the bellhousing with the correct bolts, together with the two bolts which secure the sump reinforcing plate to the bellhousing. Tighten these bolts to the recommended torque setting.
4 Refit the bellhousing cover plate, tighten the bolts to the recommended torque setting.
5 Lower the engine/gearbox unit into the car and reverse the removal and disconnection procedure described in Section 5.
6 Check, and renew if necessary, the rubber mounting blocks on the gearbox crossmember.
7 Reconnect the throttle cable and check that both carburettor throttle levers are at their stop positions. If these have been disturbed or work has been carried out on the carburettors then it will be necessary to readjust them as described in Chapter 3.
8 Reconnect the choke control cable ensuring that the cable is correctly adjusted.
9 Refit the cooling fan blades to the viscous coupling. Tighten the bolts evenly to the recommended torque setting.
10 If the gearbox has been drained then remember to refill it with the correct grade of oil.
11 Similarly replenish the engine oil.
12 Fill the cooling system with the correct mixture of antifreeze and/or inhibitor (See Chapter 2).
13 Before starting the engine give the whole job a final and thorough check out and remove any stray spanners and other tools from the engine compartment.
14 After starting up, immediately check that the oil warning light goes out. If the light remains on, stop engine at once, as it will be necessary to prime the oil pump (see this Chapter, Section 29).
15 Check the cooling system for leaks.
16 If necessary check and adjust the engine idling speed (Chapter 3).
17 If necessary check and adjust the ignition timing (Chapter 4).
18 Allow the engine to cool and check the coolant level in the expansion tank.
19 During and after test run re-check for coolant and oil leaks.

51 Engine/automatic transmission – refitting

1 Fit the automatic transmission unit to the engine as described in Chapter 6 (part 2).
2 Refitting of the combined engine/transmission is similar to that described for manual gearbox types in the preceding Section.
3 Reconnect the speed selector mechanism and check for correct operation (see Chapter 6).
4 Reconnect the inhibitor switch plug and speedometer drive cable.
5 Refill the transmission with the correct grade and quantity of fluid.

Fault diagnosis overleaf

52 Fault diagnosis – engine

Symptom	Reason/s
Engine will not turn over when starter switch is operated	Flat battery Bad battery connections Bad connections at solenoid switch and/or starter motor Defective starter motor
Engine turns over normally but fails to start	No spark at plugs No fuel reaching engine Too much fuel reaching the engine (flooding)
Engine starts but runs unevenly and misfires	Ignition and/or fuel system faults Sticking or leaking valves Burnt out valves Worn out piston rings
Lack of power	Ignition and/or fuel system faults Burnt out valves Worn out piston rings
Excessive oil consumption	Oil leaks from crankshaft oil seals, timing cover gasket, rocker cover gasket, oil filter gasket, sump gasket, sump plug Worn piston rings or cylinder bores resulting in oil being burnt by engine Worn valve guides and/or defective inlet valve stem seals
Excessive mechanical noise from engine	Worn crankshaft bearings Worn cylinders (piston slap) Slack or worn timing chain and sprockets

Note: *When investigating starting and uneven running faults do not be tempted into snap diagnosis. Start from the beginning of the check procedure and follow it through. It will take less time in the long run. Poor performance from the engine in terms of power and economy is not normally diagnosed quickly. In any event the ignition and fuel systems must be checked first before assuming any further investigation needs to be made.*

Chapter 2 Cooling system

For modifications, and information applicable to later models, see Supplement at end of manual

Contents

Specifications

Type .... Pressurised, pump and fan assisted

Cap pressure .... 15 lbf/in^2 (1.05 kgf/cm^2)

Fan .... Seven bladed, sixteen inch diameter, viscous unit to limit fan speed to 2500 rpm

Thermostat
Type .... Wax
Starts to open .... 82° C (180° F)

Fan belt adjustment .... 0.2 to 0.3 in (5 to 8 mm) deflection

Capacity (coolant) .... 19.5 pints (11.08 litres)

Coolant type .... Ethylene glycol based antifreeze suitable for mixed metal engines (Duckhams Universal Antifreeze and Summer Coolant)

Torque wrench settings ....

	lbf ft	Nm
Water pump housing bolts	20	27.5
Water outlet elbow to inlet manifold	20	27.5
Water outlet pipe to inlet manifold bolts	20	27.5
Fan blade retaining nuts and bolts	9	11.5

1 General description

The engine cooling system is conventional, acting on the thermo-syphon pump assisted principle. The coolant flow is controlled by a thermostat which is fitted at the forward end of the inlet manifold casting and behind the outlet elbow. The purpose of this thermostat is to prevent the full flow of the coolant around the system before the most efficient operating temperature is reached.

The purpose of pressurising the cooling system is to prevent premature boiling in adverse conditions and also to allow the engine to operate at its most efficient running temperature.

The overflow pipe from the radiator is connected to an expansion tank which makes topping-up unnecessary. The coolant expands when hot, and instead of being forced down an overflow pipe and lost, it flows into the expansion tank. As the engine cools the coolant contracts and, because of the pressure differential, flows back into the top tank of the radiator. Excess pressure is vented to the atmosphere via a pressure relief valve fitted to the expansion tank filler cap.

The cooling system comprises the radiator, water pump, thermostat, interconnecting hoses and waterways in the cylinder block and heads. The water pump is driven from the engine crankshaft pulley by a V-belt.

The cooling fan is connected to a Holset viscous coupling which limits the fan speed at high engine revolutions. This works in a similar manner to a torque converter, and provides a 'slipping clutch' effect; its aim is to reduce noise and engine loading.

2 Cooling system – draining

With the car on level ground, and the system *Cold*, proceed as follows:
1 Move the heater control lever to the *Hot* position.
2 Depress and remove slowly the expansion tank filler cap (photo).
3 Unscrew and remove the hexagon radiator filler plug (photo).
4 If antifreeze is used in the cooling system, and has been in use for less than two years, drain the coolant into a container of suitable

2.2 Remove the expansion tank filler cap

2.3 Remove the hexagon radiator filler plug

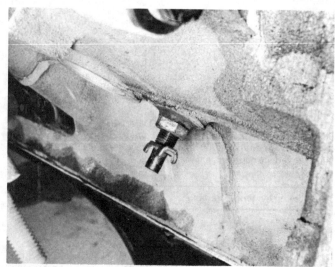
2.6A Location of the left-hand cylinder bank drain tap

capacity.

5   To drain the radiator, reach up through the hole provided in the underbelly panel and turn the drain tap in an anti-clockwise direction.

6   Drain taps are provided in each of the cylinder banks and positioned directly beneath the exhaust manifolds (photos). Turn the taps in an anti-clockwise direction to drain the coolant.

3   Cooling system – flushing

1   With the passing of time, the cooling system will gradually lose its efficiency as the radiator becomes choked with rust, scale deposits from water and other sediment. To clear the system out, initially drain the system as described previously, then detach the lower radiator hose.

2   Using a garden hose allow water to enter the radiator via the radiator filler plug. It will be necessary to close the cylinder block drain taps during this operation.

3   Allow the water from the hose to run through the radiator for several minutes until it emerges clean, then refit the lower hose.

4   When it is desired to flush the cylinder block simply remove the radiator filler plug and the cylinder block drain taps. The removal of the cylinder block drain taps will permit speedy clearance of the sediment and scale deposits. The garden hose can be inserted in the radiator filler plug hole as described in paragraph 2.

5   If when flushing the radiator the sediment and scale deposits are very dirty then it will be found desirable to remove the radiator and reverse flush it. Reverse flushing simply means feeding the clean flushing water into the lower radiator connection and expelling the sediment from the top radiator connection.

6   The alternative to the reverse flushing method, described in paragraph 5, is the use of a proprietory brand of radiator descaler available at most motor accessory shops or garages such as Holts Radflush or Holts Speedflush. The correct usage of the descaler compound is described on the container, but generally necessitates its leaving in the cooling system for a short period to free the deposits which can then be flushed out as described in paragraphs 3 and 4.

4   Cooling system – filling

1   The importance of refilling with the correct mixture of antifreeze/inhibitor and water, or inhibitor only with water cannot be over emphasised. Antifreeze solution conforming to British Standard No. 6580 or to MIL-E-5559 should be used. Alternatively, where applicable, a Rover approved cooling system corrosion inhibitor should be used. The coolant should be changed annually to ensure adequate cooling system protection.

2   When mixing water with the antifreeze/inhibitor, or just inhibitor, it is better to use soft tap water or rain water, the mixing being carried out in a plastic bucket. It is not necessary to mix the whole amount required to fill the system, as further topping-up can be done once the initial coolant mix has been poured into the system.

3   Use the following table to ensure adequate protection according to the local climatic conditions:

Amount of antifreeze	Protection provided down to
3·25 pints (1·85 litres)	–12°C (10°F)
4·55 pints (2·59 litres)	–20°C (–4°F)
6·5 pints (3·7 litres)	–36°C (–33°F)

4   Fill the cooling system via the radiator filler orifice until the system appears to be full. Make sure that the drain taps are shut first!

5   Start the engine and run it at 1500 rpm. After five minutes running, top up the cooling system via the radiator filler orifice (with the engine still running) and refit the filler plug.

6   Still with the engine running at 1500 rpm, top up the expansion tank to the base of its filler neck and fit the cap.

7   Continue to run the engine until normal operating temperature is reached, then stop the engine and allow it to cool down.

8   Check the coolant level in the expansion tank when the system has cooled down and top up if necessary.

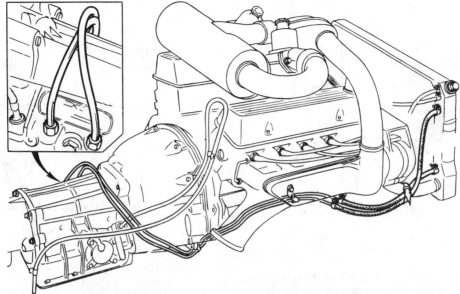

Fig. 2.1 Layout of the oil cooler hoses (automatic transmission models only)

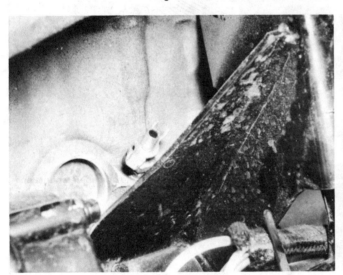

2.6B Location of the right-hand cylinder bank drain tap

5.3 The manifold vent hose and the expansion tank bottom hose connections at the radiator

5 Radiator – removal and refitting

1   For obvious safety reasons disconnect the battery negative terminal.

2   Drain the cooling system as described in Section 2. On models equipped with air conditioning, it will be necessary to have the system discharged and the condenser disconnected and removed – see Chapter 13, Section 15, paragraph 73.

3   Disconnect the following hoses at the radiator (photo):

Top hose	Manifold vent hose
Bottom hose	Expansion tank bottom hose

4   On automatic transmission models two further hoses will be found connected to the radiator. These additional hoses are the flow and return, for the automatic transmission oil cooler, which is an integral part of the radiator (Fig. 2.1).

5   Disconnect the oil cooler hoses at the radiator, and either plug or clamp then to prevent the loss of fluid and the possible ingression of dirt. Place blanking plugs in the oil cooler inlet and outlet orifices.

6   The radiator is retained by two bolts and a plate at its upper end, and rubber grommets at its base. The grommets locate the pegs fitted to the base of the radiator.

7   Undo the two retaining bolts and lift the radiator straight out vertically (photo).

5.7 Undo the radiator retaining bolts

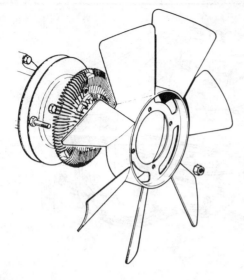

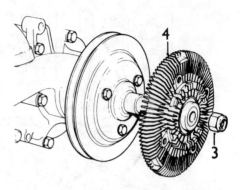

Fig. 2.3 Removing the viscous coupling

3   Retaining nut   4   Viscous coupling

Fig. 2.2 Removing the cooling fan blades from the viscous coupling

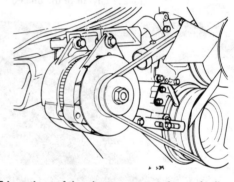

Fig. 2.5 Locations of the alternator mounting and adjuster nuts and bolts

Fig. 2.4 Removing the water pump pulley (5)

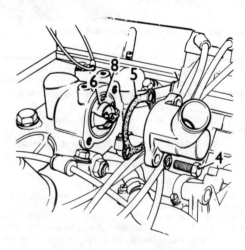

Fig. 2.7 Thermostat components

4   Housing securing bolt
5   Gasket
6   Thermostat
8   Jiggle pin (fit thermostat with this part at the twelve o'clock position)

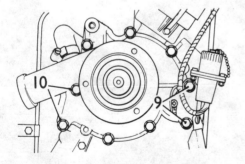

Fig. 2.6 Locations of the water pump retaining bolts

9   Diagnostic socket securing bolts
10 See text

8 When lifting the radiator away observe care as the matrix can easily be damaged by the cooling fan blade or other sharp objects (photo).

9 Refitting is a simple reversal of the removal procedure, but once again observe care as you lower the radiator into position. Check that the locating pegs attached to the base of the radiator enter the locating dowels before tightening the two securing bolts.

10 Finally refill the cooling system after reconnecting the hoses and closing the drain taps (details of refilling are given in Section 4).

11 In an emergency, minor leaks can be cured with a radiator sealant such as Holts Radweld.

6 Fan blades – removal and refitting

1 Disconnect the battery negative terminal.

2 Undo the two bolts securing the radiator to the front body panel and tilt the radiator forward sufficiently to gain access to the fan blades.

3 Remove the four nuts and bolts retaining the fan blades to the viscous coupling, and lift away the fan blades.

4 Refitting is the reverse of removal, but ensure that the fan blades are fitted the correct way round and that the retaining nuts and bolts are tightened evenly (Fig. 2.2).

7 Water pump pulley and viscous coupling – removal and refitting

1 Disconnect the battery negative terminal.

2 Remove the fan blades as described in Section 4.

3 Hold the water pump pulley still and undo the central nut retaining the viscous coupling. Note the washer located beneath the nut (Fig. 2.3).

4 Draw off the viscous coupling.

5 Undo the three bolts securing the water pump pulley (Fig. 2.4).

6 Slacken the alternator adjustment and mounting bolts. Push the alternator towards the engine to release the drivebelt tension then slip the drivebelt off the water pump pulley.

7 The water pump pulley can now be removed.

8 Refitting of the two components is the reverse of removal.

8 Fan/alternator drivebelt – removal and refitting

1 Loosen the alternator mounting and adjuster nuts and bolts (Fig. 2.5).

2 Tip the alternator towards the engine and slip the belt from the pulleys.

3 Refitting of the drivebelt is the reverse of removal, but it is important to tension the belt correctly.

4 Pull the alternator away from the engine until the tension of the drivebelt is such that it can only be deflected by 0·2 to 0·3 in (5 to 8 mm) at a point midway between the alternator and water pump pulleys.

5 With the alternator so held tighten the mounting and adjuster nuts and bolts then recheck the tension (photo).

6 If a new drivebelt has been fitted then it will need to be retensioned after approximately 250 miles (400 kms) owing to the fact that a certain amount of stretching occurs during the bedding-in stage.

9 Water pump – removal

1 Disconnect the battery negative terminal.

2 Drain the cooling system and remove the radiator as described in Sections 2 and 4.

3 Remove the cooling fan blades as described in Section 5.

4 Remove the viscous coupling and water pump pulley as described in Section 6.

5 Loosen the hose clips and pull off the water pump outlet and heater return hoses (photo).

6 Undo the two bolts and move the diagnostic socket and its bracket to one side.

5.8 Lift the radiator out taking care to prevent damaging the matrix

8.5 Checking the tension of the fan/alternator drivebelt

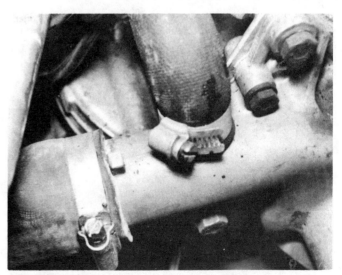
9.5 The water pump hoses

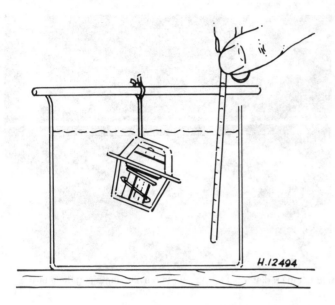

H.12494

Fig. 2.8 Testing a thermostat

7   Refer to Fig. 2.6 and remove the two bolts shown as parts 10 noting that the upper one is longer.

8   Now remove the five remaining bolts and pull the water pump away from the locating dowels.

9   Clean the threads of the pump securing bolts ready for reassembly. The threads of these bolts have a coating of thread lubricant sealant which will harden if left in contact with air.

10 It is in most cases cheaper and less frustrating to replace worn assemblies with an exchange unit. The water pump is no exception to this rule and though it is possible to replace bearings, shafts and seals, it is advised that the former course is adopted.

10 Water pump – refitting

1   Refitting is mainly a matter of reversing the removal procedure. However, there are one or two points to note during the operation.

2   Ensure that the mating surfaces of pump and engine front cover are scrupulously clean.

3   Using a smear of light grease, secure the new gasket to the pump body.

4   Apply a light smear of grease to the other gasket surface and offer the unit to the engine taking care to ensure the dowels locate in the pump body holes.

5   The pump securing bolts should be cleaned, and treated with lubricant sealant 3M EC776.

6   The securing bolts should be tightened to the recommended torque setting.

7   When refitting the cooling fan blades ensure that they are fitted correctly ie the larger diameter of the moulded boss must face the front of the car.

8   Adjust the tension of the drivebelt as described in Section 7.

11 Thermostat – removal, testing and refitting

1   If the engine tends to overheat, the cause is most likely to be due to a faulty thermostat that is failing to open at a predetermined temperature setting.

2   Conversely, where the thermostat is stuck permanently open, it will be found that the engine takes a long time to warm-up. In cold weather, this results in having to drive considerable distances using the choke. If in doubt take out the thermostat and test it.

3   There is no need to drain the whole system, but simply drain coolant from the radiator until the level of the coolant is down to the top of the cylinder block. This level will have to be achieved by trial and error. Drain off some coolant, and close the radiator drain tap. Carefully remove the engine outlet hose at the elbow. If water is present, replace the hose quickly and drain some more coolant.

4   Once the coolant has reached a suitable low level then the elbow can be removed and the thermostat exposed.

5   There are two bolts securing the thermostat housing elbow to the front of the engine. These should be removed, and the housing elbow lifted off (Fig. 2.7).

6   Remember to have a new gasket available for reassembly.

7   Carefully remove the thermostat which should just lift out.

8   With the engine cold examine it carefully to ascertain whether or not it is stuck open. If so, there is no point in making further tests; it should be renewed.

9   If the thermostat looks normal then proceed as follows.

10 Place the unit in a saucepan of cold water. Do not allow it to touch the bottom. Suspend it or support it with a piece of wire or string (Fig. 2.8).

11 Heat the saucepan and raise the temperature to that at which the thermostat is specified to open. The specified opening temperature is stamped on either the upper or lower face of the thermostat.

12 Should the thermostat fail to operate correctly, renew it with one of the correct type.

13 If it happens that you do not have a spare, the car will run quite well for a day or so without a thermostat until a replacement can be obtained, but the engine will take much longer to reach operating temperature.

14 Refit the elbow and thermostat housing cover using a new gasket.

15 When fitting the new thermostat, make sure that the small split pin, called a jiggle pin, which pokes through the valve face, is placed at the 12 o'clock position in the housing. This will prevent airlocks occurring in this area.

16 Finally reconnect the radiator hose, top-up the cooling system and check for leaks.

12 Fault diagnosis – cooling system

Symptom	Reason/s
Overheating	Insufficient water in cooling system
	Fan belt slipping (accompanied by a shrieking noise on rapid engine acceleration)
	Radiator core blocked or radiator grille restricted
	Thermostat not opening properly
	Ignition timing incorrectly set (accompanied by loss of power, and perhaps misfiring)
	Carburettors incorrectly adjusted (mixture too weak)
	Exhaust system partially blocked
	Oil level in sump too low
	Blown cylinder head gasket (water/steam being forced down the radiator overflow pipe under pressure)
	Engine not yet run-in
	Brakes binding
Overcooling	Thermostat jammed on
	Incorrect thermostat fitted allowing premature opening of valve
	Thermostat missing
Loss of cooling water	Loose clips on water hoses
	Top, bottom, or by-pass water hoses perished and leaking
	Radiator core leaking
	Expansion tank pressure cap spring worn or seal ineffective
	Blown cylinder head gasket (pressure in system forcing water/steam down overflow pipe)
	Cylinder wall or head cracked

Chapter 3
Fuel, exhaust and emission control systems

For modifications, and information applicable to later models, see Supplement at end of manual

Contents

Specifications

Fuel pump .... Electric type, immersed in fuel tank

Carburettors

Type	Twin SU
Model	HIF6
Needle	BAK
Bore	1.75 in (44 mm)
Jet size	0.100 in (2.54 mm)
Float level	0.020 to 0.060 in (0.57 to 1.5 mm)
Choke	1.2 mm orifice
Piston spring	Yellow
Damper oil	Clean engine oil (Duckhams QXR Hypergrade, or 10W/40 Motor Oil)

Idling speed .... 725 to 775 rpm

Fast idle .... 110 to 1200 rpm

CO emission .... 3 to 4.5% at idle

Air cleaner element .... Champion V420

Fuel tank capacity .... 14.5 gallons (65.9 litres)

Torque wrench settings	lbf ft	Nm
Exhaust manifold bolts	16	22
Inlet manifold bolts	30	40
Inlet manifold gasket clamp bolts	15	20
Front of fuel tank to body set-screw	20	27.5
Fuel tank rear mounting set-screw	40.5	54
Fuel tank rear mounting nut	20	27.5

1 General description

The fuel system comprises a fuel tank at the rear of the car, from which the electrically operated pump delivers fuel to the carburettors.

The electrical fuel pump is not fitted in a conventional way. It is immersed in the fuel tank and not externally mounted as is the usual practice of car manufacturers. At the inlet side of the fuel pump is a filter. Another filter of the in-line type is incorporated in the fuel delivery line just ahead of the carburettors.

2 Air cleaner and air intake temperature control system – general description

1   The air cleaner is a metal cylindrical canister, into the ends of which are fitted two disposable paper type filter elements. Elbow pieces at either end of the canister, channel the filtered air to the carburettor intakes.
2   The temperature of the incoming air to the air cleaner is maintained to approximately 100°F (38°C) by an air temperature control system. The air temperature control unit consists basically of two inlet connections and a sponge rubber flap valve connected to a bi-metallic strip (photo). One of the inlet connections feeds air to the air temperature control unit from the atmosphere via flexible trunking, whilst the other inlet is connected by a further length of trunking to a heat chamber which is bolted to the exhaust manifold.
3   The system works basically as follows. When the engine is cold the flap valve closes the cold air intake and the air supplied to the carburettors is heated, being drawn from the exhaust manifold region. As the engine warms up the bi-metallic strip expands and in so doing lifts the flap valve away from the cold air intake and a controlled mixture of both heated and cool air is drawn into the carburettors. Further warming-up of the engine will cause the bi-metallic strip to expand even further until eventually the hot air intake is closed and the incoming air is drawn only from the atmosphere via the cold air intake.
4   The air temperature control system helps to establish low emission levels and reduces the amount of choke usage, thus bringing about a fuel saving. A general improvement in cold engine performance is also a further benefit of employing such a system.

3 Air cleaner assembly – removal and refitting

1   Release the hose clips securing the alloy intake elbows to the air cleaner end pieces.
2   The right-hand elbow can be pulled away from the air cleaner and the carburettor intake.
3   In order to remove the left-hand elbow, pull off the hoses from the left-hand rocker cover to the filter and from the rear of the air cleaner. The left-hand elbow can now be withdrawn complete with attached filter and hoses (photo).
4   Lift the air temperature control valve off its locating pegs and move it forwards towards the radiator until it is separated from the air cleaner.
5   Now lift the air cleaner off its mounting pegs (photo).
6   The filter elements are retained to the air cleaner end pieces by a single plate and screw. Note the positions of the sealing rings as shown in Fig. 3.1.
7   Reassembly and refitting is the reverse of removal and dismantling.

4 Carburettors – general description

1   The SU carburettors fitted to the Rover 3500 are of the variable choke type. The fuel, which is drawn into the air passage through a jet orifice, is metered by a tapered needle which moves in and out of the jet, thus varying the effective size of the orifice. This needle is attached to, and moves with, the air valve piston which controls the variable choke opening. The jet is held in position by a horizontal arm. This is made of a bi-metallic spring, which will vary the jet height to give compensation for temperature changes. These would otherwise give mixture variation due to the fuel viscosity altering. This jet mounting arm is connected through a pivot to a lever. The lever is moved by a screw in the side of the carburettor body to adjust the mixture. The

2.2 The air temperature control flap valve assembly

3.3 Withdraw the left-hand elbow and filter element

3.5 Lifting the air cleaner housing off its mounting pegs

5.1 Side view of the carburettors with air cleaner assembly removed

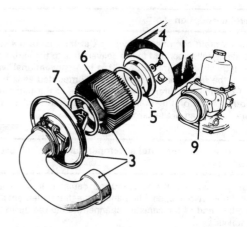

Fig. 3.1 Exploded view of the air filter/elbow assembly

1	Air cleaner housing	5	End plate retainer
3	Elbow assembly	6	Filter element
4	Central retaining screw and washer	7	Sealing ring
		9	Rubber sealing ring

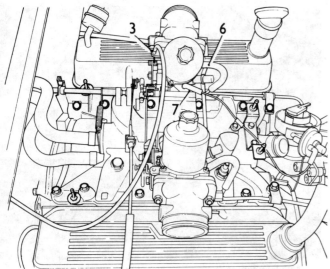

Fig. 3.2A Removing the left-hand carburettor

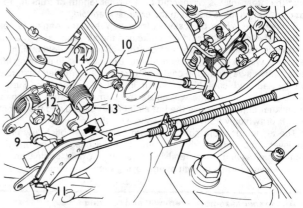

Fig. 3.2B Removing the right-hand carburettor

3	Choke control cable	10	Throttle link connection at left-hand carburettor
6	Float chamber vent pipe	11	Throttle cable end nipple
7	Distributor vacuum take-off pipe	12	Throttle lever spring
9	Left-hand carburettor choke connecting rod	13	Throttle lever retaining nut
		14	Throttle lever

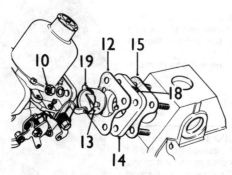

Fig. 3.3 Carburettor attachments to manifold (typical for left and right-hand carburettors)

10	Retaining nut	15	Inner gasket
12	Gasket (outer)	18	Locating arrow on insulator
13	Liner	19	Locating lug on liner
14	Insulator		

screw head is hidden by a plastic blanking plug.

2   The enriched mixture needed for cold starting is provided by a special jet. This has a progressive control to allow partial enrichment and is worked by a cam lever on the carburettor side, opposite to that having the mixture control screw. The cam mechanism is arranged so that as it is moved to enrich the mixture the cam will push up the fast idle screw to open the throttle. The valve that controls this cold start mixture comprises a hollow inner core that is twisted within a cylindrical sleeve allowing a hole in the core and one in the sleeve to coincide.

3   An emulsion bypass passage runs from the jet bridge to the throttle. At small throttle openings unevaporated fuel drops will be drawn along this passage, and mixed more efficiently with this faster travelling air. To match this slot there is a passage cut out of the base of the piston. When fitting a needle, its base should be flush with this slot.

4   The carburettor needle is held in a spring loaded mounting in the piston, biased to one side, so that it always rubs on the side of the jet. The normal type (fixed needle) which is meant to be set central within the jet actually will always vary slightly from true and give uncontrolled variations of mixture. By using this biased needle the effect on mixture will be a known constant.

5   A further feature on H1F6 carburettor is a spring loaded valve on the throttle butterfly. This valve allows air to be drawn in on the overrun thus ensuring that an over rich mixture is not permitted to enter the cylinders, which would otherwise cause high emission output levels.

5   Carburettor (left-hand) – removal and refitting

1   Remove the air cleaner and air temperature control valves as described in Section 3 (photo).
2   Disconnect the choke cable assembly by undoing the pinchbolt and retaining clip.
3   Disconnect the fuel feed lines to the carburettors at the two unions.
4   Disconnect the brake servo vacuum hose at the inlet manifold connection.
5   Pull off the float chamber vent hose.

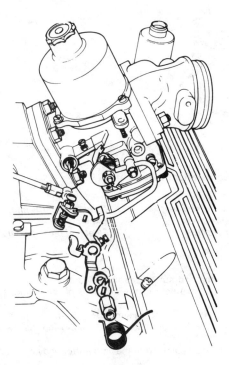

Fig. 3.4 Removing the throttle actuating lever and stop lever (right-hand carburettor)

6   Pull off the distributor vacuum supply pipe at the carburettor connection.
7   Disconnect the countershaft joining link by sliding the upper sleeve away from the centre of the link.
8   Disconnect the choke cable connecting rod at the left-hand carburettor.
9   The throttle link can now be released from the left-hand carburettor.
10 Slide the throttle cable upwards out of its retaining bracket then slip the nipple end of the inner cable out from the throttle quadrant.
11 In order to gain access to the lower right-hand carburettor retaining nut it will be necessary to dismantle the following items.
12 Unhook and remove the throttle lever return spring.
13 Bend back the locking tab washer and remove the throttle lever retaining nut. The throttle lever can now be withdrawn.
14 Undo the four carburettor securing nuts and withdraw the left-hand carburettor followed by the outer gasket, liner, insulator and inner gasket.
15 Refitting of the left-hand carburettor is the reverse of the removal procedure, but the following points should be noted.
16 Clean both the mating faces of the carburettor and induction manifold.
17 Fit the inner gasket, followed by the insulator making sure that the arrow points towards the centre of the manifold.
18 Refit the liner taking care to ensure that the lugs locate properly in the insulator recesses and do not stand proud. **Note**: *The liner can only be fitted one way round, that is with the the blade pointing downwards.*
19 The remainder of the fitting procedure as a direct reversal of the removal sequence.
20 After installation it will be found necessary to tune and adjust the carburettors as described in Section 8.

6   Carburettor (right-hand) – removal and refitting

1   Remove the air cleaner and temperature control valve as described in Section 3.
2   Disconnect the fuel feed at the union.
3   Disconnect the throttle interconnecting link rod at the right-hand carburettor.
4   Undo the pinchbolt and separate the choke interconnecting link rod at the right-hand carburettor.
5   Pull off the float chamber vent pipe at the carburettor connection.
6   In order to gain access to the lower left-hand carburettor securing nut it will be necessary to dismantle the following components.
7   Unclip and remove the throttle return spring.
8   Bend back the ends of the tab washer and remove the actuating lever and the carburettor stop lever retaining nut (Fig. 3.4).
9   The actuating lever and the stop lever can now be slid off.
10 Remove the four carburettor securing nuts and spring washers and withdraw the right-hand carburettor followed by the outer gasket, liner, insulator and inner gasket.
11 Refitting of the right-hand carburettor is the reverse of the removal procedure taking note of the points given in Section 5, paragraphs 15 to 19 of this Chapter.

7   Carburettors – overhaul

1   Remove the carburettors from the car. (See Sections 5 or 6 of this Chapter).
2   Give both carburettors a preliminary clean by washing in a clean petrol bath. Wipe dry with a clean rag.
3   Unscrew the damper and give it a sharp tug to release the retaining clip. Withdraw the damper and sealing washer.
4   Mark the relationship of the suction chamber (dashpot) and carburettor body. Undo the fixing screws and identity tag. Lift the chamber away without tipping it (photo).
5   Remove the piston return spring.
6   Carefully withdraw the piston assembly and empty the oil in the piston rod (photo).
7   To remove the jet needle, remove the needle locking screw and withdraw the needle complete with the spring and guide (Fig. 3.6).
8   Remove the circlip holding the piston lift pin and remove the pin and spring.

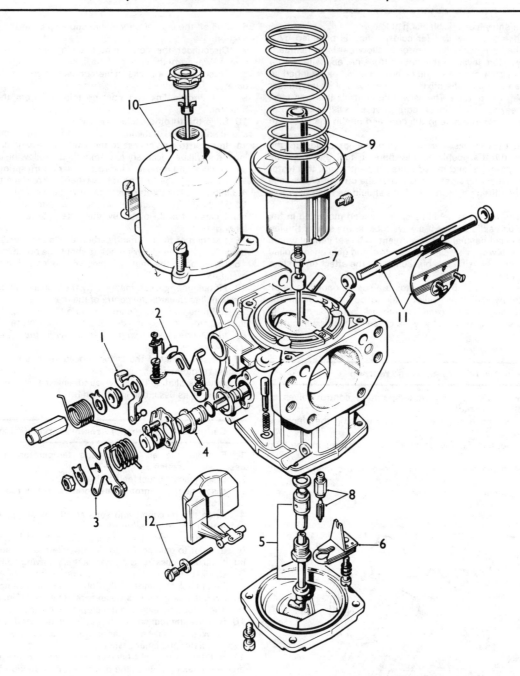

Fig. 3.5 Exploded illustration of the SU HIF6 carburettor (right-hand version shown)

1	Throttle operating lever	5	Jet assembly
2	Throttle stop lever	6	Bi-metal blade
3	Fast idle cam	7	Needle assembly
4	Cold start mechanism		

8	Needle valve and seat	11	Throttle butterfly and
9	Piston and spring		spindle
10	Suction chamber and	12	Float and pivot assembly
	damper		

9   Remove the screws holding the bottom cover plate and remove the plate with its sealing ring (photo).

10 Remove the spring loaded screw securing the bimetal strip and adjusting lever (Fig. 3.7).

11 Withdraw the bimetal strip and jet assembly; disengage the jet from the bimetal strip (photos).

12 Remove the pivot pin for the float spindle. Note the sealing washer (photo).

13 Remove the float, and the needle, fuel control valve (photos).

14 Remove the float needle valve seating (Fig. 3.8).

15 Unscrew the locknut for the jet bearing, and withdraw the jet bearing complete with its sealing washer.

16 Remove the end nut on the choke cam spindle, and remove the cam assembly. Take note of the positions of the spring, spacers and washers.

17 Dismantle the cold start assembly (Fig. 3.9).

18 Remove the throttle butterfly by removing its two retaining screws.

19 Withdraw the spindle from the carburettor body complete with the end seals.

20 This is as far as the dismantling should go to effect an overhaul. It is emphasised that on no account should the jet height setting be altered. This setting is preset at the factory using special flow test rigs. It is for this reason that the access hole to the jet adjustment

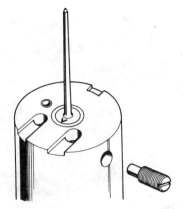

Fig. 3.6 Removing the jet needle assembly

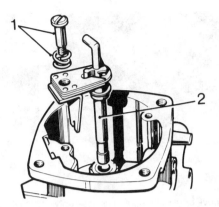

Fig. 3.7 Removing the jet assembly and bi-metal strip

1   Retaining screw and spring   2   Jet assembly

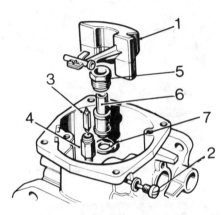

Fig. 3.8 Exploded view of the float, needle valve and jet bearing assemblies

1   Float
2   Float spindle
3   Needle valve
4   Needle valve seat
5   Jet bearing locknut
6   Jet bearing
7   Sealing washer

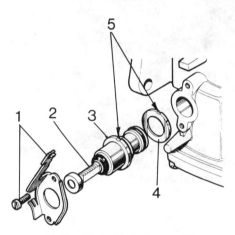

Fig. 3.9 The cold start assembly

1   Cold start retaining plate and screw
2   End seal
3   Cold start valve assembly
4   Valve flange gasket
5   Cut-out for correct alignment

7.3 Remove the suction chamber

7.6 Carefully remove the piston assembly

7.9 Bottom cover plate removed

7.11A Remove bi-metal strip and jet assembly

7.11B How to separate the jet from bi-metal strip

7.12 Removing the float hinge pin and float

7.13 Removing the needle valve

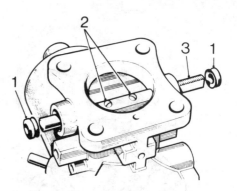

Fig. 3.10 The throttle butterfly assembly

1   Rubber seals
2   Butterfly to spindle retaining screws
3   Butterfly/throttle spindle

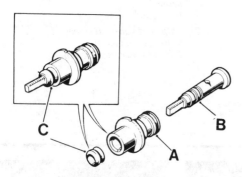

Fig. 3.11 Cold start reassembly

A   O-ring
B   spindle
C   spindle shoulder end seal

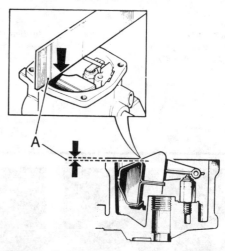

Fig. 3.12 Checking float adjustment gap A = 0.040 in (1.0 mm)

screw is plugged. All other parts can be renewed from the service spares kit available from any Rover dealer or SU stockist – with the exception of the jet adjustment screw. If after overhaul, the carburation still proves to be unsatisfactory, a complete replacement unit will be advisable.

21 Clean all the parts thoroughly in methylated spirit or other suitable solvent.

22 All the seals should be renewed during the rebuild and if the car has covered a high mileage, then it is advised that the jet metering needle be renewed also. Similarly should the throttle butterfly spindle

and its bearings be regarded with a degree of suspicion, it is advisable to have all these new parts to hand, possibly on a use-or-return basis, by arrangement with your local stockist.

23 Plug the transfer holes in the piston assembly and reassemble the piston into the suction chamber, refitting the damper and sealing washer. Turn the whole assembly up-side-down and estimate the time taken for the piston to drop down into the suction chamber. It should take five to seven seconds for H1F6 with 1.750 in (44.5 mm) bore. If a longer time is taken, then re-examine for congealed, or thick oil remaining on the piston rod the piston itself or the suction chamber.

Re-clean and carry out the test once more.

24 Reassemble the butterfly spindle and butterfly (Fig. 3.10) ensuring that the threaded end protrudes from the cold start side of the carburettor body. Note that the edges of the butterfly are chamfered. The butterfly should fit so that the bottom edge moves away from the manifold fitting flange when the throttle is opened. Make sure that the chamfered edges are a good mating fit to the bore.

25 Refit the butterfly securing screws (which should be new), but do not tighten fully at this stage.

26 **Note:** *Emission controlled cars are fitted with a butterfly that has a poppet valve set into the butterfly face.*

27 Operate the throttle spindle several times to centralise the butterfly; then, fully tighten the screws. Lock by gently peening over the protruding ends of the screws. Take great care not to bend the shaft.

28 Replace the new spindle seals with the dished ends towards the throttle. Push the seals in to within 0.035 in (0.9 mm) below the surface of the spindle housing flange.

29 To refit the cold start assembly, first oil the O-ring and fit it to the valve body (Fig. 3.11). Insert the spindle into the valve body from the O-ring end. Locate the end seal with the dished end leading.

30 Turn the carburettor on to its side and support it to give free access to the cold start valve bore. Place the valve gasket (Fig. 3.9) in position with its cut-out slot nearest the top screw hole.

31 Offer up the cold start assembly to the housing ensuring that the cut-out slot in the valve flange lines up with that of the gasket.

32 Assemble the end seal to the cover and fit the retaining plate with the slotted flange facing towards the throttle spindle. Tighten the screws evenly. Do not overtighten.

33 Locate the cam return spring. The straight end slots into the top cut-out in the retaining plate.

34 Offer the cam lever to the spindle with the right-angled extension towards the carburettor body and opposite the cast stop piece.

35 Lock up with the tab washer and nut.

36 Use a wire hook to locate the spring bent end under the extended tab on the cam lever. Move the straight end of the spring from the upper to the lower cut-out in the cold start retaining plate.

37 Refit the jet bearing assembly into the carburettor body, not forgetting to fit the fibre washer, then tighten the locking nut.

38 Refit the float chamber fuel control needle valve seating and tighten.

39 Support the carburettor body for two handed access to the float chamber. Place the needle valve into position in the valve seating – pointed end first. Offer up the float to the float chamber with the Part No lettering uppermost, and the hinged tab abutting against the needle valve. Locate the pivot pin into the carburettor body engaging it through the float hinge. Do not forget the fibre sealing washer. Tighten the pivot pin.

40 To check the correct positioning of the float in relation to the float chamber proceed as follows: support the carburettor with the float chamber uppermost, the needle valve closed by the weight of the float alone, lay a straight edge across the carburettor body flange face and measure with a feeler gauge the clearance between the straight edge and the centre of the float ridge (Fig. 3.12). The clearance should be 0.04 in ± 0.02 in (1.0 mm ± 0.5 mm). If required, bend the float hinge tab to adjust to the correct height.

41 Assemble the bimetal strip and the jet. Position the jet into the jet bearing – the jet head should run parallel with the longer arm of the bimetal strip. The longer arm must engage over the end of the jet adjusting screw. Engage the pivot screw and spring and tighten carefully until the shoulder is tight against the body.

42 Refit the float chamber bottom cover plate, not forgetting the sealing ring which fits into the groove in the cover plate (Fig. 3.13). Ensure that the cut-out section of the plate lines up with the carburettor inlet fitting flange.

43 Refit the piston lifting pin, spring and circlip assembly.

44 Refitting the jet needle to the piston: locate the spring on the top end of the needle ensuring that it fits snugly into the annular groove (Fig. 3.14). Insert the needle through its guide, from the end of the guide carrying the small protrusion. Offer up the complete assembly to the piston, positioning the guide so that the etching marked on its bottom face aligns centrally to the slot between the air holes in the piston. Push the guide into the recess in the piston until the guide face is level with the bottom face of the slot. Lock in this position with the locking screw.

45 Carefully locate the piston assembly on to the carburettor body

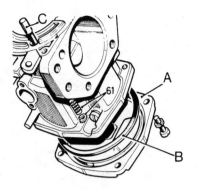

Fig. 3.13 Float chamber cover and piston lifting pin

A   Cover plate
B   Sealing ring

C   Piston lifting pin

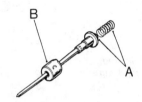

Fig. 3.14 Jet metering assembly

A   Jet needle and spring
B   Needle guide

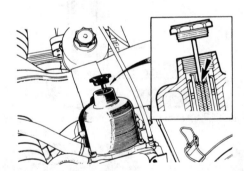

Fig. 3.15 Top up the damper oil to the level arrowed in the insert

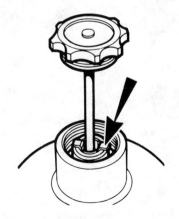

Fig. 3.16 Damper retaining clip (arrowed) must be securely pushed into piston rod

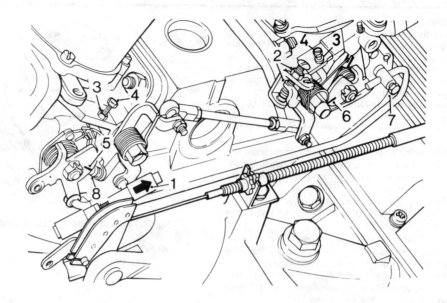

Fig. 3.17 Carburettor linkage and adjustment points (idling speed)

1   Countershaft link rod
2   Lost motion adjusting screw
3   Idle adjustment screw

     locknuts
4   Idle adjustment screws
5   Fast idle cam (left-hand

carburettor)
6   Fast idle cam (right-hand
    carburettor)

7   Choke connecting rod bolt
8   Fast idle screw (left-hand
    carburettor)

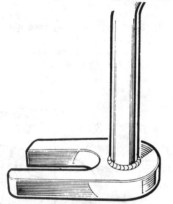

Fig. 3.18 Special tool for carburettor idle adjustment

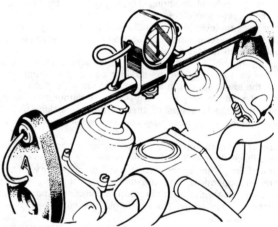

Fig. 3.19 The Rover-recommended air flow meter

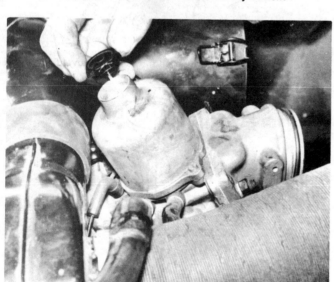

8.6 Unscrew and lift the damper plug to check the damper oil level

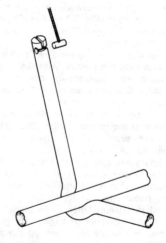

Fig. 3.20 Throttle cable end connection at pedal

and lightly oil the surface of the piston rod. Refit the spring, and by first visually lining up the position, fit the suction chamber without rotation or tilting. The identification tag goes under the rear screw. Tighten the retaining screws evenly – do not overtighten.

46 The damper oil can be introduced at this stage or left until the carburettors are refitted to the car. Make sure that the damper retainer is secure on completion (Fig. 3.15 and 3.16).

47 Finally check the free movement of the piston before refitting the carburettor (see Section 5 or 6).

8 Carburettor adjustments – general

1 The carburettor mixture ratio has been preset at the Rover works and should not be interfered with.

2 However, adjustment can be carried out to the engine idle speed and fast idle speed, without great difficulty.

3 In order to obtain accurate results, the following points must be strictly observed:

   (a) *The ignition timing, distributor pick-up air gap and automatic advance should all be checked for correct settings.*
   (b) *To produce accurate results, an independent and 'accuracy checked' tachometer should be used. The instrument fitted to the car is not suitable.*
   (c) *Ideally, any adjustments to carburettors settings should be carried out wherever possible in an ambient air temperature of between 60°F and 80°F (15.5 to 26.5°C).*

4 The engine idle speed for all models is 725 to 775 rpm.

5 Before attempting any checks upon the settings, a thorough visual and physical examination should be carried out on the throttle cable and linkages, particularly between the pedal and carburettors to ensure that there is no tendency to jerky action or sticking. Ensure that the choke control is operating to its full extent.

6 Unscrew the damper caps and lift the piston and damper to the top of their travel (photo). Fill the retainer recess with clean engine oil and then push the damper down until the cap contacts the top of the suction chamber. Continue this topping-up procedure until oil just remains visible at the bottom of the retainer recess with the piston down. Finally, screw down the cap and repeat this check for the other carburettor.

7 If it should become necessary to adjust the throttle linkage on cars fitted with automatic transmission, then it must follow that an additional check and possible re-adjustment may have to be carried out on the downshift cable, so ensuring, that the downshift cable has not suffered any movement or change in relation to the new linkage adjustment. **Note**: *Incorrect setting of the downshift cable will result in the wrong oil pressure, which in turn will give rise to possible transmission clutch failure.*

8 Before commencing operations upon the engine idle adjustment, the engine should be warmed up to the point when the thermostat has fully opened. Continue running for about 5 minutes, after which, the car should be taken for a run of at least 5 minutes duration, during which, the rpm should remain as near as possible to around the 2500 mark. This warming up cycle may be repeated as often as required during idle adjustments, but the driver is warned against overheating the engine which will cause erratic results.

9 Idling speed – adjustment

1 For automatic cars, move the gear selector lever into the P (park) position.

2 Warm up the engine as outlined in the preceding Section.

3 Stop the engine and remove the air cleaner.

4 Disconnect the countershaft link rod from the left-hand carburettor by sliding the sleeve upwards.

5 Refer to Fig. 3.17 and slacken the locknut on the lost motion adjusting screw. Loosen the screw until it is well clear of the spring loaded pad. This will allow independent adjustment of the carburettors.

6 With the engine running, use the special tool (Fig. 3.18) to slacken off the idle adjusting screw locknuts.

7 Adjust the idle screws equally to obtain the correct engine speeds given in the preceding Section.

8 When both carburettors have been adjusted satisfactorily, lock up the adjusting screw locknuts, holding the adjusting screw in position with a screwdriver, then turn the lost motion adjusting screw to eliminate the free movement and tighten the locknut.

10 Fast idling speed – adjustment

1 Lift the choke control lever on the centre console until the scribed datum mark on the left-hand carburettor fast idle cam is directly opposite the centre line of the fast idle adjustment screw (Refer to Fig. 3.17).

2 In this position the datum mark on the right-hand carburettor fast idle cam should also be in alignment with the centre line of its fast idle adjustment screw.

3 If the right-hand carburettor is misaligned then slacken the choke connecting rod bolt at the right-hand carburettor, and turn the fast idle cam until the screw head centre line and fast idle cam datum mark are in alignment. Tighten the connecting rod bolt.

4 Using the special locknut spanner (Tool no 605927) release the fast idle screw locknut on each carburettor.

5 Adjust the fast idle screws by equal amounts until a fast idle speed of between 1100 and 1200 rpm is achieved.

6 After tightening the locknuts recheck the idle speed.

11 Balancing carburettors – using a flow meter

1 In order to accurately balance or synchronise the carburettors it is essential to use an air flow meter. Various types of air flow meter are marketed but all operate on the same basic principle. The type shown in the illustration (Fig. 3.19) is that recommended by Rover and the correct usage of this tool is described in the text below.

2 Zero the gauge pointer by means of the adjusting screw.

3 Fit the balancing flow meter to the carburettor intakes making sure that there are no air leaks.

4 With the engine running, note the reading on the gauge. If the pointer remains or settles in the zero area of the scale, then no adjustment is necessary. If needle moves to the right, reduce the air flow entering the left-hand carburettor by **unscrewing** the idle adjustment screw. Alternatively increase the air flow through right-hand carburettor by **screwing up** the idle adjuster on that carburettor. If conversely, the needle moves to the left, then reverse the procedure.

5 If the idling speed rises too high or drops during these checks, adjust to the correct idle speed, maintaining the gauge needle in the zero area.

6 The difference in engine speeds set with and/or without the balancer in position will be negligible, being in the region of plus or minus 25 rev/min. However, a wide variation in speeds would indicate a basic carburettor fault that may only be remedied by an overhaul, or replacement units. It should be borne in mind that with the SU H1F6, only limited overhaul is possible (see Section 7 of this Chapter).

7 Hold the left-hand carburettor lever against its idling screw and then screw down the lost motion screw on the right-hand carburettor until it just touches the spring loaded pad and then tighten the locknut.

12 Throttle cable – removal and refitting

1 Remove the air cleaner assembly as described in Section 3.

2 Slide the outer throttle cable adjustment nut upwards from its slotted locating post.

3 Release the inner cable end nipple from the throttle quadrant (photo).

4 Open the driver's glovebox, detach the support straps and remove the two retaining screws at the rear. Detach the glovebox from the spigot of the pivot brackets.

5 Release the nipple end of the inner cable from the slotted cutout of the throttle pedal (Fig. 3.20).

6 Pull the cable through the bulkhead and extract the rubber grommet.

7 Refitting of the throttle cable is the reverse of the removal, but the following points should be observed:

8 Fit the rubber grommet to the bulkhead so that the sleeve end is facing into the engine compartment.

9 Lubricate, with a multi-purpose grease, the accessible parts of the inner cable and then feed the complete cable through the bulkhead

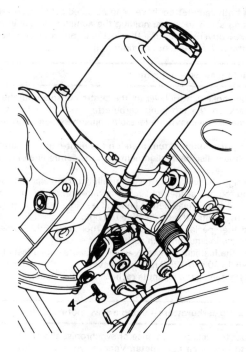

Fig. 3.21 Choke cable connection at carburettor

4   Trunnion pinchbolt

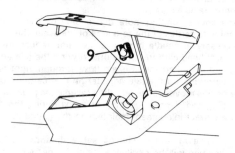

Fig. 3.22 Choke cable connection at console control lever

9   Spring retainer

12.3 Release the throttle inner cable from the throttle quadrant

from the engine compartment side.
10 Attach the nipple end of the inner cable to the throttle pedal cutout.
11 Refit the driver's glovebox.
12 Fit the nipple end of the throttle cable to the throttle quadrant and slide the adjustment nut down on to its slotted retaining bracket.
13 Turn the adjuster nut to eliminate any undue slackness or tightness.
14 Refit the air cleaner assembly as detailed in Section 3.

13 Choke cable – removal and refitting

1   Disconnect the engine breather filter from the left-hand rocker cover and the air cleaner housing. **Note**: *the breather filter is fitted with the IN face towards the inlet manifold.*
2   Unscrew the hose clip and remove the left-hand air cleaner housing elbow.
3   Undo the nut securing the fuel feed pipe support bracket to the left-hand carburettor intake face. Loosen the screws clamping the pipe to the bracket and slide the bracket along the pipe to gain access to the choke cable trunnion bolt.
4   Undo the trunnion pinchbolt and remove the outer cable retaining clip. The forward section of the choke cable can now be pulled away from the carburettor (Fig. 3.21).
5   Remove the driver's glovebox as described in Section 12, paragraph 4.
6   Prise up the centre console rear panel and remove the screw retaining the choke control lever assembly.
7   Remove the inner cable rod retaining clip and disconnect the electrical leads to the choke warning light switch.
8   Remove the centre console as described in Chapter 12.
9   Lubricate the outer part of the cable so allowing the complete cable assembly to be drawn through the bulkhead grommet from within the car.
10 Refitting of the choke cable is the reverse of the removal procedure, but the following points should be noted to ensure easy fitment and satisfactory choke operation.
11 Remove the choke inner cable from the outer cable. Apply a multi-purpose grease to the inner cable and refit it into the outer one.
12 Apply a small quantity of grease to the outer cable to assist in feeding it up through the bulkhead grommet.
13 Route the cable past the underside of the heater unit and through the bulkhead grommet.
14 Refit the centre console and the glovebox by reversing the removal procedures.
15 When fitting the cable to the choke lever ensure that the outer cable locates correctly in the integral clip located underneath the lever (see Fig. 3.22).
16 After connecting the choke cable to the carburettor, check the choke operation.

14 In-line fuel filter – removal and refitting

1   Rover recommend that the in-line fuel filter be renewed at 12 000 mile (20 000 km) intervals or annually whichever occurs first (photo).
2   Undo the union nuts at either end of the filter.
3   Loosen the clip securing the filter to the bracket.
4   Withdraw the filter and discard.
5   Refitting of the new filter is the reverse of the removal procedure but it is important to ensure that the end of the fuel filter marked 'IN' is connected to the fuel supply pipe. In some instances the new filter may only have an arrow marked on it and in such cases the arrow denotes the fuel flow direction, ie towards the carburettors.
6   After fitting the new filter start the engine and check for leaks.

15 Fuel tank – removal and refitting

Warning: *Due to the high fire risk do not use a naked light. It is preferable to work on the car out in the open taking advantage of the natural light and the breeze to dispel any petrol vapours.*
1   For safety reasons, immobilise all electrical circuits, by disconnecting the battery negative terminal connection.
2   Should the fuel tank be over a quarter full, then for ease of handl-

ing, syphon out into a suitable clean container using a length of hose.

3   Fold down the rear seat squab and pull the luggage compartment covering back to reveal a large rubber grommet.

4   Pull out the grommet and disconnect the wiring plug from the socket.

5   Disconnect the fuel feed pipe from the pump/tank outlet.

6   Chock the front wheels, raise the rear of the car and support it on axle stands or strong packing blocks.

7   Remove the left-hand rear roadwheel to gain access to the fuel filler pipe connecting hose (Fig.3.23).

8   Clean away the road dirt in the area around the fuel filter connecting hose then loosen the clips sufficiently to enable the hose to be slid up clear of the tank filler neck.

9   Pull off the fuel tank vent hose.

10   Place a trolley jack directly underneath the fuel tank to support it. Insert a suitable piece of flat wood between the tank and the jack lifting pad to prevent damage to the tank.

11   Release the fuel feed pipe from the right-hand side of the fuel tank. Access to these is from beneath the car.

12   Ensure that the jack is supporting the fuel tank centrally then remove the remaining two bolts (front end) and the two nuts (rear end), securing the tank (Fig. 3.24).

13   Lower the jack slowly and draw the fuel tank out from underneath the car.

14   If the tank is to be renewed then it will be necessary to remove the vent hose and the fuel feed line clips in order to extract the fuel pump and tank unit assembly. In addition, any surplus fuel left in the old tank will have to be drained out.

15   Non-professional home repairs on the fuel tank if split or leaking are not recommended. The only remedy for such faults is to fit a new tank or a professionally reconditioned unit. Generally it will be found that a radiator repair specialist will also undertake fuel tank repairs.

16   Refitting of the fuel tank is the reverse of the removal procedure. **Note**: *when fitting the fuel pump and tank gauge unit, use a new gasket.* Details of the fuel pump/tank gauge assembly is covered in Section 16.

16 Fuel pump and tank gauge unit – removal and refitting

1   Disconnect the negative battery terminal.

2   Fold the rear seat squab forward and then roll the luggage compartment floor covering back towards the rear of the car.

3   Roll back the extreme left-hand felt strip and remove the large rubber grommet from the luggage compartment floor panel (photo).

4   Disconnect the wiring plug from the socket fitted into the upper exposed section of the fuel tank.

5   Undo the fuel outlet union connection situated next to the wiring

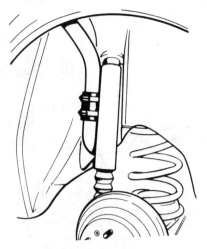

Fig. 3.23 Location of the filler pipe connecting hose

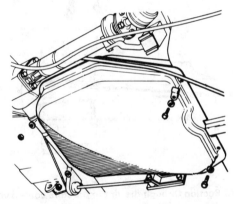

Fig. 3.24 Locations of the nuts and bolts which retain the fuel tank

14.1 The in-line fuel filter unit

16.3 Access to the fuel pump/tank gauge unit is through a hole in the rear floor panel

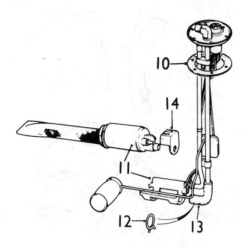

Fig. 3.25 The fuel pump and tank gauge unit

10 Gasket   13 Elbow hose
11 Pump and retaining clip 14 Terminal cover
12 Spring clip

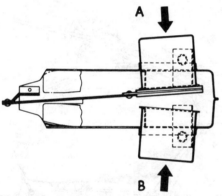

Fig. 3.26 Section through the air temperature control valve

A   Cold air intake from atmosphere
B   Hot air intake from exhaust manifold heat chamber

17.5 Layout of the crankcase breather hoses

socket.

6   Remove the six retaining screws securing the fuel pump/tank gauge unit to the fuel tank.

7   Withdraw the assembly up through the top of the fuel tank and remove the gasket (Fig. 3.25).

8   The pump can be separated from the assembly after releasing the spring clip, elbow hose, terminal cover and two electrical leads.

9   Refitting the pump to the tank gauge unit is the reverse of removal. When connecting the pump cables the black cable is fitted to the (–) terminal and the red cable to the (+) terminal.

10   When fitting the assembly use a new gasket and reverse the removal procedure.

11   **Note**: *The electric feed supply to the fuel pump is taken from the starter motor solenoid and the engine oil pressure switch; consequently, the fuel pump is only operative when the engine is being turned by the starter motor or is running with sufficient oil pressure.*

17   Emission control systems – general description

1   The engine fitted to this Rover model is a well tried and proven unit having been modified to deliver a higher power output with a lower fuel consumption. It is therefore obvious that this modified engine is more efficient when compared with its predecessors and as a consequence the emission output levels from it are substantially less.

2   The emission control system comprises basically of the following two systems although it must be emphasised that many other components play a contributory part in maintaining the low emission levels.

3   *Air intake temperature control system:* A description of this system is given in Section 2.

4   *Crankcase emission control system:* In this system the crankcase fumes and blow-by gases are recirculated through the induction manifold and burned in the normal combustion process.

5   The breathing cycle is initiated by clean air being drawn from the back of the air cleaner, which is then fed into the left-hand rocker cover via hoses and an in-line filter (photo).This clean air enters the crankcase and the crankcase fumes rise through the pushrod tubes and are collected in the right-hand rocker cover. These fumes then pass through the flame trap and are directed to the depression side of the carburettors by rubber hoses. These fumes are then drawn into the combustion chamber and burned.

18   Emission control systems – maintenance

Air intake temperature control system
1   This system is basically maintenance free, apart from a periodic inspection of the hot and cold air flexible hoses.

2   A function test can be carried out quite simply, to check the operation of the flap valve and bi-metallic strip.

3   With the engine cold, disconnect the cold air intake flexible hose and check that the flap valve is covering the cold air inlet port. Reconnect the hose and run the engine until normal operating temperature is reached, then disconnect the hot air intake flexible hose. The flap valve should in this condition be covering the hot air intake port. Reconnect the hot air intake hose (Fig. 3.26).

4   If the function of the air intake temperature control system does not follow that described in paragraph 3, the only remedy is to renew the assembly.

Crankcase emission control system
5   Periodically, disconnect the interconnecting hoses between the carburettors and the flame trap. Inspect the hoses carefully for deterioration and clean them by passing a short length of cloth through them.

6   The flame trap can be unscrewed from the right-hand rocker cover and cleaned by immersing it in a suitable solvent, ie paraffin. After cleaning, shake the flame trap vigorously to expel all of the cleaning solvent.

7   An in-line breather filter is fitted in the system and lies between the left-hand rocker cover and the air cleaner housing. This filter should be renewed at periods of 12 000 miles (20 000 kms) or annually whichever occurs first. When fitting the filter, the end marked 'IN' must face towards the inlet manifold.

19.3 Examine the rubber support rings for deterioration

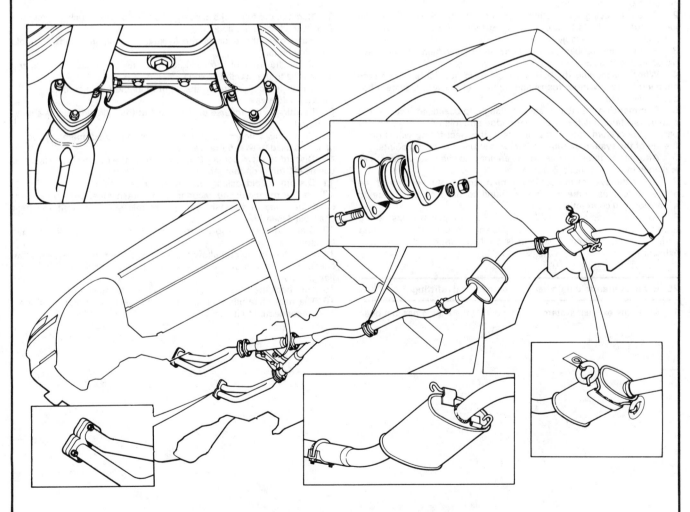

Fig. 3.27 Layout and detail of the exhaust system

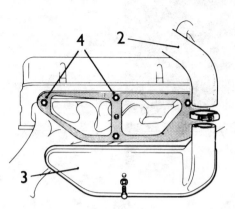

Fig. 3.28 The heat chamber is connected to the right-hand exhaust manifold

2   *Hot air intake hose*   4   *Heat chamber backplate bolts*
3   *Heat chamber cover*

19 Exhaust system – general

1   The exhaust system is of a conventional design consisting of several short sections with flanged connections for easy renewal of corroded or damaged parts.
2   When removing any section, apply penetrating oil liberally to the flange nuts and bolts before unscrewing them, and obtain new joint gaskets before reassembly.
3   Examine the rubber support rings and renew them if they have perished due to oil contamination or heat (photo).
4   When assembling the exhaust system do not tighten the flange coupling bolts any more than finger tight until the whole system has been connected.
5   Commencing at the manifold flange, proceed to secure the exhaust system, but take care that undue strain is not placed on any part of the system due to misalignment. Incorrect fitting will shorten the life of the system by causing fractures at the connecting points.
6   After fitting the system start the engine and check for exhaust gas leakages from the couplings and flanges.
7   Allow the system to cool down, then recheck the security of the entire system as some settling is bound to have occurred due to expansion and contraction.
8   Holts Flexiwrap and Holts Gun Gum exhaust repair systems can be used for effective repairs to exhaust pipes and silencer boxes, including ends and bends. Holts Flexiwrap is an MOT approved permanent exhaust repair.

20 Exhaust manifold (left-hand) – removal and refitting

1   Allow the exhaust system to cool down if the engine has just been running, then bend back the locking tabs on the eight manifold retaining bolts.
2   Raise the front of the car and undo the three nuts securing the downpipe to the manifold flange.
3   Lower the car and undo the eight manifold to cylinder head retaining bolts and lift the manifold away.
4   Refitting is the reverse of removal, but it is necessary to renew the two copper O-rings which are fitted to the down pipe flange.
5   Between the manifold and the cylinder head is a 'face joint' having no gasket. It is therefore, imperative that both faces are scrupulously clean.
6   Secure the manifold in position using new locking tabs and tighten the bolts to the recommended torque setting. Do not bend the locking tab ends back on to the bolt heads at this stage.
7   Secure the down pipe to the manifold flange having fitted the new copper O-rings in position. Tighten the securing nuts to the recommended torque setting.
8   Start the engine and check for exhaust gas leakages. Stop the engine and allow the exhaust system to cool down. Now check the tightness of the exhaust manifold and down pipe flange. The tab washer ends can now be bent back over the bolt heads.

21 Exhaust manifold (right-hand) – removal and refitting

1   Allow the exhaust system to cool down sufficiently if the engine has just been running. Remove the washer fluid reservoir.
2   Undo the hose clip and pull off the hot air intake hose from the heat chamber cover.
3   Remove the bolt and washer, then lift away the heat chamber cover.
4   Remove the four bolts securing the back plate of the heat chamber and lift the back plate away.
5   Bend back the ends of the locking tabs on the eight manifold retaining bolts.
6   Raise the front of the car and undo the three nuts securing the down pipe to the manifold flange.
7   Lower the car and undo the eight manifold retaining bolts and lift the manifold away.
8   Refitting is the reverse of removal, but the following points should be noted.
9   Clean the cylinder head and manifold faces scrupulously, as no gasket is used between the two parts.
10   Discard the two copper O-rings fitted to the down pipe flange and use new O-rings on reassembly.
11   Discard the old locking tabs and use new ones.
12   Fit the manifold and reconnect the down pipe, but do not turn back the ends of the tab washers at this stage, or refit the heat chamber assembly.
13   Start the engine, allow it to warm up and check for exhaust gas leakage.
14   Stop the engine and allow the exhaust system to cool down. Now check the tightness of the exhaust manifold bolts and the down pipe flange nuts.
15   Turn back the ends of the locking tabs on to the bolt heads.
16   The heat chamber assembly can now be refitted and the hot air hose reconnected to it.

22 Fault diagnosis – fuel system

Symptom	Reason/s
Carburation and ignition faults	Air cleaner choked and dirty giving rich mixture Fuel leaking from carburettor/s or fuel lines Float chamber flooding Generally worn carburettor/s Balance weights or vacuum advance mechanism in distributor faulty
Poor performance	Carburettor/s incorrectly adjusted, mixture too rich or too weak Idling speed too high Distributor pick-up air gap incorrect Carburettors require balancing Incorrectly set spark plugs Tyres under-inflated Wrong spark plugs fitted Brakes dragging Petrol tank air vent restricted Partially clogged fuel pump or in-line filter Dirt lodged in float chamber needle housing Incorrectly seating valves in fuel pump Too little fuel in fuel tank (prevalent when climbing steep hills)
Air leaks	Union joints on pipe connections loose Inlet manifold to block joint, or inlet manifold to carburettor/s gasket leaking
Fuel pump faults	Disconnected cables at pump Wires disconnected at oil pressure switch; this switch affects the fuel pump operation Fuel pump filter clogged Suction pipe of fuel pump disconnected

Chapter 4 Ignition system

For modifications, and information applicable to later models, see Supplement at end of manual

Contents

Specifications

Distributor
Type .... Lucas 35 DE8 (Opus electronic)
Rotation .... Clockwise
Pick-up air gap .... 0.014 to 0.016 in (0.36 to 0.41 mm)

Ignition coil
Type .... Lucas 22 C 12 (electronic)
Ballast resistor type 9BR

Spark plugs
Type .... Champion N9YCC or N9YC
Electrode gap .... 0.032 in (0.80 mm)

Ignition timing
Static .... 6° BTDC
Dynamic (with distributor vacuum pipe removed) .... 10° BTDC at 1200 rpm
17° BTDC at 1800 rpm
22° BTDC at 2600 rpm
Location of timing marks .... Scale on crankshaft damper and notch on pointer attached to timing cover

Engine firing order .... 1,8,4,3,6,5,7,2 (No 1 front, left bank odd, right bank even)

Torque wrench settings

Torque wrench settings	lbf ft	Nm
Spark plugs	12	16
Distributor clamp plate bolt	14	19

1 General description

In order that the engine may run correctly, it is necessary for an electrical spark to ignite the fuel/air charge in the combustion chamber at exactly the right moment in relation to engine speed and load.

The system fitted to all Rover 3500 models is of the electronic type. In comparison with the conventional type of distributor the cam, contact breaker points and capacitor are replaced by an oscillator, timing rotor, pick-up amplifier and power transistor. These components are all housed in a standard Lucas distributor body.

Basically the transistorised ignition functions are as follows: during operation, the oscillator supplies pulses to the pick-up in a continuous sequence. As the timing rotor, which is driven by the distributor shaft and has a ferrite rod for each lobe, passes the pick-up,

one of its ferrite rods catches one of the pulses and applies it to the amplifier. This amplified pulse causes the power transistor to switch off; this results in a collapse of the ignition coil primary circuit and a high secondary voltage is induced similarly to a conventional system.

The ignition timing is advanced and retarded automatically to ensure that the spark occurs at just the right instant for the particular load at the prevailing engine speed.

The ignition advance is controlled by a mechanical and vacuum operated system. The mechanical governor mechanism comprises two weights which move out under centrifugal force from the central distributor shaft as the engine speed rises. As they move outwards they rotate the cams relative to the distributor shaft, and so advance the spark. The movement of the weights is governed by two springs, and it is the tension of the springs which is largely responsible for correct spark advancement.

The vacuum control comprises a diaphragm in a sealed casing, one side of which is connected, via a small bore tube, to a carburettor, and the other side of the moving plate. Depression in the inlet manifold and carburettors, which varies with engine speed and throttle opening, causes the diaphragm to move, so moving the plate. This advances or retards the spark. A fine degree of control is achieved by a spring in the vacuum assembly.

2 Pick-up air gap – adjustment

Caution: Do not attempt to check the pick-up air gap with the ignition switched on.

1 Disconnect the battery negative lead.
2 Spring back the retaining clips and lift away the distributor cap.
3 Pull off the rotor arm and remove the plastic anti-flash cover.
4 Slide a 0·014 to 0·016 in (0·34 to 0·41 mm) feeler gauge between the timing rotor and the pick-up coil contact. It should be a firm sliding fit, if too tight or too loose, adjustment will be required.
Note: *The angular position of the rotor is not important.*
5 To adjust, slacken the pick-up retaining screws and reposition as necessary. Recheck the gap after the screws have been tightened (Fig. 4.1).
6 Whilst the distributor cap is removed, wipe it clean with a clean dry cloth. If the electrodes in the cap are badly burnt the cap will need to be renewed. Otherwise, light corrosion or scoring can be removed with a penknife or small screwdriver.
7 Push the carbon brush (located in the centre of the distributor cap) inwards a few times and make sure that it is free to move.
8 Fit the anti-flash cover, rotor and distributor cap.
9 Reconnect the battery negative lead.

3 Distributor – removal and refitting

1 Disconnect the battery negative lead.
2 Remove the two straps which secure the distributor wiring harness to the bracket.
3 At the ignition coil disconnect the two relevant Lucar connectors noting their exact positions for refitting.
4 At the ballast resistor pull out the appropriate harness plug.
5 Pull off the vacuum supply hose at the distributor vacuum capsule.
6 Pull off the ignition HT lead at the ignition coil.
7 Pull off the spark plug leads and release them from the plastic retainers attached to the rocker covers.
8 Spring back the distributor cap securing clips and lift off the cap (photo).
9 Pull off the rotor arm and extract the anti-flash cover (photo).
10 Temporarily refit the rotor arm.
11 Rotate the crankshaft pulley until the TDC mark on the pulley is aligned with the pointer and No 1 cylinder is firing. This position can be checked by observing if the rotor arm is pointing to the No 1 segment if the distributor cap were to be refitted.
12 Remove the distributor clamping plate bolt. Lift away the clamp plate and withdraw the distributor together with the wiring harness.
13 Before fitting the distributor rotate the oil pump shaft until the tongue of the shaft is visible.
14 Turn the rotor arm until it is lying in the position as shown in Fig. 4.4A and refit the distributor into its locating bore. Some degree of movement may be required to engage the slotted adaptor to the oil pump shaft tongue.
15 With the distributor base resting against the timing cover, the rotor arm should now be positioned as shown in Fig. 4.4B.
16 Reposition the clamp bracket, but only screw in the retaining bolt finger tight.
17 Pull off the rotor arm and check the static ignition timing as described in Section 6.
18 Reconnect the vacuum advance pipe.
19 Reconnect the harness plug at the ballast resistor.
20 Reconnect the two Lucar connectors to the ignition coil. The black cable with both a white and a green identification mark must be fitted to the negative (–) terminal.
21 Refit the anti-flash cover, the rotor arm and distributor cap.
22 The HT leads can now be refitted to their respective sparking plugs and clipped to the rocker cover fixings. The remaining HT lead fits into the ignition coil.

Fig. 4.1 Adjusting the pick-up air gap

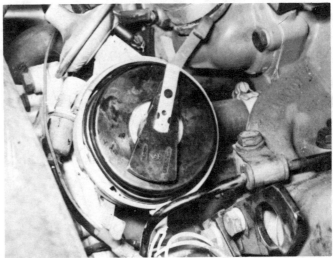

3.8 The distributor after removal of the distributor cap

3.9 The distributor after removal of the rotor arm and anti-flash cover

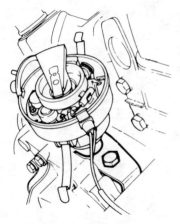

Fig. 4.2 Location of the distributor clamping plate bolt

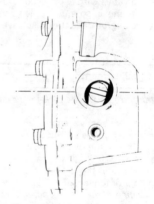

Fig. 4.3 Positioning the oil pump shaft prior to installing the distributor

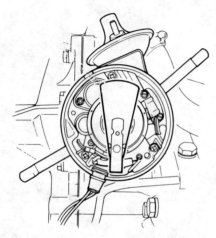

Fig. 4.4A Position the rotor arm as shown prior to fitting

Fig. 4.4B On entry the rotor arm will turn and assume this position

23 Refit the two straps securing the wiring harnesses to the cantilever bracket.
24 Reconnect the battery and check the ignition timing as described in Section 6.

4 Distributor – dismantling, overhaul and reassembly

1 Remove the distributor from the car as previously described, and take off the cap.
2 Remove the rotor arm and anti-flash cover, and withdraw the felt lubrication pad.
3 Using a pair of small external circlip pliers, remove the circlip retaining the timing rotor.
4 After removing the circlip, extract the plain washer followed by a rubber O-ring and then withdraw the timing rotor.
5 Undo the retaining screws and lift away the pick-up unit and the electronic assembly plate together with the wiring grommet which is a push fit into the distributor body.
6 At this side of the distributor body remove two further screws and withdraw the vacuum unit and gasket, together with the capacitor unit.
7 Use a small pin punch to drive out the roll pin retaining the drive gear. Remove the drive gear and thrust washer.
8 Ensure that there are no burrs on the driveshaft, then withdraw it.
9 Extract the elastic distance collar and remove the control springs. When removing the control springs exercise care as they can easily be

distorted and ruined.
10 Remove the O-ring from the distributor body. No further dismantling should be attempted.
11 Clean the mechanical parts carefully in petrol, then examine them for wear as described in the following paragraphs.
12 Check the fit of the balance weights on the distributor shaft. If the pivots are loose or the holes excessively worn, the relevant parts must be renewed. The springs are best renewed anyway.
13 Examine the driving gear teeth for wear and renew if necessary.
14 Check the fit of the driveshaft in the housing. If excessive wear is present, the parts must be renewed.
15 Check that the vacuum unit is working correctly by sucking through the tube and checking that the linkage moves.
16 Check the metal contact on the distributor rotor for security of fixing and burning. Small burning marks can be removed with a smooth file or very fine emery paper, but if anything else is wrong the rotor should be renewed. Look also for cracks in the plastic moulding.
17 Check the distributor cap in a similar manner, renewing it if necessary.
18 Reassembly is essentially the reverse of the dismantling procedure, but the following points should be noted:

    (a) Lubricate the weight assembly with a dry lubricant
    (b) Lubricate the shaft with a dry lubricant
    (c) Lubricate the moving plate pin with a dry lubricant
    (d) Adjust the pick-up coil air gap as described in Section 2
    (e) Lubricate the distributor as described in Section 5

Are your plugs trying to tell you something?

Normal.
Grey-brown deposits, lightly coated core nose. Plugs ideally suited to engine, and engine in good condition.

Heavy Deposits.
A build up of crusty deposits, light-grey sandy colour in appearance.
Fault: Often caused by worn valve guides, excessive use of upper cylinder lubricant, or idling for long periods.

Lead Glazing.
Plug insulator firing tip appears yellow or green/yellow and shiny in appearance.
Fault: Often caused by incorrect carburation, excessive idling followed by sharp acceleration. Also check ignition timing.

Carbon fouling.
Dry, black, sooty deposits.
Fault: over-rich fuel mixture.
Check: carburettor mixture settings, float level, choke operation, air filter.

Oil fouling.
Wet, oily deposits. Fault: worn bores/piston rings or valve guides; sometimes occurs (temporarily) during running-in period.

Overheating.
Electrodes have glazed appearance, core nose very white – few deposits. Fault: plug overheating. Check: plug value, ignition timing, fuel octane rating (too low) and fuel mixture (too weak).

Electrode damage.
Electrodes burned away; core nose has burned, glazed appearance. Fault: pre-ignition. Check: for correct heat range and as for 'overheating'.

Split core nose.
(May appear initially as a crack). Fault: detonation or wrong gap-setting technique. Check: ignition timing, cooling system. fuel mixture (too weak).

WHY DOUBLE COPPER IS BETTER FOR YOUR ENGINE.

Unique Trapezoidal Copper Cored Earth Electrode — — 50% Larger Spark Area

— Copper Cored Centre Electrode

Champion Double Copper plugs are the first in the world to have copper core in both centre <u>and</u> earth electrode. This innovative design means that they run cooler by up to 100°C – giving greater efficiency and longer life. These double copper cores transfer heat away from the tip of the plug faster and more efficiently. Therefore, Double Copper runs at cooler temperatures than conventional plugs giving improved acceleration response and high speed performance with no fear of pre-ignition.

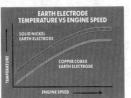

Champion Double Copper plugs also feature a unique trapezoidal earth electrode giving a 50% increase in spark area. This, together with the double copper cores, offers greatly reduced electrode wear, so the spark stays stronger for longer.

 FASTER COLD STARTING

 FOR UNLEADED OR LEADED FUEL

 ELECTRODES UP TO 100°C COOLER

 BETTER ACCELERATION RESPONSE

 LOWER EMISSIONS

 50% BIGGER SPARK AREA

 THE LONGER LIFE PLUG

Plug Tips/Hot and Cold.
Spark plugs must operate within well-defined temperature limits to avoid cold fouling at one extreme and overheating at the other.
Champion and the car manufacturers work out the best plugs for an engine to give optimum performance under all conditions, from freezing cold starts to sustained high speed motorway cruising.
Plugs are often referred to as hot or cold. With Champion, the higher the number on its body, the hotter the plug, and the lower the number the cooler the plug. For the correct plug for your car refer to the specifications at the beginning of this chapter.

Plug Cleaning
Modern plug design and materials mean that Champion no longer recommends periodic plug cleaning. Certainly don't clean your plugs with a wire brush as this can cause metal conductive paths across the nose of the insulator so impairing its performance and resulting in loss of acceleration and reduced m.p.g.
However, if plugs are removed, always carefully clean the area where the plug seats in the cylinder head as grit and dirt can sometimes cause gas leakage.
Also wipe any traces of oil or grease from plug leads as this may lead to arcing.

DOUBLE COPPER

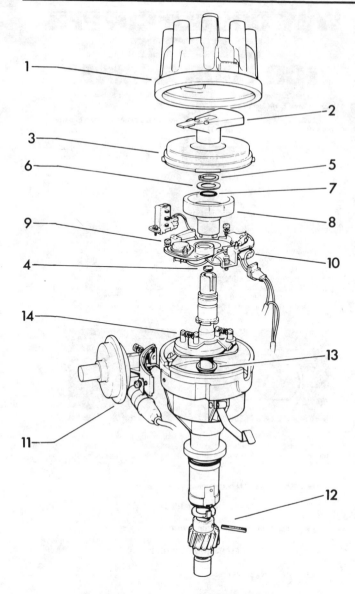

Fig. 4.5 Exploded view of the distributor

1	Distributor cap	9	Pick-up unit
2	Rotor arm	10	Electronic assembly plate
3	Anti-flash cover	11	Vacuum unit, rubber gasket and
4	Felt lubrication pad		capacitor
5	Circlip	12	Drive gear roll pin
6	Plain washer	13	Distance piece collar
7	Rubber O-ring	14	Control springs and advance/
8	Timing rotor		retard unit

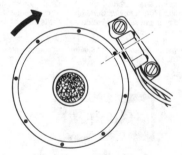

Fig. 4.6 Static timing check

6.2 The crankshaft timing marks and fixed pointer (timing set at TDC or 0° in photograph)

5   Distributor – lubrication

1   During routine maintenance, and where otherwise stated in this Chapter, the distributor should be lubricated as follows.
2   Remove the distributor cap, rotor arm and anti-flash cover.
3   Apply a few drops of engine oil to the felt pad in the cavity below the rotor.
4   Inject a few drops of engine oil through the apertures to lubricate the centrifugal advance mechanism.
5   Refit the anti-flash cover, rotor arm and distributor cap.

6   Ignition timing – checking and adjustment

1   In this Section, procedures are given for static and dynamic checking. With conventional distributors, the static setting is satisfactory for most practical purposes. This is not however true in the case of transistorised types; here, the static setting may only be regarded as a basic setting-up point when the dynamic setting has been lost.

Static setting

2   Rotate the crankshaft in the normal direction of rotation until the fixed pointer is in alignment with the 6° BTDC mark on the crankshaft pulley damper (photo).
3   Remove the distributor cap, rotor and anti-flash cover.
4   If the static timing is correctly set the relationship of the nearest ferrite rod in the timing rotor to the pick-up should be as shown in Fig. 4.6.
5   If correction is required, loosen the distributor clamping plate bolt and rotate the distributor body as required.
6   Tighten the distributor clamp plate bolt, then recheck the static timing.
7   Fit the anti-flash cover, rotor arm and distributor cap, then carry out the dynamic setting check as described below.

Dynamic setting

8   Connect the battery negative lead.
9   If possible, connect an external tachometer to the engine; if not available, use the car tachometer.
10 Using a proprietary stroboscopic timing light connected in accordance with the manufacturer's instructions, run the engine at the various speeds indicated in the Specifications and check the timing.
Note: *During these tests the vacuum advance unit pipe should be removed from the distributor and plugged.*
11 Should the timing not be as quoted then loosen the distributor

clamp plate bolt and rotate the distributor body anti-clockwise to advance, or clockwise to retard. This must only be done with the engine stopped.

12 Should the ignition timing be satisfactory at the lower engine speeds, but fail to remain accurate as the engine speed is increased, then it is reasonable to assume that the mechanical advance weights are sticking. One possible cause of sticking advance weights is the use of a non-specified lubricant.

13 On completion, remove the stroboscopic timing light and reconnect the No 1 spark plug HT lead.

7 Spark plugs and HT leads

1 The correct functioning of the spark plugs is vital for the correct running and efficiency of the engine. It is essential that the plugs fitted are appropriate for the engine, and the suitable type is specified at the beginning of this chapter. If this type is used and the engine is in good condition, the spark plugs should not need attention between scheduled replacement intervals. Spark plug cleaning is rarely necessary and should not be attempted unless specialised equipment is available as damage can easily be caused to the firing ends.

2 The condition of the spark plugs will also tell much about the overall condition of the engine.

3 If the insulator nose of the spark plug is clean and white, with no deposits, this is indicative of a weak mixture, or too hot a plug (a hot plug transfers heat away from the electrode slowly, a cold plug transfers heat away quickly).

4 If the top and insulator nose is covered with hard black deposits, then this is indicative that the mixture is too rich. Should the plug be black and oily, then it is likely that the engine is fairly worn, as well as the mixture being too rich.

5 If the insulator nose is covered with light tan to greyish brown deposits, then the mixture is correct and it is likely that the engine is in good condition.

6 The spark plug gap is of considerable importance, as, if it is too large or too small, the size of the spark and its efficiency will be seriously impaired. The spark plug gap should be set to the specified gap.

7 To set it, measure the gap with a feeler gauge, and then bend open, or close, the outer plug electrode until the correct gap is achieved. The centre electrode should never be bent as this may crack the insulation and cause plug failure, if nothing worse.

8 Replace the distributor HT leads in the correct firing order, which is 1 8 4 3 6 5 7 2; No 1 cylinder being the one nearest the radiator in the left-hand cylinder bank.

9 The plug leads require no routine maintenance other than being kept clean and wiped over regularly.

8 Fault diagnosis – ignition system

Caution: *The HT voltage generated by the transistorised ignition system is considerably higher than that in a conventional system. Take care to avoid personal electric shocks when testing the system. Always use insulated tools or non-conductive material when handling live HT leads. Persons equipped with an artificial cardiac pacemaker should not risk handling live HT leads at all.*

Engine fails to start

1 If the engine fails to start and the car was running normally when it was last used, first check there is fuel in the fuel tank. If the engine turns over normally on the starter motor and the battery is evidently well charged, then the fault may be in either the high or low tension circuits. **Note:** *If the battery is known to be fully charged, the ignition light comes on, and the starter motor fails to turn the engine check the tightness of the leads on the battery terminal and also the secureness of the earth lead to its connection to the body. It is quite common for the leads to have worked loose, even if they look and feel secure. If one of the battery terminal posts gets very hot when trying to work the*

starter motor this is a sure indication of a faulty connection to that terminal.

2 One of the commonest reasons for bad starting is wet or damp spark plug leads and distributor. Remove the distributor cap; if condensation is visible internally, dry the cap with a rag and also wipe the leads. Refit the cap. A moisture dispersant, such as Holts Wet Start, can be very effective. To prevent the problem recurring, Holts Damp Start can be used to provide a sealing coat, so excluding any further moisture from the ignition system. In extreme difficulty, Holts Cold Start will help to start a car when only a very poor spark occurs.

3 If the engine still fails to start, check that current is reaching the plugs by disconnecting each plug lead in turn at the spark plug end, and hold the end of the cable about $\frac{1}{8}$ in (3 mm) away from the cylinder block. Spin the engine on the starter motor.

4 Sparking between the end of the cable and the block should be fairly strong with a regular blue spark. (Hold the lead with a dry cloth or rubber glove to avoid electric shocks). If current is reaching the plugs, remove them, clean and regap them. The engine should now start.

5 If there is no spark at the plug leads, take off the HT lead from the centre of the distributor cap and hold it to the block as before. Spin the engine on the starter once more. A rapid succession of blue sparks between the end of the lead and block indicates that the coil is in order and that the distributor cap is cracked, the rotor arm faulty, or the carbon brush in the top of the distributor cap is not making good contact with the spring on the rotor arm.

6 If there are no sparks from the end of the lead from the coil, check the connections at the coil end of the lead. If it is in order start checking the low tension circuit.

Engine misfires

7 If the engine misfires regularly, run it at a fast idling speed. Pull off each of the plug caps in turn and listen to the note of the engine. Hold the plug cap in a dry cloth or with a rubber glove as additional protection against a shock from the HT supply.

8 No difference in engine running will be noticed when the lead from the defective circuit is removed. Removing the lead from one of the good cylinders will accentuate the misfire.

9 Remove the plug lead from the end of the defective plug and hold it about $\frac{1}{8}$ in (3 mm) away from the block. Restart the engine. If the sparking is fairly strong and regular, the fault must lie in the spark plug.

10 The plug may be loose, the insulation may be cracked, or the electrodes may have burnt away giving too wide a gap for the spark to jump. Worse still, one of the electrodes may have broken off. Either renew the plug, or clean it, reset the gap, and then test it.

11 If there is no spark at the end of the plug lead, or if it is weak and intermittent, check the ignition lead from the distributor to the plug. If the insulation is cracked or perished, renew the lead. Check the connections at the distributor cap.

12 If there is still no spark, examine the distributor cap carefully for tracking. This can be recognised by a very thin black line running between two or more electrodes or between an electrode and some other part of the distributor. These lines are paths which conduct electricity across the cap thus letting it run to earth. The only remedy is a new distributor cap.

13 Apart from the ignition timing being incorrect, other causes of misfiring have already been dealt with under the section dealing with the failure of the engine to start. To recap – these are that:

(a) the coil may be faulty giving an intermittent misfire
(b) there may be a damaged wire or loose connection in the low tension circuit
(c) there may be a mechanical fault in the distributor

14 If the ignition timing is too far retarded, it should be noted that the engine will tend to overheat, and there will be a quite noticeable drop in power. If the engine is overheating and the power is down and the ignition timing is correct, then the carburettor should be checked, as it is likely that this is where the fault lies.

15 If the tests above do not indicate or isolate a fault, then it probably lies within the transistorised ignition system. In such circumstances it is advisable to arrange for your nearest Rover or Lucas dealer to carry out a further diagnostic check.

Chapter 5 Clutch

Contents

Specifications

Type . . . . Borg and Beck

Clutch driven plate diameter . . . . 9.5 in (240 mm)

Fluid . . . . Hydraulic fluid to FMVSS 116 DOT 3 or SAE J1703 (Duckhams Universal Brake and Clutch Fluid)

Torque wrench settings	lbf ft	Nm
Cover bolts	20	27.5
Slave cylinder bolts	25	34
Release arm pivot post	37	50

1 General description

The clutch fitted to manual transmission models is of single dry plate diaphragm spring type and is hydraulically operated.

The unit comprises a steel cover which is dowelled and bolted to the rear face of the flywheel and contains the pressure plate, diaphragm spring and fulcrum rings.

The clutch disc is free to slide along the splined first motion shaft and is held in position between the flywheel and the pressure plate by the pressure of the pressure plate spring. Friction lining material is riveted to the clutch disc and it has a spring cushioned hub to absorb transmission shocks and to help ensure a smooth take off.

The circular diaphragm spring is mounted on shoulder pins and held in place in the cover by two fulcrum rings. The spring is also held to the pressure plate by three spring steel clips which are riveted in position.

The clutch release mechanism consists of a hydraulic master cylinder and slave cylinder and the interconnecting pipework, a release arm and sealed ball type release bearing – the latter being in permanent contact with the fingers of the pressure plate assembly.

As the friction linings on the clutch driven plate wear, the pressure plate automatically moves closer to the driven plate to compensate. This makes the centre of the diaphragm spring move nearer to the release bearing, so decreasing the release bearing clearance. Depressing the clutch pedal actuates the clutch release arm by means of hydraulic pressure. The release arm pushes the release bearing forwards to bear against the release fingers, so moving the centre of the diaphragm spring inwards. The spring is sandwiched between two annular rings which act as fulcrum points. As the centre of the spring is pushed in, the outside of the spring is pushed out, so moving the pressure plate backwards and disengaging the pressure plate from the clutch disc.

When the clutch pedal is released the diaphragm spring forces the pressure plate into contact with the high fulcrum linings on the clutch disc and at the same time pushes the clutch disc a fraction of an inch forwards on its splines so engaging the clutch disc with the flywheel. The clutch disc is now firmly sandwiched between the pressure plate and the flywheel so the drive is taken up.

2 Maintenance

1   This consists of occasionally checking the security of the bolts which retain the master and slave cylinders and applying a little engine oil to the operating rod clevis joints.
2   Periodically check the hydraulic pipes and unions for leaks, corrosion or deterioration.
3   At weekly intervals remove the clutch master cylinder cap and check the fluid level (photo). Before unscrewing the cap wipe it clean to prevent the ingress of dirt. Use only the recommended type of clutch fluid. If topping-up becomes a common occurrence then carry out a visual inspection of the clutch hydraulic system. Any leakage of fluid would then be evident.

3 Master cylinder – removal and refitting

1   From within the car remove the split pin, washer and clevis pin securing the clutch master cylinder pushrod to the clutch pedal.
2   From the engine compartment disconnect the metal hydraulic pipe at the master cylinder union. Plug the end of the pipe and the hole in the master cylinder to prevent the escape of the fluid. Remember that the fluid is corrosive and will have a detrimental effect on paintwork. If

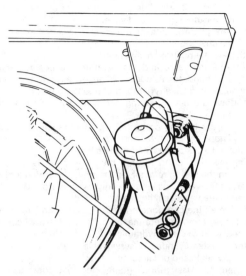

Fig. 5.1 Remove the nuts, spring washers and plain washers which retain the clutch master cylinder

2.3 Checking the clutch master cylinder reservoir fluid level

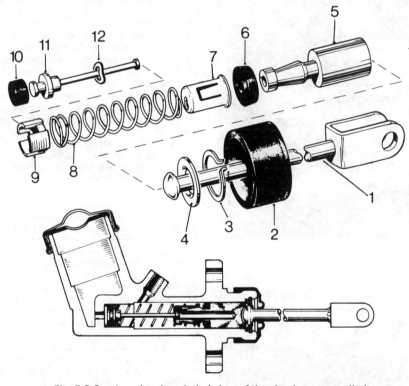

Fig. 5.2 Sectioned and exploded view of the clutch master cylinder

1	Pushrod	4	Dished washer	7	Thimble	10	Seal
2	Rubber boot	5	Piston	8	Spring	11	Valve stem
3	Circlip	6	Piston seal	9	Valve seal spacer	12	Dished washer

you should spill any fluid wipe it up immediately.

3   Remove the two nuts, spring washers and plain washers securing the master cylinder to the scuttle/pedal assembly (Fig. 5.1).

4   The master cylinder can now be withdrawn.

5   Refitting is the reverse of the removal procedure, but the following points should be noted.

6   Fit a new split pin to the clevis pin and remember to separate the ends of the split pin to prevent it from falling out.

7   Bleed the clutch hydraulic system as detailed in Section 8.

---

4   Master cylinder – overhaul

1   Remove the master cylinder as described in the previous Section.

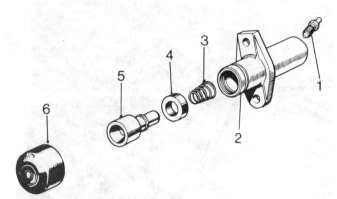

Fig. 5.3 Slave cylinder components

1	Bleed nipple	4	Piston seal
2	Cylinder body	5	Piston
3	Spring	6	Boot

5.5 Removing the clutch slave cylinder

5.6 The clutch slave cylinder removed revealing the pushrod

2   Unscrew the reservoir cap and drain out the fluid.
3   Refer to Fig. 5.2 and slide the rubber boot off the master cylinder and ease it over the pushrod end yoke.
4   From the pushrod end of the master cylinder extract the circlip retaining the pushrod.
5   Withdraw the pushrod dished washer.
6   Invert the master cylinder and bump the pushrod end into the palm of your hand to dislodge the piston assembly or alternatively apply air supplied from a tyre foot pump to the outlet port.
7   Withdraw the piston, spring and seal assembly from the master cylinder bore.
8   Prise up the locking prong that retains the spring and separate it from the piston.
9   Remove the piston seal and discard it.
10   Compress the spring so that the valve stem is in line with the larger hole in the spring retainer, and remove the spring and retainer.
11   Remove the valve spacer and spring washer from the valve stem.
12   Remove the valve seal and discard it.
13   Examine all the component for scores or 'bright' wear areas and if evident, renew the complete master cylinder. Wash all components in methylated spirit or clean hydraulic fluid.
14   If the master cylinder is serviceable, obtain a repair kit which includes new seals and other components.
15   Reassembly: Use rubber grease to coat the new seals. The remaining parts should be smeared with brake fluid.
16   The new valve seal should be fitted (flat side on first) to the end of the valve stem.
17   The spring washer, fits over the small end of the stem, domed side first.
18   Now fit the spacer, again over the small end, legs first.
19   Place the spring in position on the valve stem and insert the retainer into the spring. Compress the spring holding the retainer and engage the valve stem into the keyhole slot in the retainer.
20   Fit the new piston seal to the piston, making sure that the larger diameter goes on last.
21   Bring the piston and the spring retainer together fitting the piston into the retainer until the locking prong engages.
22   Apply rubber grease to the piston and seal, and insert the whole assembly, valve end first, into the cylinder.
23   Refit the pushrod and secure with its retaining washer and circlip.
24   Having rechecked that all the operations have been correctly carried out and there are no components left on the workbench, the unit can now be refitted to the car.

5   Slave cylinder – removal and refitting

1   Unscrew the clutch master cylinder reservoir cap and place a thin sheet of polythene over the reservoir then refit the cap. This measure prevents the fluid syphoning out when the slave cylinder is removed.
2   Raise the car and support it securely.
3   Clean the external surface of the slave cylinder especially in the region of the fluid pipe and union nut.
4   Undo the union nut, pull aside the fluid pipe and plug the end.
5   Remove the two bolts and spring washers securing the slave cylinder to the bellhousing (photo).
6   Withdraw the slave cylinder gently, avoid jerking it in a forward direction as the pushrod can easily dislodge the release arm. If the release arm is dislodged then it will be necessary to remove the gearbox in order to refit it (photo).
7   Refitting of the slave cylinder is the reverse of removal, but make sure that the bleed nipple is located above the fluid pipe union nut as it is possible to install the slave cylinder in an upside-down position.
8   After refitting it will be necessary to bleed the clutch hydraulic system as described in Section 8.

6   Slave cylinder – overhaul

1   Remove the slave cylinder as detailed in Section 5.
2   Clean the exterior of the unit, prior to dismantling, using clean brake fluid or methylated spirit.
3   Obtain the necessary servicing kit of spares which will include the required seal and dust cover. In the case of a high mileage car, the piston return spring should also be renewed.

4   Dismantle the unit by first removing the dust cover after which the piston can usually be dislodged by bumping the open end down onto the palm of your hand. Alternatively apply compressed air generated by a tyre foot pump to the fluid inlet port (Fig. 5.3).

5   Extract the piston assembly follow by the conical spring.

6   Unscrew the bleed nipple and clean all the components in clean hydraulic fluid or methylated spirit.

7   Discard the rubber piston seal and the dust cover.

8   Examine the piston surface and cylinder bore for scoring or 'bright' wear areas. If these are evident, renew the complete slave cylinder.

9   Treat the new piston seal with a smear of rubber grease, and to the remainder of the internal parts apply a film of clean hydraulic fluid.

10 Fit the seal (smaller diameter first) to the piston.

11 Locate the spring, again with the smaller diameter towards the piston.

12 Apply a smear of rubber grease to the piston assembly, and insert (spring first) into the slave cylinder body.

13 Smear the inside of the new rubber boot with rubber grease and fit it over the end of the slave cylinder.

14 Screw in the bleed nipple and fit the slave cylinder as described in Section 5.

7   Clutch pedal assembly – removal and refitting

This procedure is covered in Chapter 9, Section 13.

8   Bleeding the hydraulic system

Whenever the clutch hydraulic system has been overhauled, a part is renewed, or the level in the reservoir is too low, air will have entered the system necessitating its bleeding. During this operation the level of hydraulic fluid in the reservoir should not be allowed to fall below half full, otherwise air will be drawn in.

1   Obtain a clean, dry, glass jar, a length of plastic or rubber tubing which will fit the bleed nipple of the clutch slave cylinder and which is about 12 in (300 mm) long, a supply of the correct type of fluid and the services of an assistant.

2   Check that the master cylinder reservoir is full and, if not, fill it to within $\frac{1}{4}$ in (6·5 mm) of the top. Also add about one inch of fluid to the jar.

3   Remove the rubber dust cap from the slave cylinder bleed nipple, wipe the nipple clean then attach the bleed tube.

4   With the other end of the tube immersed in the fluid in the jar (which can be supported on the subframe if required), and the assistant ready inside the car, unscrew the bleed nipple one full turn.

5   The assistant should now pump the clutch pedal up and down until the air bubbles cease to emerge from the end of the tubing. Check the reservoir frequently to ensure that the hydraulic fluid does not drop too far, so letting air into the system.

6   When no more air bubbles appear, tighten the bleed nipple at the bottom of a downstroke.

7   Fit the rubber dust cap over the bleed nipple.

8   Discard the fluid which has been bled from the system as it is unfit for re-use.

9   A 'one-man' or pressure bleeding kit may be used if wished – refer to Chapter 13 for details.

9   Clutch – removal, inspection and refitting

1   Remove the gearbox as described in Chapter 6.

2   The clutch cover is secured to the flywheel by a peripheral ring of bolts. Mark the position of the clutch cover in relation to the flywheel.

3   Unscrew the securing bolts evenly, a turn at a time in diametrically opposite sequence, to avoid distortion. The three bolts located in the deep recesses of the cover should not be disturbed.

4   When the bolts are finally removed, withdraw the pressure plate assembly from the flywheel and catch the driven plate as it is released from the face of the flywheel.

5   The pressure plate assembly should not be dismantled but if worn, cracked or distorted, it should be renewed on an exchange basis.

6   Examine the driven plate for wear. If the linings are worn almost down to the rivets then a factory reconditioned unit should be obtained

on an exchange basis – do not waste your time trying to reline the plate, it seldom proves satisfactory.

7   If there is evidence of oil staining, find the cause which will probably be a faulty gearbox input shaft oil seal or a crankshaft rear oil seal.

8   Check the machine surfaces of the flywheel and pressure plate; if grooved or scored then the flywheel should be machined (within the specified limits – see Chapter 13), and the pressure plate assembly renewed.

9   Check the release bearing for smooth operation. There should be no harshness or slackness in it and it should spin reasonably freely bearing in mind that it is grease sealed. (Refer to next Section).

10 It is important that no oil or grease gets on the clutch plate friction linings or the pressure plate and flywheel faces. It is advisable to replace the clutch with clean hands and to wipe down the pressure plate and flywheel faces with a clean rag before assembly begins.

11 Place the clutch plate against the flywheel, ensuring that it is the correct way round. The flywheel side of the driven plate has the shorter hub boss. If the plate is fitted the wrong way round, it will be quite impossible to operate the clutch.

12 Replace the clutch cover assembly loosely on the dowels. Replace the six bolts and spring washers and tighten them finger tight so that the clutch plate is gripped but can still be moved. The clutch disc must now be centralised so that when the engine and gearbox are mated, the gearbox first motion shaft splines will pass through the splines in the centre of the driven plate.

13 Centralisation can be carried out quite easily by inserting a round bar or long screwdriver through the hole in the centre of the clutch, so that the end of the bar rests in the small hole in the end of the crankshaft containing the spigot bush. Ideally an old first motion shaft should be used.

14 Using the first motion shaft spigot bush as a fulcrum, moving the bar sideways or up and down will move the clutch disc in whichever direction is necessary to achieve centralisation.

15 Centralisation is easily judged by removing the bar and viewing the driven plate hub in relation to the hole in the centre of the clutch cover plate diaphragm spring. When the hub appears exactly in the centre of the hole, all is correct. Alternatively the first motion shaft will fit the bush and centre of the clutch hub exactly, obviating the need for visual alignment.

16 Tighten the clutch bolts firmly in a diagonal sequence to ensure that the cover plate is pulled down evenly and without distortion of the flange. Finally tighten the bolts down to the recommended torque setting.

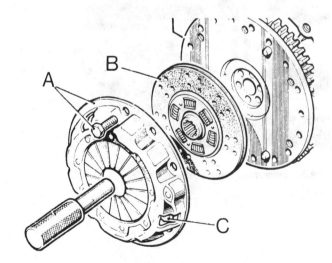

Fig. 5.4 Major clutch components

A   *Clutch cover and bolt*
B   *Driven plate*
C   *Recessed bolts*
     (not to be unscrewed)

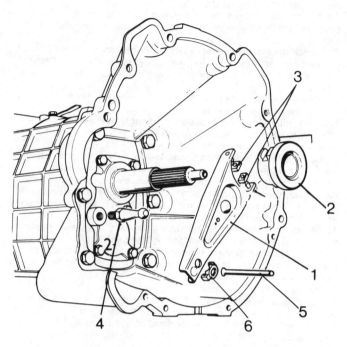

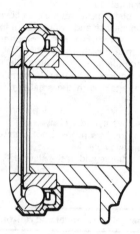

Fig. 5.6 Sectional view of the release bearing and sleeve

Fig. 5.5 Clutch release lever and bearing

1	Release lever	4	Pivot post
2	Release bearing assembly	5	Pushrod
3	Slipper pads	6	Pushrod retainer

10.4 The release bearing in position

10 Clutch withdrawal mechanism – removal, inspection, overhaul and refitting

1   Remove the gearbox as described in Chapter 6.
2   Using the service tool ST 1136 or a suitably cranked spanner, unscrew the release arm pivot post.
3   Withdraw the release arm together with the pivot ball post and the release bearing.
4   The release bearing can now be slid sideways away from the release arm slipper pads (photo).
5   Clean all the components, excluding the release bearing, in either paraffin or a suitable cleaning solution.
6   Examine the various components for wear and renew as found necessary.
7   The release bearing is sealed for life and as such cannot be cleaned or repacked with grease. (Fig. 5.6).
8   Spin the bearing by hand whilst holding the sleeve. If the bearing is unserviceable it can be pressed or driven off the sleeve and a new one fitted. When pressing on the new bearing, the pressure must only be applied to the inner race. Ensure the release face is outermost.
9   Before reassembly apply a light smear of general purpose grease to the slipper pads, the ball part of the pivot post and the inner bore of the release bearing sleeve.
10   Fit the release arm assembly by following the reverse of the removal procedure.

11 Fault diagnosis – clutch

Symptom	Reason/s
Judder when taking up drive	Loose engine mountings Worn or oil contaminated driven plate friction linings Worn splines on driven plate hub or first input shaft Worn crankshaft spigot bush (pilot bearing)
Clutch slip	Damaged or distorted pressure plate assembly Driven plate linings worn or oil contaminated
Noise on depressing clutch pedal	Dry-worn or damaged clutch release bearing Excessive play in input shaft splines
Noise as clutch pedal is released	Distorted driven plate Broken or weak driven plate hub cushion coil springs Distorted or worn input shaft Release bearing loose
Difficulty in disengaging clutch for gearchange	Fault in master cylinder or slave cylinder Air in hydraulic system Driven plate hub splines rusted on shaft

Chapter 6
Manual gearbox and automatic transmission

For modifications, and information applicable to later models, see Supplement at end of manual

Contents

Specifications

Manual gearbox
Type . . . .   5-speed, synchromesh on all forward gears

Ratios

5th	0.833 : 1
4th	1.000 : 1
3rd	1.396 : 1
2nd	2.087 : 1
1st	3.321 : 1
Reverse	3.428 : 1

Gearbox lubricant
Type/specification:

Up to VIN 133000 . . . . Hypoid gear oil, viscosity SAE 75W EP (refill), or SAE 80EP (top-up only) to API-GL5 or MIL-L-2105B (Duckhams Hypoid 75 – refill or Hypoid 80S – top-up only)

Later models . . . . Type 'G' ATF to M2C 33F or M2C 33G (Duckhams Q-Matic)

Quantity . . . . 2.7 pints (1.5 litres) approx

Torque wrench settings

	lbf ft	Nm
Flange to mainshaft	150	200
Drain/filler plugs	26	35
Sump bolts	4.5 to 7.0	6.1 to 9.5
Bellhousing to engine bracing set-screws	37	50
Bellhousing to sump bracing set-screws	37	50
Bellhousing to gearbox casing bolts and set-screws	59	80
Bellhousing to cylinder block bolts	21	28
Bellhousing cover plate bolts	21	28

Automatic transmission
Type . . . . Borg Warner model 65 or 66

Transmission conversion range

3rd	1.00 to 2.08
2nd	1.45 to 3.02
1st	2.39 to 4.97
Reverse	2.09 to 4.35

Shift speeds

Throttle position		Selection	Shift	Speed mph (km/h)
Closed . . . . —		1	2 to 1	16 to 26 (27 to 44)
Light throttle . . . . —		2	1 to 2	9 to 15 (15 to 25)
		D	2 to 3	14 to 19 (24 to 32)
Part throttle . . . . —		D	3 to 2	–
Kick-down . . . . —		D	1 to 2	40 to 50 (68 to 85)
		D	2 to 3	73 to 83 (123 to 140)
		D	3 to 2	51 to 64 (86 to 108)
		1	2 to 1	28 to 40 (47 to 68)
		D	3 to 1	28 to 40 (47 to 68)
		2	1 to 2	40 to 50 (68 to 85)
		2	2 to 1	28 to 40 (47 to 68)

Automatic transmission fluid . . . .   Type 'G' ATF to M2C 33F or M2C 33G (Duckhams Q-Matic)

Automatic transmission fluid capacity (including oil cooler . . . .   12.25 pints (6.96 litres)

Torque wrench setting
Driving flange securing bolt (use thread locking compound) . . . .

lbf ft	Nm
35 to 50	48 to 68

Part A Manual gearbox

1 General description

This gearbox was designed specifically for the Rover 3500, but was fitted to the Triumph TR7 as an option. The most unusual feature of this gearbox is the use of taper roller bearings for the mainshaft/input shaft and layshaft, which provide for a less bulky gearbox using standard bearings, and also simplifies assembly.

The gearbox is built up on a centre plate, a rigid iron casting between the tailpiece and the main housing. Since taper rollers come apart easily, the shafts and gears can be simply placed in position and jiggled around until the gears mesh; all that is needed is for the shaft end play to be adjusted, which is a relatively straightforward operation.

A single shaft selector mechanism is used for the gear selection. Gears 1 to 4 are arranged in the usual H-pattern, but reverse and 5th are left-forward and right-forward respectively. The single shaft has two operating dowels, the rear one engaging reverse and the front one engaging the forward gears, via bosses on the selector forks. An interlock arrangement prevents engagement of more than one gear at the same time.

The selector mechanisms are mounted on the centre plate. A simple externally mounted hairpin-type spring give the gear lever a natural bias to the 3/4 plane. This bias has to be overcome in progressive steps to obtain the 1/2 plane, 5th gear and reverse gear in order, the latter having a separate biassing arrangement.

With the exception of fifth, which overhangs the centre plate to the rear, the gear layout and mode of operation is conventional.

2 Gearbox – removal and refitting

1   Detach the battery negative lead.
2   With neutral selected, unscrew and remove the gear lever knob and pull out the gear lever shroud and top panel assembly (photo).
3   Withdraw the sponge rubber insert, followed by the draught excluder and flange assembly.
4   Remove the single bolt and lift off the ball cap. Remove the countersunk screw and the bolt which retain the hairpin bias screw clamp, then remove the clamp. Carefully prise the ends of the spring aside and lift out the gear lever, taking care not to lose the strong anti-rattle spring and nylon plunger (photos).
5   Raise the car and support it on blocks placed beneath the body frame sidemembers, for access to the gearbox area.
6   Remove the propeller shaft as described in Chapter 7.
7   Remove the forward exhaust system sections at the manifold and intermediate pipe; refer to Chapter 3 for further information as necessary.
8   Disconnect the speedometer cable from the gearbox by undoing the single bolt and lifting away the 'U' shaped clamp plate. Pull away the speedometer cable and tie it back out of the way (photo).
9   Pull off the electrical leads of the reverse light switch and discon-

2.2 Remove the gear lever knob

2.4A Remove the single bolt (arrowed) which retains the ball cap

2.4B Spring the ends of the hair spring to one side and lift out the gear lever. Spring clamp (arrowed) should have been removed first to avoid distorting spring

2.4C The anti-rattle spring and nylon plunger

2.8 Disconnect the speedometer cable

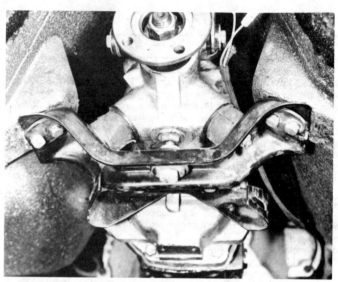

2.13 The gearbox rear mounting crossmember

3.4 Removing the flange nut

3.6 Selector shaft nut (arrowed)

Fig. 6.1 5th gear synchro and associated parts

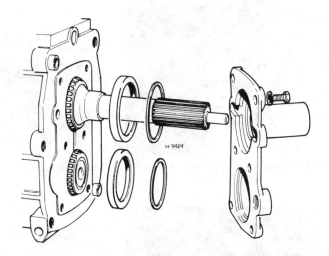

Fig. 6.2 Gearbox front cover, spacers and bearing tracks

3.7 Note the plastic bushes and tubular spacers

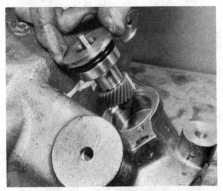

3.8 Removing the speedometer driven gear

3.11 Oil pump showing the driveshaft

nect the cable from the retainer clip fitted to the upper face of the gearbox casing. Remove the starter motor.

10 Place a jack underneath the sump with a wooden protective block inserted between the two. Raise the jack to just take the weight of the engine.

11 Undo the two bolts securing the clutch slave cylinder and carefully withdraw it. Tie the slave cylinder to one side, taking care not to strain the flexible hydraulic hose.

12 Remove the two bolts from the sump stiffening plate.

13 Remove the bolts retaining the rear mounting to the body underframe (photo).

14 Carefully lower the support jack to gain access to the bellhousing bolts. Take care when lowering the support jack to prevent the air cleaner assembly from fouling the bulkhead.

15 Remove the bolts securing the flywheel cover plate to the bellhousing.

16 Now remove the eight bolts, noting their lengths and positions, which secure the gearbox bellhousing to the rear engine plate.

17 Whilst suitably supporting the gearbox ie on a trolley jack, withdraw it from the engine taking care that load is not taken on the input shaft. The gearbox is fairly heavy, weighing in the region of 110 lbs (50 kg) and help from an assistant is recommended.

18 Refitting the gearbox is basically the reverse of the removal procedure. When connecting the transmission rear mounting to the body underframe, make sure that the gap between the snubber and the underside of the crossmember is 0.118 in (3.0 mm). Adjust if necessary by releasing the locknut and turning the centre bolt.

19 Refitting the gear lever anti-rattle spring and plunger is rather awkward. The method is to install the gear lever, minus spring and

plunger, and select second or fourth gear. Withdraw the gear lever and refit it together with the spring and plunger. A large screwdriver can be used to slightly compress the plunger and spring to assist the entry of the assembly.

20 Check if the gearbox has been drained of lubricant then refill it after refitting, if necessary.

3 Manual gearbox – dismantling

1 Before commencing to dismantle the gearbox, clean the exterior with a water-soluble solvent. This will make the gearbox easier to handle, and possibly prevent dirt from contaminating the internal parts. Drain the gearbox oil, then refit the plug.

2 Remove the clutch release bearing and lever arm as described in Chapter 5.

3 Remove the bolts and washers, and withdraw the bellhousing.

4 Make up a suitable bracket which can be bolted to the mainshaft flange, which will wedge against the remote control extension, then unscrew the flange nut and washer (photo).

5 Pull off the mainshaft drive flange.

6 Remove the nut and pin which are used to connect the remote control shaft to the selector shaft (photo).

7 Remove the four bolts, spring washers and plain washers securing the remote control housing to the gearbox rear cover. Note the positions of the plastic bushes and tubular spacers when the housing is removed (photo).

8 Remove the clamp plate, and withdraw the speedometer driven

3.12 Removing the selector fork and bracket

3.13 Removing the selector shaft circlip

3.15 Removing the layshaft 5th gear

3.18 Removing the front selector spool locating boss

3.24 Selector lever pivot pin (arrowed)

3.29 The layshaft showing the bearings

3.30 Removing the oil pump cover and intake pipe

3.31 The oil pump gears in the cover

5.2 Driving the mainshaft out of the 1st gear

gear and housing (photo).

9   Remove the two bolts and spring washers, and withdraw the locating boss for the 5th gear (rear) selector spool.

10   Remove the ten bolts, spring washers and flat washers, and withdraw the rear cover and gasket. Note the positions of the tubular dowels.

11   Remove the oil pump driveshaft from 5th gear or oil pump so that the shaft is not lost (photo).

12   Remove the two bolts and spring washers, and take off the 5th gear selector fork and bracket (photo).

13   Remove the circlip from the selector shaft and withdraw the 5th gear selector spool. Note that the longer cam is pointing downwards (photo).

14   Remove the circlip, and withdraw the 5th gear synchro assembly, 5th gear and spacer from the mainshaft.

15   Remove the circlip retaining the layshaft 5th gear, then use a 2 or 3 legged puller to remove the gear (photo).

16   Remove the six bolts and spring washers, then remove the gearbox front cover.

17   Remove the selective washers from the input shaft and layshaft.

18   Remove the two bolts and spring washers, and withdraw the locating boss for the front selector spool (photo).

19   Remove the selector plug, spring and ball from the drilling in the centre plate.

20   Support the gearbox on the centre plate and pull off the main casing.

21   Remove the 1st gear synchro cone from the input shaft.

22   Withdraw the layshaft gear cluster from the centre plate.

23   Using a vice with protective jaw covers support the centre plate.

24   Remove the retaining circlip and take out the reverse lever pivot

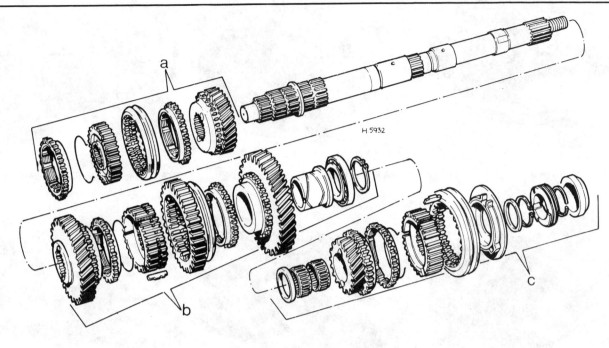

H 5932

Fig. 6.3 Exploded view of the mainshaft gears

a   3rd/4th synchro hub and sleeve, and 3rd gear   b   1st/2nd gear assembly, including reverse gear   c   5th gear assembly

pin. The reverse lever and slipper pad can now be taken out (photo).

25 Slide the reverse shaft rearwards so that the reverse gear spacer, mainshaft, selector shaft, selector shaft fork and spool can be drawn forwards and away from the centre plate.

26 Withdraw the selector fork and spool. Note that the shorter cam is pointing towards the bottom of the gearbox.

27 Remove the nut and spring washers, if necessary, and remove the reverse gear pivot shaft.

28 If subsequent inspection shows the input shaft bearing to be defective, the outer race can be driven out of the casing using a soft drift. The inner race and bearing can then be pulled or levered off.

29 If subsequent inspection shows the layshaft bearings to be faulty, the outer races can be driven out of the casing and centre plate. Then the inner race and bearings can be pulled or levered off (photo).

30 Remove the bolts and spring washers, and take off the oil pump and intake pipe (photo).

31 Remove the oil pump gears (photo).

32 Remove the rear cover oil seal, bearing, speedometer, gear, circlip and sleeve, and oil sleeve.

33 If subsequent inspection shows the mainshaft bearing to be defective, the outer race can be driven out of the centre plate. Removal of the inner race and bearing is dealt with in Section 5.

---

4 Manual gearbox – examination

1 The gearbox has been stripped probably, because of wear or malfunction, possibly excessive noise, ineffective synchromesh or failure to stay in a selected gear. The cause of most gearbox ailments is the failure of the taper bearings on the input or mainshaft and wear on the synchro-rings, both the cup surfaces and the dogs. Wear may be found in the mainshaft/input shaft taper roller bearing. This is easily renewed, and it is very rare for the nose of the mainshaft to wear unless it has been spinning in the bearing race (inner track).

2 Examine the teeth of all gears for signs of uneven or excessive wear and, of course, chipping. If a gear on the mainshaft requires replacement check that the corresponding lay gear is not equally damaged. If it is, the whole lay gear may need replacing also.

3 All gears should be a good running fit on the shaft with no signs of rocking. The hubs should not be a sloppy fit on the splines.

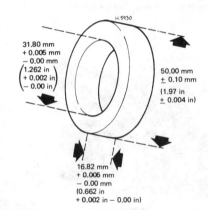

H.5930

31.80 mm
+ 0.005 mm
− 0.00 mm
(1.262 in
+ 0.002 in
− 0.00 in)

50.00 mm
± 0.10 mm
(1.97 in
± 0.004 in)

16.82 mm
+ 0.006 mm
− 0.00 mm
(0.662 in
+ 0.002 in − 0.00 in)

Fig. 6.4 Spacer dimensions for checking 1st gear bush endfloat

4 Selector forks should be examined for signs of wear or ridging on the faces which are in contact with the operating sleeve.

5 Check for wear on the selector rod and interlock spool.

6 The taper bearings may not be obviously worn, but if one has gone to the trouble of dismantling the gearbox it would be advantageous to renew them. The same applies to the synchronizer rings although for these, the mainshaft has to be completely dismantled for the new ones to be fitted.

7 Examine for wear the bush in the reverse idler gear. If any is found, press out the old bush, and then press in a new one so that it is flush with the boss opposite the collar of the operating lever. It may be found necessary to ream the bush after installation.

8 Examine the oil pump gears for wear and damaged teeth, renewing parts as necessary.

9 Examine the oil pump driveshaft, if worn or damaged then renew it.

10 It is recommended that new oil seals are fitted. These should be fitted with the lip towards the gearbox.

11 Before finally deciding to dismantle the mainshaft and replace parts, it is advisable to make enquiries regarding the availability of parts and their cost. It may still be worth considering an exchange gearbox even at this stage. Your old gearbox will have to be reassembled for exchange.

5.3 Pull off the 3rd gear

5.18A Fitting the baulk ring ...

5.18B ... and synchro-hub and sleeve

5.18C ... fitting the input shaft/mainshaft pilot bearing

5.19A Fit the 2nd gear and baulk ring ...

5.19B ... synchro hub and sleeve (including reverse gear), and baulk ring ...

5.19C ... 1st gear and selective bush ...

5.19D ... bearing ...

5.19E ... and circlip

6.4A Two views of the mainshaft and layshaft assembled ...

6.4B ... to the centre plate

6.11 Input shaft ready for assembly into the casing

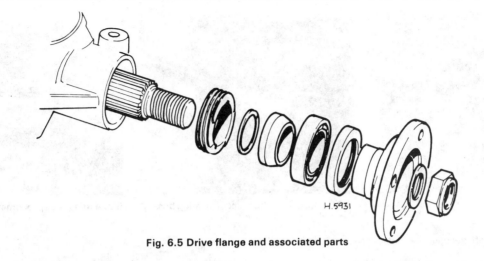

Fig. 6.5 Drive flange and associated parts

5 Manual gearbox mainshaft – dismantling and reassembly

1   From the front end of the mainshaft remove the pilot bearing and spacer.

2   Remove the mainshaft bearing circlip, then use a lead hammer or similar item to drive the mainshaft out of the 1st gear. In this way the gear, bush and bearing can be removed together (photo).

3   From the front end of the mainshaft, pull off the 3rd gear and the 3rd/4th synchronizer hub and sleeve (photo).

4   Now take off the 1st/2nd gear hub, sleeve, synchro cones and 2nd gear (this assembly incorporates the reverse gear).

5   Clean all parts in petrol or paraffin, and dry them in a lint-free cloth.

6   On the assembled synchro assemblies, check that a load of 18 to 22 lbf (8·2 to 10 kgf) is required to push the synchro hub through the outer sleeve in either direction.

7   Manufacture a spacer to the dimensions shown in Fig. 6.4, so that the 1st gear bush endfloat can be checked as described in paragraphs 8 to 11 below.

8   Fit 2nd gear, 1st/2nd synchro hub and 1st gear to the mainshaft; then fit the spacer.

9   Using an old circlip and a set of feeler gauges, check the clearance between the spacer and circlip. This should be 0·0002 to 0·002 in (0·005 to 0·055 mm).

10 If necessary select a new bush with a collar thickness which will give this dimension.

11 Remove the circlip, spacer, bush, synchro hub, and 2nd gear from the mainshaft.

12 Check the 5th gear endfloat as described in paragraphs 13 to 16 below.

13 Fit the 5th gear assembly to the mainshaft (this comprises the front spacer, 5th gear, synchro hub, rear plate and spacer).

14 Using an old circlip and the feeler gauges, check the endfloat. This should be 0·0002 to 0·002 in (0·005 to 0·055 mm).

15 If necessary select a new rear spacer to provide this clearance.

16 Remove the circlip, spacer and 5th gear assembly from the mainshaft.

17 Ensure that the 1st/2nd synchro is assembled with the short splines on the inner member towards 2nd gear.

18 Fit 3rd gear, baulk ring, and the synchro sleeve and hub, so that the longer boss of the hub is towards the front of the gearbox. Also fit the bearing (photos).

19 Fit the 2nd gear, baulk ring, synchro hub and sleeve (selector fork annulus towards the rear of the gearbox), baulk ring, 1st gear and selective bush, bearing and a new circlip. *During fitment, the circlip internal diameter must not be opened out beyond* 1·272 in (32·3 mm) (photos).

6 Manual gearbox – reassembly

1   Commence reassembly by installing new layshaft bearings, if the original ones were removed.

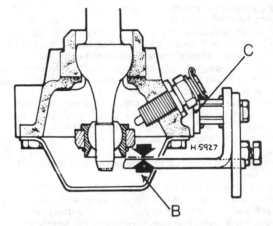

Fig. 6.6 Remote control assembly adjustment

B   *Gearlever bush/baulk plate clearance*
C   *1st/2nd gate stop shims*

2   At this point it is also convenient to fit new bearing tracks in the front of the casing and in the centre plate, if the original ones were removed.

3   Using protective jaw clamps, mount the centre plate in a vice.

4   Engage the forks of the assembled selector shaft (1st/2nd selector fork, front spool and 3rd/4th selector fork) in their respective synchro sleeves on the mainshaft. At the same time, engage the selector shaft and mainshaft assemblies in the centre plate (photos).

5   Fit the spacer, 5th gear, baulk ring, synchro hub and sleeve, endplate, selective spacer (see paragraph 15 of Section 5) and a new circlip. *During fitment, the circlip internal diameter must not be opened out beyond* 1·088 in (27·63 mm).

6   Fit the layshaft to the centre plate, and fit the 5th gear, spacer and a new circlip. *During fitment, the circlip internal diameter must not be opened out beyond* 0·886 in (22·5 mm).

7   Fit the reverse gear so that the lip for the slipper pad is towards the front of the gearbox; fit the front and rear spacers, and the reverse shaft.

8   Fit the reverse lever, slipper pad, pivot pin and a new circlip. If a new reverse gear pivot shaft is being used, ensure that its radial location permits engagement and clearance of the reverse slipper pad. Secure the shaft with a spring washer and nut, then recheck the engagement and clearance.

9   Remove the assembled centre plate from the vice and locate it on a suitable stand with the front of the mainshaft upwards, taking care that the reverse shaft does not slide out.

10 Fit a new front gasket to the centre plate.

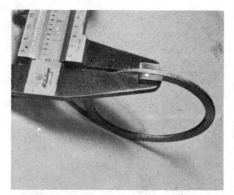

6.20 Selecting a mainshaft spacer

6.31 Cable clip on front spool locating boss

6.32 Fitting the speedometer driving gear

11 Fit the input shaft bearing, then insert the input shaft into the casing (photo).

12 Carefully slide the casing and input shaft into position over the gear assemblies, ensuring that the centre plate dowels and selector shaft engage in their respective locations.

13 Using slave bolts and flat washers, to prevent damage to the rear face of the centre plate, draw the casing evenly onto the centre plate.

14 Place the layshaft spacer on the layshaft bearing track at the front end of the casing and temporarily fit the cover and gasket.

15 Using a dial gauge, check and record the total layshaft endfloat. **Note:** *If no layshaft endfloat can be detected, repeat paragraph 14 using a spacer of 0·040 in (1·02 mm) and recheck.*

16 Remove the front cover and spacer, then select a replacement spacer to obtain a preload of 0.001 to 0.002 in (0.025 to 0.05 mm). The spacer thickness can be determined by adding together the provisional spacer thickness, the measured endfloat and the required preload.

17 Refit the front cover using the selected spacer and recheck the specified endfloat.

18 Place a small steel ball on the machined centre of the end of the input shaft so that the stylus of a dial gauge can be rested on it.

19 Check and record the combined endfloat of the input shaft and mainshaft. If it is found that side movement of the input shaft prevents an accurate reading from being obtained, it is permissible to remove the front cover and wrap about 6 turns of masking tape around the input shaft below the splines; this will stop any side movement.

20 Having determined the endfloat, select a spacer for the front cover by subtracting 0.002 in (0.05 mm) from the measured endfloat (photo).

21 Remove the front cover (and tape, if used). If the front cover oil seal has not yet been renewed, this should be done now. Fit it with the lips facing the gearbox, then lubricate the lips with gearbox oil.

22 Carefully fit the front cover so that the seal lips are not marked by the shaft splines.

23 Remove the slave bolts from the centre plate.

24 Fit the 5th gear spool with the longer cam towards the bottom of the gearbox, then fit the circlip.

25 Fit the 5th gear selector bracket and fork.

26 Fit a new selector shaft O-ring in the rear cover, and fit the oil ring bush.

27 Fit a new gasket to the rear of the centre plate, then engage the oil pump driveshaft in the layshaft end.

28 Fit the oil pump gears, then fit the cover.

29 Carefully fit the rear cover so that the oil pump drive engages correctly.

30 Fit the selector shaft ball, spring and screwed plug to the centre plate.

31 Fit both spool locating bosses to the gearbox casing assembly. Note the cable clip on the front one (photo).

32 Fit the speedometer driving gear to the mainshaft, ensuring that it engages properly with the mainshaft flats (photo).

33 Fit the circlip and sleeve, followed by the ballrace, to the mainshaft.

34 Fit the rear oil seal and lubricate the lips with gear oil (photo).

35 Fit the mainshaft flange, then fit and tighten the nut and washer to the specified torque. Use the bracket and bolt which were used when the flange nut was removed.

6.34 Rear oil seal being fitted

36 Fit the speedometer gear and housing, securing it with the plate washers and bolt.

37 If the bellhousing was removed during the dismantling procedure then refit it.

38 Fit the clutch release bearing and lever, referring to Chapter 5.

39 Install the remote control assembly, and adjust it as described in the following paragraphs.

40 Remove the remote control assembly bottom cover plate.

41 With the gear lever vertical and neutral selected, loosen the baulk plate adjusting bolts until the plate contacts the backing plate.

42 Tighten the adjusting bolts equally until they just start to move the baulk plate away from the backing plate.

43 Attach a spring balance to the gear knob end of the gear lever and measure the force required to move the lever into the reverse gate. The force should be between 30 and 35 lbf (13.6 and 15.9 kgf). Adjust if necessary by tightening or slackening the two bolts and locknuts on the right-hand side of the reverse baulk plate. On completion the clearance 'B' in Fig. 6.6 must be not less than 0.01 in (0.25 mm).

44 With first gear engaged, check that a clearance of between 0.01 and 0.05 in (0.25 and 1.25 mm) exists between the side of the gear lever and the edge of the baulk plate. Add or remove shims as necessary to achieve this.

45 Repeat the measurement in paragraph 44 with 2nd gear engaged. When all is correct, refit the bottom cover plate.

46 Engage 3rd gear, then position the gear lever hairpin spring bias screws, so that there is a clearance of 0·020 in (0·5 mm) between the spring and crosspin on each side. Do not tighten the locknuts.

47 Apply a light load to move the gear lever to the right to take up the free play, then adjust the right-hand screw downwards until the spring leg just makes contact with the crosspin.

48 Repeat paragraph 47, moving the gear lever to the left, then adjust the left-hand screw downwards to just contact the crosspin.

49 Move the gear lever to neutral, rock it across the gate and check that it comes to rest in the 3rd/4th plane.
50 Tighten the locknuts.
51 Adjust the reverse light switch as described in Chapter 10.
52 Top-up the gearbox with the specified grade and quantity of oil after refitting.

7 Manual gearbox gearchange remote control assembly – dismantling and reassembly

1 With the assembly removed from the transmission as described in Section 3, remove the two bolts and countersunk head screws securing the bias spring bridge plates.
2 Remove the bridge plates, bridge plate lines and hairpin-type bias spring.
3 Remove the bias spring adjustment bolts and locknuts.
4 Remove the two bolts and washers securing the reverse baulk plate assembly; withdraw the reverse baulk plate, springs and spacers.
5 Remove the four bolts and washers, and take off the bottom cover plate (photo).
6 Remove the reverse light switch and locknut, referring to Chapter 10 if necessary.
7 Remove the square-headed pinchbolt and take off the selector shaft elbow. Now withdraw the selector shaft.
8 Press out the selector shaft bushes from the casing.
9 Remove the circlips. Press out the pivot balls and bushes from the selector shaft elbows.
10 Reassembly is the reverse of the dismantling procedure. On com-

pletion, with the assembly attached to the gearbox, the reverse baulk plate, 1st/2nd stop gate and gear lever hairpin bias spring should each be adjusted by following the procedure given in paragraph 40 onwards of Section 6.

7.5 Bottom cover plate removed

8 Fault diagnosis – manual gearbox

Symptom	Reason/s
Weak or ineffective synchromesh	Synchronising cones worn, split or damaged
	Synchromesh dogs worn or damaged
Jumps out of gear	Gearbox coupling dogs badly worn
	Selector forks or slipper pads badly worn
Excessive noise	Incorrect grade of oil in gearbox or oil level too low
	Bushes or bearings worn or damaged
	Gear teeth excessively worn or damaged

Part B Automatic transmission

9 General description

The Borg-Warner 65 automatic transmission is available as an optional extra for certain versions of the Rover 3500. It is a light-weight version of the earlier Borg-Warner 35 and due to the resighting of the hydraulic control unit to within the sump, the unsightly bulge in the transmission tunnel which was associated with former versions, is no longer necessary. The system comprises two main components: (a) A three element hydrokinetic torque converter coupling capable of torque multiplication at an infinitely variable ratio between 2·08 : 1 and 1: 1. (b) A torque/speed responsive hydraulic epicyclic gearbox comprising a planetary gear set providing three forward ratios and one reverse ratio. Selection of the required ratio is by means of a console-mounted lever, with the selector positions, P, R, N, D, 2, 1 marked.

It is not possible to start the engine unless the selector is in the P or N positions. This prevents inadvertent movement of the vehicle, and is controlled by an inhibitor switch mounted on the transmission unit.

The six selector positions are stepped to control the selector lever movement. The positions normally used in a particular sequence are grouped together. To prevent accidental engagement of R or P the selector lever is spring loaded and so biassed away from the operating plane of these selector positions

Note: *A transmission oil cooler is fitted on vehicles with automatic transmission – see Chapter 2, Fig. 2.1.*

Owing to the complexity of the automatic transmission unit, it is

not recommended that stripping the unit is attempted. Where the unit is known to be faulty, and the fault cannot be rectified by following the procedures given in the following Sections of this Chapter, the repair should be entrusted to a Rover dealer or an automatic transmission specialist.

10 Automatic transmission – removal and refitting

1 Initially drive the car onto ramps, or have available adequate jacks and axle stands to permit access to the underside of the car.
2 Select N and chock the roadwheels remaining on the ground.
3 Open the bonnet and disconnect the battery negative terminal.
4 Remove the air cleaner assembly as described in Chapter 3.
5 Disconnect the downshift.
6 Release the transmission dipstick/filler tube from its cylinder head fixing and likewise release the transmission breather pipe from the clip at the rear of the cylinder head.
7 Unscrew the union at the base of the filler pipe and drain the fluid into a container of at least 9·5 pints (5·4 litres) capacity.
8 Disconnect the exhaust system from the manifold flanges to the intermediate pipe. Remove the bolts and nuts securing the exhaust pipes to the transmission bracket and lift away this forward section.
9 Remove the propeller shaft as described in Chapter 7.
10 Remove the selector rod by withdrawing the split-pins and clevis pins at either end. Do not alter the adjustment of this rod during the removal procedure and remember to remove the nylon bushes from the levers.

10.12 Removing the torque converter to engine drive plate bolts (engine shown removed for clarity)

10.21 The torque converter showing the drive fingers of the converter hub (engine removed for clarity)

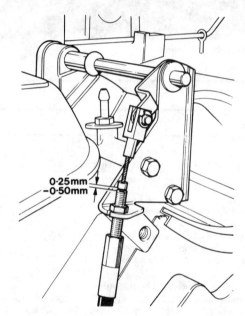

0·25mm – 0·50mm

Fig. 6.7 Checking the adjustment of the downshift cable

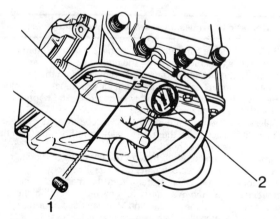

Fig. 6.8 Checking the downshift cable (pressure test)

1   *Blanking plug*
2   *Pressure gauge (scale up to 100 lbf/in² – 7 kgf/cm²)*

11   Remove the rear, right-hand engine sump bolt and then undo the bolts securing the torque converter access plate in position. Lift the access plate away.
12   Through the access hole remove the four bolts and thick washers securing the torque converter to the engine drive plate (photo).
13   Support the transmission unit using an ordinary jack or ideally a trolley jack. A flat piece of timber placed between the jack lifting pad and the transmission sump pan will spread the load and prevent damaging the sump.
14   Remove the two bolts, spring washers and plain washers securing the sump reinforcement plate to the torque converter bellhousing.
15   Remove the four bolts, spring washers and plates retaining the transmission rear mounting platform.
16   Lower the transmission support jack sufficiently to gain access to the torque converter bellhousing bolts and oil cooler pipe unions.
17   With the engine/transmission assembly so inclined disconnect the following units:

(a) *oil cooler pipes*
(b) *speedometer cable*
(c) *starter/inhibitor reverse lamp switch leads*

18   Place a support under the engine sump in a similar manner to that employed under the transmission sump.
19   Undo and remove the bolts and spring washers which secure the transmission unit to the engine. Note the positions of any wiring harness clips.
20   Draw the transmission unit away from the engine but do not lower it until the torque converter is clear of the crankshaft spigot. Some fluid is certain to flow out during this operation so conveniently placed newspapers or rags will be useful.
21   When refitting the automatic transmission unit, first align the slots in the pump driving gear with the driving fingers of the converter hub (photo).
22   Whilst employing an assistant to turn the crankshaft pulley as necessary, raise the transmission unit and insert the input shaft into the torque converter. As the input shaft splines align, the unit can be pushed fully home.
23   The remainder of the refitting procedure is the reverse of that used during removal.
24   On completion, top up the transmission to the *Cold-High* mark on the transmission dipstick.
25   After warming up the engine, recheck the fluid level as described in Section 24.

11 Downshift cable – checking and adjustment

Note: *The downshift cable has been preset at the Rover factory during manufacture and should not normally require adjustment. However, if the carburettors have been adjusted or a previous owner has interfered with the cable adjustment the following checks can be carried out.*

1 Select P, start the engine and run it until normal operating temperature has been reached (ie five minutes after the opening of the thermostat).
2 Refer to Chapter 3 and tune the carburettors. Check that the throttle linkage is set correctly.
3 Remove the air cleaner assembly to gain access to the downshift cable and throttle linkage.
4 With the engine idling turn the accelerator coupling shaft until the engine idling speed just increases.
5 Hold the coupling shaft in this position and measure the clearance gap between the crimped stop on the downshift cable and the end of the adjuster. This clearance gap should be between 0·010 and 0·020 in (0·25 and 0·50 mm) (Fig. 6.7).
6 Where this clearance gap is outside the defined dimensions make adjustments, by means of the cable adjuster, only after having checked that all the throttle rods and linkage are set to the correct dimensions.
7 Where possible carry out the downshift cable pressure test (as described in Section 12) before adjusting the cable.

12 Downshift cable – pressure test

1 Run the engine until the normal operating temperature is reached.
2 Refer to Chapter 3 and tune the carburettors.
3 Stop the engine and raise the car to provide access to the transmission. If jacks are used, adequately chock the wheels. Remove the plug situated in the cut-away on the lower edge of the transmission rear extension flange and fit a pressure gauge suitable for reading up to 100 lbf/in² (7 kgf/cm²).
4 Lower the car to the ground and apply the footbrake and handbrake as well as having the wheels chocked.
5 Start the engine and select D, and check that the gauge pressure is between 55 and 70 lbf/in² (3·8 and 4·9 kgf/cm²) at idle speed.
6 Increase the speed to 1250 rpm and check that the pressure increases by 15 to 20 lbf/in² (1·0 to 1·4 kgf/cm²).
7 Stop the engine.
8 If the downshift cable has been set correctly as described in Section 10, but the operating pressures are incorrect, then the gearbox can be suspected of having an internal fault. **Note:** *an incorrect pressure reading will result if the fluid level is incorrect.*
9 It is not a satisfactory practice to adjust the downshift cable merely as an attempt to correct the pressure readings. In such instances it is advisable to seek the expertise of your Rover dealer or automatic transmission specialist.

13 Front brake band – adjustment

1 Raise the car for access to the transmission and select N.
2 Slacken the locknut on the adjustment screw then tighten the adjuster screw (using a torque wrench) to a torque setting of 5 lbf ft (0·7 kgf m), then back if off ¾ of a turn.
3 Hold the adjuster screw stationary in this position and tighten the locknut.
4 Lower the car to the ground.

14 Rear brake band – adjustment

1 Select N and raise the car for access to the transmission unit.
2 Slacken the locknut and then tighten the adjuster screw to a torque setting of 5 lbf ft (0·7 kgf m). Remember to use a torque wrench for this operation as 'guess work' is not at all satisfactory.
3 Having tightened the adjuster screw to this setting back it off by ¾ of a turn.
4 Hold the adjuster screw stationary in this position and tighten the locknut.
5 Lower the car to the ground.

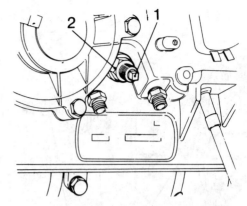

Fig. 6.9 Front brake band adjustment point

1 Adjuster   *2 Locknut*

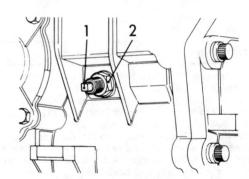

Fig. 6.10 Rear brake band adjustment point

1 Adjuster   *2 Locknut*

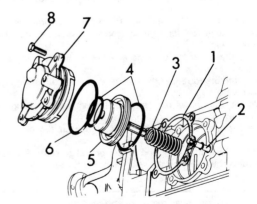

Fig. 6.11 Component parts of front servo

1 Joint washer (gasket)   *5 Piston*
2 O-ring   *6 Cover O-ring*
3 Spring   *7 Cover*
4 Piston O-rings   *8 Screw*

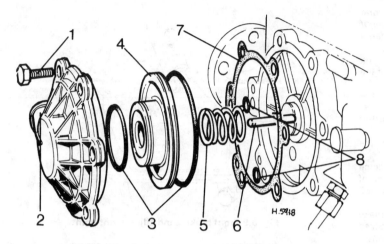

Fig. 6.12 Component parts of rear servo

1 Screw	5 Spring
2 Cover	6 Pushrod
3 Piston O-rings	7 Joint washer (gasket)
4 Piston	8 O-rings

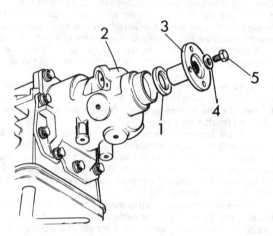

Fig. 6.13 Rear extension oil seal

1 Oil seal	4 Bolt
2 Rear extension	5 Washer
3 Drive flange	

15 Front servo – removal, overhaul and refitting

1   With the handbrake on and N selected raise the vehicle to gain access to the transmission unit. If you are using a jack remember to use some supplementary method of support as mentioned previously.
2   Disconnect and remove the forward section of the exhaust system between the manifolds and the intermediate pipe.
3   Remove the propeller shaft as described in Chapter 7.
4   Disconnect the selector arm and rod from the transmission unit.
5   Support the transmission unit with a suitable jack placed beneath the sump. Use a block of timber to spread the load.
6   Undo the four bolts securing the transmission crossmember to the chassis frame.
7   Lower the support jack just enough to gain access to the front servo unit. Do not lower the jack too far as the air cleaner body will foul the bulkhead.
8   Take out the four cover bolts and withdraw the servo assembly, spring and joint washer.
9   Remove the spring and withdraw the piston.
10 Take off all the O-rings from the piston and body, and discard them.
11 Clean all parts in petrol and wipe them dry with a lint-free cloth.
12 Inspect the piston for scoring, corrosion or other damage and renew if necessary.
13 Inspect the cover for damage and check that the passages are unobstructed.
14 It is preferable to renew the spring, if possible, unless it is known to be serviceable.
15 Assemble the unit in reverse order to dismantling, using new O-rings and a new gasket.
16 Raise the support jack, relocate and tighten the crossmember bolts.
17 Refit the selector arm and lever, propeller shaft and exhaust system section by reversing the removal procedures.

16 Rear servo – removal, overhaul and refitting

1   With the handbrake on and N selected raise the vehicle and support it to gain access to the transmission unit.
2   Remove the forward section of the exhaust system between the manifolds and the intermediate pipe.
3   Refer to Chapter 7 and remove the propeller shaft.

4   Disconnect the selector arm and rod, from the transmission unit.
5   Locate a support jack under the transmission sump pan. Place a flat block of wood on the jack lifting pad to prevent damaging the sump pan.
6   Having supported the transmission in this manner remove the four bolts securing the transmission crossmember to the chassis frame.
7   Lower the support jack just enough to gain access to the rear servo unit. If the jack is lowered too far the air cleaner body will foul the bulkhead and possibly cause damage to other components.
8   Take out the six bolts securing the rear servo cover.
9   Withdraw the servo assembly, joint washer, spring and pushrod.
10 Remove the pushrod and spring, then withdraw the piston.
11 Take off all the O-rings from the piston and body, then discard them.
12 Clean all the parts in petrol and wipe them dry with a lint-free cloth.
13 Inspect the piston for scoring, corrosion or other damage and renew if necessary.
14 Inspect the cover for damage and check that the passages are unobstructed.
15 It is preferable to renew the spring if possible, unless it is known to be serviceable.
16 Assemble the unit in the reverse order to dismantling using new O-rings and a new gasket.
17 Raise the support jack, relocate and tighten the four crossmember bolts.
18 The selector arm and lever, propeller shaft and front exhaust section can all be refitted by reversing the removal procedures.

17 Rear extension – removal and refitting

1   Drive the car onto a ramp or have jacks and axle stands available, chock the wheels and select N.
2   Disconnect the transmission fluid filler tube from the cylinder head and sump pan. Have ready a container of at least 9·5 pints (5·5 litres) as the fluid will drain from the transmission when the union at the base of the filler tube is unscrewed.
3   Disconnect and remove the forward section of the exhaust system between the manifolds and the intermediate pipe.
4   Remove the four bolts securing the front end of the propeller shaft. Move the propeller shaft to one side and support it.
5   In order to prevent the output flange from turning when undoing the flange retaining bolt, it will be necessary to construct a simple tool.

A flat steel bar is ideal and can be drilled and then bolted to the flange. Hold the bar and undo the flange bolt, then pull off the flange.

6   Support the transmission unit under its sump using a suitable jack. Place a flat wooden block on top of the jack lifting pad to spread the load.

7   Unscrew and remove the four bolts, spring washers and the two plates securing the transmission crossmember to the chassis frame.

8   Undo the two nuts and separate the crossmember bracket from the extension housing.

9   Unscrew two bolts and remove the exhaust system support bracket.

10   Lower the transmission support jack sufficiently to gain access to the extension housing retaining bolts.

11   Disconnect the speedometer cable by undoing the single bolt, removing the U-shaped clamp and pulling the cable away.

12   Undo the extension housing retaining bolts and withdraw the rear extension housing.

13   Refitting is a straightforward reversal of the removal procedure, but make sure that a new flange gasket is used.

18 Extension rear oil seal – renewal

1   Drive the car on to a ramp or have jacks and axle stands available. Chock the wheels and select N.

2   Mark the relationship of the propeller shaft and transmission drive flanges for re-alignment purposes.

3   Remove the four bolts securing the front end of the propeller shaft. Move the propeller shaft to one side and support it.

4   In order to undo the transmission flange bolt it will be found necessary to construct a simple tool to hold the drive flange still. A flat steel bar is ideal for this purpose and can be drilled and then bolted to the flange.

5   Hold the end of the tool firmly with one hand and undo the flange retaining bolt.

6   Pull off the drive flange.

7   Prise out the old oil seal.

8   Using a suitable drift, carefully drive in a new oil seal. Lightly lubricate the lip of the seal.

9   Refit the parts in the reverse order of removal.

19 Governor – removal, overhaul and refitting

1   Remove the rear extension as described in Section 16.

2   Withdraw the speedometer drive gear.

3   Unscrew the counterweight from the base of the governor, taking note of the spring washer.

4   Withdraw the governor from the shaft.

5   Prise off the retaining circlip and remove the weight.

6   Withdraw the stem, spring and valve.

7   Wash all the parts in petrol and dry with a lint-free cloth.

8   Check the parts for burrs and scoring, and for any signs of thread damage.

9   It is best to renew the spring, if at all possible, even if apparently satisfactory.

10   When reassembling, first insert the valve into the body.

11   Next, fit the spring to the stem, then fit both parts into the body.

12   Refit the weight and a new circlip.

13   Refit the governor and replace the counterweight and spring washer.

14   Refit the speedometer drive gear, followed by the rear extension. Remember to use a new gasket.

20 Selector rod – adjustment

1   Drive the vehicle onto a ramp or raise it up using jacks and axle stands.

2   Select P and apply the handbrake.

3   Slacken the locknut on the selector rod. Remove the split-pins and clevis pins, then lift the rod away. Note the locations of the spacer washers.

4   Check that the hand selector lever and the transmission selector lever are both in the P position.

5   Fit the selector rod to the gearbox selector lever.

6   Lift the front of the rod up and adjust the clevis fork until the clevis

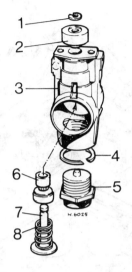

Fig. 6.14 Removing the governor

1	Circlip	5	Counterweight
2	Weight	6	Valve
3	Governor body	7	Stem
4	Spring washer	8	Spring

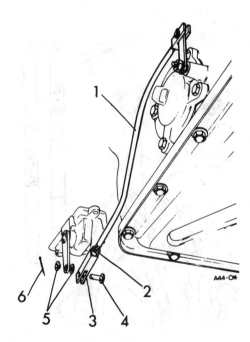

Fig. 6.15 Adjusting the selector rod

1	Selector rod	4	Clevis pin
2	Locknut	5	Spacer washers
3	Clevis fork	6	Split pin

pin holes in the fork and cross-shaft lever are aligned.

7   Fit the clevis pin, washers and split pins.

8   Tighten the locknut.

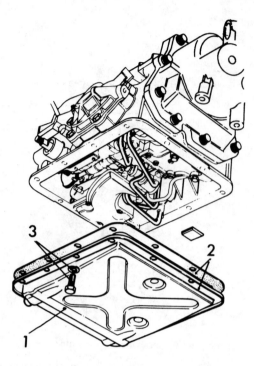

Fig. 6.16 The sump

1 Sump pan   3 Bolt and spring washer
2 Gasket

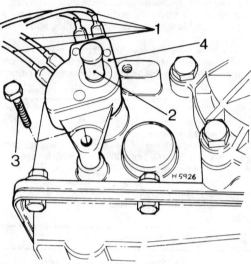

Fig. 6.17 Starter inhibitor/reverse light switch

1 Electrical leads   3 Bolt
2 Thread protector   4 Switch

4   Wipe around the area of the filler tube union at the transmission
and then unscrew the union; drain the contents into a suitable container. **Note**: *It is not possible to drain the torque converter completely.*
5   Tighten the union nut; then add fresh fluid via the filler tube until
the level is no higher than the 'cold high' mark on the dipstick.
6   Give the car a warming-up run and re-check the fluid level when
hot, by following the procedure given in Section 24.

22 Transmission sump – removal and refitting

1   Drive the vehicle on to a ramp or raise it up using jacks to gain
access to the underside of the transmission. Select P and apply the
handbrake.
2   Unscrew the filler tube union at the transmission and drain the
contents into a suitable size container.
3   Unscrew the twelve sump pan bolts and remove the sump with its
gasket.
4   When refitting the sump, make sure that the mating surfaces are
clean. Use a new gasket and tighten the bolts evenly to the recommended torque setting.
5   Refit the filler tube and then refill with new fluid as described in
Section 21.

23 Starter inhibitor/reverse lamp switch – removal and refitting

1   Drive the car on to a ramp or have adequate jacks to permit access
to the transmission. Select P and apply the handbrake.
2   Disconnect the battery negative terminal connection.
3   Take off the thread protector from the switch cover (where fitted).
4   Disconnect the switch leads. Note their colour coding and their
relative positions for correct refitting later.
5   Take out the retaining bolt and remove the switch.
6   Refitting is a reversal of the removal procedure.

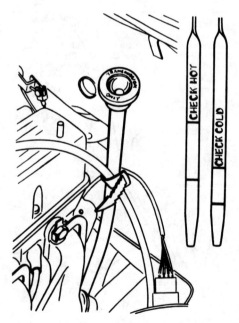

Fig. 6.18 The transmission fluid dipstick – location and detail

21 Transmission sump – draining and refilling

1   Drive the vehicle on to a ramp or have adequate jacks to provide
access to the underside of the car.
2   Select P and apply the handbrake.
3   Raise the ramp, or jacks.

24 Fluid level – checking

The automatic transmission fluid level check can be carried out
with the system either *'Cold'* or *'Hot'* as follows:

Cold check

1   Park the vehicle on a level surface, apply the footbrake and handbrake. Start the engine.

2   With the engine running move the selector through the complete range of shift positions. Continue this operation for a period of two minutes to ensure that the system is fully primed.
3   After this period select P, still allowing the engine to idle.
4   Open the bonnet, withdraw the transmission dipstick, wipe it clean.
5   Insert the dipstick fully and withdraw it immediately.
6   The fluid level should be on the 'cold' side of the dipstick blade.
7   Top-up as required to the 'high cold' mark, but do not overfill.
8   Repeat paragraphs 1 to 7 as necessary.

Hot check

9   The transmission should be at normal operating temperature when carrying out this check, ie after a run of approximately 20 miles (30 km).
10   Park the vehicle on a level surface, apply the footbrake and handbrake.
11   While holding the brakes on in this manner, allow the engine to idle and move the selector lever through the complete range of shift positions.
12   Continue to move the shift lever through the shift range for a period of two to three minutes in order to fully prime the transmission.
13   Having primed the system, move the selector lever to P and allow the engine to remain at idling speed.
14   Open the bonnet, withdraw the transmission dipstick and wipe it clean.
15   Insert the dipstick to its full depth and withdraw it immediately.
16   The fluid level should be read on the 'hot' side of the dipstick blade.
17   Top-up as necessary to the 'high hot' mark, but do not overfill.
18   Repeat paragraphs 9 to 17 as necessary.

25 Stall test

This test can only be satisfactorily carried out with an engine which is in good condition and capable of developing full power. **Note:** *during the test it is important that the temperature of the transmission fluid does not exceed 110°C (230°F) at any time.*
1   Run the engine until normal operating temperature has been reached and then check the fluid level as described in Section 23 (hot check).
2   Chock the rear wheels. Also apply the foot and handbrakes for the duration of the test.
3   If possible connect an auxiliary type of tachometer which can be observed from the driver's seat.
4   Start the engine, and with the brakes applied select D and allow the engine to idle for approximately one minute to ensure full circulation of the transmission fluid.
5   After this period, depress the accelerator pedal to the full throttle position *Not Kick-down*, and take a note of the tachometer reading which should be in the region between 1900 and 2100 rpm. *Under no circumstances hold the throttle pedal in this position for longer than ten seconds as the transmission will overheat.*
6   If the tachometer reading obtained during the test is between 1300 and 1900 rpm, then the engine is probably not developing full power. Readings less than 1300 rpm indicate suspected stator slip in

the torque converter. Where readings in excess of 2300 rpm are obtained, this is usually an indication of defective brake bands or clutches within the transmission unit.
7   If the test is to be repeated, allow 10 to 15 minutes for the transmission fluid to dissipate.

26 Road tests

The following tests will give an indication of the condition of the automatic transmission. Check that the unit functions properly in all the tests mentioned.

Owing to the complicated construction, and the finely adjusted settings within the unit, it is recommended that any repairs or adjustments, other than those we explain, should be entrusted to an appointed Rover workshop or an automatic transmission specialist.
Note: *The term full throttle refers to approximately seven-eighths of the available pedal travel and kick-down is equivalent to full pedal travel.*

Procedure

1   Check that the starter motor operates only with the selector lever at P or N and that the reverse lights operate only at R.
2   Apply the handbrake. With the engine idling select N-D, N-2, N-R. Engagement should be positive (a cushioned 'thump' under fast idling conditions is to be expected).
3   With the transmission at normal running temperature, select D. Release the brakes and accelerate with minimum throttle. Check the 1-2 and 2-3 shift speeds and the smoothness of the change.
4   Stop the vehicle, select D then re-start using full throttle. Check the 1-2 and 2-3 shift speeds and the smoothness of the change.
5   At a maximum speed of 50 mph (80 km/h) kick-down fully. The transmission should immediately change down into second gear.
6   Stop the vehicle, select D, then re-start using kick-down, check the 1-2 and 2-3 gearchange speeds.
7   At 65 mph (107 km/h), select 2 and simultaneously release the throttle; check the 3-2 changedown.
8   At 35 mph (56 km/h) select 1 and simultaneously release the throttle; check the 2-1 changedown.
9   With 1 still engaged, stop the car and using kick-down accelerate to over 40 mph (65km/h). Check for 'slip', 'squawk' and loss of upward gearchanges.
10   Park the vehicle on a gradient. Apply the handbrake and select P then release the handbrake and check that the parking pawl holds. Check that the selector lever is firmly locked in P.

Converter diagnosis

Inability to start on steep hills, combined with poor acceleration from rest and low stall speeds (1300 rpm), indicates that the converter stator unidirectional clutch is slipping. This permits the stator to rotate in an opposite direction to the impeller and turbine preventing torque multiplication. Poor acceleration in third gear above 30 mph (50 km/h) and reduced maximum speed, indicates that the unidirectional clutch has seized. The stator will not rotate with the turbine and impeller and the 'fluid flywheel' effect cannot occur. This condition will also be indicated by excessive overheating of the transmission although the stall speed will be satisfactory.

Chapter 7 Propeller shaft

Contents

Specifications

Type . . . . Single piece, tubular with constant velocity joints at either end

Torque wrench settings

	lbf ft	Nm
Gearbox and rear axle flange bolts/nuts	37	50

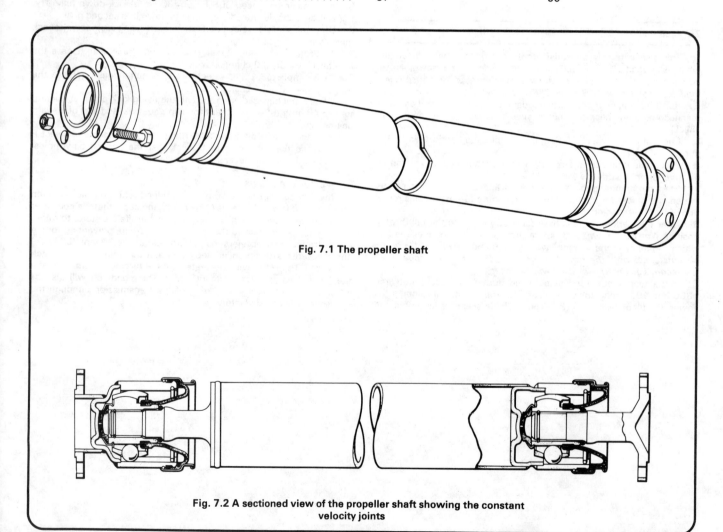

Fig. 7.1 The propeller shaft

Fig. 7.2 A sectioned view of the propeller shaft showing the constant
velocity joints

2.5 The propeller shaft connection to the final drive extension shaft flange. Note the painted index mark for correct installation

2.7 Disconnecting the forward end of the propeller shaft from the gearbox flange

1 General description

Drive is transmitted from the gearbox unit to the rear axle by a finely balanced tubular propeller shaft. At either end of the shaft are constant velocity joints, which allow for vertical movement of the rear axle. The design of the constant velocity joint also permits a small amount of longitudinal movement to allow for the fore-and-aft movement of the rear axle.

Flanges are used at each end for attachment to the gearbox mainshaft flange and rear axle drive flange.

No provision is made for lubrication during service life.

2 Propeller shaft – removal and refitting

1   Jack up the rear of the car and position on firmly based axle stands located at the body jacking points. Alternatively, position the rear of the car over an inspection pit or on a ramp.
2   If the rear of the car is jacked up, always supplement the jack with supporting axle stands or blocks so that danger is minimised, should the jack fail.
3   When the rear wheels are off the ground, place the car in gear, or apply the handbrake. This is to ensure that the propeller shaft does not turn when an attempt is made to loosen the nuts securing the propeller shaft universal joint flanges to the rear of the gearbox and to the final drive extension shaft flange.
4   The propeller shaft is carefully balanced to fine limits and it is important that it is replaced in exactly the same position it was in prior to its removal. Index mark the edges of the propeller shaft flanges and the corresponding edges of the front and rear driving flanges.
5   Undo and remove the four nuts and bolts which hold the rear flange of the propeller shaft to the flange on the final drive extension shaft (photo).
6   Push the propeller shaft forwards, lower the rear end of the propeller shaft, and support it.
7   Undo and remove the four nuts and bolts which hold the forward flange of the propeller shaft, to the flange at the rear of the gearbox unit (photo).
8   Remove the propeller shaft from the car.
9   Refitting is the reverse of the removal procedure, but ensure that the index marks are aligned. **Note:** *owing to the fact that the spacing of the propeller shaft front and rear flange holes are not the same, it will be found that the propeller shaft can be fitted in one position only (photo).*

2.9 The rear flange of the propeller shaft

3 Constant velocity joints – checking for wear

1   Wear in the propeller shaft constant velocity joints can be indicated by vibration or 'clunks' in the transmission, particularly when the drive is being taken up or when going to over-run. (Backlash in the rear axle has the same effect, so check both assemblies, if symptoms occur).
2   It is easy to check the constant velocity joints whilst the propeller shaft is still in position. Try to turn the shaft with one hand and grip the other side of the joint with the other hand. There should be no movement across the joint. Check also by trying to lift the shaft and noting any movement in the joints.
3   If any wear is detected when carrying out the checks mentioned above, then a replacement propeller shaft will have to be obtained as the constant velocity joints are non-repairable items.

4 Fault diagnosis – propeller shaft

Symptom	Reason/s
Vibration	Misalignment Wear in constant velocity joints Loose flange nuts
Noisy operation	Wear in constant velocity joints Loose flange nuts

Chapter 8 Rear axle

For modifications, and information applicable to later models, see Supplement at end of manual.

Contents

Specifications

Type .... Semi-floating live axle with hypoid bevel gears and two pinion differential

Oil capacity .... 1.6 pints (0.91 litres)

Oil type .... Hypoid gear oil, viscosity SAE 90EP to BLS 22-OL-03 or MIL-L-2105B (Duckhams Hypoid 90S)

Final drive ratio .... 3.08 : 1

Torque wrench settings

	lbf ft	Nm
Halfshaft bearing retainer plate set-screws	37	50
Extension housing to axle casing (nuts and bolts)	37	50
Extension housing mounting bracket bolts	37	50
Oil filler level plug	26	35
Oil seal housing to hypoid housing set-screws	37	50
Brake pipe bracket set-screws	21	28
Damper locknut	22	32
Damper nut	15	20
Radius rod nuts	41	54
Watts linkage pivot nut	41	54

1 General description

The semi-floating, 'live' rear axle consists of a conventional hypoid final drive and differential units.

The axle casing is located at its forward end by semi-trailing arms and a torque tube (pinion housing extension). Self-levelling damper struts and coil springs also assist. Sideways location of the rear axle is provided by a Watts type, pivoting linkage arrangement, which is transversely mounted at the rear of the axle casing.

Drive from the propeller shaft is taken to the bevel pinion via the extension shaft. From the bevel pinion the drive is transmitted to the crownwheel and differential unit which together form the differential assembly.

The differential assembly (including the crownwheel but excluding the bevel pinion) is free to revolve within the axle casing, being mounted at either side on taper roller bearings and retained to the casing by two semi-circular bearing housing caps. This arrangement enables the differential assembly to be removed, from the rear axle casing, without the necessity to remove the rear axle.

The procedures given in this Chapter enable the owner to carry out certain operations, but owing to the need for specialised tools and the

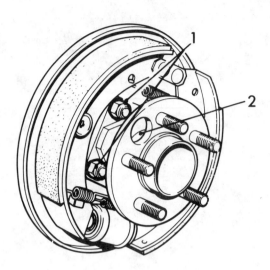

Fig. 8.1 Halfshaft location

1   *Retaining nuts (4 off)*
2   *Access hole in halfshaft flange*

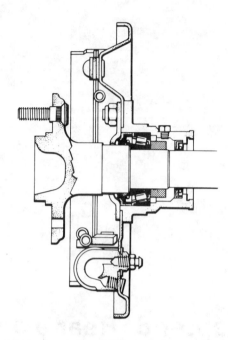

Fig. 8.2 Sectional view of the rear hub assembly

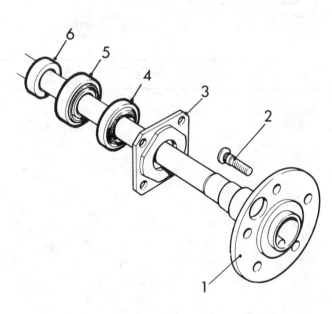

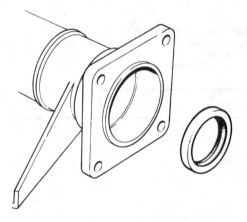

Fig. 8.4 Axle tube and oil seal

Fig. 8.3 Halfshaft and bearing/seal arrangement

1	*Halfshaft*	4	*Oil seal*
2	*Wheel stud*	5	*Bearing*
3	*Retainer plate*	6	*Lock ring*

necessary expertise, it is not recommended that the owner should attempt to either remove, dismantle or make adjustments to the differential or bevel pinion assemblies. It is far better to entrust work of this complex nature to your local Rover dealer who will have the necessary equipment and trained personnel at hand.

2   Halfshaft – removal and refitting

1   The halfshafts may be withdrawn without disturbing the differential gear.
2   Chock the front roadwheels and raise the appropriate rear roadwheel clear of the ground. Support the car with either an axle stand or strong wooden packing blocks.
3   Remove the rear roadwheel and release the handbrake.
4   Undo the single countersunk screw and withdraw the brake drum. Should it be found difficult to remove refer to Chapter 9 for further

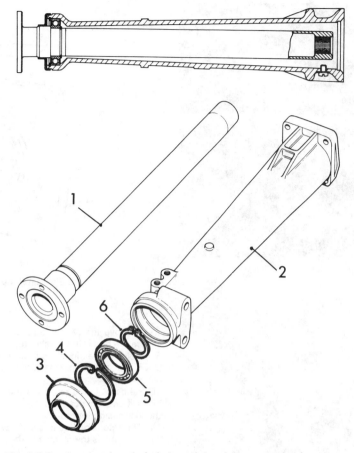

Fig. 8.5 Sectional and exploded view of the pinion extension housing assembly

1	Extension shaft	4	Circlip
2	Extension housing	5	Bearing
3	Mudshield	6	Circlip

details.

5   Through the large hole in the halfshaft flange undo the four bolts and nuts securing the halfshaft assembly and brake backplate to the axle tube flange.

6   Rover recommend that a slide hammer tool be used to withdraw the halfshaft, but if such a tool is not at hand the brake drum and a heavy soft faced hammer will suffice.

7   Temporarily install the brake drum so that the inside of the drum is facing towards you. Retain the drum to the halfshaft by using the wheelnuts screwed on the 'wrong' way round (taper edge outwards).

8   Using a heavy soft faced hammer, or an ordinary hammer and a hardwood block, tap the drum from behind whilst rotating it to draw out the halfshaft complete with the bearing.

9   Refitting is basically tne reverse of the removal procedure, but the following points should be noted:

  (a) *The interior of the axle tube/halfshaft bearing area should be smeared with a lithium-based grease*

  (b) *Likewise smear a little lithium-based grease on the bearing and the oil seal*

  (c) *Slide the halfshaft carefully in through the axle tube and turn it slowly until its splined end engages with the differential splines*

  (d) *Push the halfshaft inwards and check that the bearing and oil seal enter the axle tube squarely*

  (e) *Fit the securing bolts and nuts, taking care to tighten them evenly*

  (f) *Wipe away any surplus lubricant and grease, to prevent the possibility of brake lining contamination*

3   Halfshaft bearing and oil seals – removal and refitting

1   Because of the special tools required to draw off the spacer ring and halfshaft bearing retainer oil seal, this job should be entrusted to a Rover dealer. However, the halfshaft can be removed as described in the previous Section to minimise labour costs.

2   To remove the oil seal from the axle tube, first remove the half-shaft, as described in Section 2.

3   Prise out the seal from the axle tube.

4   Smear the replacement seal with axle oil, ensure that the bore of the axle tube is clean, then install the seal with the lip towards the differential.

5   Install the halfshaft as described in Section 2.

4   Pinion extension housing – removal and refitting

1   Chock the front roadwheels, raise the rear of the car and support it on strong wooden packing blocks or axle stands.

2   Release the handbrake.

3   Disconnect the propeller shaft at the extension housing drive flange.

4   Remove the clip retaining the handbrake cable to the extension housing.

5   Undo the two bolts securing the flexible brake hose bracket to the extension housing.

6   Place a support jack under the differential pinion ensuring that it is clear of the extension housing flange.

4.3 The extension housing bracket

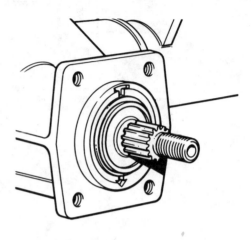

Fig. 8.6 Installing the pinion oil seal

7　　Remove the two bolts, together with their spring washers, which secure the mounting bracket to the extension housing.
8　　Release the mounting bracket from the extension housing.
9　　Lower the support jack until the extension housing is clear of the car body.
10　Remove the three bolts and spring washers, and one bolt, nut bracket and locknut which secure the extension housing rear flange to the axle casing (photo).
11　The extension housing can now be withdrawn.
12　Refitting is the reverse of the removal procedure.

4.10 The extension housing rear flange

5　Pinion extension housing bearing – removal and refitting

1　　Remove the pinion extension housing as described in Section 4.
2　　Scribe a line on the extension housing to coincide with the amount of overlap of the mudshield. This facilitates accurate refitment later.
3　　Using a wedge shaped drift, tap the mudshield forwards towards the drive flange. Great care must be taken when doing this as the mudshield will distort if tapped unevenly or too hard.
4　　Using a suitable pair of circlip pliers extract the end circlip which retains the bearing and shaft.
5　　Pull the shaft and bearing out of the extension housing.
6　　Remove a further circlip directly behind the bearing.
7　　The bearing can now be either pressed or driven off the shaft.
8　　Fit the new bearing and locate it with the circlip.
9　　Fit the bearing and shaft into the housing and fit the circlip to the housing.
10　Slide the mudshield back along the shaft into its original position. When correctly fitted there should be a gap of $\frac{5}{32}$ in (4 mm) between the edge of the mudshield and the machined lip of the extension housing.
11　Refit the extension housing by reversing the removal procedure.

6　Differential pinion oil seal – renewal

Note: *Rover recommend that certain special service tools are used to carry out this operation, but in all probability this task can be carried out without them if some care is exercised.*
1　　Remove the pinion extension housing as described in Section 4.
2　　Carefully remove the pinion seal housing.
3　　Extract the pinion seal from the housing.
4　　Fit a new pinion oil seal to the housing taking great care to prevent damaging the seal lip. The lip of the seal must face away from the arrow-marked housing face.
5　　Wrap a narrow strip of masking tape over the pinion shaft. This measure will protect the seal during fitment of the seal housing. Posi-

6.9 Location of the rear axle level/filler plug

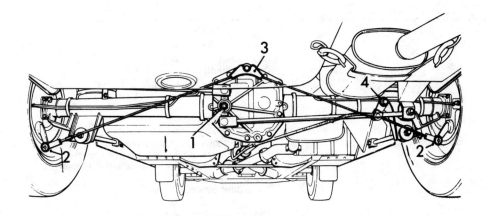

Fig. 8.7A Removing the rear axle (illustrations indicating some of...

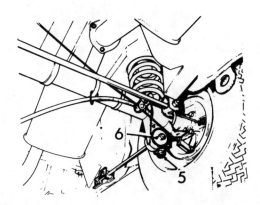

Fig. 8.7B ... the components which must be either removed or disconnected)

1	Watts linkage pivot		unit
2	Handbrake cable fork ends	5	Damper lower mounting
3	Handbrake cable guide	6	Radius rod end nut
4	Handbrake compensator		

tion the masking tape in such a way that it can be easily removed after fitting the seal housing.

6   Lubricate the lip of the seal and the masking tape.

7   Fit the seal and housing and insert them evenly into the axle casing. Note that the arrow-marked face must be fitted outermost and the arrow must point downwards. Tap the seal housing evenly and gently into position.

8   Fit the extension housing by reversing the removal procedure.

9   Finally check and if necessary top-up the rear axle (photo).

7   Rear axle – removal and refitting

1   Raise the rear of the car and support it using suitable stands or blocks beneath the bodyframe side-members. Chock the front wheels for safety.

2   Remove the rear roadwheels and release the handbrake.

3   Place a supporting jack, ideally a trolley jack, under the differential unit.

4   Disconnect the rear end of the propeller shaft from the final drive flange. Move the propeller shaft to one side and support it.

5   Disconnect the flexible brake hose from the bracket attached to the pinion extension housing.

6   Undo the two bolts securing the bracket to the pinion extension housing. Ease the bracket off the locating dowels.

7   Loosen the clip on the extension housing and separate the handbrake cable support clip from it.

8   Disconnect the handbrake cable fork ends from the backplate levers by withdrawing the split pins and clevis pins.

9   Release the handbrake cable from the guide fitted to the rear of the axle casing.

10 Disconnect the handbrake cable compensator by removing the nut and bolt clamping the compensator and releasing the handbrake cable trunnion.

11 Tie the handbrake cables back out of the way.

12 Disconnect the radius arms from the axle brackets by undoing the nuts and withdrawing the large plain washers and rubber bushes.

13 Undo the nut and remove the plain washer securing the Watt's linkage to the differential housing. Pull the Watt's linkage central pivot arm back clear of the central pivot post.

14 Disconnect the dampers from the axle simply by removing the locknut, nut and washer.

15 Lower the support jack slowly and at the same time draw the axle clear of the radius rods.

16 The axle can now be pulled out from under the car.

17 Refitting is basically the reverse of the removal procedure, but the following points should be noted.

18 When locating the axle tighten each of the various nuts and bolts only finger tight at first. After everything is reconnected is this manner, progressively tighten the nuts and bolts to the recommended torque setting.

19 One of the final tasks will be to bleed the brakes. This operation is described in Chapter 9.

8 Fault diagnosis – rear axle

Symptom	Reason/s
Vibration	Worn halfshaft bearings Loose drive flange bolts Propeller shaft out-of-balance Wheels require balancing
Noise	Insufficient lubricant Worn differential gears
'Clunk' on acceleration or deceleration	Incorrect crownwheel and pinion mesh Excessive backlash due to wear in differential gears Worn halfshaft or differential side gear splines Loose drive flange bolts Worn drive pinion flange splines
Oil leakage	Faulty pinion or halfshaft seals Blocked axle housing breather

Chapter 9 Braking system

For modifications, and information applicable to later models, see Supplement at end of manual

Contents

Specifications

System type ....   Dual hydraulic, front disc and rear drums, with vacuum servo and rear wheel pressure reducing valve. Cable operated handbrake to rear wheels

Front brakes
Type ....   Disc and caliper
Disc diameter (nominal) ....   10.15 in (258 mm)
Disc thickness:
  New......................................   0.55 in (14 mm)
  Minimum after refinishing ....   0.51 in (13 mm)
Pad lining minimum thickness ....   0.12 in (3 mm)

Rear brakes
Type ....   Drum, self adjusting
Drum internal diameter (nominal) ....   9 in (228 mm)
Drum width (internal) ....   2.25 in (57 mm)
Shoe lining minimum thickness ....   0.12 in (3 mm)

Vacuum servo unit
Boost ratio ....   3.08 : 1

Handbrake
Type ....   Cable operated to rear wheels from floor mounted lever

Brake fluid specification ....   Hydraulic fluid to FMVSS 116 DOT 3 or SAE J1703 (Duckhams Universal Brake and Clutch Fluid)

Torque wrench settings

	lbf ft	Nm
Pedal bracket to dash bracket screw	20	27.5
Pressure reducing valve to body nut	20	27.5
Front caliper to suspension bolt	55	75
Disc to hub bolt	41	54.5
Disc shield set-screw	8	11
Handbrake lever to body bolt	20	27.5
Handbrake fulcrum to rear axle nyloc nut (M10)	12.5	17
Brake compensator lever to handbrake nut (M6)	8	11
Servo and pedal bracket to dash nut	20	27.5

1 General description

The brakes fitted to the front two wheels are of the rotating disc and static caliper type, with one caliper per disc, each caliper containing two piston operated friction pads, which on application of the footbrake, pinch the disc rotating between them.

Application of the footbrake creates hydraulic pressure in the master cylinder and fluid from the cylinder travels via steel and flexible pipes to the cylinders in each half of the calipers, the fluid so pushing the pistons, to move the friction pads, into contact with each side of each disc.

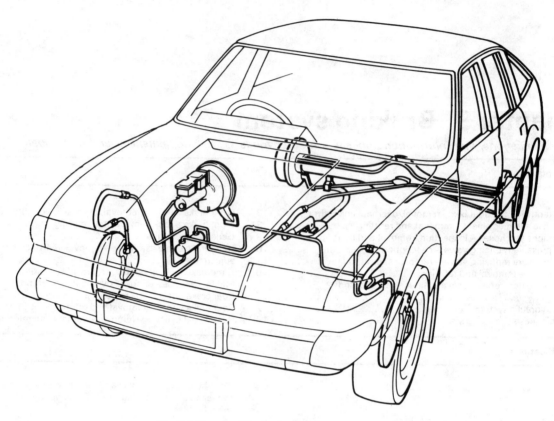

Fig. 9.1 Layout of the brake system

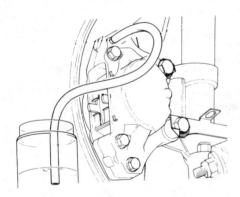

Fig. 9.2 Bleeding a front brake caliper

Two rubber seals are fitted to the operating cylinders. The outer seal prevents moisture and dirt from entering the cylinder. The inner seal, which is retained in a groove inside the cylinder, prevents fluid leakage and provides a running clearance for the pad irrespective of how worn it is, by moving it back a fraction when the brake pedal is released.

As the friction pad wears so the pistons move further out of the cylinders and the level of the fluid in the hydraulic reservoir drops; disc pad wear is thus taken up automatically and eliminates the need for periodic adjustments by the owner.

The rear brakes are of the self-adjusting, leading and trailing shoe type, with one brake cylinder per wheel for both shoes. A lever assembly is fitted between the two shoes of each brake unit and attached to this is a system of cables which in turn is connected to the handbrake lever. It is unusual to have to adjust the handbrake system as the efficiency of this system is largely dependent on the condition of the brake linings and the adjustment of the brake shoes. The hand-

brake can, however, be adjusted independently from the footbrake operated hydraulic system.

Connected to the brake pedal is a servo unit onto which is mounted the master cylinder. It increases the hydraulic line pressure whilst decreasing the driver's pedal effort. The master cylinder is a dual-type which means that the front and rear brakes operate independently of each other through a common pedal pushrod. Should one half of the system fail to operate, the brakes on the other half will still operate, although the system efficiency is reduced. A brake pressure regulator is fitted and is designed to prevent the rear wheels from locking. A separate description of this is given in the text.

2   Brake hydraulic system – bleeding

1   Removal of all the air from the hydraulic system is essential to the correct working of the braking system, but before undertaking this, examine the fluid reservoir cap to ensure that the vent hole is clear; check the level of fluid and replenish if required.
2   Check all brake line unions and connections for possible seepage, also check the condition of the rubber hoses. These may be perished.
3   If the condition of the wheel cylinders is in doubt, check for signs of possible fluid leakage.
4   If there is any possibility of incorrect fluid having been put into the system, drain all the fluid out and flush through with isopropyl-alcohol or methylated spirit. Renew all piston seals and cups since they will be affected and could possibly fail when under pressure.
5   Gather together a clean jam jar, a 9 in (230 mm) length of tubing which fits tightly over the bleed nipple and a supply of the correct type of fluid. You will also require the services of an assistant. Additional bleeding methods are described in Chapter 13, Section 12.
6   Disconnect the wires from the brake pressure failure switch, and unscrew the switch from the underside of the master cylinder.
7   To bleed the system, make sure that the car is on a level surface and release the handbrake. To gain better access to the bleed nipples it may be preferable to lift one roadwheel at a time. If this is the case, chock the roadwheels which remain on the ground.

8 Commence at the front wheel caliper furthest from the master cylinder, remove the rubber cap and wipe carefully around the bleed nipple (photo).
9 Fit one end of the rubber tube over the nipple and place the other end of the tube in a clean glass jar containing sufficient fluid to keep the end of the tube submerged during the operation.
10 Open the bleed valve with a spanner and quickly press down the brake pedal. After slowly releasing the pedal, pause for a moment to allow the fluid to recoup in the master cylinder and then depress again. This will force air from the system. Continue until no more air bubbles can be seen coming from the tube, then, with the pedal depressed, close the bleed nipple. At frequent intervals during the operation, make certain that the reservoir is kept topped-up, otherwise air will enter the system again. Always discard any fluid which is bled off since it probably contains air, dirt and moisture.
11 Now repeat the operation on the other front caliper in the same way. Do not forget to replace the rubber protective cap on the bleed nipple afterwards. This completes the bleeding of the front brakes.
12 The rear brakes should now be bled. There is only one bleed nipple; this is on the right-hand backplate.
13 When the system has been fully bled the pedal action should be firm, and free from any 'sponginess'. If this still appears to be present, there is a likelihood that one of the seals in the master cylinder has failed.
14 On completion, refit the brake pressure failure switch. Note that the tightening torque is only 15 lbf in (0·17 kgf m).

2.8 Front brake caliper bleed nipple (arrowed)

3 Brake disc and disc shield – removal and refitting

1 Remove the front hub, as described in Chapter 11.

Brake disc

2 Remove the five disc-to-hub retaining bolts, and withdraw the disc.
3 Refitting is the reverse of the removal procedure. Tighten the retaining bolts evenly to the specified torque.

Disc shield

4 Remove the three bolts and spring washers. Detach the disc shield from the vertical link.
5 Refitting is the reverse of the removal procedure.

4 Front brake pads – removal and refitting

1 Apply the handbrake, then jack-up the front of the car and remove the roadwheel.
2 Straighten the ends of the split pins, slightly depress the pad retaining springs and withdraw the split pins (photo).
3 Lift the retaining springs away and withdraw the pads and shims taking note of their positions (photo).
4 Carefully press the caliper pistons back into their bores. **Note:** *This will cause the reservoir fluid level to rise. Prevent it from overflowing by loosening the caliper bleed nipple as the piston is being moved, then close it when movement is complete.*
5 Refitting is now the reverse of the removal procedure, but the following points should be noted:

   (a) *Ensure that the pad location area in the caliper is free from dust and dirt*
   (b) *If the shims are corroded, obtain new ones; they should be fitted as shown in the photograph*
   (c) *Use new pad retaining springs and split pins. Fold back one leg of each split pin*
   (d) *Depress the brake pedal several times on completion to correctly locate the pads*
   (e) *Check the reservoir fluid level on completion*

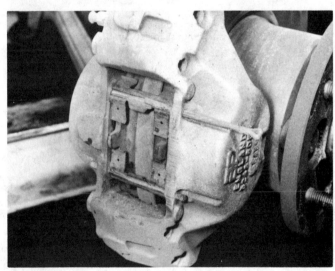
4.2 Withdraw the pad retaining pins

5 Front brake caliper – removal, overhaul and refitting

1 Apply the handbrake, then jack-up the front of the car and remove the roadwheel.
2 Disconnect the brake union from the caliper. Seal the fluid connections to prevent the ingress of dirt.

4.3 Withdraw the pads and shims

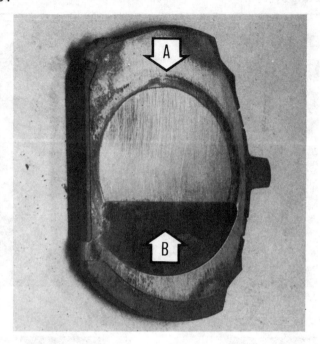

4.5 Correct installation of the shim to the brake pad. Indent A of pad must be uppermost with shim cut-out B at bottom

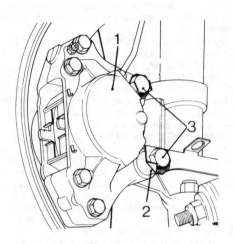

Fig. 9.3 Front brake caliper

1 Caliper   3 Retaining bolts
2 Tab washers

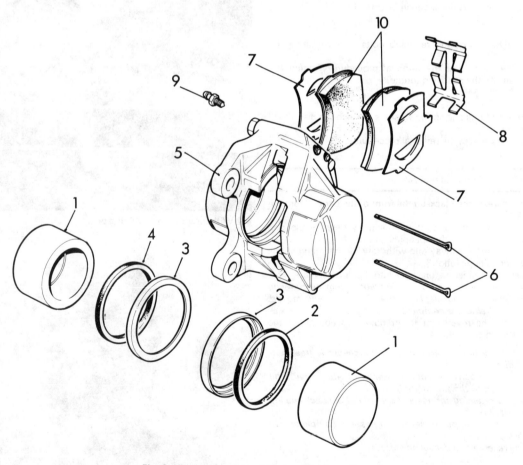

Fig. 9.4 Exploded view of the front brake caliper

1 Pistons	5 Caliper	8 Pad retaining spring
2 Fluid seal	6 Split pins	9 Bleed screw
3 Wiper seals	7 Shims	10 Brade pads
4 Fluid seal		

3   Straighten the ends of the tab washers and undo the two bolts retaining the caliper to the damper unit and stub axle assembly.
4   The caliper can now be withdrawn.
5   Remove the brake pads and shims (refer to Section 4, if necessary).
6   Using a small 'G' clamp and a thin flat strip of wood, clamp one of the pistons in position. Apply a low pressure air line or alternatively a tyre foot pump to the fluid port and eject the piston.
7   Having removed one of the pistons, remove the 'G' clamp and place the flat piece of wood over the hole vacated by the piston that has just been removed. Carefully clamp the piece of wood in position.
8   Apply the low pressure air source to the fluid port and eject the other piston.
9   Note the exact positions of the two pistons. Under no circumstances swop their caliper positions. Should one of the pistons be seized in the caliper, the whole caliper must be renewed.
10 Using a blunt screwdriver, carefully prise out the wiper seal retainers. Do not scratch any metal parts.
11 Extract the wiper dust seals and fluid seals from the bores.
12 Thoroughly clean the metal parts using clean brake fluid, methylated spirit or isopropyl-alcohol. Inspect the caliper bores and pistons for wear, scoring and corrosion, renew parts as necessary. *Do not attempt to separate the two halves of the caliper.*
13 Position new fluid seals in the caliper bores, ensuring that they are properly located. They will stand proud of the bore at the edge furthest away from the mouth of the bore.
14 Lubricate the bores with new brake fluid and squarely insert the pistons in their original positions. Leave about $\frac{5}{16}$ in (8 mm) of each piston projecting.
15 Fit a new wiper seal into each seal retainer, and slide an assembly into each bore.
16 Press the seals and pistons fully home.
17 Refitting of the caliper is now the reverse of the removal procedure. Fit the retaining bolts only finger tight at first and reconnect the fluid pipe.
18 Tighten the retaining bolts to the recommended torque setting and bend back the ends of the tab washers. The fluid coupling can now be fully tightened.
19 On completion of this installation the brakes will have to be bled as described in Section 2. Fitting of the brake pads is covered in Section 4.

6   Rear brake shoes – removal and refitting

1   Jack-up the rear of the car and support it on stands or blocks beneath the rear axle. Chock the front wheels for safety.
2   Remove the roadwheel and release the handbrake.
3   Remove the single countersunk screw and pull off the brake drum (photo). **Note:** *If the drum is difficult to remove, remove the rubber plug on the rear of the backplate and insert a small screwdriver to engage in the small adjusting lever. Press downwards to contact the brake shoes.*
4   Note the installed positions of the shoes and springs. Remove the steady pin cups and springs by depressing the cups and turning the pins through 90 degrees. The pins can now be withdrawn from the rear of the backplate.
5   Lever the ends of the brake shoes out from the slots in the wheel cylinder piston heads (photo).
6   Remove the clevis pin securing the yoke end of the handbrake cable to the backplate operating lever.
7   Detach the pull-off springs and the cross-lever tension spring, to remove the brake shoes. Retain the piston in the cylinders using a wire clip or strong rubber band.
8   Clean any dust etc. from the brake drum and backplate. *Take care that the dust is not inhaled since it can be very harmful to the lungs.* If there are signs of fluid leakage from the hydraulic wheel cylinder or oil leakage from the halfshaft or bearing these points should be investigated and if necessary, remedied at this stage – see Section 7 and Chapter 8. Renew the brake shoes where the linings have worn down to the specified minimum thickness or are likely to wear down to this point during the next few thousand miles of motoring.
9   When fitting the shoes, insert the tension spring hook in the cross-lever and engage the other end in the web of the leading shoe. **Note:** *The springs are in sets for left and right-hand brakes.*
10 Ease the shoe and cross-lever towards the backplate; engage the

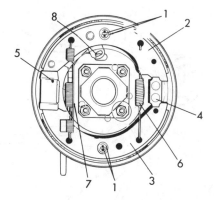

Fig. 9.5 Layout of the right-hand rear brake

1 Steady pin and cup	*5 Wheel cylinder*
2 Leading shoe	*6 Front pull-off spring*
3 Trailing shoe	*7 Rear pull-off spring*
4 Abutment plate	*8 Cross-lever tension spring*

6.3 The rear brakes with drum removed

6.5 The wheel cylinder showing the locations of the brake shoe webs

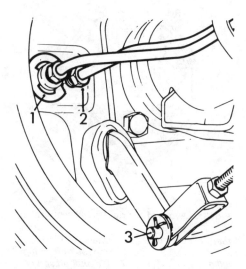

Fig. 9.6 Left-hand rear wheel cylinder fixing at backplate

1 Spring clip   *3 Handbrake cable fork clevis pin*
2 Feed/transfer pipe

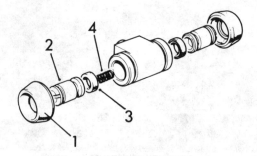

Fig. 9.7 Exploded view of the rear wheel cylinder unit

1 Rubber boot   3 Seal
2 Piston   4 Spring

9.2 The flexible brake hose to the rear axle

toe in the piston slot and heel in the abutment slot.

11 Hold the cross-member and shoe against the backplate, and fit the steady pin, spring and cup.

12 Hook the pull-off springs into the holes in the shoe webs. Note that they run on the backplate side of the shoes.

13 Pull the trailing shoe into position with the heel in the piston slot, and the toe in the abutment slot. Ensure that the cross-lever cut-out engages in the adjuster plate slot.

14 Fit the second steady pin, spring and cup.

15 Refit the second steady pin, spring and cup.

16 Refit the handbrake cable and clevis pin to the backplate operating lever using a new split-pin.

17 Provided that care is exercised to prevent the pistons from being forced out, the automatic adjuster action can be checked by gently pressing the brake pedal. As the shoes expand, the ratchet will operate; this can be cancelled by raising the ratchet plate to separate the ratchet teeth and allowing the shoes to retract under spring action.

18 Fit the brake drum and roadwheel, then depress the brake pedal several times to centralize and adjust the brakes.

19 If the brake action is unsatisfactory, test run the car and apply moderately high pedal effort during several test runs at a speed around 20 mph (33 kph).

7 Rear wheel cylinder – removal, overhaul and refitting

1   Remove the brake shoes as described in the previous Section.

2   Disconnect the handbrake cable from the lever behind the backplate by removing the split pin and clevis pin.

3   Disconnect the pipe union and remove the bleed screw, or the feed and transfer pipe unions from the rear of the wheel cylinder, as applicable.

4   Remove the spring clip, and take off the wheel cylinder.

5   Remove the rubber boots and take out the pistons; also remove the spring from the bore.

6   Remove the seal from each piston.

7   Thoroughly clean the metal parts using clean brake fluid, methylated spirit or isopropyl alcohol. Inspect the pistons and cylinder bores for wear, scoring and corrosion; renew parts as necessary.

8   Smear the cylinder bore with new brake fluid, then fit a new seal to the large groove of each piston, so that the lip of the seal faces away from the slot.

9   Locate the rubber boots into the smaller groves of the piston, then insert the pistons into the bore with the spring between them.

10 Refitting is the reverse of the removal procedure, but bleed the brakes before test running the car.

8 Rear brake backplate – removal and refitting

1   Remove the halfshaft assembly as described in Chapter 8. Insert a piece of lint-free cloth in the end of the open axle tube to prevent the oil from running. Providing the axle is not overfilled and the car has been raised high enough, no oil should run out.

2   Refer to the procedure given in paragraphs 2 and 3 of the previous Section.

3   Remove the four nuts, spring washers and bolts securing the backplate. Withdraw the backplate.

4   Refitting is the reverse of the removal procedures, but bleed the brakes on completion (see Section 2).

9 Brake pipes and hoses – inspection, removal and refitting

1   Inspection of the braking system hydraulic pipes and flexible hoses is part of the maintenance schedule. Carefully check the rigid pipes along the rear axle, underbody and in the engine compartment, not forgetting the short runs to the front wheel calipers. Any pipes showing signs of corrosion or damage should be renewed, following which it will be necessary to bleed the system as described previously.

2   Carefully inspect the flexible hoses. There is one flexible pipe to the rear axle and one on each suspension arm (photo). Look for any signs of swellings, cracking and/or chafing. If any of these maladies is evident, renew the hoses straight away. Remember that your life could depend on it.

3   Where flexible hoses are to be renewed, unscrew the metal pipe

union nut from its connection to the hose, and then holding the hexagon on the hose with a spanner, unscrew the attachment nut and washer.
4   The body end of the flexible hose can now be withdrawn from the chassis mounting bracket and will be quite free.
5   Refitting is the reverse of the removal procedure, following which it will be necessary to bleed the system, as described in Section 2.

10 Brake pressure reducing valve – description of operation

The reducing valve is installed in the brake circuit between the master cylinder, and the front and rear brakes. Its purpose is to limit the pressure applied to the rear brakes relative to the front brake pressure, thus minimising the possibility of rear wheel locking. In the event of a failure in the front circuit the cut-off pressure is increased and the pressure reduction ratio is altered (Fig. 9.8).

Fluid from the master cylinder primary chamber is fed into the pressure reducing valve at port 'A' and out to the front brakes via ports 'C' and 'D'. The master cylinder secondary chamber feeds into port 'B', through the internal passages in the valve plunger, past the metering valve and then to the rear brakes via port 'E'. The large spring 'S' biases the valve plunger to the left. Hydraulic pressure therefore acts on the annular area (a1 – a2) forcing the plunger to the left while the force acting on the area 'a1' and annular area (a4 – a3) tries to move the plunger to the right where it is opposed by the spring. When the net force acting to the right overcomes the pre-load provided by the spring, the plunger assembly shifts to the right and closes the metering valve 'F'. Thus, pressure at the rear outlet port 'E' falls relative to the input pressure. As pressure is increased at ports 'A' and 'B', the plunger is forced to the left, opening the metering valve 'F' and allowing a metered quantity of fluid to be fed to the rear brakes. The resultant increase in pressure acting on area 'a1' causes the plunger to again shift to the right, thus closing the metering valve. This procedure continues until there is no further increase in applied pressure from the master cylinder.

The resultant pressure at outlet 'E' is reduced after cut-off in proportion to the area 'a2' and the difference between the two annular areas (a1 – a2) and (a4 – a3). This cut-off pressure is equal to the pre-load in the spring 'S' divided by the combined areas 'a2' and (a4 – a3). Should the front brake circuit fail, there will be no pressure acting on annular area (a4 – a3) so that the net force tending to move the plunger to the right will equal the product of the input pressure and area 'a2'. Thus, as the value of the pre-load spring is unchanged, the cut-off pressure will increase considerably.

As the annular area (a4 – a3) is now redundant, the reduction ratio after cut-off changes the area 'a2'. Should the rear brake circuit fail, the pressure reducing valve is completely inoperative.

11 Brake pressure reducing valve – removal and refitting

1   Loosen the brake pipe union at the master cylinder and remove the two inlet pipes from the top of the reducing valve (photo).
2   Disconnect the remaining pipes at the pressure reducing valve.
3   Undo the nut, plain washer, spring washer and bolt. Lift the pressure reducing valve from the wheel arch. Wrap it in a lint-free cloth before lifting it clear to avoid the spillage of brake fluid.
4   Refitting is the reverse of the removal procedure, but bleed the brakes on completion.

12 Master cylinder – removal, overhaul and refitting

1   Noting their installed position, detach the fluid lines from the master cylinder. Plug the pipes and ports to prevent the loss of brake fluid and the ingress of dust, dirt, etc. (photo).
2   Detach the leads from the brake pressure failure and low fluid level switches, then remove the master cylinder retaining nuts and washers. Withdraw the master cylinder from the servo.
3   Clean all dirt from the external surfaces of the master cylinder.
4   Unscrew and remove the brake pressure failure switch.
5   Secure the master cylinder in a vice fitted with jaw protectors and remove the two crosshead screws which secure the fluid reservoir. Withdraw the reservoir from the master cylinder body.
6   Extract the two reservoir sealing rings after noting their exact posi-

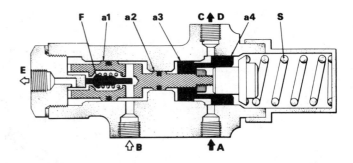

Fig. 9.8 Sectional view of the brake pressure reducing valve

11.1 The brake pressure reducing valve

12.1 The brake master cylinder

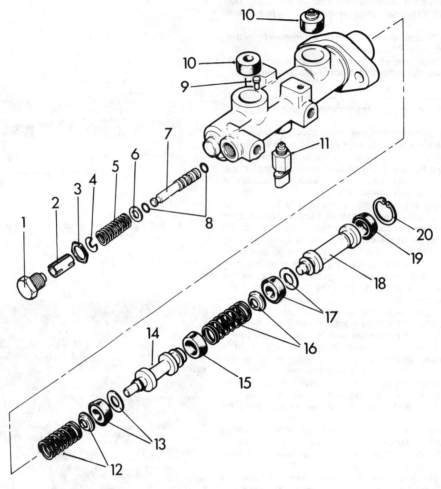

Fig. 9.9 Exploded view of the master cylinder

1 End plug	7 Pressure differential	switch	16 Primary piston return
2 Distance piece	piston	12 Secondary piston return	spring and cup
3 Copper washer	8 O-ring seals	spring and clip	17 Piston seals
4 Spring retainer	9 Stop pin	13 Piston seals	18 Primary piston
5 Spring	10 Seals	14 Secondary piston	19 Primary piston seal
6 Washer	11 Pressure differential	15 Secondary piston seal	20 Circlip

tions.

7   Extract the circlip from the end of the cylinder bore.

8   Withdraw the primary piston and return spring.

9   Using a copper or brass rod, insert it into the cylinder and depress the secondary piston so that the stop pin (situated next to the secondary piston fluid feed port) can be extracted.

10 Withdraw the secondary piston, spring retainer and the return spring.

11 Take a note of the sizes and pistons of the various rubber seals, piston washers and spring retainers.

12 Unscrew and remove the end plug and washer but do not prise off the distance piece from the end plug spigot.

13 Extract the pressure differential assembly, either by shaking it from the body or by applying air pressure to the secondary outlet port.

14 Wash all components in methylated spirit, isopropyl alcohol or clean hydraulic fluid, and examine the surfaces of the pistons and cylinder bore for scoring or 'bright' wear areas. Where these are evident renew the complete master cylinder.

15 If the components are in good condition, discard all seals and obtain the appropriate repair kit.

16 Fit new 'O' ring seals to the pressure warning piston.

17 Install a shim washer to the primary and secondary pistons.

18 Using the fingers only, manipulate the two identical piston seals into place on the primary and secondary piston (lips facing away from the washers).

19 Of the two remaining seals contained in the repair kit, fit the thinner one to the secondary piston (lip towards primary spring seat). Fit the thicker one to the primary piston (lip towards piston seal).

20 Fit the shorter return spring and cup to the secondary piston, dip the assembly into clean hydraulic fluid and insert it into the master cylinder body. Take care not to turn back the lip of the seal.

21 Depress the secondary piston and insert the stop pin after the head of the piston has been seen to pass the feed port.

22 Fit the return spring and cup to the primary piston, dip the assembly into clean hydraulic fluid and insert it into the master cylinder body. Take care not to turn back the seal lips. Refit the retaining circlip.

23 Insert the pressure differential piston into its bore and then fit a new copper sealing washer to the end plug and screw it in, tightening it to the specified torque.

24 Fit new reservoir seals into the cylinder body recesses.

25 Fit the reservoir and tighten the retaining screws to the recommended torque setting.

26 Fit the brake pressure failure switch.

27 Refitting the master cylinder is the reverse of the removal procedure, but on completion bleed the hydraulic system, as described in Section 2.

13 Brake (and clutch) pedal box – removal, overhaul and refitting

1   Remove the driver's side glovebox and hinge.

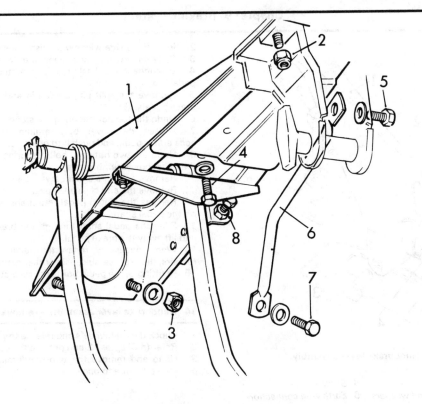

Fig. 9.10 The brake pedal box assembly

1 Pedal box
2 Steering column to pedal box bolts and nuts
3 Nuts retaining pedal box to fascia and bulkhead
4 Steering column to pedal box nuts and bolts
5 Steady bracket to pedal box bolt
6 Steady bracket
7 Steady bracket to accelerator pedal bolt
8 Pedal height adjustment bolt and locknut

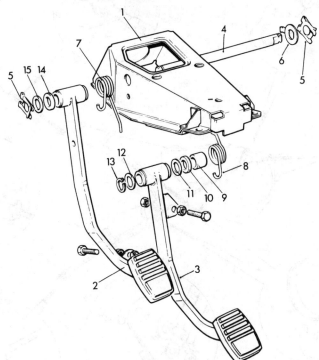

Fig. 9.11 Exploded view of the pedal box, brake and clutch pedal components

1 Pedal box
2 Clutch pedal
3 Brake pedal
4 Pedal shaft
5 Retaining clip
6 Locking washer
7 Return spring (clutch pedal)
8 Return spring (brake pedal)
9 Thrust washer
10 Felt seal
11 Spacer
12 Spacer
13 Circlip
14 Felt seal
15 Spacer

2   Pull off the side window demister hose.
3   Pull off the wiring block connector to the stop lamp switch.
4   Disconnect the flasher unit from the brackets mounted to the pedal box.
5   Remove the split pin, clevis pin and washer from the clutch and brake pedals.
6   Undo the top bolt securing the steady bracket to the pedal box.
7   Loosen the cover bolt retaining the steady bracket to the accelerator pedal and push it to one side.
8   Undo the two nuts and bolts securing the bulkhead and fascia. Lift the pedal box assembly away.
10   Remove the bolts and lift away the pedal stop bracket.
11   Remove the end clips and spacers.
12   Release the clutch pedal return spring and slide the clutch pedal off the pedal shaft.
13   Slide the pedal shaft through the brake pedal, remove the circlip and lift away the brake pedal.
14   Where necessary, renew the pedal pivot bushes, and the pedal rubbers, then reassemble, using other new parts as necessary.
15   Refitting of the pedal box is the reverse of the removal procedure.

14 Handbrake lever assembly – removal and refitting

1   Chock the roadwheels and release the handbrake lever.
2   Refer to Chapter 12 and remove the centre console.
3   Undo and remove the two handbrake lever mounting bolts and pull the earth wire to one side.

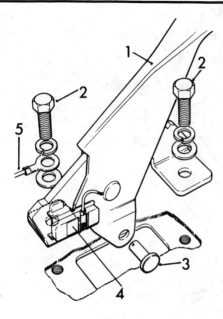

Fig. 9.12 Handbrake lever assembly

1 Handbrake lever   4 Switch
2 Retaining bolts and washers 5 Earth wire connection
3 Clevis pin

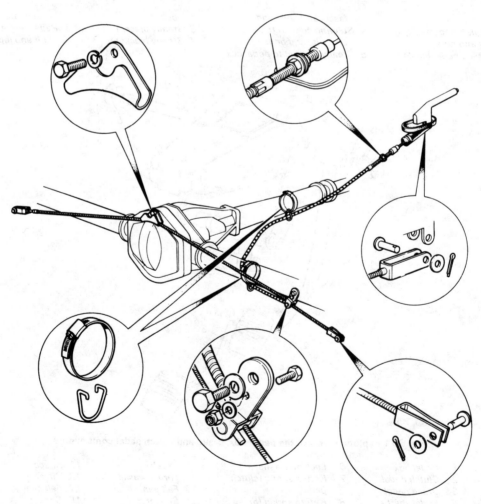

Fig. 9.13 Layout of the handbrake cable assembly

4   Separate the single wiring connector to the handbrake warning light switch.

5   Lift the handbrake lever slightly to gain access to the split pin and clevis pin securing the handbrake cable end to the operating lever.

6   Remove the split pin and clevis pin and lift the handbrake lever away.

7   Reverse the removal procedure for refitting, and then check the handbrake cable adjustment as described in Section 15.

15 Handbrake cable assembly – removal, refitting and adjustment

1   Raise the rear of the vehicle to gain access to the underside. Remember to provide additional support such as axle stands or packing blocks.

2   Release the handbrake lever.

3   Pull the rubber protective boot away from the underside of the handbrake lever and remove the split pin and clevis pin securing the yoke end of the handbrake inner cable to the lever end.

4   Loosen the adjuster locknuts at the abutment bracket and slide the cable away from the bracket via the slotted hole.

5   Pull the protective rubber boot off the cable.

6   Remove the split pin, washer and clevis pin at each rear brake operating lever on the backplate.

7   Release the cable from the guide piece on the axle tube.

8   Loosen the small nut and bolt at the compensator in order to release the trunnion.

9   Pull the cable assembly out from the rear taking care to guide the forward section through the two support clips attached to the axle casing.

10   Refitting is the reverse of removal but the handbrake cable will require adjustment as described in the text below.

11   Ensure that the handbrake lever is fully off.

12   Slacken all handbrake cables by loosening the adjuster locknuts at the abutment bracket and at the left-hand backplate lever end (photo).

13   Disconnect the handbrake cable at the backplate lever ends.

14   Apply the footbrake hard at least three times with the engine running. Stop the engine.

15   Reconnect the left-hand handbrake cable and adjust it so that the compensator takes up an angle of 30° to the left of the vertical, viewed from the rear of the car (Fig. 9.14). Tighten the adjuster locknut when adjustment is correct.

16   Reconnect the right-hand cable end.

17   At the abutment bracket, pull the outer cable rearwards to take up the slack (until the right-hand lever just moves). Secure the cable in this position with the adjusting nut, then make one more complete turn of the adjusting nut before securing with the locknut.

18   Apply the handbrake by one notch only and check that both rear

wheels can be revolved without binding, a small amount of drag is permissible. Pull the handbrake on by two more notches and check that both rear wheels are locked. If the rear wheels can still be turned after the application of the handbrake by three notches, then the handbrake will require readjustment to remove a further amount of slackness. Conversely, if the brakes lock up before the application of the handbrake by three notches, then the handbrake cable has been overtightened and re-adjustment will be necessary.

16 Brake servo – removal and refitting

1   Remove the driver's glovebox.

2   Remove the split pin, washer and clevis pin securing the pushrod end to the brake pedal.

3   Remove the brake master cylinder as described in Section 12.

4   Disconnect the vacuum hose from the servo non-return valve.

5   Remove the four retaining nuts and spring washers, and withdraw the servo.

6   Refitting is the reverse of the removal procedure, but bleed the brakes on completion (see Section 2).

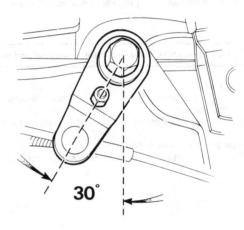

Fig. 9.14 When adjusting the handbrake cable on the left-hand side, the compensator should be brought to the angle shown

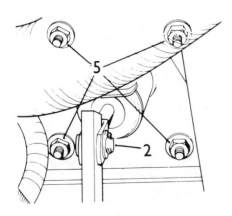

Fig. 9.15 Servo fixing points to bulkhead

2   Clevis pin (pushrod fork to brake pedal)
5   Servo retaining nuts

15.12 The handbrake cable adjuster at the abutment bracket

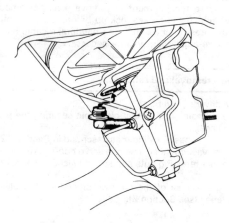

Fig. 9.16 Withdrawing the servo non-return valve

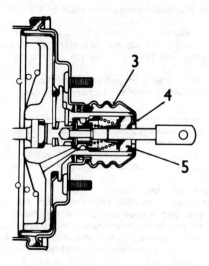

Fig. 9.17 Cross section through the servo/filter assembly

    3 Rubber boot   *5 Felt and filter*
    4 Steel ring

17 Brake servo non-return valve and filter – removal and refitting

Non-return valve
1   With the engine stopped, depress the brake pedal several times to release the servo vacuum.
2   Pull the vacuum hose off at the non-return valve elbow on the servo.
3   Withdraw the non-return valve.
4   Refitting is the reverse of the removal procedure; where

necessary, renew the sealing rubber.

Filter
5   Remove the driver's glovebox.
6   Remove the split pin, washer and clevis pin securing the servo pushrod end to the brake pedal.
7   Pull the rubber pushrod boot back off the pushrod.,
8   Remove the steel ring from the pushrod housing and withdraw the felt and filter.
9   Refitting is the reverse of the removal procedure.

18 Fault diagnosis – braking system

Symptom	Reason/s
Pedal travels almost to floorboards before brakes operate	Brake fluid too low Caliper leaking Master cylinder leaking (bubbles in master cylinder fluid) Brake flexible hose leaking Brake line fractured Brake system unions loose Rear automatic adjusters seized
Brake pedal feels springy	New linings not yet bedded-in Brake discs or drums badly worn or cracked Master cylinder securing nuts loose
Brake pedal feels spongy and soggy	Caliper or wheel cylinder leaking Master cylinder leaking (bubbles in master cylinder reservoir) Brake pipe line or flexible hose leaking Unions in brake system loose Air in hydraulic system
Excessive effort required to brake car	Pad or shoe linings badly worn New pads or shoes recently fitted – not yet bedded-in Harder linings fitted than standard causing increase in pedal pressure Linings and brake drums contaminated with oil, grease or hydraulic fluid Servo unit inoperative or faulty One half of dual brake system inoperative
Brakes uneven and pulling to one side	Linings and discs or drums contaminated vwith oil, grease or hydraulic fluid Tyre pressures unequal Radial ply tyres fitted at one end of the car only Brake caliper loose Brake pads or shoes fitted incorrectly Different type of linings fitted at each wheel Anchorages for front suspension or rear suspension loose Brake discs or drums badly worn, cracked or distorted
Brakes tend to bind, drag or lock-on	Air in hydraulic system Wheel cylinders seized Handbrake cables too tight

Chapter 10 Electrical system

For modifications, and information applicable to later models, see Supplement at end of manual

Contents

Specifications

System type . . . .   12 volt, negative earth

Battery . . . .   50 or 68 Ah

Alternator

Type	Lucas 23ACR (machine sensed)
Brush length, new	0.5 in (12.70 mm)
Brush length, minimum	0.2 in (5.0 mm) protrusion
Brush spring pressure	9 to 13 ozf (255 to 370 kgf)
Stator windings	Three phase – delta connected
Field winding resistance at 20°C (68°F)	3.201 ohms
Regulator type	14 TR
Nominal output, hot:	
Alternator speed	6000 rpm
Engine speed	2250 rpm
Control voltage	14 volts
Current	55 amp
Drivebelt tension	0.2 to 0.3 in (5 to 8 mm)

Starter motor

Type	Lucas 3M100 PE
Brush length, new	0.71 in (18 mm)
Brush length, minimum	0.35 in (9 mm)

Brush spring pressure	36 ozf (1 kgf)
Shaft endfloat, maximum	0.01 in (0.25 mm)
Solenoid pull-in winding resistance	0.25 to 0.27 ohms
Solenoid hold-in winding resistance	0.76 to 0.80 ohms

Windscreen wiper motor

Type	Lucas
Armature endfloat	0.002 to 0.008 in (0.05 to 0.20 mm)
Brush length, new	0.380 in (9.7 mm)
Brush length, minimum	0.180 in (4.8 mm) or when narrow section is worn away on high speed brush
Brush spring pressure	5 to 7 ozf (140 to 200 gf)

Wiper blades

Champion C45-01

Bulbs

	Wattage
Headlamps (main beam)	55
Headlamps (dip/main beam)	60/55
Front indicator lamp	21
Front parking lamp	5
Tail lamp	4
Reverse lamp	21
Stop lamp	21
Number plate lamp	6
Rear fog lamp	21
Instrument panel illumination	1.2
Hazard warning light	1.5
Door open guard lamp	5
Interior lamp	6
Map light	6
Glovebox light	6
Fibre optic light source	5
Front fog lamp	55
Boot light	5
Underbonnet light	5
Brake failure warning light	5
Handbrake warning light	1.2
Cigar lighter illumination	2.2
Clock illumination	2.2

Fuses (main fuse box)

	Circuits protected
No 1 – 2	Spare fuse
No 3 – 4 (35 amp)	Heater
No 5 – 6 (25 amp)	Battery control
No 7 – 8 (25 amp)	Hazard flashers
No 9 – 10 (25 amp)	Ignition
No 11 – 12 (35 amp)	Screen washers
No 13 – 14 (25 amp)	RH main beam
No 15 – 16 (25 amp)	LH main beam
No 17 – 18 (15 amp)	RH dipped beam
No 19 – 20 (15 amp)	LH dipped beam
No 21 – 22 (15 amp)	Side/tail, rear fog and panel lights
No 23 – 24 (25 amp)	Front fog lamps

In-line fuses

50 amp (near fuse box)	Heated rear screen
50 amp (RH footwell)	Central door locking system
2 amp (behind radio)	Radio supply

Torque wrench settings

	lbf ft	Nm
Alternator mounting bolts	17	24
Alternator pulley nut	30	40
Starter motor securing bolts	35	47

1 General description

The electrical system is of the 12 volt type and the major components comprise a 12 volt battery, of which the negative terminal is earthed. A Lucas alternator is fitted to the front right-hand side of the engine and is driven from the engine crankshaft pulley. A pre-engaged Lucas starter motor is mounted on the rear right-hand side of the engine.

The battery supplies current for the ignition, lighting and other electrical circuits, and provides a reserve of electricity when the current consumed by the electrical equipment exceeds that being replaced by the alternator. Normally the alternator is able to meet any demand placed upon it.

A feature of the electrical system is the centralised door locking system which is standard on all models. Electrically operated windows can be specified as an optional extra. Further details of these features are given in the text.

When fitting electrical accessories to cars with a negative earth system, it is important, if they contain silicone diodes or transistors, that they are connected correctly, otherwise damage may result to the components concerned. Before purchasing any electrical accessory check that it has or can be adjusted to the correct polarity to suit the car.

It is important that the battery leads are always disconnected if the battery is to be boost charged, or if any body or mechanical repairs

3.1 Checking the battery electrolyte level

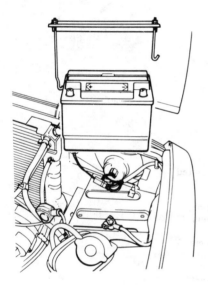

Fig. 10.1 The battery and retainer

are to be carried out using electric arc welding equipment, otherwise, serious damage can be caused to the more delicate instruments specially those containing semi-conductors.

2 Battery – removal and refitting

On models with central door locking, make sure before reconnecting the battery that both front door interior locking buttons are in the unlocked (raised) position.

1   Detach the negative battery lead followed by the positive battery lead from the battery terminal lugs. Disconnecting the leads in this order prevents the possibility of 'shorting' the battery.
2   Loosen the nuts and swing the battery retainer downwards.
3   Lift out the battery.
4   Before refitting, ensure that the retainer is in the downward position and that the hooks are engaged in the body aperture. Check that the leads and loom wires are not trapped.
5   Fit the battery, then connect the terminal leads, positive first. Do not hammer them on. They may jam or at the worst the battery will crack.

6   Finally, smear the battery terminals and lead ends with a little petroleum jelly or a proprietary brand of battery corrosion inhibitor. Do not use regular lubricating grease as a substitute.

3 Battery – maintenance and inspection

1   Normal weekly battery maintenance consists of checking the electrolyte level of each cell to ensure that the separators are covered by $\frac{1}{4}$ in (6 mm) of electrolyte. If the level has fallen, top-up the battery using distilled water only. Do not overfill. If a battery is overfilled or any electrolyte spilled, immediately wipe away the excess as electrolyte attacks and corrodes any metal it comes into contact with very rapidly.
2   If the battery has the 'Auto-fill' device fitted, a special topping-up sequence is required. The white balls in the 'Auto-fill' battery are part of the automatic topping-up device which ensures correct electrolyte level. The vent chamber should remain in position at all times except when topping-up or taking specific gravity readings. If the electrolyte level in any of the cells is below the bottom of the filling tube top-up as follows:

(a) *Lift off the vent chamber cover*
(b) *With the battery level, pour distilled water into the trough until all the filling tubes and trough are full*
(c) *Immediately replace the cover to allow the water in the trough and tubes to flow into the cells. Each cell will automatically receive the correct amount of water*

3   As well as keeping the terminals clean and covered with petroleum jelly, the top of the battery, and especially the top of the cells, should be kept clean and dry. This helps prevent corrosion and ensures that the battery does not become partially discharged by leakage through dampness and dirt.
4   Once every three months remove the battery and inspect the battery securing bolts, the battery clamp plate, tray and battery leads for corrosion (white fluffy deposits, on the metal, which are brittle to the touch). If any corrosion is found, clean off the deposits with ammonia or a solution of bicarbonate of soda and warm water, and paint over the clean metal with anti-rust and anti-acid paint.
5   At the same time inspect the battery case for cracks. If a crack is found, clean and plug it with one of the proprietary compounds marketed for this purpose. If leakage through the crack has been excessive then it will be necessary to refill the appropriate cell with fresh electrolyte as detailed later. Cracks are frequently caused to the top of the battery case by pouring in distilled water in the middle of winter *after* instead of *before* a run. This gives the water no chance to mix with the electrolyte and so the former freezes and splits the battery case.
6   If topping-up the battery becomes too frequent and the case has been inspected for cracks that could cause leakage, but none are found, the battery is being overcharged and the alternator will have to be checked. Generally, this indicates that the regulator (housed within the alternator end cover) is at fault thus allowing the alternator to operate uncontrolled, delivering full output even when the battery is fully charged. A fairly basic check can be carried out (see Section 7), but as a general principle this sort of job is best left to a competent auto-electrician or your Rover dealer.
7   With the battery on the bench at the three monthly interval check, measure the specific gravity with a hydrometer to determine the state of charge and condition of the electrolyte. There should be very little variation between the different cells, and, if a variation in excess of 0.025 is present, it will be due to either:

(a) *Loss of electrolyte from the battery at some time caused by spillage or a leak, resulting in a drop in the specific gravity of the electrolyte when the deficiency was replaced with distilled water instead of fresh electrolyte*
(b) *An internal short circuit caused by buckling of the plates or similar malady pointing to the likelihood of total battery failure in the near future*

8   The specific gravity of the electrolyte for fully charged conditions at the temperatures indicated, is listed in Table A. The specific gravity of a fully discharged battery at different temperatures of the electrolyte is given in Table B.

Table A

Specific gravity – battery fully charged
1.268 at 100°F or 38°C electrolyte temperature
1.272 at 90°F or 32°C electrolyte temperature
1.276 at 80°F or 27°C electrolyte temperature
1.280 at 70°F or 21°C electrolyte temperature
1.284 at 60°F or 16°C electrolyte temperature
1.288 at 50°F or 10°C electrolyte temperature
1.292 at 40°F or 4°C electrolyte temperature
1.296 at 30°F or -1.5°C electrolyte temperature

Table B

Specific gravity – battery fully discharged
1.098 at 100°F or 38°C electrolyte temperature
1.102 at 90°F or 32°C electrolyte temperature
1.106 at 80°F or 27°C electrolyte temperature
1.110 at 70°F or 21°C electrolyte temperature
1.114 at 60°F or 16°C electrolyte temperature
1.118 at 50°F or 10°C electrolyte temperature
1.122 at 40°F or 4°C electrolyte temperature
1.126 at 30°F or -1.5°C electrolyte temperature

4 Battery electrolyte – replenishment

1   With the battery fully charged, check the specific gravity of the electrolyte in each of the cells. If one or more of the cells reads 0.025, or more, below the others, it is likely that some electrolyte has been lost. Check each cell for short circuits with a voltage meter. A four to seven second test should give a steady reading of between 1.2 and 1.8 volts.
2   Top the cell up with a solution of 1 part sulphuric acid to 2.5 parts of water. If the cell is already fully topped up draw some electrolyte out of it with a pipette. The total capacity of each cell is ¾ pint.
3   When mixing the sulphuric acid and water, *NEVER ADD WATER TO SULPHURIC ACID* – always pour the acid slowly onto the water in a glass container. *IF WATER IS ADDED TO SULPHURIC ACID IT WILL EXPLODE.*
4   Continue to top up the cell with the freshly made electrolyte and then recharge the battery and check the hydrometer readings.

5 Battery charging

Note: *Before charging the battery disconnect the terminal leads, check the electrolyte level and if possible, remove the battery from the car.*
1   In winter time when heavy demand is placed upon the battery, such as when starting from cold and much electrical equipment is continually in use, it is a good idea to occasionally have the battery fully charged from an external source at the rate of 3.5 to 4 amps.
2   Continue to charge the battery at this rate until no further rise in specific gravity is noted over a four-hour period.
3   Alternatively, a trickle charger, charging at the rate of 1.5 amps can be safely used overnight.
4   Specially rapid 'boost' charges which are claimed to restore the power of the battery in 1 to 2 hours are most dangerous as they can cause serious damage to the battery plates through overheating.
5   Whilst charging the battery note that the temperature of the electrolyte should never exceed 100°F.
6   Always disconnect both battery cables before the external charger is connected otherwise serious damage to the alternator may occur.

6 Alternator – general description, maintenance and precautions

1   Briefly, the alternator comprises a rotor and stator. Voltage is induced in the coils of the stator as soon as the rotor revolves. This is a 3-phase alternating voltage which is then rectified by diodes to provide the necessary current for the electrical system. The level of the voltage required to maintain the battery charge is controlled by a regulator unit.
2   Maintenance consists of occasionally wiping away any oil or dirt which may have accumulated on the outside of the unit.

3   No lubrication is required as the bearings are sealed for life.
4   Check the drivebelt tension at intervals given in the 'Routine Maintenance' Section. Refer to Section 8, for the procedure.
5   Due to the need for special testing equipment and the possibility of damage being caused to the alternator diodes if incorrect testing methods are adopted, it is recommended that overhaul or major repair is entrusted to a Lucas or Rover dealer. Alternatively, a service exchange unit should be obtained.
6   Alternator brush renewal is dealt with in Section 9.
7   Take extreme care when connecting the battery to ensure that the polarity is correct, and never run the engine with a battery charger connected. Do not stop the engine by removing a battery lead as the alternator will almost certainly be damaged. When boost starting from another battery ensure that it is connected positive to positive and negative to negative.

7 Alternator – testing in position in the car

If the alternator is suspected of being faulty, a test can be carried out which can help in isolating any such fault. A dc voltmeter (range 0 to 15V) and a dc ammeter (suitable for the nominal output current – see Specifications) will be required.
1   Check the alternator drivebelt tension and adjust if necessary – see Section 8.
2   Disconnect the brown cable from the starter motor solenoid. Connect the ammeter between this cable and the starter motor solenoid terminal.
3   Connect the voltmeter across the battery terminals.
4   Run the engine at 2250 rpm (6000 rpm of the alternator); the ammeter reading should stabilize.
5   If the ammeter reads zero, an internal fault in the alternator is indicated.
6   If less than 10 amps is indicated, and the voltmeter shows 13.6 to 14.4 volts, where it is known that the battery is in a low state of charge, the alternator is suspect and should be checked by an auto-electrician. The nominal output is given in the Specifications.
7   If the ammeter reads less than 10 amps and the voltmeter reads less than 13.6 volts, a fault in the alternator internal regulator is indicated. A fault in the regulator is also indicated when the voltage exceeds 14.4 volts.

8 Alternator – removal, refitting and drivebelt adjustment

1   Detach the battery earth lead.
2   Slide the harness plug lock inboard and down to unlock it, then remove the plug.
3   Slacken the adjustment bolt and the mounting bolts in that order.
4   Push the alternator towards the engine so that the drivebelt can be removed.
5   Remove the adjustment bolt and washer, and the main mounting

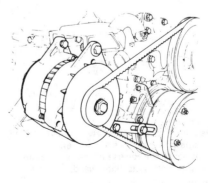

Fig. 10.2 The alternator showing the mounting and adjustment link nuts and bolts

8.8 The adjuster link bolt

11.1 The starter motor (engine removed for clarity)

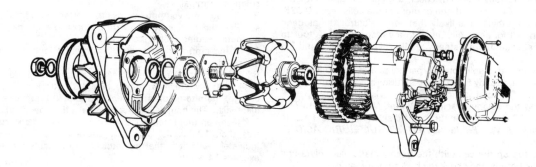

Fig. 10.3 Exploded view of the Lucas 23ACR alternator

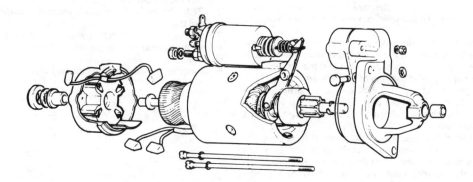

Fig. 10.4 Starter motor components

bolts, nuts and washers.

6   Support the alternator and withdraw the main mounting bolts and washers. The alternator can now be lifted clear.

7   Refitting is basically the reverse of the removal procedure, but do not tighten the nuts and bolts until the drivebelt tension has been checked as described below.

8   Where necessary, slacken the adjustment bolt, and the mounting bolts (photo).

9   Pull the alternator away from the engine and tighten the adjust-ment bolt. Check for a total movement of the belt of 0.2 to 0.3 in (5 to 8 mm) under firm thumb pressure at the midpoint of the longest belt run. Re-adjust, if necessary. **Note:** *It is permissible to apply leverage at the drive end bracket, if necessary to obtain the correct tension, but only a softwood lever, or similar item may be used.*

10   Tighten the mounting bolts on completion.

11   If a new belt has been fitted, the belt tension should be rechecked after about 150 miles (250 km) of travelling.)

9 Alternator – brush renewal

1   With the alternator removed from the car, remove the two set-screws retaining the plastic end cover.
2   Remove the end cover and disconnect, where applicable, the radio interference suppressor (capacitor) lead.
3   Remove the four small set-screws positioned in the centre of the brush box. When removing the set-screws take a note of the exact positions of the various wires located by the screws.
4   Remove the single set-screw retaining the regulator unit and lift away the flat metal connector strip coupling the regulator to one of the smaller set-screws (referred to in paragraph 3).
5   The brushes can now be lifted out of their locations in the brush box.
6   Examine the slip rings for discolouration before fitting the new brushes.
7   Where necessary the slip rings can be cleaned by polishing them with fine glass paper, crocus paper or metal polish. Ensure that no residue is left afterwards.
8   Better access to the slip rings can be achieved after removing the brush box which is retained by two set-screws. Note that the black wire from the regulator unit is located under the head of one of these set-screws.
9   Reassemble the alternator by reversing the dismantling procedure.

10 Starter motor – general description

When the ignition switch is turned, current flows through the solenoid pull-in winding and starter motor, moving the solenoid armature. At the same time a much smaller current flows through the solenoid hold-in winding directly to earth.

The movement of the solenoid armature causes the drive pinion to move and engage with the starter ring gear on the flywheel. At the same time the main contacts close and energise the motor circuit. The pull-in winding now becomes ineffective and it remains in the operated condition by the action of the hold-in winding only.

A special one-way clutch is fitted to the starter drive pinion, so that when the engine commences to fire there is no possibility of it driving the starter motor.

When the ignition key is released, the solenoid is de-energised and returns to its original position. This breaks the supply to the motor and returns the drive pinion to the disengaged position.

11 Starter motor – removal and refitting

1   Detach the battery earth lead and raise the front of the car to a suitable working height for access to the starter motor (photo).
2   Remove the nut and spring washer, then disconnect the heavy battery feed cable to the starter motor solenoid.
3   Disconnect the white/yellow and white/brown wires at the solenoid by removing the two cross-head screws. Note the locations of the wires.
4   Using a socket, extension and ratchet spanner remove the starter motor mounting flange bolts.
5   Lift the starter motor out and downwards from the engine.
6   Refitting is the reverse of removal, but check that the solenoid wires are connected correctly.

12 Starter motor – overhaul

1   Slacken the nut which secures the connecting link to the solenoid terminal 'STA'.
2   Remove the two screws which secure the solenoid to the drive end bracket.
3   Lift the solenoid plunger upwards and separate it from the engagement lever. Extract the return spring seat and dust excluder from the plunger body.
4   Withdraw the block from between the drive end bracket and the starter motor yoke.
5   Remove the armature end cap from the commutator end bracket.
6   Chisel off some of the claws from the armature shaft spire nut so that the nut can be withdrawn from the shaft.

7   Remove the two tie-bolts and then withdraw the commutator and cover and starter motor yoke from the drive end bracket.
8   Separate the commutator end cover from the starter motor yoke, at the same time disengaging the field coil brushes from the brush box to facilitate separation.
9   Withdraw the thrust washer from the armature shaft.
10 Remove the spire nut from the engagement lever pivot pin and then extract the pin from the drive end bracket.
11 Withdraw the armature and roller clutch drive assembly from the drive end bracket.
12 Using a piece of tubing, drive back the thrust collar to expose the jump ring on the armature shaft. Remove the jump ring and withdraw the thrust collar and roller clutch.
13 Remove the spring ring and release the engagement lever, thrust washers and spring from the roller-clutch drive.
14 Remove the dust excluding seal from the bore of the drive end bracket.
15 Inspect all components for wear. If the armature shaft bushes require renewal, press them out or screw in a $\frac{1}{2}$ in tap. Before inserting the new bushes, soak them in engine oil for 24 hours.
16 If the brushes have worn below the minimum specified length, renew them by cutting the end bracket brush leads from the terminal post. File a groove in the head of the terminal post and solder the new brush leads in to the groove. Cut the field winding brush leads about $\frac{1}{4}$ in (6 mm) from the joint of the field winding. Solder the new brush leads to the ends of the old ones. Localise the heat to prevent damage to the field windings.
17 Check the field windings for continuity using a torch battery and test bulb. If the windings are faulty, removal of the pole shoe screws should be left to a service station having a pressure screwdriver, as they are very tight.
18 Check the insulation of the armature by connecting a test bulb and torch battery. Use probes placed on the armature shaft and each commutator section in turn. If the test bulb lights at any position then the insulation has broken down, and the armature must be renewed. Discolouration of the commutator should be removed by polishing it with a piece of glass paper (not emery cloth). Do not undercut the insulation.
19 Reassembly is a reversal of dismantling, but apply grease to the moving parts of the engagement lever, the outer surface of the roller clutch housing and to the lips of the drive end bracket dust seal. Fit a new spire nut to the armature shaft, positioning it to give the specified shaft endfloat. Measure this endfloat by inserting feeler blades between the face of the spire nut and the flange of the commutator end bush.

13 Headlamp unit – removal and refitting

1   Open the bonnet.
2   If the left-hand unit is to be removed carry out the following operations:

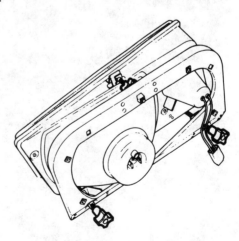

Fig. 10.5 Headlamp unit and retaining screws

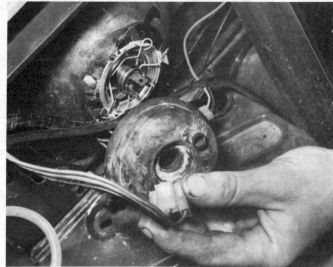

14.2 The wiring harness plug connected to the rear of the outer headlamp

14.3 Remove the protective rubber cover

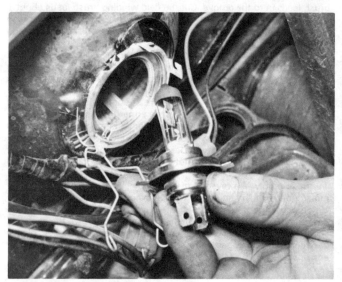

14.5 Withdraw the bulb

14.9 Slide the rubber cover back along the wires

14.11 Withdraw the bulb

15.2 The vertical beam adjustment knob

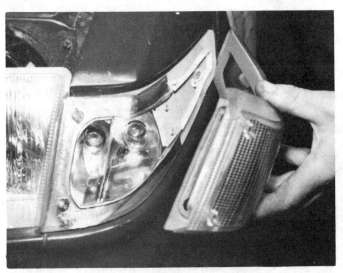

16.1 Removing the front parking/flasher lamp lens

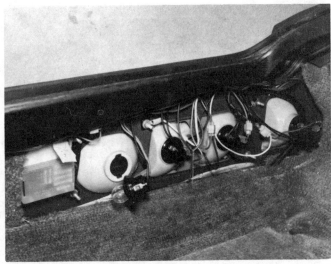

18.3 Removing the rear fog lamp bulb holder

(a) *Remove the screen washer reservoir*
(b) *Undo the four bolts securing the radiator in position*
(c) *Tip the radiator back to gain access to the lower inboard headlamp retainer screw*

3   If the right-hand unit is to be removed, then it will be necessary to remove the battery (Section 2) for better access.
4   From the rear of the light units pull off the harness plugs for the dipped/main beam and the main beam lamp.
5   Loosen one of the bolts securing the headlamp sealing panel. Push the panel inwards slightly to provide clearance.
6   Remove the screws securing the headlamp assembly by manoeuvering it upwards and forwards from the vehicle body.
7   Refitting is the reverse of the removal procedure.

14 Headlamp – bulb renewal

1   Open the bonnet.

Main/dip beam bulb (outer)

2   Pull off the wiring harness plug from the rear of the light unit (photo).
3   Remove the protective rubber cover (photo).
4   Squeeze the ends of the spring retainer clip together, and tip the retainer clip outwards to release the bulb holder.
5   Withdraw the bulb, but do not handle the glass part (photo).
6   Insert the new bulb without touching the glass part. It will locate in one position only, this being indicated by the positioning of the pegs and cut-outs. If the glass is accidentally touched, clean it with methylated spirit, using a clean lint-free cloth.
7   Secure the bulb by relocating the spring retainer clip.
8   Refit the rubber cover and wiring harness plug.

Main beam bulb (inner)

9   Disconnect the rubber cover by tilting it and then pull it back along the two wires (photo).
10 Disconnect the two wiring spade connectors.
11 Disengage the wire retainer clip and lift out the bulb. Do not handle the bulb by its glass portion (photo).
12 Fit the bulb so that it is positioned correctly, then refit the spring retainer and wiring connections.
13 Slide the rubber cover up the wires and relocate it.

15 Headlamp beam – alignment

1   It is recommended that adjustment of the headlamp beams should only be carried out by a dealer or garage having beam setting equip-

ment. This should always be carried out if a headlamp shell or bulb has been fitted.
2   Where the headlamp beam is known to be greatly out of alignment, it is permissible to make adjustments using the three large plastic knobs located at the rear of the headlamp unit (photo). However, this must only be regarded as a temporary adjustment, and when in doubt the beams should be set to aim perhaps more towards the ground, in order to obviate glare. This adjustment must be checked at the earliest opportunity by a suitably equipped dealer.
3   Holts Amber Lamp is useful for temporarily changing the headlight colour to conform with the normal usage on Continental Europe.

16 Front parking/flasher lamps

Bulb renewal

1   Remove the three screws and withdraw the lens, then remove the desired bayonet-fitting bulb. Refitting of the bulb is the reverse of this procedure (photo).

Removal and refitting

2   Open the bonnet and disconnect the wiring harness plug.
3   Remove the single retaining nut, spring washer and plain washer.
4   Push out the stud and withdraw two front spigots from the grommets in the vehicle body.
5   Lift the lamp assembly away and extract the rubber gasket.
6   Refitting is the reverse of the removal procedure.

17 Fog lamp (front)

Bulb renewal

1   Prise the rim of the fog lamp out of its housing.
2   Support the weight of the lamp and pull off the two wiring connectors at its rear.
3   Disengage the ends of the wire retainer clip and withdraw the bulb. Do not touch the glass part of the bulb.
4   Refitting of the bulb rim assembly, to the housing, is the reverse of the removal procedure. Reconnection of the lamp wires is as follows. The grey wire is the bulb feed and the black wire connects to the lamp body earth terminal.

Removal and refitting

5   Open the bonnet and disconnect the fog lamp wiring harness located next to the rear of the headlamp unit.
6   Attach a short length of cord to the fog lamp harness and tie the other end of the cord to a suitable anchorage. This measure will prevent the wiring harness from being pulled completely through during the removal operation.

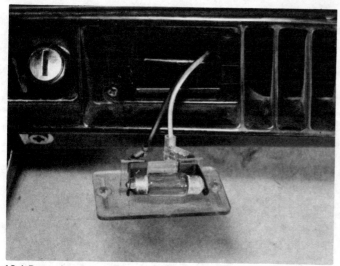

19.1 Removing the number plate lamp bulb

22.2 Removing the luggage compartment courtesy lamp

7   Disconnect the two snap connectors.
8   Unscrew the fog lamp adjustment screw counting the number of turns in order to obtain a satisfactory setting on refitting.
9   Through a hole in the underbelly panel, insert a probe and depress the inner spring retainer. With the spring retainer so depressed, lower the lamp and withdraw the harness.
10   Refitting is the reverse of the removal operation. When reconnecting the snap connectors the blue/yellow cable must be connected into the grey cable and the two remaining black cables connected together.
11   Turn the adjustment screw to its original position and make the final adjustment at night on a suitable stretch of road.

18 Rear lamp assembly

Bulb renewal
1   Open the tailgate.
2   Undo the thumb screws and lift away the cover panel from the rear of the lamp assembly.
3   All the bulb holders except the tail lamp can be removed by twisting them in an anti-clockwise direction (photo). The tail lamp bulb holder is simply a push fit in the lamp body.
4   Withdraw the bayonet-fitting bulb. Refitting is the reverse of the removal procedure.

Removal and refitting
5   Remove the bulb holders as described in paragraph 3.
6   Disconnect the single connector and terminal end from the tail lamp bulb holder.
7   Undo the six nuts and extract the special anti-vibration washers.
8   Where the left-hand lamp is being removed, the bulb failure indicator unit will have to be removed from the mounting bracket inner studs.
9   Remove the harness earth tag(s) and the single star washer from the upper inboard stud.
10   Remove the harness strap from the upper centre stud and withdraw the lamp assembly, together with the rubber gasket, from the vehicle.
11   Refitting is the reverse of removal. Where any wiring connections have been disconnected they should be refitted as shown in Fig. 10.6.

19 Number plate lamp

Bulb renewal
1   Remove the two screws and withdraw the lens, then remove the festoon-type bulb. Refitting is the reverse of this procedure (photo).

Removal and refitting
2   Remove the two retaining screws and withdraw the lamp from the body, forward edge first.
3   Remove the festoon-type bulb and pull off the two wiring connectors.
4   Refitting is the reverse of removal.

20 Under bonnet lamp

Bulb renewal
1   Remove the two lens retaining screws and lift away the lens and rubber seal.
2   Pull the capless-type bulb straight out of the lamp body.
3   Refitting is the reverse of removal.

Removal and refitting
4   Disconnect the battery negative earth terminal connection.
5   Remove the two lens retaining screws and lift away the lens and rubber seal.
6   Locate the wiring connectors enclosed in the bonnet channel and disconnect them.
7   Withdraw the lamp body together with a short harness.
8   Refitting is the reverse of removal.

21 Courtesy lamp (centre pillar)

Bulb renewal
1   Disconnect the battery earth terminal connection, for safety reasons.
2   Gently pull the lens out from its centre pillar mounting.
3   Prise out the festoon-type bulb. Refitting is the reverse of removal.

Removal and refitting
4   Pull the lens out from the centre pillar and remove the festoon-type bulb as described in paragraphs 1 to 3 above.
5   Pull out the single spade connector.
6   Note the positions of the other two terminal wires, then pull them out of their respective location points.
7   Refitting is the reverse of removal.

22 Courtesy lamp (luggage compartment)

Bulb renewal
1   Disconnect the battery negative lead.

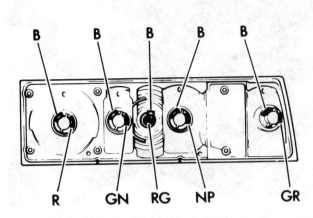

Fig. 10.6 Rear lamp wiring connections

B	Black	RG	Red/green
GR	Green/red	GN	Green/brown
NP	Brown/purple	R	Red

24.1 The door open guard lamp

2   Carefully prise out the lamp assembly and remove the bayonet-type bulb (photo). Refitting is the reversal of removal.

Removal and refitting
3   Extract the lamp assembly from the rear panel as described in paragraphs 1 to 2 above.
4   Note the positions of the two leads and pull them off. Withdraw the lamp.
5   Refitting is the reverse of removal.

23 Map reading lamp

Bulb renewal
1   Pull the lens away from the dashboard sufficiently to deflect the two plastic clips.
2   Withdraw the festoon-type bulb. Refitting is the reverse of removal.

Removal and refitting
3   Remove the lamp as described in paragraph 1. Open the glove box, then disconnect the two wiring connections.
4   Refitting is the reverse of removal. The purple wire is connected to the bulb contact and the black wire to the switch contact.

24 Door 'open guard' lamp

Bulb renewal
1   Open the door and carefully draw the lens out from the plastic rim (photo).
2   Remove the bayonet-type bulb. Refitting is the reverse of removal.

Removal and refitting
3   Disconnect the battery earth lead.
4   Open the door and draw the lens out from the plastic rim.
5   Carefully prise the plastic moulding out from the door frame.
6   Owing to the length and awkward run of the wiring harness, it is advisable to cut the two lamp wires at a distance of approximately 3 in (75 mm) from the lamp to facilitate removal.
7   Refitting of the lamp necessitates joining the wires up. The method recommended is to solder, or crimp bullet connectors to the cable ends and then rejoin the cables using single snap connectors. The remainder of the refitting procedure is the reverse of removal.

25 Cigar lighter

Bulb renewal
1   Carefully prise the cigar lighter and plate clear of the console, unclip the bulb and remove the bayonet-type bulb.
2   Refitting is the reverse of removal.

Removal and refitting
3   Disconnect the battery negative lead.
4   Withdraw the heating unit and prise up the centre console panel in order to release the three plastic spigots.
5   Disconnect the two spade connectors and the single snap connector. Note the positions of the leads.
6   Squeeze the sides of the bulb cowl and withdraw it.
7   Using a pair of long-nosed pliers on the inner well cross-piece, unscrew the inner well from the outer well, and then remove the bezel.
8   Refitting is the reverse of the removal procedure; position the bulb cowl as necessary. When connecting the wires the purple wire should be corrected to the centre terminal and the black wire to the unit body.

26 Fibre optic lamp

Bulb renewal
1   Remove the glovebox and locate the fibre optic lamp, fitted to the hinge assembly, next to the heater.
2   Pull the bulb holder out and remove the bayonet-type bulb. Refitting is the reverse of removal.

Removal and refitting
3   Refer to paragraphs 1 and 2 above and pull out the bulb holder.
4   Pull out the fibre element terminal ends (four on manual transmission models and five on automatic transmission models).
5   Undo the two screws securing the lamp to the hinge bracket and lift the lamp away.
6   Refitting is the reverse of removal.

27 Glovebox lamp

Bulb renewal
1   Open the glovebox and carefully prise open the two connector clips to remove the festoon-type bulb. Refitting is the reverse of

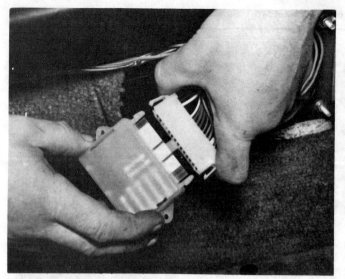

28.3 Withdrawing the bulb failure indicator unit

29.4 Remove the small panel housing to gain access to the warning light bulbs

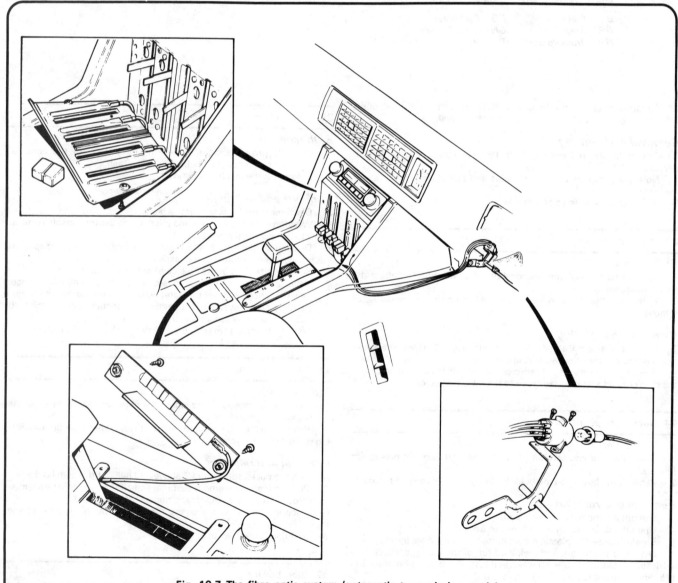

Fig. 10.7 The fibre optic system (automatic transmission model shown)

removal.

Removal and refitting

2 Carry out the removal instructions detailed in paragraph 1 for bulb removal.

3 Disconnect the two wiring connections and lift away the lamp.

4 Refitting is the reverse of removal.

28 Bulb failure indicator

1 If the bulb failure indicator should fail to illuminate when the ignition switch is in the start position, then move the master light switch to the side light position and check that the side lamps are illuminated. Should the side lights fail to illuminate, then it is reasonable to assume that the bulb failure indicator has become defective.

2 The bulb failure indicator is mounted adjacent to the left-hand rear light cluster.

3 The bulb failure indicator unit can be temporarily by-passed by withdrawing the wiring block connector, breaking off the central locating lug and re-installing the block connector after rotating it by 180°. **Note**: *this procedure is only intended as a 'get you home' repair, and a new unit should be fitted as soon as possible (photo).*

29 Instrument illumination and panel warning lights

1 Disconnect the battery negative terminal lead.

2 Turn the knob at the left-hand end of the instrument panel through 90°, and withdraw the instrument panel fuse box end cover.

3 Lift the top cover of the instrument panel off and disconnect the two snap connectors which are located in the radio speaker supply cables.

4 If a panel warning light bulb is to be renewed then pull the small panel housing, at the front of the instrument panel, away to gain access to the bulbs (photo).

5 Instrument illumination bulbs can, in most cases, be extracted via the top of the instrument panel. This simply entails withdrawing the respective bulb holder unit.

6 Refitting is the reverse of removal.

30 Fibre optic system components – removal and refitting

Refer to Fig. 10.7 for details of the layout.

Fibre optic lamp

1 Details are given in Section 26 of this Chapter.

Selector panel illumination (automatic transmission models)

2 Remove the two screws at either end of the panel.

3 Lift the panel sufficiently to expose the fibre optic illumination system.

4 Pull off the single wiring spade connector and withdraw the fibre element terminal end.

5 Lift the panel away.

6 Refitting is the reverse of removal, but take care to prevent the fibre element from being trapped by the panel.

Heater control illumination

7 Pull off the heater control knobs and remove the two panel retaining screws.

8 Tip the top of the panel away from the housing and pull off the four wiring spade connectors and withdraw the four fibre element terminal ends.

9 Lift the panel away.

10 Refitting is the reverse of removal.

31 Relays and flasher units – removal and refitting

Hazard flasher unit

1 The hazard flasher unit is located together with the turn signal flasher unit and attached to the brake pedal mounting bracket.

2 Identify the hazard flasher unit by the wire colour codes blue/brown and light green/purple.

3 Pull the flasher unit away from its retainer clip and pull off the two wiring connections mentioned in paragraph 2. Refitting is the reverse of removal.

Turn signal flasher unit

4 Refer to paragraph 1 for the location of the unit.

5 Identify the turn signal flasher unit by the colour coding of the supply cables attached to it, which are both of the same colour light green/brown.

6 Removal and refitting is as described in paragraph 3.

Heated rear window relay

7 Disconnect the battery earth lead and remove the passenger glovebox.

8 Loosen the two bolts which locate the relay mounting bracket.

9 Push the relay bracket forwards to disengage its slots from the bolts and allow the bracket to hang down.

10 Identify the heated rear window relay by the brown/yellow, brown/red, white/slate and black wires attached to it.

11 Remove a single nut, spring washer and bolt and disconnect the harness plug.

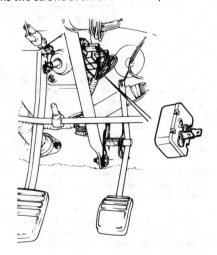

Fig. 10.8 Location of the turn signal flasher unit

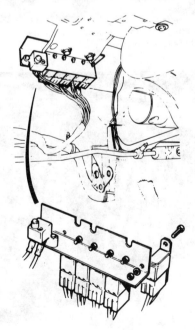

Fig. 10.9 Location of the heated rear window relay

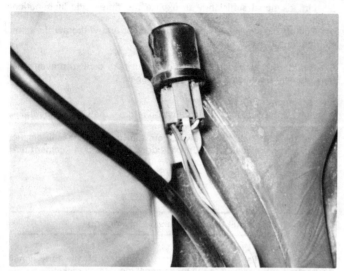

31.16 The starter motor relay is positioned adjacent to the radiator expansion tank

```
LOCATION OF FUSES AS VIEWED
  2              1   14  HEADLAMP        13
                         R.H. MAIN
                         25 AMP.
  4  HEATER     3   16  HEADLAMP        15
     25 AMP.             L.H. MAIN
                         25 AMP.
  6  BATTERY    5   18  HEADLAMP        17
     CONTROL            R.H. DIP
     25 AMP.             15 AMP.
  8  HAZARD     7   20  HEADLAMP        19
     WARNING            L.H. DIP
     25 AMP.             15 AMP.
 10  IGNITION   9   22  SIDE, TAIL &    21
     CONTROL            FOG GUARD LTS.
     25 AMP.             15 AMP.
 12  SCREENWIPER 11 24  FRONT FOG       23
     MOTOR             LAMPS
     35 AMP.            25 AMP.
HEATED REAR SCREEN AND ALL
OPTION FUSES LOCATED BENEATH
TOP COVER BEHIND FUSE BOX.
```

32.1 A list of the fuses and the circuits which they protect is shown on the inside of the fuse box cover

32.2A The main fuse box located in the end of the instrument housing

12 Refitting is the reverse of removal.

Heater motor supply line relay

13 This relay is mounted together with the heated rear window relay, and is identified by the brown, brown/blue, white and black wires attached to it.
14 Removal and refitting are identical to the procedures described in paragraphs 7 to 12.

Lighting supply line relay

15 The location, removal and refitting of this relay is identical to that described in paragraphs 7 to 12. The lighting supply line relay can be identified by the brown, red/blue, red/green and black wires attached to it.

Starter motor relay

16 The starter motor relay is located in the engine bay next to the radiator overflow (expansion) tank (photo).
17 Pull the wiring connector block off the relay and undo the single retaining screw.
18 Refitting is the reverse of removal.

Window lift supply line relays (where applicable)

19 These relays, where applicable, are mounted together with the heated rear window, heater motor supply line and lighting supply line relays.
20 Removal and refitting is as described in paragraphs 7 to 12.
21 The rear window lift supply line relay can be identified by the brown/green, light green, brown/purple and black wires attached to it. The front window lift supply line relay has brown/green, green, brown/purple and black wires attached to it.

Door lock relays

22 Relays which operate the door locking and unlocking operations are included in Section 36.

32 Fuses

1   A list of fuse ratings and the circuits protected by these fuses are given in the Specifications Section; further details can be obtained by reference to the appropriate wiring diagram or the end of the fuse box end cover (photo).
2   The bulk of the fuses are located in the end of the instrument panel housing (photo). Access to these fuses is achieved by turning the end cover knob through 90°. Additional in-line fuses for the heated rear screen and radio supply are located beneath the instrument panel top cover, well forward behind the speedometer (photo). To remove the instrument panel top cover, remove the screw and clip located at the top of the main fuse box and pull the cover left to release the three cover securing lugs. Lift off the cover (photo). Refitting the cover is the reverse of the removal procedure. The in-line fuse for the central door locking system (if fitted) is located in the right-hand footwell, adjacent to the accelerator pedal.
3   If any item of electrical equipment fails to operate, first check the appropriate fuse. If the fuse has blown the first thing to do is to find the cause, otherwise it will merely blow again – (fuses can blow through age fatigue, but this is the exception rather than the rule). Having found the faulty fuse, switch off the electrical equipment and then fit a new fuse. From the Specifications note which circuits are served by the blown fuse and then start to switch each one on separately in turn. (It may be necessary to have the ignition circuit switched on at the same time. The fuse should blow again when the faulty item is switched on. If the fuse does not blow immediately, start again, but this time leave the circuits switched on and build up the cumulative total lead on the fuse. If and when it blows you will have an indication of which circuits may be causing the problem. If a new fuse does not blow until the car is moving then look for a loose, chafed or pinched wire.
4   When fitting a new fuse always use a fuse of the correct rating. Do not, under any circumstances, fit a fuse of a higher rating or use a piece of tin foil as a substitute. It should be clearly understood that fuses are the weakest link in a circuit. Any fault causing shorting or an overload of a particular circuit will cause the fuse wire to melt and thus break the circuit. A higher rated fuse or a piece of tin foil will not break the circuit and in such cases overheating and the risk of fire at the fault source, could easily occur.
5   If a fault occurs in one accessory or component and its rectification defies all efforts, always remember than it could be a relay at fault.

32.2B The heated rear screen and radio supply in-line fuses

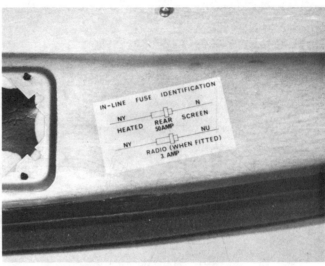

32.2C Instrument panel top cover carries a fuse information label

Relays cannot be repaired or adjusted and, if faulty, should be renewed as a unit (details given in other Sections of this Chapter).

33 Ignition/starter switch – removal and refitting

1   Disconnect the battery earth lead.
2   Slacken the steering column clamp knob and lower the steering column to its lowest position.
3   Remove the steering column nacelle halves (one screw each).
4   In order to obtain better access remove the door glass demist hose from the heater outlet.
5   Note the run of the switch harness and remove the three retaining straps (two securing it to the steering column and the third securing it to the mounting bracket).
6   Pull the harness away from the steering column to expose the ignition/starter switch harness plug.
7   Disconnect the harness plug and remove the two screws securing the switch.
8   Remove the switch together with the wiring harness.
9   Refitting is the reverse of removal.

34 Multi-function stalk switch assembly – removal and refitting

1   Disconnect the battery earth lead.
2   Slacken the steering column clamp knob and lower the steering column to its lowest position.
3   Remove the steering column nacelle halves (one screw each).
4   Refer to Chapter 11 and remove the steering wheel.
5   In order to gain better access remove the door glass demist hose from the heater outlet.
6   Note the run of the switch harness and remove the three retaining straps (two securing the harness to the steering column, the third retaining it to the mounting bracket).
7   Pull the harness away from the steering column to expose the four harness plugs.
8   Disconnect the three harness plugs which are associated with the steering column multi-function switch and the master light switch assembly.

9   Loosen the switch assembly clamp screw and remove the assembly complete with its harness.
10 If one of the switches is faulty, then it can be renewed individually by removing the single spire clip and undoing the two outer hexagon screws. Do not loosen or remove the two similar hexagon screws, located at the centre of the switch assembly. Where necessary the master light switch can be removed as described in Section 35.
11 Refitting is the reverse of removal, but where possible renew the spire clip. Before installing the switch assembly ensure that the turn signal cancelling collar is correctly aligned by checking that the arrow on the collar is pointing towards the centre of the trafficator stock. Refer to Chapter 11 for the correct refitting of the steering wheel.

35 Switches – removal and refitting

Master light switch
1   Disconnect the battery negative lead.
2   Slacken the steering column clamp knob and lower the steering column to its lowest position.
3   Remove the steering column nacelle halves (one screw each).
4   Press the two spring clips on the side of the switch body inwards and withdraw the switch from the mounting.
5   Note the positions and cable colour codes and pull off the three single pin connectors.
6   Refitting is the reverse of removal. When reconnecting the switch cables ensure that the brown cable is connected to terminal 3, the red/green cable to terminal 2 and the blue cable to terminal 1.

Heated rear screen, hazard flasher, front fog lamp, rear fog lamp and rear window lift isolate (where applicable) switches
7   Disconnect the battery earth lead.
8   Remove the instrument housing end panel by turning the locking knob through 90°.
9   Lift off the lid of the instrument housing and push the appropriate switch out from its housing.
10 Disconnect the appropriate harness plug and withdraw the switch and its attached harness.
11 Refitting is the reverse of the removal procedure.

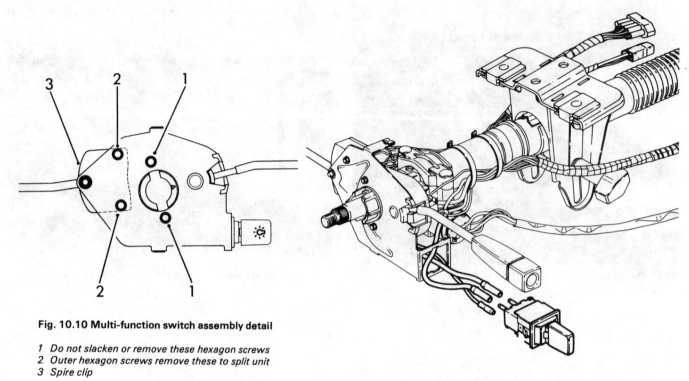

Fig. 10.10 Multi-function switch assembly detail

1 *Do not slacken or remove these hexagon screws*
2 *Outer hexagon screws remove these to split unit*
3 *Spire clip*

Fig. 10.11 The master light switch and wiring connections

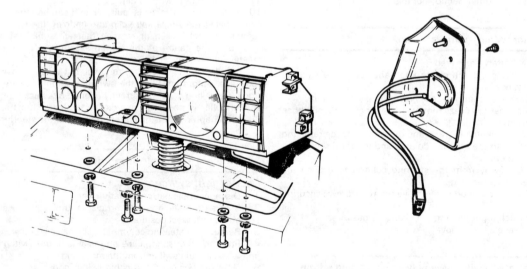

Fig. 10.12 The instrument housing and panel rheostat switch

Panel rheostat switch

12 Disconnect the battery negative lead.

13 Remove the instrument housing end panel by turning the locking knob through 90°.

14 Lift off the lid of the instrument housing and disconnect the two wiring connectors for the radio speaker.

15 Under the facia locate and remove the three bolts, spring washers and plain washers securing the instrument housing.

16 Release two plastic clips on the fuse box and swing the fuse box into the instrument housing in order to gain access to a further retaining bolt.

17 Remove this retaining bolt and carefully raise the rheostat switch end of the instrument housing to gain access to the end cover screws.

18 Remove the rheostat end cover screws. Withdraw the end cover, and disconnect the rheostat multi-plug connector.

19 Pull the control knob off the rheostat switch, undo the switch retaining nut and remove the switch from the end panel. Note the position of the spring washer.

20 Refitting is the reverse of removal.

Door switch (courtesy lights)

21 With the door open, remove the single screw, withdraw the switch

and detach the wiring connector.

22 Refitting is the reverse of the removal procedure.

Glovebox lamp switch

23 Open the glovebox, remove the single retaining screw and pull off the wiring connector.

24 Refitting is the reverse of the removal procedure.

Seat belt (belt switch)

25 Undo the single bolt to release the switch assembly and separate the harness plug after releasing the harness from the clip fixed to the seat frame.

26 Refitting is the reverse of the removal procedure.

Passengers seat belt (seat) switch

27 Remove the passenger seat as described in Chapter 12.

28 Remove the four screws and prise out the four studs to release the seat side trim mouldings.

29 Release the clip which retains the harness plug to the appropriate seat side trim moulding.

30 Remove the four bolts and any distance washers present in order to separate the squab from the cushion.

31 Remove the four wire retainer clips which secure the cushion cover to the seat frame just behind the harness plug.

32 Remove the four clips to release the cushion cover cord from the seat frame.

33 Remove a further five clips which secure the rear flap of the seat cushion cover to the seat frame.

34 Fold the cushion cover forward to reveal the switch which is glued to the cushion.

35 Break the adhesive to free the switch and then trace the loom into the cushion and disconnect two single pin harness plugs.

36 Refitting is the reverse of the removal procedure.

Handbrake switch

37 Disconnect the battery negative lead.

38 Prise out carefully the two screw head covers.

39 Using a wide blade screwdriver, carefully prise up the rear panel of the centre console in order to release the four plastic spigots. Prise up the centre console panel between the handbrake and choke to release a further four plastic spigots.

40 Remove the six screws, two at the centre console side panel and four securing the centre console to the body. Raise the rear of the console to gain access to the handbrake switch.

41 Disconnect the switch feed wire connector, undo the single retainer screw and lift the switch away.

42 Refitting is the reverse of the removal procedure.

Choke switch

43 Disconnect the battery negative lead.

44 Remove the screw retaining the choke control lever assembly.

45 Lift the rear of the choke control assembly to an angle of approximately 45° and pull it back slightly to release the forward hook.

46 Lift the bonnet and slide the choke cable through the bulkhead grommet by approximately 2.36 in (60 mm).

47 Pull the choke control assembly rearwards by approximately 2.36 in (60 mm) to obtain access to the choke switch.

48 Pull off the two wiring connectors at the switch. Disconnect the choke control rod from the control lever by removing the retaining clip.

49 Remove a single screw and lift away the choke switch.

50 Refitting is the reverse of the removal procedure.

Luggage compartment lamp switch

51 Open the tailgate and pull off the two spade connectors at the switch.

52 Remove the single retaining screw and lift away the switch.

Engine compartment lamp switch

53 Open the bonnet and disconnect the single feed wire at the switch.

54 Remove the single retaining screw and lift away the switch.

55 Refitting is the reverse of removal.

Stop light switch

56 Remove the driver's side glovebox and pull off the two spade connectors at the stop light switch. Undo the special nut and withdraw the

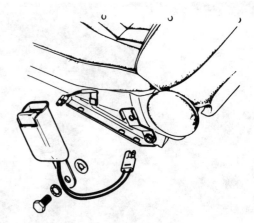

Fig. 10.13 The passenger's seat belt switch

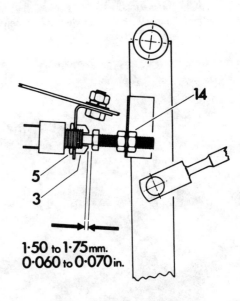

Fig. 10.14 Stop light switch adjustment

3   Special nut   14 Brake pedal bolt and nuts
5   Thin nut

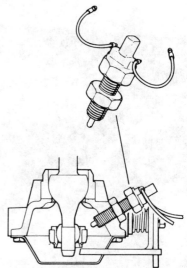

Fig. 10.15 Reversing lamp switch

35.67 The reverse lamp switch wires as viewed from beneath

35.72 The oil pressure switch (arrowed)

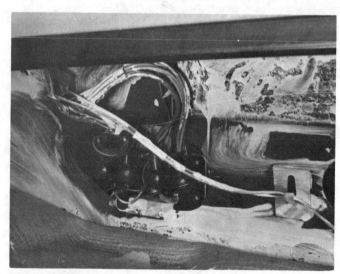

36.1 The door lock control system

stop light switch from the support bracket.
57 Where a new stop light switch is being fitted, transfer the thin nut to the new switch.
58 Refitting is basically the reverse of removal, but initially screw the thin nut on to the bottom of the thread.
59 Place the special nut in position between the brake pedal and bracket. Insert the switch through the bracket so that the locating flat is at the bottom.
60 Screw the special nut onto the switch until the nut recess contacts the switch body. Screw the thin nut up to the bracket and tighten it.
61 Measure the gap between the brake pedal bolt and the outer edge of the special nut with the brake pedal in the fully released position. If this clearance gap is between 0.060 and 0.070 in (1.50 to 1.75 mm) then the adjustment is satisfactory and the next paragraph can be ignored.
62 Where found necessary the clearance gap can be adjusted by loosening the brake pedal bolt nuts and altering the effective length of the bolt. After tightening the nuts recheck the clearance gap.
63 Reconnect the switch wires and refit the driver's glovebox.

Reverse lamp switch (automatic transmission)
64 The reverse lamp switch is integral with the starter inhibitor switch.
65 Refer to Chapter 6, Section 23, for removal and refitting procedures.

Reverse lamp switch (manual transmission)
66 Unscrew the gear lever knob and prise out the upper panel housing.
67 Withdraw the rubber draught excluder and the foam rubber insert. Separate the switch wires at the single snap-connectors, slacken the locknut and unscrew the switch (photo). When installing the switch, select reverse gear and screw in the switch until it just makes contact (this can be checked with a continuity tester or a test lamp and battery), then screw it in a further 3 flats (180°). Hold the switch in this position and tighten the locknut.
68 The remainder of the refitting procedure is the reverse of that used when removing.

Brake line failure switch
69 Release the harness plug claws and disconnect the plug from the switch on the lower side of the master cylinder.
70 Unscrew the switch.
71 Refitting is the reverse of the removal procedure. Note that the switch tightening torque is only 15 lbf in (0.17 kg fm).

Oil pressure switch
72 Detach the leads from the switch on the right-hand side of the engine adjacent to the alternator (photo).
73 Unscrew the adaptor unit from the oil pump and then unscrew the switch from the adaptor.
74 Refitting of the assembly is the reverse of removal, but note that the threads of the adaptor unit are tapered so avoid overtightening it.

36 Central door locking system components – removal and refitting

Door lock control assembly
1   The door lock control assembly is located behind the carpet covering the right-hand side panel of the luggage compartment (photo).
2   Disconnect the battery negative lead and pull the carpet aside to gain access to the assembly.
3   Remove the four screws and single star washer then carefully manoeuvre the control assembly out from the aperture in the side panel.
4   Disconnect the wires from the six terminals shown in Fig. 10.17.
5   Refitting is the reverse of removal.

Door lock (locking and unlocking) resistors
6   Remove the door lock control assembly as described in paragraphs 1 to 3.
7   In order to gain better access to the resistors, pull back the rubber covers at the inner terminal studs of the relay units. Undo the retaining nuts at these studs and lift away the four harness tags.
8   Identify the required resistor by tracing the appropriate brown/red wire from its relay. Identify the relay by the wires attached to it as shown below:

Locking relay:
Brown
Brown/red
Green/black
Green/slate

Unlocking relay:
Brown
Brown/red
Blue/black
Blue/orange

9 Note the location of the wires on the terminal block and loosen the two screws in order to remove the appropriate resistor.
10 Refitting is the reverse of removal.

Door lock (locking and unlocking) relays

11 Remove the door lock control assembly as described in paragraphs 1 to 3.
12 Identify the required relays as described in paragraph 8.
13 Pull off the two spade connectors.
14 Pull back the two rubber covers at the relay terminal studs. Undo the two nuts and lift off the four harness tags.
15 Remove the two nuts, spring washers, plain washers and bolts to release the relay.
16 Refitting is the reverse of the removal procedure.

Door lock interior switch

17 Remove the door trim pad as described in Chapter 12.
18 Release the two fixing claws and separate the harness plug (photo).
19 Push the single plastic clip on the switch inwards and withdraw the switch upwards from the door pull.
20 Refitting of the switch is the reverse of removal, but make sure that the 'door lock open' symbol is facing towards the rear of the car.

Door lock key switch assembly

21 Refer to Chapter 12.

Door lock solenoids

22 Refer to Chapter 12.

37 Instrument housing – removal and refitting

1   Disconnect the battery earth lead.
2   Rotate the recessed control on the end cover through 90° until it releases.
3   Pull off the top cover and disconnect the wiring connectors joining the radio speaker leads.
4   Disconnect the speedometer cable by depressing the locking prong and drawing away the cable.
5   From inside the instrument housing remove the bolt together with the spring washers and plain washers retaining the instrument housing to the top of the dashboard at a point next to the fuse panel (Fig. 10.19).
6   Open the driver's glovebox and undo the three bolts, spring washers and plain washers securing the instrument housing.
7   Pull off the corrugated hose from the air duct at the rear of the instrument housing.
8   Pull the instrument forward and disconnect the wiring harness multi-plugs.
9   Pull out the bulb and the white/green lead from the triangular plate at the rear of the gauge housing.
10 Disconnect the leads from the bulb holders fitted to the speedometer, tachometer and turn signal warning lights.
11 Depress the rear retaining lugs on the fuse holder housing and release it from the instrument housing.
12 The instrument housing can now be removed.
13 Refitting is the reverse of removal, but note the following points:

    (a)   The pin arrangement pattern of the multi-plugs is designed to avoid incorrect assembly.
    (b)   Red/white and black leads are connected to the bulb holders of the speedometer and tachometer.
    (c)   Green/white and black leads are connected to the right-hand

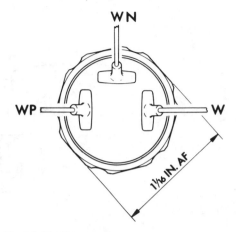

Fig. 10.16 Oil pressure switch wiring connections

WN   *White/brown*   W   *White*
WP   *White/purple*

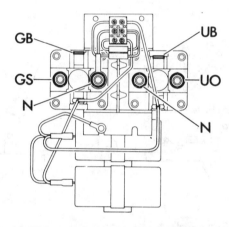

Fig.10.17 Door lock control wiring cable colour codes

UB   *Blue/black*   GS   *Green/slate*
UO   *Blue/orange*   GB   *Green/black*
N   *Brown*

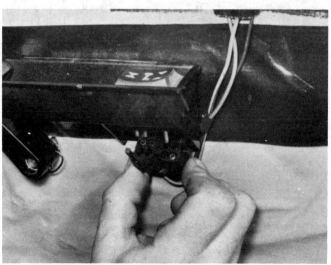

36.18 Disconnecting the harness plug from the interior central door lock switch

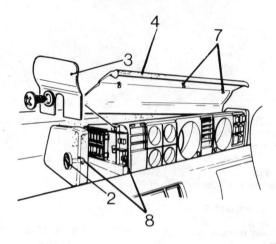

Fig. 10.18 The instrument housing end and top cover panels

2 *Recessed control*   4 *Top cover*   8 *Locking prong and retainer slot*
3 *End clip*   7 *Retaining pins*

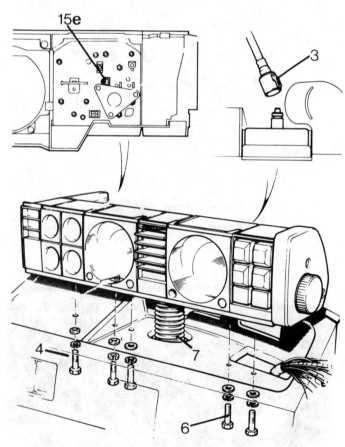

Fig. 10.19 Instrument housing fixings

3 *Speedometer cable*   *underneath dash)*
4 *Retaining bolt (access from* 7 *Air duct hose*
   inside housing)   15E *White/green lead connection*
6 *Retaining bolts (access from*   *point*

turn signal warning light.
(d)   Green/red and black leads are connected to the left-hand turn signal warning light.
(e)   White/green lead connects to the terminal at the rear of the gauge housing.

38 Panel instruments and sender units – removal and refitting

Battery condition indicator, oil gauge, temperature gauge and fuel gauge
1   Disconnect the battery negative lead.
2   Remove the instrument housing and cover by turning the recessed knob through 90°.
3   Lift off the top panel of the instrument housing and disconnect the leads to the radio speaker at the wiring connectors.
4   Press the top retaining lugs down on the front cover of the gauge housing and pull away the cover from the housing.
5   Remove the two gauge housing retaining screws and draw the gauge housing forward.
6   Press down the locking prong at the rear of the housing and with-draw the multi-plug.
7   Pull out the bulb holder from the triangular plate and disconnect the white/green lead from the back of the gauge housing.
8   Withdraw the gauge housing, remove the two screws and lift away the front lens holder.
9   In order to remove any individual gauge simply undo the retaining nuts and remove the wavy washers. The gauge can now be withdrawn.
10 Refitting is the reverse of removal.

Clock
Note: *The clock is non-adjustable apart from moving the 'hands' to correct small discrepancies. If the clock should continually gain or lose more than five minutes per week a new clock should be fitted.*
11 Disconnect the battery earth lead.
12 Open the passenger's glovebox, reach in and push the back of the clock from behind, to remove it from the facia.
13 Disconnect the electrical leads from the clock and withdraw the bulb holder.
14 Refitting is the reverse of the removal procedure.

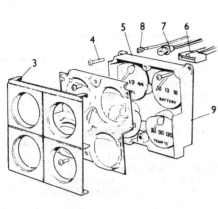

Fig. 10.20A Fixing details of the panel instruments

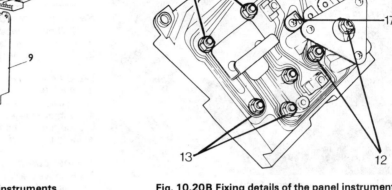

Fig. 10.20B Fixing details of the panel instruments

3 Front cover retaining lugs
4 Screw retaining gauge
   housing
5 Gauge housing
6 Multi-plug
7 Bulb holder
8 White/green lead
11 Nuts retaining battery

condition indicator
12 Nuts retaining oil pres-
    sure gauge
13 Nuts retaining temperature
gauge
14 Nuts retaining fuel gauge
17 Connection point for
    white/green lead

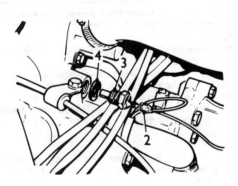

Fig. 10.21 Temperature gauge transmitter

2 Wiring connector   4 Sealing washer
3 Transmitter unit

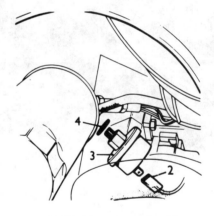

Fig. 10.22 Oil pressure transmitter

2 Wiring connector   4 Sealing washer
3 Oil pressure transmitter unit

Speedometer

15 Disconnect the battery negative lead.
16 Remove the instrument housing end and top panels as described in paragraphs 2 and 3.
17 Depress the locking prong and pull out the speedometer cable from the rear of the speedometer head.
18 Depress the upper retaining lug on the speedometer front cover and lift the cover away from the instrument housing.
19 Undo the two retaining screws and draw the speedometer forward sufficiently to remove the bulb holders.
20 Refitting is the reverse of removal.

Tachometer

21 Disconnect the battery negative lead.
22 Remove the instrument housing end and top panels as described in paragraphs 2 and 3.
23 Pull out the wiring plug connector from the rear of the tachometer (photo).
24 Depress the upper retaining lugs on the tachometer front cover and lift the cover away.'

25 Undo the two tachometer retaining screws. Draw the tachometer forwards and pull out the bulb holders (photo).
26 Refitting is the reverse of the removal procedure.

Temperature gauge transmitter

27 Disconnect the battery negative lead.
28 Pull off the wiring connector from the coolant temperature transmitter fitted to the front of the inlet manifold.
29 Unscrew the transmitter and withdraw the sealing washer.
30 Refitting is the reverse of the removal procedure, but remember to fit a new sealing washer.

Oil pressure transmitter

31 Disconnect the battery earth lead.
32 Pull off the electric lead at the transmitter.
33 Unscrew the transmitter and withdraw the sealing washer.
34 If the transmitter is suspect, then it can be checked by substitution or by temporarily fitting a pressure gauge in its place.
35 Installation of the transmitter is the reverse of the removal procedure, but remember to fit a new sealing washer.

38.23 Rear view of the tachometer as fitted in the instrument panel

38.25 Locations of the tachometer retaining screws

39.8 The screen washer pump is retained by two nuts and bolts

Fuel gauge tank unit

36   The fuel gauge tank unit is an integral part of the fuel pump assembly. Removal and refitting details for this assembly are given in Chapter 3.

39 Windscreen washers

Reservoir – removal and refitting

1   Pull off the washer reservoir pipe from the washer pump, then lift the reservoir from its retaining bracket.
2   Refitting is the reverse of the removal procedure.

Washer jet – removal and refitting

3   Pull off the pipe, then remove the nut and anti-vibration washer, taking care that they are not dropped.
4   Remove the jet and sealing washer.
5   Refitting is the reverse of this procedure. If necessary, rotate the jet using a screwdriver to direct the jet satisfactorily.

Washer pump – removal and refitting

6   Remove the washer reservoir, as previously described.
7   Pull off the two electrical leads from the pump.
8   Undo the two nuts and bolts securing the washer pump to its mounting bracket (photo).
9   Lift the pump and pull off the inlet and outlet pipes.
10 Refitting is the reverse of removal, but make sure that the inlet and outlet pipes are connected correctly. The direction of water flow is usually denoted by an arrow at the pump inlet and outlet connections. The lime green and black power wire should be connected to the (+) terminal of the washer pump.

40 Windscreen wiper arms and blades – removal and refitting

Wiper arm

1   Open the bonnet and carefully prise off the plastic cap from the pivot end of the wiper arm (photo).
2   Undo the nut retaining the arm to the spindle.
3   Tilt the arm and blade assembly away from the windscreen and withdraw the wiper arm from the spindle.
4   Refitting is the reverse of the removal procedure. Position the arm on the splines to obtain the most suitable 'Park' position.

Wiper blade

5   Lift the arm and blade away from the windscreen, then simultaneously depress the clip and withdraw the blade pin from the pivot block (photo).
6   Refitting is the reverse of the removal procedure.

40.1 Prise off the plastic cap from the pivot end of the wiper arm

41 Windscreen wiper motor and drive assembly – removal and refitting

1 Open the bonnet and disconnect the battery earth lead.
2 Remove the air cleaner (see Chapter 3).
3 Remove the four bolts, plate and screw securing the bonnet lock to the body and move the lock to one side. The locations of these bolts are shown in Fig. 10.24.
4 Remove the wiper arms (see Section 40).
5 Undo the two wheel box retaining nuts and extract the spacing washers and rubber seals.
6 Disconnect the wiper motor earthing strap at the wiper motor mounting plate.
7 Remove the nut, bolt and washers securing the wiper motor. mounting plate to the body.
8 Pull off the electrical multi-plug connector from the wiper motor.
9 Tip the assembly to allow the wheel box spindles to fall clear of their location holes and withdraw the assembly from the body aperture.
10 Refitting is the reverse of the removal procedure. Before refitting the wiper arms switch the wipers on and off in order to obtain the 'Park' position.

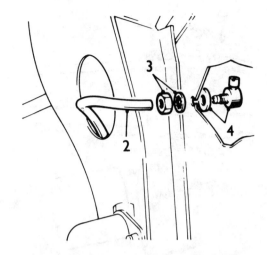

Fig. 10.23 Screenwasher jet fixing detail

2 Delivery pipe   4 Jet and sealing washer
3 Nut and anti-vibration washer

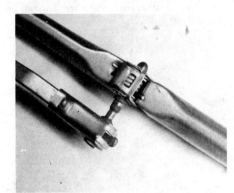

40.5 Depress the clip and withdraw the wiper blade assembly

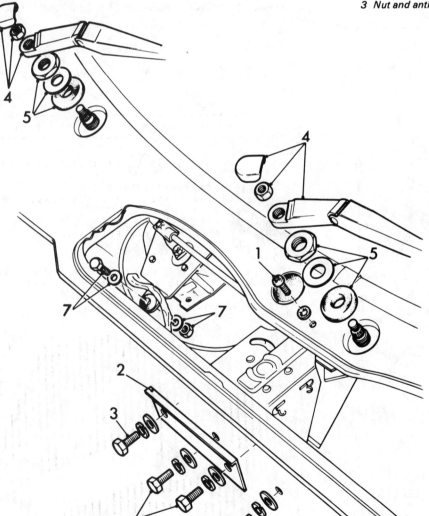

Fig. 10.24 Wiper motor and drive assembly fixing detail

1 Bonnet lock fixing screw   3 Bonnet lock fixing bolts   5 Wheel box fixing nuts, spacing   7 Wiper motor mounting plate to
2 Retainer plate   4 Wiper arm, nut and plastic cap   washers and seals   body fixing

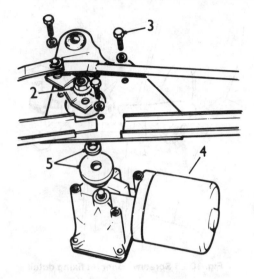

Fig. 10.25 Wiper motor to linkage fixing detail

2 *Special serrated nut*
3 *Wiper motor to mounting plate*
   bolt
4 *Wiper motor*
5 *Shim washer and rubber seal*

42 Windscreen wiper motor – removal, overhaul and refitting

1   Remove the wiper motor and drive assembly from the car as described in Section 41.
2   Remove the special, serrated face, nut from the wiper motor shaft.
3   Undo the three bolts securing the wiper motor to its mounting plate.
4   Withdraw the wiper motor from its linkage and note the positions of the shim washer and rubber seal fitted to the wiper motor shaft.
5   Undo the three screws retaining the gearbox cover and lift it off.
6   Make sure that the end of the wiper motor shaft is free from burr, then withdraw it and extract the dished washer.
7   Remove the thrust screw, or thrust screw and locknut from the side of the wiper body.
8   Remove the through bolts and slowly withdraw the cover and armature. The brushes will drop clear of the commutator, but do not allow them to become contaminated with grease from the worm gear.
9   Pull the armature out of the cover.
10 Undo the three screws retaining the brush assembly.
11 Lift and slide the limit switch sideways, to release it from the spring clip.
12 The brush assembly and limit switch can now be lifted away together.
13 Examine the various components for wear and renew as necessary.

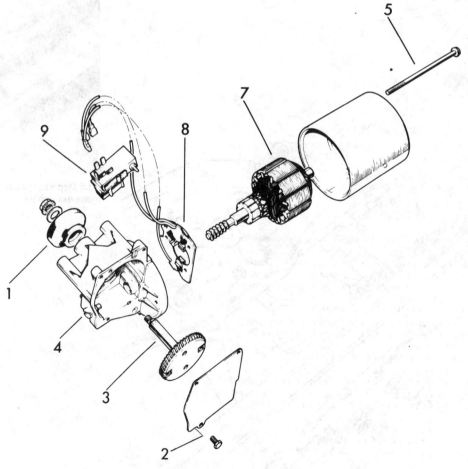

Fig. 10.26 Exploded view of the wiper motor assembly

1 *Rubber seal*
2 *Gearbox cover plate*
3 *Wiper motor shaft*
4 *Thrust screw*
5 *Through bolts*
7 *Armature*
8 *Brush assembly*
9 *Limit switch*

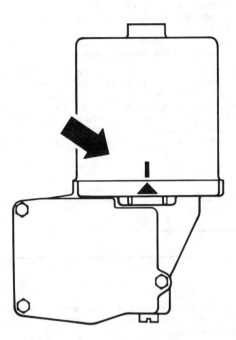

Fig. 10.27 Cover to gearbox casing alignment marks

Fig. 10.28 Wiper motor delay unit

14 Commence the reassembly procedure by sliding the limit switch in position and securing it with the clip.

15 Refit the brush assembly and secure it with the three screws.

16 Lubricate the cover bearing and soak the covering bearing felt washer with Shell Turbo 41 oil.

17 Refit the armature to the cover, lubricate the self-aligning bearing with Shell Turbo 41 oil, then insert the armature shaft through the bearing whilst restraining the three brushes. Take care when inserting the armature shaft to prevent the brushes from becoming contaminated with grease.

18 Position the cover against the gearbox casing so that the datum lines are correctly aligned.

19 Insert the cover through bolts and tighten them.

20 Refit the thrust screw, or the thrust screw and locknut and then check the armature endfloat.

21 On types with an adjustable thrust screw loosen the locknut and screw the adjustment screw inwards until resistance is felt. Turn the screw back by a quarter of a turn and tighten the locknut.

22 On types with a non-adjustable thrust screw, push the armature towards the cover and place a feeler gauge between the armature shaft and the thrust screw. The endfloat at this point should be 0.002 to 0.008 in (0.005 to 0.20 mm). Where the endfloat is insufficient, the only solution is to place a packing washer under the head of the thrust screw. If the endfloat is excessive, then have metal machined from under the head of the thrust screw.

23 Lubricate the final gear bushes with Shell Turbo 41 oil and apply Ragosine Listate grease to the final gear cam.

24 Fit the dished washer with its concave surface facing the final drive gear then insert the shaft.

25 Pack the area around the worm and final gear with Ragosine Listate grease.

26 Reposition the gearbox cover and fit the rubber seal.

27 The wiper motor can now be refitted to the mounting plate by reversing the removal procedure.

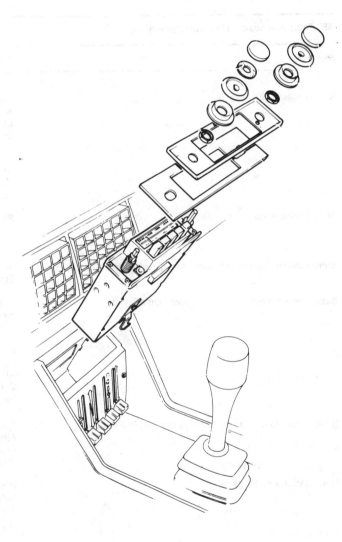

Fig. 10.29 Radio fixing detail

43 Wiper motor delay unit – removal and refitting

1 The wiper motor delay unit is retained by a clip and mounted alongside similar units on the body panel behind the driver's glove compartment.

2 Before removing the unit, disconnect the battery negative lead.

3 Open the driver's glove compartment and identify the unit by the colour coding of the wires jointed to it.

Terminal 1   *White with green tracer*
Terminal 2   *Brown with light green tracer*
Terminal 3   *Yellow with light green tracer*
Terminal 4   *Brown with green tracer*

4 Pull off the wiring connections and pull the wiper motor delay unit from its retaining clip.

5 Refitting is the reverse of the removal procedure.

44 Radio – removal, refitting and trimming

1   Disconnect the battery earth lead.
2   Pull off the upper knob, felt washer, lower knob and nut cover from the left-hand control.
3   Pull off upper knob, lower knob and nut cover from the right-hand control.
4   Undo the two thin nuts and lift away the face panel and support plate.
5   Hold the radio by the two control spindles. Push it downwards and tilt it slightly to release the catch on the lower retaining bracket.
6   Withdraw the radio from the aperture sufficiently and disconnect the following:

(a)   *Earthing wire at the radio terminal connection*
(b)   *Supply wire, by releasing the bayonet type fitting at the in-line choke*
(c)   *Speaker wires, at the harness plug*
(d)   *The aerial lead, at the plug connector*

7   Refitting is the reverse of removal, but do not fit the right-hand control knob components until the radio has been trimmed.
8   Switch on the radio and tune it to a weak position eg 250 metres (1.2 MHz). Insert a thin screwdriver through the small aperture adjacent to the right-hand control spindle and adjust the trim screw to obtain the maximum volume.
9   Switch off the radio and refit the right-hand control knob components.

45 Fault diagnosis – electrical system

Symptom	Reason/s
Starter fails to turn engine	Battery discharged
	Battery defective internally
	Battery terminal leads loose or earth lead not securely attached to body
	Loose or broken connections in starter motor circuit
	Starter motor switch or solenoid faulty
	Starter motor pinion jammed in mesh with flywheel gear ring
	Starter brushes badly worn, sticking, or brush wires loose
	Starter motor armature faulty
	Field coils earthed
Starter turns engine very slowly	Battery in discharged condition
	Starter brushes badly worn, sticking or brush wires loose
	Loose wires in starter motor circuit
Starter motor noisy or excessively rough engagement	Pinion or flywheel gear teeth broken or worn
	Starter motor retaining bolts loose
Battery will not hold charge for more than a few days	Battery defective internally
	Electrolyte level too low or electrolyte too weak due to leakage
	Plate separators no longer fully effective
	Battery plates severely sulphated
	Fan belt slipping
	Battery terminal connections loose or corroded
	Alternator not charging
	Short in lighting circuit causing continual battery drain
	Regulator unit not working correctly
Ignition light fails to go out, battery runs flat in a few days	Fan belt loose and slipping or broken
	Alternator brushes worn, sticking, broken or dirty
	Alternator brush springs weak or broken
	Internal fault in alternator
Horn operates all the time	Horn push either earthed or stuck down
	Cable to horn push earthed
	Relay faulty
Horn fails to operate	Blown fuse
	Cable or cable connection loose, broken or disconnected
	Horn has an internal fault
	Relay faulty
Horn emits intermittent or unsatisfactory noise	Cable connections loose
	Horn incorrectly adjusted
Lights do not come on	If engine not running, battery discharged
	Wire connections loose, disconnected or broken
	Light switch shorting or otherwise faulty
Lights come on but fade out	If engine not running, battery discharged
	Light bulb filament burnt out or sealed beam units broken
	Wire connections loose, disconnected or broken
	Light switch shorting or otherwise faulty

Lights give very poor illumination

Lamp glasses dirty
Lamps badly out of alignment

Lights work erratically – flashing on and off, especially over bumps

Battery terminals or earth connection loose
Lights not earthing properly
Contacts in light switch faulty

Wiper motor fails to work

Blown fuse
Wire connections loose, disconnected or broken
Brushes badly worn
Armature worn or faulty
Field coils faulty

Wiper motor works very slowly and takes excessive current

Commutator dirty, greasy or burnt
Armature bearings dirty or unaligned
Armature badly worn or faulty
Brushes badly worn
Commutator dirty, greasy or burnt
Armature badly worn or faulty

Wiper motor works but wiper blades remain static

Wiper motor gearbox parts badly worn

Fig. 10.30 (see page 140) Typical wiring diagram (right-hand drive models)

COLOUR CODE

B	Black	P	Purple
G	Green	R	Red
K	Pink	S	Slate
LG	Light Green	U	Blue
N	Brown	W	White
O	Orange	Y	Yellow

1 Alternator
2 Battery
3 Door lock fuse
4 Resistor (lock)
5 Resistor (unlock)
6 Capacitor (lock)
7 Capacitor (unlock)
8 Relay (lock)
9 Relay (unlock)
10 Front door lock solenoid and key switch
11 Rear door lock solenoid
12 Tailgate lock solenoid
13 Interior switch
14 Radio fuse
15 Radio choke
16 Radio
17 Speaker
18 Main beam warning light
19 Fuse
20 Main beam (RH)
21 Main beam (LH)
22 Dip beam (RH)
23 Dip beam (LH)
24 Front fog light switch
25 Front fog light
26 Rear fog light switch
27 Rear fog light
28 Rear fog light warning light
29 Fibre optic light
30 Clock illumination
31 Cigarette lighter illumination
32 Number plate illumination light
33 Bulb failure indicator
34 Tail light
35 Stop light
36 Front parking light
37 Turn signal switch
38 Flasher warning light (RH)
39 Front flasher light (RH)
40 Rear flasher light (RH)
41 Rear flasher light (LH)
42 Front flasher light (LH)
43 Flasher warning light (LH)
44 Starter motor
45 Ignition/starter switch
46 Starter inhibitor switch (automatic transmission only)
47 Starter motor relay
48 Heater motor supply line relay
49 Lighting supply line relay
50 Master light switch
51 Main/dip/flash switch
52 Choke warning light
53 Choke switch
54 Brake warning light
55 Brake fluid level switch
56 Brake line failure switch
57 Handbrake warning light
58 Handbrake switch
59 Panel rheostat
60 Tachometer illumination
61 Instrument illumination
62 Speedometer illumination
63 Horn push
64 Horn
65 Stop light switch
66 Passenger's seat switch
67 Passenger's seat belt switch
68 Seat belt warning light
69 Driver's seat belt switch
70 Bulb failure warning light
71 Hazard flasher unit
72 Hazard switch
73 Turn signal flasher unit
74 Glovebox light
75 Glovebox light switch
76 Engine bay light
77 Engine bay light switch
78 Cigarette lighter
79 Ignition warning light
80 Oil pressure switch
81 Oil pressure warning light
82 Fuel pump
83 Ballast resistor
84 Ignition coil
85 Ignition distributor
86 Tachometer
87 Heated rear window switch
88 Heated rear window warning light
89 Heated rear window relay
90 Heated rear window fuse
91 Heated rear window
92 Windscreen wiper switch
93 Windscreen wiper delay unit
94 Windscreen wiper motor
95 Windscreen washer switch
96 Windscreen washer pump
97 Fuel gauge
98 Fuel tank unit
99 Fuel warning light delay unit
100 Fuel warning light
101 Temperature gauge
102 Temperature sender unit
103 Oil pressure gauge
104 Oil pressure sender unit
105 Battery condition indicator
106 Reverse light switch
107 Reverse light
108 Heater motor
109 Heater resistor
110 Heater switch
111 Luggage compartment light
112 Luggage compartment light switch
113 B-post light
114 Front door guard light
115 Door switch
116 Clock
117 Map light
118 Engine diagnosis socket
119 Engine diagnosis timing transducer

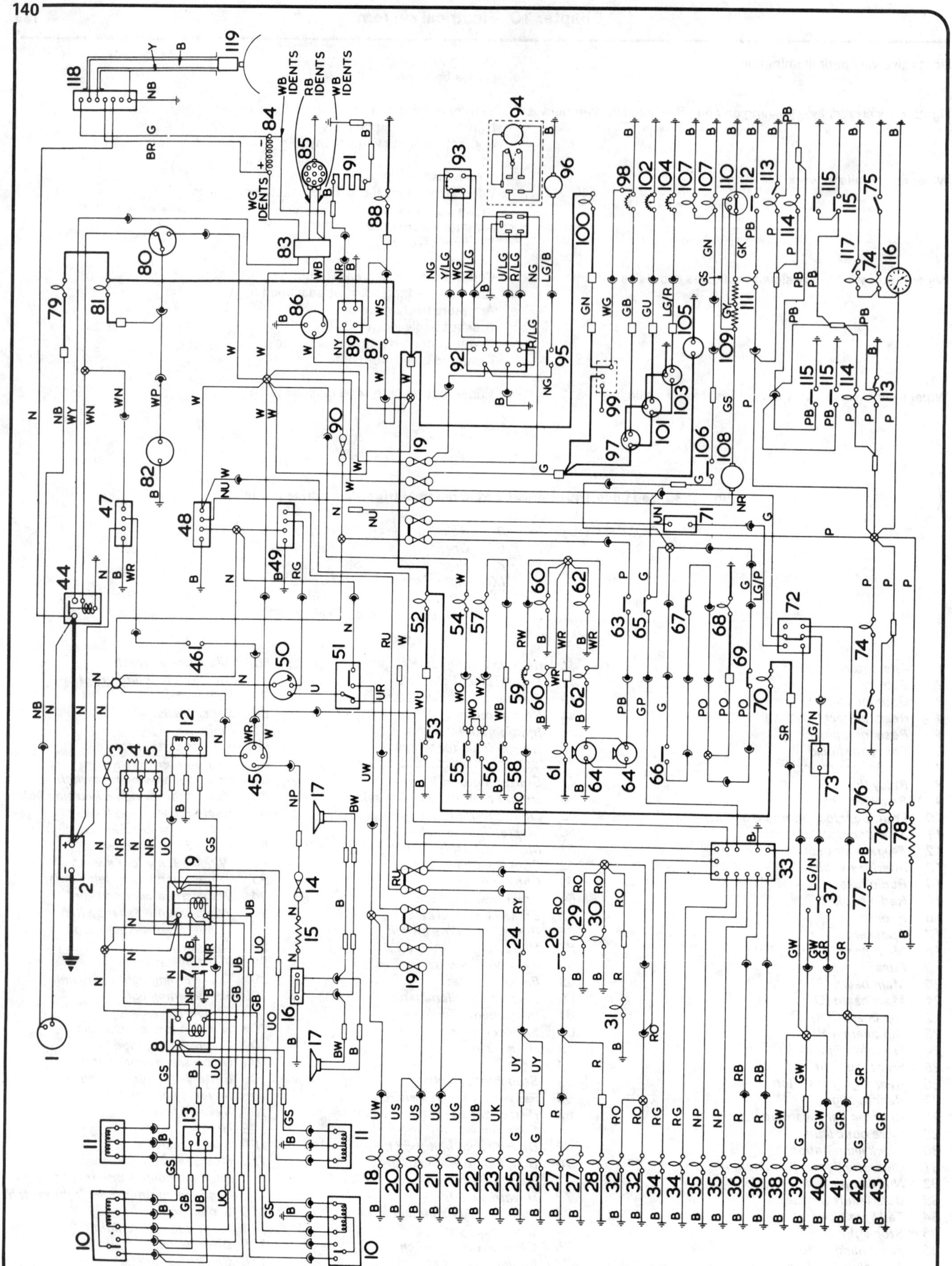

Chapter 11 Suspension and steering

For modifications, and information applicable to later models, see Supplement at end of manual

Contents

Specifications

Front suspension .... MacPherson strut with telescopic dampers, eccentrically mounted coil springs and anti-roll bar

Rear suspension .... Axle located by semi-trailing arms, torque tube and transverse Watts linkage. Suspension provided by Boge Nivomat self-energising, self-levelling damper struts and coil springs, with progressive-rate bump stop rubbers

Steering
Type .... Power-assisted rack-and-pinion
Steering wheel turns, lock-to-lock 2.7
Power steering fluid type .... Type 'G' ATF to M2C 33F or M2C 33G (Duckhams Q-Matic)
Steering/front suspension geometry ....

	Unladen	Laden
Camber	0°	+ 0° 55'
Castor	2° 00'	2° 00'
Kingpin inclination	13° 20'	10° 15'
Wheel alignment (toe-in)	0 – $\frac{1}{8}$ in (0 – 3·17 mm)	0 – $\frac{1}{8}$ in (0 – 3·17 mm)

Wheel bearings
Lubricant type .... Multi-purpose lithium based grease to NLGI 2 (Duckhams LB 10)

Wheels
Standard .... Pressed steel
Optional .... Aluminium alloy or 'Denovo'
Size .... 6J x 14

Tyre sizes .... 185 HR 14, 195/70 HR 14 or 195/65 HR 375*
Denovo type manufactured by Dunlop

Tyre pressures

	Front	Rear
185 HR 14:		
Normal	26 lbf/in² (1·8 kgf/cm²)	26 lbf/in² (1·8 kgf/cm²)
Fully laden	26 lbf/in² (1·8 kgf/cm²)	30 lbf/in² (2·1 kgf/cm²)
195/70 HR 14:		
Normal	26 lbf/in² (1·8 kgf/cm²)	26 lbf/in² (1·8 kgf/cm²)
Fully laden	26 lbf/in² (1.8 kgf/cm²)	28 lbf/in² (2.0 kgf/cm²)
195/65 HR 375*:		
Normal	23 lbf/in² (1·6 kgf/cm²)	23 lbf/in² (1·6 kgf/cm²)
Fully laden	26 lbf/in² (1·8 kgf/cm²)	28 lbf/in² (2·0 kgf/cm²)

Torque wrench settings

	lbf ft	Nm
Front suspension		
Anti-roll bar to crossmember	32	43
Anti-roll bar to lower link	71	95
Subframe attachments	30	40
Lower link to crossmember	59	80
Lower link to strut assembly	36	48
Strut mounting to body	21	28
Steering arm to strut	55	75
Rear suspension		
Trailing link to fork end	41	54
Trailing link fork end to body	41	54
Trailing link to rear axle	41	54
Watts linkage to rear axle	41	54
Rear crossmember body to outer mounting	34	46
Levelling unit to axle and body (nut)	15	20
Levelling unit to axle and body (locknut)	22	32
Bump stop to upper spring cup	20	27·5
Rear crossmember to axle extension	41	54
Steering		
Rack to crossmember	32	43
Balljoint to steering arm	36	48
Steering wheel	20	27
Wheel nuts	66	88
Coupling set-screw	20	27·5
Column mounting bracket to dash	20	27·5
Power steering pump valve cap	35	47

1   General description

The front suspension is of the MacPherson strut type with telescopic dampers, offset coil springs and an anti-roll bar. The single lower links are pivoted at their inner ends in rubber bushes set in the subframe assembly. This subframe also carries the anti-roll bar and steering rack assembly. At the upper ends, the springs and dampers are retained in housings in the front wing valances.

The rear suspension comprises a live rear axle, coil springs and separately mounted Boge Nivomat self-levelling damper units. The axle is located by semi-trailing arms and the long nose of the final drive housing (acting as a torque tube) at its forward end. Sideways location is provided by a transverse Watts linkage system mounted at the rear of the axle.

The steering is of the power-assisted rack-and-pinion type with twin tie-rods connecting to the steering arms through balljoints. The power steering pump is belt driven from the engine crankshaft.

The steering wheel connects through a steering shaft, a universal joint, an intermediate shaft and a second universal joint to the steering gear pinion.

The steering and suspension is relatively maintenance-free apart from periodically checking the tension of the steering pump drive belt, power steering fluid level and renewing the power steering fluid reservoir filter. It is advisable to periodically inspect the entire steering and suspension systems.

2   Anti-roll bar – removal and refitting

1   Apply the handbrake then raise the front of the car, and support it on blocks or axle stands beneath the subframe or body frame members. For convenience, also remove the roadwheels.
2   Remove the two bolts and nyloc nuts on each side which secure the anti-roll bar saddle brackets to the subframe.
3   Remove the spring pin, nyloc nut, flat and dished washer, and bush at each end of the anti-roll bar.
4   Remove the bolt and nyloc nut securing one of the bottom links to the subframe.
5   Pull the bottom link from the subframe bracket, withdraw the anti-roll bar from the car, then take off the inner bush and dished washer from each end.
6   If the rubbers have deteriorated, they should be cut away with a sharp knife. When installing replacements, ensure that the anti-roll bar is clean, then smear it with a proprietary rubber grease or glycerine and slide on the bushes.
7   Refitting is basically the reverse of the removal procedure. Attach the bottom link first and secure it with the bolt and nyloc nut.
8   Offer up the anti-roll bar and align the ends with the mounting holes in each of the bottom links. The saddle brackets can now be refitted.

3   Front spring and strut – removal and refitting

1   Apply the handbrake, then raise the front of the car at the appropriate side. Support it beneath the subframe or bodyframe member.
2   Remove the roadwheel.
3   Fit a brake hose clamp and disconnect the brake caliper pipe union from the brake hose. The use of the brake hose clamp is to prevent the loss of brake fluid due to the syphoning action. The alternative to this method is to remove the master cylinder filler cap, place a thin film of polythene over the top and replace the cap. When the brake union is disconnected the end can be plugged to prevent any fluid loss.
4   Remove the nyloc nut and plain washer from the track rod end and separate the track rod end from the steering arm using either a balljoint separator or split wedges. If neither tool is available a flat lever bar and a hammer can be used to release the taper pin.
5   Remove the nyloc nut and washer securing the suspension balljoint to the base of the strut. Separate the balljoint taper pin from the strut using the method described in paragraph 4.
6   Remove the three nyloc nuts at the top damper mounting, then pull the strut clear of the car.
7   Using proprietary spring compressors, compress the spring evenly.
8   Prise out the plastic dust cover from the top bearing assembly and undo the nyloc nut from the top of the damper piston rod.
9   Remove the washer, lift off the upper swivel assembly complete with the upper spring pan and shim(s).
10 Withdraw the spring, gaiter retaining plate, gaiter and two rubber

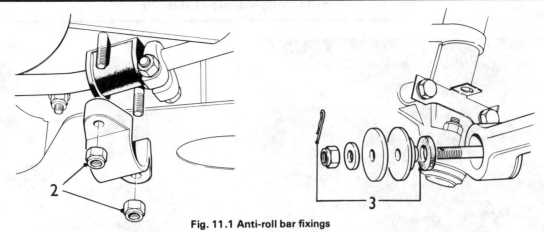

Fig. 11.1 Anti-roll bar fixings

2 Saddle bracket retaining nuts   3 Spring pin, nyloc nut, flat and dished washers

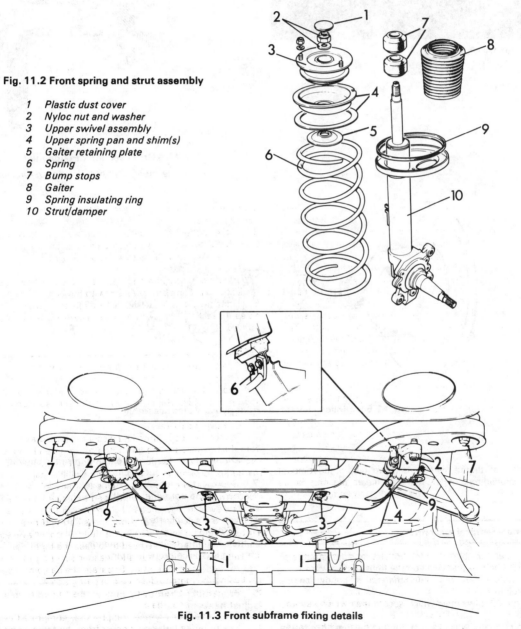

Fig. 11.2 Front spring and strut assembly

1 Plastic dust cover
2 Nyloc nut and washer
3 Upper swivel assembly
4 Upper spring pan and shim(s)
5 Gaiter retaining plate
6 Spring
7 Bump stops
8 Gaiter
9 Spring insulating ring
10 Strut/damper

Fig. 11.3 Front subframe fixing details

1 Support jacks
2 Anti-roll bar fixing to subframe
3 Steering rack to subframe fixing
4 Nuts and bolts securing lower links to subframe
6 Engine mounting and stabiliser bar
7 Subframe retaining bolts
(long)
9 Subframe retaining bolts (short)

5.6 Removing the grease cap

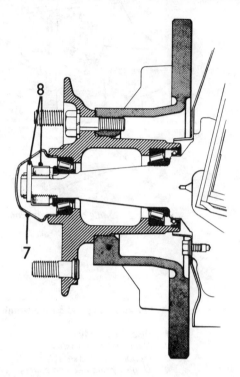

Fig. 11.4 Cross section through the front hub

7 Grease cap   8 Split-pin and nut retaining cap

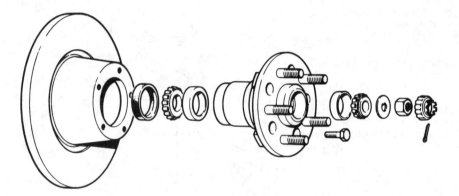

Fig. 11.5 Exploded view of the front hub and disc assembly

bump stops.

11 Reassembly and refitting of the strut is the reverse of the removal and dismantling procedures. After refitting, bleed the brakes as described in Chapter 9.

4 Front subframe – removal and refitting

1   Jack-up the car, and support it on the bodyframe sidemembers so that the weight of the body is just taken off the front suspension.

2   Undo the four nuts and bolts, securing the anti-roll bar and engine stabiliser to the subframe.

3 Undo the four nuts and washers which secure the steering rack to the subframe.

4   Undo the two nuts and washers securing the bottom links to the subframe. Withdraw the bolts and release the links. If the bolts cannot be withdrawn, adjust the support jacks to relieve the load on the bolts.

5   Support the engine with a jack placed beneath the sump coupling plate.

6   Disconnect the engine mounting from the subframe and stabiliser by removing the four nuts, bolts and washers.

7   Support the subframe. Remove the two long bolts, nuts and washers at the front end, and the two short bolts, nuts and washers at the rear.

8   Lower the supports and withdraw the subframe.

9   Refitting is the reverse of the removal procedure, but remember to tighten the nuts to the recommended torque setting. Ensure that the steering rack is correctly located.

5 Front hub – removal, dismantling, reassembly, refitting and adjustment

1   Apply the handbrake, then raise the front of the car at the appropriate side. Support it beneath the subframe or bodyframe member.

2   Remove the roadwheel, clamp the flexible brake hose or alternatively remove the master cylinder reservoir cap and spread a piece of

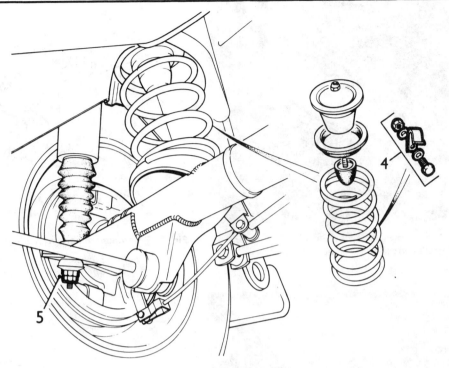

Fig. 11.6 Rear spring and bump stop detail

4 Spring retaining clip assembly   5 Damper retaining nuts (lower)

thin polythene sheeting over the top, then refit the cap. This measure will prevent the excessive loss of brake fluid when the union is disconnected.

3   Disconnect the caliper metal pipe at its union with the flexible hose.

4   Bend the tab washer ends back from the caliper retaining bolt heads and remove the two bolts.

5   Lift the brake caliper away.

6   Prise off the grease cap and wipe away the surplus grease from the end of the stub axle (photo).

7   Remove the split pin, retaining cap, nut and washer.

8   Withdraw the hub and disc, complete with bearings and oil seal.

9   Remove the outer bearing; remove the inner seal and inner bearing.

10 Drive out the bearing inner races from the hub.

11 Clean all the parts carefully in petrol or paraffin, and check for obvious wear, scoring, signs of overheating (a bluish colour), etc. Brown grease stains are of no significance. Ensure that the bearings run smoothly when assembled in their outer tracks. Replace bearings, where necessary, as complete assemblies, and on no account mix up parts of bearings from one side of the car to the other.

12 Press in the bearing outer tracks, then lubricate the bearing races with a general purpose grease, working it well in with the fingers.

13 Partially pack the hub with grease, then install the bearing races.

14 Fit a new oil seal with the lips facing the inner bearing then push on the hub. Take care that the outer bearing is not dislodged.

15 Fit the washer to the stub axle and screw on the nut finger-tight only.

16 Fit the caliper and reconnect the brakepipe. Fit a new caliper lock tab and tighten to the recommended torque setting (Chapter 9).

17 Adjust the hub by tightening the nut to a torque setting of 5 lbf ft (0.69 kgf m) then back it off one flat.

18 Install the retaining cap and retain it with a new split pin. Replace the hub grease cap (there is no need to fill it with grease).

19 Before replacing the roadwheel bleed the brakes as described in Chapter 9.

6   Front suspension lower link and balljoint assembly – removal and refitting

1   Apply the handbrake, then raise the front of the car at the appropriate side. Support it beneath the subframe or the bodyframe member.

2   Remove the roadwheel, then detach the end of the anti-roll bar from the lower link (refer to Section 2, if necessary).

3   Remove the nyloc nut and plain washer securing the lower link balljoint to the base of the strut/stub axle assembly.

4   Pull back the rubber boot from the balljoint, then use a proprietary balljoint separator or split wedges to separate the balljoint taper pin from the strut/stub axle assembly. If neither tool is available, strike opposite sides of the taper pin eye simultaneously with two club hammers.

5   Remove the bolt and nyloc nut securing the lower link to the subframe.

6   Withdraw the lower link and balljoint assembly.

7   Refitting is the reverse of the removal procedure.

7   Rear spring and bump stop – removal and refitting

1   Jack-up the rear of the car and support it on blocks or an axle stand beneath the bodyframe member. Chock the front wheels for safety.

2   Place a jack under the axle to support its weight, but ensure that the car's body weight is still taken by the support placed beneath the bodyframe member.

3   Remove the two 'power lock' bolts which secure the forked end of the trailing link assembly to the inner sill.

4   Undo and remove the bolt, nyloc nut and washer, securing the spring retainer clip to the axle.

5   Disconnect the two nuts securing the self-levelling damper unit to the axle bracket.

6   Carefully lower the axle support jack, then withdraw the spring and insulating ring.

7   If the bump stop is to be removed then undo the nut securing the bump stop to the spring top mounting.

8   Refitting is the reverse of the removal procedure.

8   Rear suspension trailing link – removal and refitting

1   Chock the front roadwheels, raise the rear of the car and support it on axle stands, or packing blocks, placed under the bodyframe sidemember.

8.2 Trailing link connection to the axle locating bracket

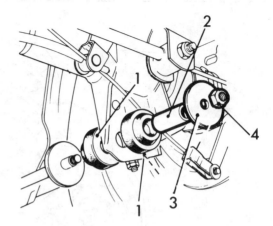

Fig. 11.7 Component parts at rear end connection of trailing link

1 Bushes
2 Spacer sleeve
3 Washer
4 Nyloc nut

10.2 Watts linkage – side link and bracket

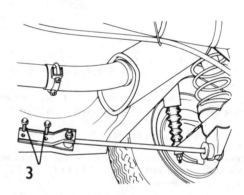

Fig. 11.8 Front fixing of trailing link

3 Power lock bolts

10.3 Watts linkage centre pivot

11.6 Lower steering coupling

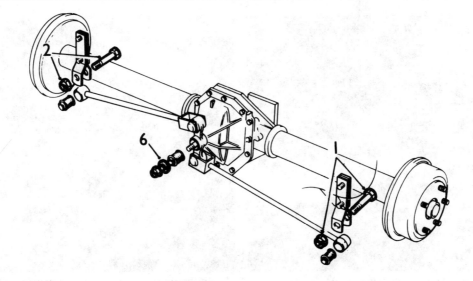

Fig. 11.9 Layout of Watts linkage system

1 Side link bolt and nut (right-hand)
2 Side link bolt and nut (left-hand)
6 Bush, washer and nyloc nut (centre pivot)

2 Disconnect the trailing link from the axle locating bracket by removing the nyloc nut, plain washer, rubber bush and distance tube (photo).
3 Undo the two 'power lock' bolts retaining the forked bracket to the inner body sill panel.
4 Pull the trailing link away from the axle and extract the rubber bush from the rear end.
5 If necessary remove the nut and bolt securing the eyed end of the trailing link to the fork bracket.
6 Renew the bushes as necessary and refit by reversing the removal procedure.

9 Rear dampers (self-levelling units) – removal and refitting

1 Raise the rear of the car and support it with packing blocks or stands, placed under the bodyframe sidemember. Remember to chock the front roadwheels.
2 Fold down the rear seat and pull away the carpet from the region of the wheel arch to expose the top mounting of the self-levelling unit.
3 Place a support jack under the axle to support its weight.
4 Undo the locknut, nut and dished washer securing the self-levelling unit to the body.
5 Lower the axle support jack. Undo the locknut and nut securing the lower end of the self-levelling unit to the axle bracket. Note that a dished washer is positioned above these retaining nuts.
6 Withdraw the self-levelling unit. Remove the metal spacing sleeves from the body and axle bracket rubber bushes.
7 Remove the rubber bushes from the body and axle mounting holes.
8 Refitting is the reverse of the removal procedure. When fitting the rubber bushes it may be found beneficial to lubricate them with a proprietary brand of rubber grease.

10 Watts linkage assembly – removal and refitting

1 Chock the front roadwheels, raise the rear of the car and support it on axle stands or strong packing blocks.
2 Remove the bolts and nyloc nuts securing the side links to the side brackets (photo).
3 Undo the central pivot nut, remove the plain washer and slide the complete assembly off (photo).
4 With the assembly removed from the car, check the condition of the pressed-in rubber bushes. Renew the bushes as necessary.

5 Refitting of the assembly is the reverse of the removal procedure.

11 Steering rack and pinion – removal and refitting

Note: *When dismantling or disconnecting any part of the power steering system it is very important to ensure that complete cleanliness is observed. Exposed ends of pipes, hoses or parts should be sealed in some way to prevent the ingress of foreign matter. Do not at any time start the engine until the fluid reservoir has been filled, otherwise the hydraulic pipe will be seriously damaged.*
1 Lift the bonnet and remove the air cleaner assembly as described in Chapter 3.
2 Apply the handbrake then raise the front of the car, and support it on blocks or axle stands placed beneath the bodyframe members. For convenience also remove the roadwheels.
3 With the wheels in the straight-ahead position, index mark the pinion shaft and the lower steering coupling to assist with alignment when refitting. (This is not necessary if the steering rack is to be renewed).
4 Remove the nuts from the tie-rod balljoints on the steering arms.
5 Pull back the rubber boot on each balljoint then use a proprietary balljoint separator, or split wedges to separate the balljoint from the steering arm. If neither tool is available, strike opposite sides of the taper pin eye simultaneously with two club hammers.
6 Remove the nut and bolt securing the lower steering universal joint coupling to the rack pinion (photo).
7 Loosen the bolt and nut securing the universal joint coupling to the intermediate shaft.
8 Remove the bolt retaining the flexible pipe clip to the rack body.
9 Place a suitable receptacle under the steering rack valve housing. Disconnect the feed and return flexible hoses from the valve housing and allow the fluid to drain. **Note:** *do not re-use the fluid drained from the system.*
10 Position a jack under the engine sump. Place a flat block of wood on the lifting pad to spread the load and to prevent damaging the sump.
11 With the engine so supported, remove the engine mounting bolts and nyloc nuts.
12 Remove the two bolts securing the right-hand engine tie-rod to the subframe and lift the tie-rod away.
13 Raise the engine support jack to lift the engine clear of the rack.
14 Turn the right-hand front wheel to the full right-hand lock position.
15 Remove the four bolts, washers and nuts securing the steering rack to the subframe.

12.1 Steering tie-rod balljoint (right-hand side shown)

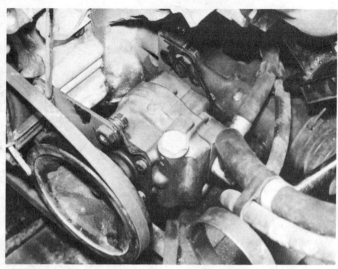

14.5 The power steering pump upper mounting bolts

16 Separate the lower coupling from the rack pinion shaft and manoeuvre the rack out of the right-hand wheel arch.

17 If the steering rack is worn or faulty then it is advisable to entrust the repairs to your local Rover dealer, or obtain a new or reconditioned unit.

18 Refitting is the reverse of the removal procedure. If a different rack is being fitted then it will be necessary to centralise it. To centralise the rack, remove the centre plug from the thrust pad. Locate the dimple in the rack shaft by passing stiff wire through the plug aperture. Move the pinion shaft as necessary to get the dimple in the centre of the aperture. Fit a bolt in place of the centre plug and lightly tighten it to hold the rack in the centred position.

19 After installation, refit the damper plug, fill and bleed the hydraulic system as described in Section 18. The front wheel alignment will need checking and possibly adjusting. Refer to Section 13 for details.

12 Steering tie-rod balljoints and rack gaiters – removal and refitting

1 Carefully mark the position of the tie-rod outer balljoint locknut so that it can be re-installed in the same position and thus prevent upsetting the front wheel alignment. If new balljoints are to be installed, note the distance from the beginning of the tie-rod screw thread to the centre of the outer balljoint cap. This is because a replacement may differ slightly in dimension when compared with the original one (photo).

2 Slacken the outer balljoint locknut.

3 Detach the outer balljoint, as described in paragraphs 4 and 5, of Section 11.

4 Unscrew the balljoint and locknut from the tie-rod.

5 Remove the gaiter retaining clips and slide the gaiter off the tie-rod.

6 When installing, lubricate the inner balljoint with a general purpose grease and slide on the gaiter.

7 With the rack centralised, install the inboard clip on the gaiter.

8 Fit the outboard clip on the gaiter whilst checking that the steering can be moved from lock-to-lock without the gaiter being strained.

9 Fit the balljoint on the tie-rod. If the original position is not known, screw it on until the distance between centres of the balljoints is approximately 13.33 in (338 mm).

10 The remainder of the installation procedure is the reverse of that used when removing.

11 On completion, if there is any doubt about the balljoint(s) not being fitted in their original positions, the front wheel alignment must be checked – see Section 13.

13 Front wheel alignment – checking

1 In order to minimize tyre wear, and retain the correct steering and roadholding characteristics, it is essential that the front wheels are correctly aligned. Ideally, the alignment should be checked using special gauges. It is, therefore, recommended that the job is done by a Rover dealer. However, it is possible to do the check with a reasonable amount of accuracy if care is taken.

2 The front wheels are correctly aligned when they are turning inwards at the front by the specified amount; this is the toe-in. This measurement is made with the wheels in the straight-ahead position, with the steering rack in the mid-position of its travel, the ball centres of the tie-rod equal and the steering wheel centre spot horizontal.

3 It is important that the measurement is taken on a centre line drawn horizontally and parallel to the ground through the centre-line of the hub. The exact point should be in the centre of the sidewall of the tyre and not on the wheel rim which could be distorted and so give inaccurate readings.

4 The adjustment is effected by loosening the locknut on each tie-rod outer balljoint and also slackening the rubber gaiter clip holding it to the tie-rod, both tie-rods being turned equally until the adjustment is correct.

5 Camber, castor angles and king pin inclination are set in production and any variation from specified tolerances can only be due to collision damage, or wear in the suspension components, as there is no provision for adjustment.

14 Power steering pump – removal and refitting

1 Open the bonnet and remove the filler cap of the power steering reservoir.

2 Place a suitable receptable underneath the power steering pump; detach the inlet hose from the pump and drain the fluid.

3 After draining the fluid, seal the end of the hose to prevent the ingress of dirt and replace the reservoir cap.

4 Disconnect the outlet hose from the pump and seal its end to prevent the ingress of dirt.

5 Slacken and remove the adjustment and pivot nuts and bolts (photo).

6 Lift the drivebelt forward from the pulley and lift the pump away.

7 Refitting is the reverse of the removal procedure, but before installing the drivebelt carry out the initial bleeding operation as described in Section 18 paragraph 5 after refilling the hydraulic reservoir. The drivebelt adjustment procedure is described in Section 16 and the remainder of the bleeding operation is covered in Section 18 paragraph 7 to 9.

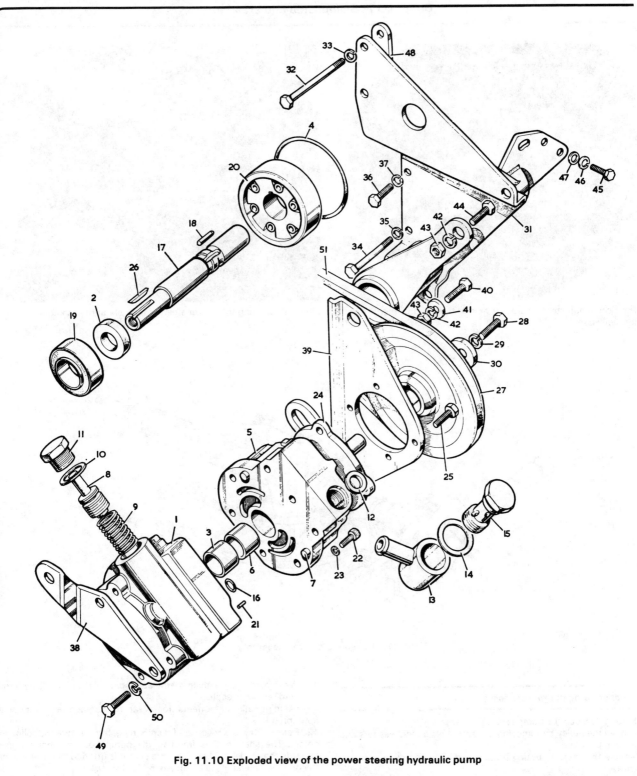

Fig. 11.10 Exploded view of the power steering hydraulic pump

1 Body	14 Fibre washer	26 Key	39 Mounting bracket
2 Oil seal	15 Banjo bolt	27 Pulley	40 Nut
3 Bush	16 O-ring	28 Bolt	41 Plain washer
4 O-ring	17 Shaft	29 Spring washer	42 Spring washer
5 End cover	18 Pin	30 Plain washer	43 Nut
6 Bush	19 Bearing	31 Pump mounting arm	44 Bolt
7 Dowel	20 Vane carrier and roller	32 Bolt	45 Bolt
8 Valve assembly	vane	33 Spring washer	46 Spring washer
9 Spring (flow control)	21 Cam lock peg	34 Mounting bracket	47 Washer
10 O-ring	22 Screw	35 Plain washer	48 Mounting bracket
11 Valve cap	23 Lock washer	36 Bolt	49 Bolt
12 Adaptor seal	24 End plate	37 Spring washer	50 Spring washer
13 Banjo	25 Screw and washer	38 Mounting bracket	51 Drive belt

16.8 The slotted adjuster link bracket viewed through the aperture in the underbelly panel

17.3 Withdrawing the power steering filter element assembly

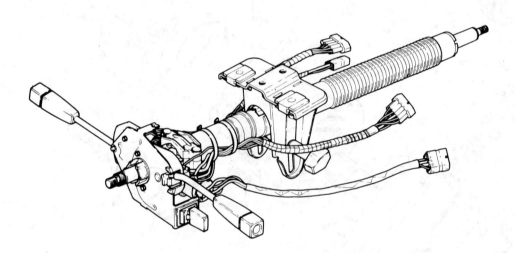

Fig. 11.11 Steering column assembly

15 Power steering pump – servicing

1   Thoroughly clean the pump exterior surfaces.
2   Remove the pulley by removing its centre bolt, spring washers and plain washers.
3   Remove the front mounting bracket and body end plate, also the rear bracket.
4   Secure the pump body in a vice and remove the adaptor screw, adaptor, fibre washer and rubber seal. Do not remove the venturi flow director which is pressed into the cover.
5   Remove the six Allen screws which secure the cover to the pump body and remove the pump from the vice, holding it vertically as the cover is removed so that the internal components do not fall out.
6   Remove the O-ring seals from the groove in the pump body and discard them.
7   Tilt the pump and extract the six rollers.
8   Draw the carrier off the shaft and remove the drive pin. Withdraw the shaft, the cam and the cam lock peg. If essential, remove the shaft key and draw off the sealed bearings.
9   Extract the shaft seal from the pump body and then withdraw the valve cap, valve and valve spring.

10 Wash all components in methylated spirit or clean pump hydraulic fluid and renew all seals.
11 Examine all components for wear or damage and renew as appropriate.
12 Reassembly is a reversal of dismantling, but observe the following points. The shaft seal is fitted to the pump body so that its lip is towards the carrier pocket. The vane carrier is fitted to the shaft so that the greater vane angle is as shown in Fig. 11.10.
13 Check the end-clearance of the carrier and rollers in the pump body using a straight edge and feeler gauges. If it is more than 0.002 in (0.05 mm) renew carrier and rollers.
14 Tighten the valve cap to the specified torque wrench setting.

16 Power steering pump drivebelt – removal, refitting and adjustment

1   Remove the fan belt as described in Chapter 2, Section 8.
2   Remove the three bolts and spring washers, securing the water pump pulley to the fan assembly.
3   Loosen the two bolts, retaining the timing pointer to the timing cover, and move the pointer to one side.

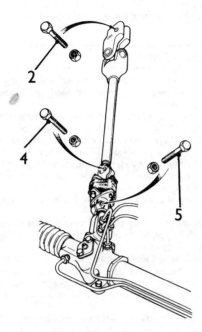

Fig. 11.12 Steering column intermediate shaft fixing detail

2 Nut and bolt securing intermediate shaft to steering column mast
4 Nut and bolt securing lower universal coupling to intermediate shaft
5 Nut and bolt securing lower universal coupling to steering rack pinion

4   Remove the single bolt and spring washer, retaining the transducer pick-up to the timing cover bracket, and move the transducer pick-up to one side.
5   Loosen the pivot and adjuster nuts and bolts. Tip the pump base inwards to release the belt tension.
6   Remove the belt.
7   Refitting of the drivebelt is basically the reverse of the removal procedure, but it will be necessary to adjust the drivebelt before tightening the pivot and adjuster nuts and bolts.
8   Check the deflection at a point midway between the crankshaft and pump pulleys, reaching the belt from underneath the car. The total deflection should be between 0.25 and 0.375 in (6.0 to 9.0 mm). Adjust by carefully levering the pump towards or away from the engine until the belt deflection is correct, then tighten the adjuster and pivot nuts and bolts (photo).

17 Power steering reservoir filter element – renewal

1   Rover recommend that the power steering reservoir filter be renewed at intervals of 20 000 miles (32 000 km) or where the steering rack or pump assemblies have been overhauled or renewed.
2   Unscrew the reservoir cap and remove the retaining bar, spring and filter from the reservoir.
3   Withdraw and discard the filter and reassemble using a new filter (photo).
4   After installation check the fluid level and top-up as necessary.

18 Power steering system – filling and bleeding

1   Turn the steering wheel so that the roadwheels are pointing in the straight-ahead position.
2   Before filling the fluid reservoir check the system completely to ensure that all the pipes, hoses and unions are satisfactory.
3   Fill the hydraulic reservoir with the recommended type of fluid (see Specifications) to a point 1 in (25 mm) below the base of the filler neck.
4   Loosen the pump adjuster/pivot bolts and nuts and relieve the

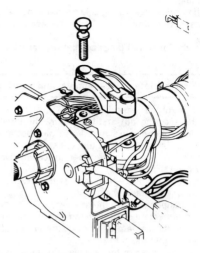

Fig. 11.13 Steering column lock clamp plate and shear head bolt

drivebelt tension.
5   Rotate the hydraulic pump pulley, by hand, several times in a clockwise direction to prime the system.
6   Re-tension the drivebelt as described in Section 16, recheck the fluid level and top-up as necessary.
7   Start the engine and whilst allowing it to idle, turn the steering wheel so that the roadwheels are deflected, from the straight-ahead position, to the full left-hand lock position. Return the roadwheels to the straight-ahead position and recheck the fluid level.
8   Repeat paragraph 7 but this time turn the steering to the right-hand lock position and then return it to the straight-ahead position. Recheck the fluid level and top-up as necessary.
9   Repeat paragraphs 7 and 8 until all air is expelled. Finally recheck and top-up the fluid level.

19 Steering wheel – removal and refitting

1   Turn the steering wheel until the roadwheels are pointing in the straight-ahead position.
2   Pull out the steering wheel trim pad and whilst grasping the rim of the steering wheel with one hand undo the central retaining nut and remove the plain washers.
3   Using Rover service tool 18G 1014, or a suitable puller, draw the steering wheel off the steering column taper. Do not, under any circumstances, attempt to drive or tap the steering wheel off the steering column as irreparable damage may result.
4   Lift the steering wheel off the steering column shaft.
5   Before installing the steering wheel check that the arrow on the trafficator cancelling collar aligns with the centre of the trafficator stock.
6   Refit the steering wheel, locating the two lugs on the wheel with the two slots in the cancelling collar.
7   Tighten the steering wheel retaining nut to the recommended torque setting and then refit the trim pad.

20 Steering column assembly – removal and refitting

1   Open the bonnet and disconnect the battery earth lead.
2   Remove the driver's side glovebox.
3   Remove the nut and bolt securing the upper universal coupling to the intermediate shaft.
4   Separate the four wiring multi-plug connectors.
5   Undo the two bolts, washers and nyloc nuts retaining the steering column mounting bracket to the body.
6   Pull the steering column away from the car.
7   Before refitting the steering column ensure that the roadwheels are in the straight-ahead position and the steering wheel centralised.

8   Engage the end of the steering column splines in the upper universal coupling.
9   Install and tighten the steering column clamp bolt and nut.
10 Lift the steering column up and refit the steering column bracket to body bolts.
11 Reconnect the four multi-plugs and battery earth lead.

21 Steering intermediate shaft – removal and refitting

1   Raise the front of the car and support it.
2   Remove the securing nut and bolt where the intermediate shaft joins the steering column mast. In order to gain better access to this nut and bolt, it may be necessary to turn the steering wheel.
3   From within the car lift the steering column inner shaft by approximately $\frac{1}{2}$ in (12.7 mm).
4   Remove the nut and bolt which secures the lower universal coupling to the steering rack pinion shaft.
5   Slide the coupling and intermediate shaft downwards to disengage the intermediate shaft from the steering column inner shaft.
6   Separate the intermediate shaft from the universal coupling and withdraw the shaft from the car.
7   Refitting is the reverse of the removal procedure, but before starting reassembly ensure that the roadwheels are in the straight-ahead position.

22 Steering lock/ignition switch – removal and refitting

1   Withdraw the key from the switch and remove the nacelle halves (two screws).
2   Either remove the two shear-head screws securing the steering lock/ignition switch using a hammer and a small chisel, or centre-punch and drill them, then use a screw extractor.

3   Remove the plug-in connector to the ignition switch and then remove the steering lock.
4   Refitting is the reverse of the removal procedure.

23 Roadwheels and tyres

1   Whenever the roadwheels are removed it is a good idea to clean the insides to remove accumulations of mud and in the case of the front one, disc pad dust.
2   Check the condition of the wheel for rust and repaint if necessary.
3   Examine the wheel stud holes. If these are tending to become elongated or the dished recesses, in which the nuts seat, have worn or become overcompressed, then the wheel will have to be renewed.
4   With a roadwheel removed, pick out any embedded flints from the tread and check for splits in the sidewalls or damage to the tyre carcass generally.
5   Where the depth of tread pattern is 1 mm or less, the tyre must be renewed.
6   Rotation of the roadwheels to even out wear is a worthwhile idea if the wheels have been balanced off the car. Include the spare wheel in the rotational pattern.
7   If the wheels have been balanced on the car then they cannot be moved round the car as the balance of the wheel, tyre and hub will be upset. In fact their exact stud fitting positions must be marked before removing a roadwheel so that it can be returned to its original 'in-balance' state.
8   It is recommended that wheels are re-balanced halfway through the life of the tyres to compensate for the loss of tread rubber due to wear.
9   Finally, always keep the tyres (including the spare) inflated to the recommended pressures and always refit the dust caps on the tyre valves. Tyre pressures are best checked first thing in the morning when the tyres are cold.

24 Fault diagnosis – suspension and steering

Symptom	Reason/s
Steering feels vague, car wanders and 'floats' at speed	Tyre pressures even Dampers worn Steering gear balljoints badly worn Steering mechanism free play excessive Front rear suspension pick-up points out of alignment
Stiff and heavy steering	Tyre pressures too low No grease in steering gear Front wheel toe-in incorrect Steering gear incorrectly adjusted too tightly Steering column badly misaligned Power steering pump defective Power steering drivebelt slack or missing
Wheel wobble and vibration	Wheel nuts loose Front wheels and tyres out of balance Steering balljoints badly worn Hub bearings badly worn Steering gear free play excessive Front springs weak or broken

Chapter 12 Bodywork and fittings

For modifications, and information applicable to later models, see Supplement at end of manual

Contents

1 General description

The combined body and chassis underframe is made of steel fabrications which are welded together to form a 'monocoque' structure. Certain areas are reinforced to provide mounting points for the suspension, steering system, engine supports etc. Special pressure pads and beams are built into the doors and body structure to transmit any impact loads evenly; in fact the doors will open normally after the car has undergone the standard 30 mph ECE 12 barrier-impact test.

All Rover 3500 (SDI) models are manufactured with five doors, the fifth door taking the form of a one-piece rear tailgate. The rear tailgate is fitted with a Triplex heated window.

The front screen is of the Triplex Ten-Twenty laminated type and is bonded into position to carry a proportion of the body torsional stress. A great deal of development went into the design of this screen and a reduction of 99% in facial injuries is claimed owing to the thick interlayer laminate.

Not only is the body designed with safety in mind, but also fuel economy, performance and roominess were all prime considerations. The aerodynamically sound bodyshape was evolved from clay 'mock-up' models which underwent wind tunnel tests. Careful planning of the layout, and the positioning of the main mechanical components, helped to create the desired space to seat five passengers comfortably with an ample reserve for luggage, parcels etc. Where maximum load space is required the rear seat backrest can be folded down flat.

2 Maintenance – bodywork and underframe

The general condition of a vehicle's bodywork is the one thing that significantly affects its value. Maintenance is easy but needs to be regular. Neglect, particularly after minor damage, can lead quickly to further deterioration and costly repair bills. It is important also to keep watch on those parts of the vehicle not immediately visible, for instance the underside, inside all the wheel arches and the lower part of the engine compartment.

The basic maintenance routine for the bodywork is washing – preferably with a lot of water, from a hose. This will remove all the loose solids which may have stuck to the vehicle. It is important to flush these off in such a way as to prevent grit from scratching the finish. The wheel arches and underframe need washing in the same way to remove any accumulated mud which will retain moisture and tend to encourage rust. Paradoxically enough, the best time to clean the underframe and wheel arches is in wet weather when the mud is thoroughly wet and soft. In very wet weather the underframe is usually cleaned of large accumulations automatically and this is a good time for inspection.

Periodically, except on vehicles with a wax-based underbody protective coating, it is a good idea to have the whole of the underframe of the vehicle steam cleaned, engine compartment included, so that a thorough inspection can be carried out to see what minor repairs and renovations are necessary. Steam cleaning is available at many garages and is necessary for removal of the accumulation of oily grime which sometimes is allowed to become thick in certain areas. If steam cleaning facilities are not available, there are one or two excellent grease solvents available such as Holts Engine Cleaner or Holts Foambrite which can be brush applied. The dirt can then be simply hosed off. Note that these methods should not be used on vehicles with wax-based underbody protective coating or the coating will be removed. Such vehicles should be inspected annually, preferably just prior to winter, when the underbody should be washed down and any damage to the wax coating repaired using Holts Undershield. Ideally, a completely fresh coat should be applied. It would also be worth considering the use of such wax-based protection for injection into door panels, sills, box sections, etc, as an additional safeguard against rust damage where such protection is not provided by the vehicle manufacturer.

After washing paintwork, wipe off with a chamois leather to give an unspotted clear finish. A coat of clear protective wax polish, like the many excellent Turtle Wax polishes, will give added protection against chemical pollutants in the air. If the paintwork sheen has dulled or oxidised, use a cleaner/polisher combination such as Turtle Extra to restore the brilliance of the shine. This requires a little effort, but such dulling is usually caused because regular washing has been neglected. Care needs to be taken with metallic paintwork, as special non-abrasive cleaner/polisher is required to avoid damage to the finish. Always check that the door and ventilator opening drain holes and pipes are completely clear so that water can be drained out. Bright work should be treated in the same way as paint work. Windscreens and windows can be kept clear of the smeary film which often appears, by the use of a proprietary glass cleaner like Holts Mixra. Never use any form of wax or other body or chromium polish on glass.

3 Maintenance – upholstery and carpets

Mats and carpets should be brushed or vacuum cleaned regularly to keep them free of grit. If they are badly stained remove them from the vehicle for scrubbing or sponging and make quite sure they are dry before refitting. Seats and interior trim panels can be kept clean by wiping with a damp cloth and Turtle Wax Carisma. If they do become stained (which can be more apparent on light coloured upholstery) use a little liquid detergent and a soft nail brush to scour the grime out of the grain of the material. Do not forget to keep the headlining clean in the same way as the upholstery. When using liquid cleaners inside the vehicle do not over-wet the surfaces being cleaned. Excessive damp could get into the seams and padded interior causing stains, offensive odours or even rot. If the inside of the vehicle gets wet accidentally it is worthwhile taking some trouble to dry it out properly, particularly where carpets are involved. *Do not leave oil or electric heaters inside the vehicle for this purpose.*

4 Minor body damage – repair

The photographic sequences on pages 158 and 159 illustrate the operations detailed in the following sub-sections.
Note: *For more detailed information about bodywork repair, the Haynes Publishing Group publish a book by Lindsay Porter called The Car Bodywork Repair Manual. This incorporates information on such aspects as rust treatment, painting and glass fibre repairs, as well as details on more ambitious repairs involving welding and panel beating.*

Repair of minor scratches in bodywork

If the scratch is very superficial, and does not penetrate to the metal of the bodywork, repair is very simple. Lightly rub the area of the scratch with a paintwork renovator like Turtle Wax New Color Back, or a very fine cutting paste like Holts Body + Plus Rubbing Compound, to remove loose paint from the scratch and to clear the surrounding bodywork of wax polish. Rinse the area with clean water.

Apply touch-up paint, such as Holts Dupli-Color Color Touch or a paint film like Holts Autofilm, to the scratch using a fine paint brush; continue to apply fine layers of paint until the surface of the paint in the scratch is level with the surrounding paintwork. Allow the new paint at least two weeks to harden: then blend it into the surrounding paintwork by rubbing the scratch area with a paintwork renovator or a very fine cutting paste, such as Holts Body + Plus Rubbing Compound or Turtle Wax New Color Back. Finally, apply wax polish from one of the Turtle Wax range of wax polishes.

Where the scratch has penetrated right through to the metal of the bodywork, causing the metal to rust, a different repair technique is required. Remove any loose rust from the bottom of the scratch with a penknife, then apply rust inhibiting paint, such as Turtle Wax Rust Master, to prevent the formation of rust in the future. Using a rubber or nylon applicator fill the scratch with bodystopper paste like Holts Body + Plus Knifing Putty. If required, this paste can be mixed with cellulose thinners, such as Holts Body + Plus Cellulose Thinners, to provide a very thin paste which is ideal for filling narrow scratches. Before the stopper-paste in the scratch hardens, wrap a piece of smooth cotton rag around the top of a finger. Dip the finger in cellulose thinners, such as Holts Body + Plus Cellulose Thinners, and then quickly sweep it across the surface of the stopper-paste in the scratch; this will ensure that the surface of the stopper-paste is slightly hollowed. The scratch can now be painted over as described earlier in this Section.

Repair of dents in bodywork

When deep denting of the vehicle's bodywork has taken place, the first task is to pull the dent out, until the affected bodywork almost attains its original shape. There is little point in trying to restore the original shape completely, as the metal in the damaged area will have stretched on impact and cannot be reshaped fully to its original contour. It is better to bring the level of the dent up to a point which is about ⅛ in (3 mm) below the level of the surrounding bodywork. In cases where the dent is very shallow anyway, it is not worth trying to pull it out at all. If the underside of the dent is accessible, it can be hammered out gently from behind, using a mallet with a wooden or plastic head. Whilst doing this, hold a suitable block of wood firmly against the outside of the panel to absorb the impact from the hammer blows and thus prevent a large area of the bodywork from being 'belled-out'.

Should the dent be in a section of the bodywork which has a double skin or some other factor making it inaccessible from behind, a different technique is called for. Drill several small holes through the metal inside the area – particularly in the deeper section. Then screw long self-tapping screws into the holes just sufficiently for them to gain a good purchase in the metal. Now the dent can be pulled out by pulling on the protruding heads of the screws with a pair of pliers.

The next stage of the repair is the removal of the paint from the damaged area, and from an inch or so of the surrounding 'sound' bodywork. This is accomplished most easily by using a wire brush or abrasive pad on a power drill, although it can be done just as

effectively by hand using sheets of abrasive paper. To complete the preparation for filling, score the surface of the bare metal with a screwdriver or the tang of a file, or alternatively, drill small holes in the affected area. This will provide a really good 'key' for the filler paste.

To complete the repair see the Section on filling and re-spraying.

Repair of rust holes or gashes in bodywork

Remove all paint from the affected area and from an inch or so of the surrounding 'sound' bodywork, using an abrasive pad or a wire brush on a power drill. If these are not available a few sheets of abrasive paper will do the job just as effectively. With the paint removed you will be able to gauge the severity of the corrosion and therefore decide whether to renew the whole panel (if this is possible) or to repair the affected area. New body panels are not as expensive as most people think and it is often quicker and more satisfactory to fit a new panel than to attempt to repair large areas of corrosion.

Remove all fittings from the affected area except those which will act as a guide to the original shape of the damaged bodywork (eg headlamp shells etc). Then, using tin snips or a hacksaw blade, remove all loose metal and any other metal badly affected by corrosion. Hammer the edges of the hole inwards in order to create a slight depression for the filler paste.

Wire brush the affected area to remove the powdery rust from the surface of the remaining metal. Paint the affected area with rust inhibiting paint like Turtle Wax Rust Master; if the back of the rusted area is accessible treat this also.

Before filling can take place it will be necessary to block the hole in some way. This can be achieved by the use of aluminium or plastic mesh, or aluminium tape.

Aluminium or plastic mesh or glass fibre matting, such as the Holts Body + Plus Glass Fibre Matting, is probably the best material to use for a large hole. Cut a piece to the approximate size and shape of the hole to be filled, then position it in the hole so that its edges are below the level of the surrounding bodywork. It can be retained in position by several blobs of filler paste around its periphery.

Aluminium tape should be used for small or very narrow holes. Pull a piece off the roll and trim it to the approximate size and shape required, then pull off the backing paper (if used) and stick the tape over the hole; it can be overlapped if the thickness of one piece is insufficient. Burnish down the edges of the tape with the handle of a screwdriver or similar, to ensure that the tape is securely attached to the metal underneath.

Bodywork repairs – filling and re-spraying

Before using this Section, see the Sections on dent, deep scratch, rust holes and gash repairs.

Many types of bodyfiller are available, but generally speaking those proprietary kits which contain a tin of filler paste and a tube of resin hardener are best for this type of repair, like Holts Body + Plus or Holts No Mix which can be used directly from the tube. A wide, flexible plastic or nylon applicator will be found invaluable for imparting a smooth and well contoured finish to the surface of the filler.

Mix up a little filler on a clean piece of card or board – measure the hardener carefully (follow the maker's instructions on the pack) otherwise the filler will set too rapidly or too slowly. Alternatively, Holts No Mix can be used straight from the tube without mixing, but daylight is required to cure it. Using the applicator apply the filler paste to the prepared area; draw the applicator across the surface of the filler to achieve the correct contour and to level the filler surface. As soon as a contour that approximates to the correct one is achieved, stop working the paste – if you carry on too long the paste will become sticky and begin to 'pick up' on the applicator. Continue to add thin layers of filler paste at twenty-minute intervals until the level of the filler is just proud of the surrounding bodywork.

Once the filler has hardened, excess can be removed using a metal plane or file. From then on, progressively finer grades of abrasive paper should be used, starting with a 40 grade production paper and finishing with 400 grade wet-and-dry paper. Always wrap the abrasive paper around a flat rubber, cork, or wooden block – otherwise the surface of the filler will not be completely flat. During the smoothing of the filler surface the wet-and-dry paper should be periodically rinsed in water. This will ensure that a very smooth finish is imparted to the filler at the final stage.

At this stage the 'dent' should be surrounded by a ring of bare metal, which in turn should be encircled by the finely 'feathered' edge of the good paintwork. Rinse the repair area with clean water, until all of the dust produced by the rubbing-down operation has gone.

Spray the whole repair area with a light coat of primer, either Holts Body + Plus Grey or Red Oxide Primer – this will show up any imperfections in the surface of the filler. Repair these imperfections with fresh filler paste or bodystopper, and once more smooth the surface with abrasive paper. If bodystopper is used, it can be mixed with cellulose thinners to form a really thin paste which is ideal for filling small holes. Repeat this spray and repair procedure until you are satisfied that the surface of the filler, and the feathered edge of the paintwork are perfect. Clean the repair area with clean water and allow to dry fully.

The repair area is now ready for final spraying. Paint spraying must be carried out in a warm, dry, windless and dust free atmosphere. This condition can be created artificially if you have access to a large indoor working area, but if you are forced to work in the open, you will have to pick your day very carefully. If you are working indoors, dousing the floor in the work area with water will help to settle the dust which would otherwise be in the atmosphere. If the repair area is confined to one body panel, mask off the surrounding panels; this will help to minimise the effects of a slight mis-match in paint colours. Bodywork fittings (eg chrome strips, door handles etc) will also need to be masked off. Use genuine masking tape and several thicknesses of newspaper for the masking operations.

Before commencing to spray, agitate the aerosol can thoroughly, then spray a test area (an old tin, or similar) until the technique is mastered. Cover the repair area with a thick coat of primer; the thickness should be built up using several thin layers of paint rather than one thick one. Using 400 grade wet-and-dry paper, rub down the surface of the primer until it is really smooth. While doing this, the work area should be thoroughly doused with water, and the wet-and-dry paper periodically rinsed in water. Allow to dry before spraying on more paint.

Spray on the top coat using Holts Dupli-Color Autospray, again building up the thickness by using several thin layers of paint. Start spraying in the centre of the repair area and then work outwards, with a side-to-side motion, until the whole repair area and about 2 inches of the surrounding original paintwork is covered. Remove all masking material 10 to 15 minutes after spraying on the final coat of paint.

Allow the new paint at least two weeks to harden, then, using a paintwork renovator or a very fine cutting paste such as Turtle Wax New Color Back or Holts Body + Plus Rubbing Compound, blend the edges of the paint into the existing paintwork. Finally, apply wax polish.

Plastic components

With the use of more and more plastic body components by the vehicle manufacturers (eg bumpers, spoilers, and in some cases major body panels), rectification of more serious damage to such items has become a matter of either entrusting repair work to a specialist in this field, or renewing complete components. Repair of such damage by the DIY owner is not really feasible owing to the cost of the equipment and materials required for effecting such repairs. The basic technique involves making a groove along the line of the crack in the plastic using a rotary burr in a power drill. The damaged part is then welded back together by using a hot air gun to heat up and fuse a plastic filler rod into the groove. Any excess plastic is then removed and the area rubbed down to a smooth finish. It is important that a filler rod of the correct plastic is used, as body components can be made of a variety of different types (eg polycarbonate, ABS, polypropylene).

Damage of a less serious nature (abrasions, minor cracks etc) can be repaired by the DIY owner using a two-part epoxy filler repair material, like Holts Body + Plus or Holts No Mix which can be used directly from the tube. Once mixed in equal proportions (or applied direct from the tube in the case of Holts No Mix), this is used in similar fashion to the bodywork filler used on metal panels. The filler is usually cured in twenty to thirty minutes, ready for sanding and painting.

If the owner is renewing a complete component himself, or if he has repaired it with epoxy filler, he will be left with the problem of finding a suitable paint for finishing which is compatible with the type of plastic used. At one time the use of a universal paint was not possible owing to the complex range of plastics encountered in body component applications. Standard paints, generally speaking, will not bond to plastic or rubber satisfactorily, but Holts Professional Spraymatch paints to match any plastic or rubber finish can be obtained from dealers. However, it is now possible to obtain a plastic body parts finishing kit which consists of a pre-primer treatment, a primer and coloured top coat. Full instructions are normally supplied with a kit, but basically the method of use is to first apply the pre-primer to the component concerned and allow it to dry for up to 30 minutes. Then the primer is applied and left to dry for about an hour before finally applying the special coloured top coat. The result is a correctly coloured component where the paint will flex with the plastic or rubber, a property that standard paint does not normally possess.

5   Major body damage – repair

Where serious damage has ocurred or large areas need renewal due to neglect, it means certainly that completely new sections or panels will need welding in and this is best left to professionals. If the damage is due to impact it will also be necessary to completely check the alignment of the body shell structure. Due to the principle of construction the strength and shape of the whole can be affected by damage to a part. In such instances the services of a Rover agent with specialist checking jigs are essential. If a body is left misaligned it is first of all dangerous as the car will not handle properly and secondly uneven stresses will be imposed on the steering, engine and transmission, causing abnormal wear or complete failure. Tyre wear may also be excessive.

6   Bumpers – removal and refitting

Front bumper
1   Refer to Fig. 12.1 and undo the four nuts, spring washers and plain washers securing the rubber end caps to the brackets.
2   Lift away the rubber ends from the bumper and brackets.
3   Whilst supporting the bumper remove the two bolts, spring washers and plain washers securing it to the brackets.
4   Lift the bumper bar away.
5   Refitting is the reverse of the removal procedure.

Rear bumper
6   The rear bumper components are retained to corner brackets in a similar manner to the front bumper (see Fig. 12.2).
7   Removal and refitting are identical procedures to that described in paragraphs 1 to 5 above.

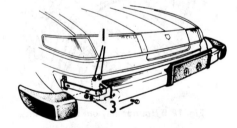

Fig. 12.1 Front bumper fixing detail

1   Nut and spring washer retaining rubber end cap
3   Bolt, spring washer and plain washer securing bumper to bracket

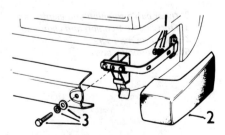

Fig. 12.2 Rear bumper fixing detail

1   Nut, spring washer and plain washer retaining rubber end cap
2   Rubber end cap
3   Bolt, spring washer and plain washer securing bumper to bracket

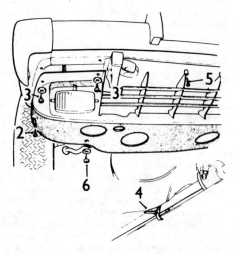

Fig. 12.3 Underbelly panel

2 *Side screw*
3 *Forward edge facing screws*
4 *Support straps*

5 *Centre fixing screw*
6 *Rear edge fixing screw*

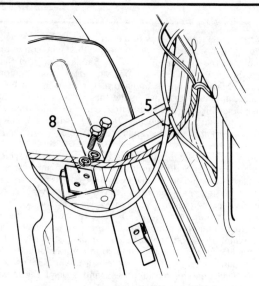

Fig. 12.4 Bonnet hinge detail (left-hand)

5 *Screenwasher 'T' piece*
8 *Hinge fixing screws and adjuster plate*

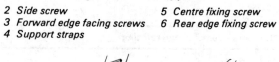

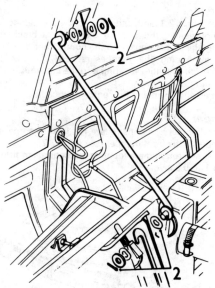

Fig. 12.5 Bonnet stay bar components

2 *washers and split pins*

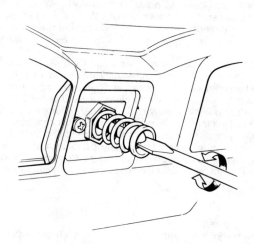

Fig. 12.6 Adjusting the bonnet catch

Fig. 12.7 Bonnet lock components

2 *Inner cable trunnion and clamp bolt*
3 *Outer cable trunnion and clamp bolt*
4 *Lock retaining screw*
5 *Lock retaining bolts*

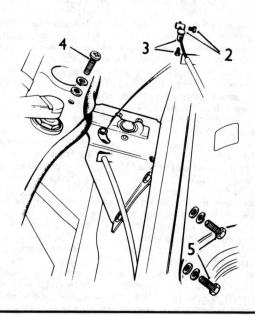

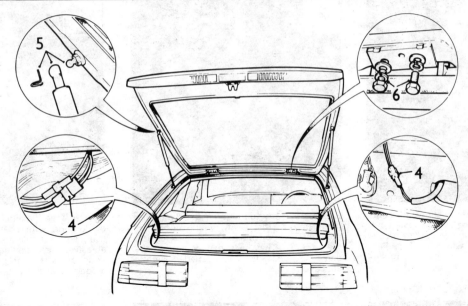

Fig. 12.8 Tailgate components

4 Harness plugs   *5 Support stay retaining clips*   *6 Tailgate to hinge bolts*

7 Underbelly panel – removal and refitting

1 Open the bonnet and locate the fog lamp wiring harness next to the rear of the headlamp unit. Disconnect the leads at the snap connectors.
2 Refer to Fig. 12.3 and remove the self-tapping screws from the locations shown at either side and the centre.
3 Lift the panel away.
4 Refitting is the reverse of the removal procedure, but ensure that the fog lamp cables are connected up as follows: black wire to black wire: blue/yellow wire to grey wire.

8 Bonnet – removal and refitting

1 Disconnect the battery earth lead.
2 Separate the two snap-connectors from the bonnet lamp leads, and the two wiring spade connectors at the bonnet lamp switch.
3 Pull the under-bonnet lamp wiring harness away from the retaining clips.
4 Separate the screenwasher hose at the 'T' piece.
5 With the help of an assistant to support the bonnet mark around the bonnet hinge positions with a pencil.
6 Remove the split pin and washers securing the stay bar to the bonnet.
7 Undo the four hinge retaining bolts and lift away the two adjuster plates securing the hinges to the body.
8 Lift off the bonnet.
9 Refitting is the reverse of the removal procedure, but after completion close the bonnet and check that it is correctly aligned. If necessary, loosen the hinge retaining bolts and adjust the bonnet position.

9 Bonnet catches and controls

Catch removal, refitting and adjustment

1 Support the bonnet in the open position then remove the two screws, spring washers and flat washers to release the catch.
2 Refitting is the reverse of the removal procedure.
3 If necessary, adjust the catch to give a positive locking action and to eliminate free movement, as described in the following paragraphs.
4 Pull back the spring and loosen the locknut on the adjuster bolt.
5 Rotate the screw in, or out, as necessary, then tighten the locknut and check the operation of the catch. Adjust further as necessary.

Bonnet lock removal and refitting

6 Remove the cable trunnion, then slacken the pinch bolt and remove the cable from the lock.
7 Remove the four bolts, single screw, spring washers and flat washers, then detach the lock.
8 Refitting is the reverse of the removal procedure.

Release cable removal and refitting

9 Initially proceed as described in paragraph 6. **Note**: *Do not close the bonnet with the release cable attached.*
10 Open the driver's side glovebox, unscrew the nut from the cable securing bracket beneath the facia, then withdraw the cable through the grommet in the bulkhead. Do not lose the nut and shakeproof washer.
11 Refitting is the reverse of the removal procedure, adjustment for satisfactory operation being made at the cable end.

10 Rear tailgate – removal and refitting

1 Disconnect the battery earth lead.
2 Open and support the tailgate.
3 Pull away the carpet from the body at the rear panel and disconnect the three wiring plug connectors (two on the left and one on the right).
4 Tie a length of string around the wiring plug connectors and pull each one through the door closing face aperture, together with its grommet. The length of string will facilitate guiding the looms through the aperture at a later stage.
5 With the tailgate open, release the retaining clips from the upper sockets on the support stays. Pull the support stays away from the ball pins.
6 Undo the four bolts securing the tailgate to the hinges and lift the tailgate away.
7 Refitting is the reverse of the removal procedure, but on completion check that the tailgate is correctly aligned with the body. Adjustment can be achieved by loosening the hinge bolts and moving the tailgate to correct any misalignment.

11 Rear tailgate hinges – renewal

1 Remove the tailgate as described in Section 10.

1

This photographic sequence shows the steps taken to repair the dent and paintwork damage shown above. In general, the procedure for repairing a hole will be similar; where there are substantial differences, the procedure is clearly described and shown in a separate photograph.

2

First remove any trim around the dent, then hammer out the dent where access is possible. This will minimise filling. Here, after the large dent has been hammered out, the damaged area is being made slightly concave.

3

Next, remove all paint from the damaged area by rubbing with coarse abrasive paper or using a power drill fitted with a wire brush or abrasive pad. 'Feather' the edge of the boundary with good paintwork using a finer grade of abrasive paper.

4

Where there are holes or other damage, the sheet metal should be cut away before proceeding further. The damaged area and any signs of rust should be treated with Turtle Wax Hi-Tech Rust Eater, which will also inhibit further rust formation.

5

For a large dent or hole mix Holts Body Plus Resin and Hardener according to the manufacturer's instructions and apply around the edge of the repair. Press Glass Fibre Matting over the repair area and leave for 20-30 minutes to harden. Then ...

5A

... brush more Holts Body Plus Resin and Hardener onto the matting and leave to harden. Repeat the sequence with two or three layers of matting, checking that the final layer is lower than the surrounding area. Apply Holts Body Plus Filler Paste as shown in Step 5B.

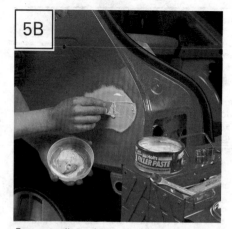

5B

For a medium dent, mix Holts Body Plus Filler Paste and Hardener according to the manufacturer's instructions and apply it with a flexible applicator. Apply thin layers of filler at 20-minute intervals, until the filler surface is slightly proud of the surrounding bodywork.

5C

For small dents and scratches use Holts No Mix Filler Paste straight from the tube. Apply it according to the instructions in thin layers, using the spatula provided. It will harden in minutes if applied outdoors and may then be used as its own knifing putty.

6

Use a plane or file for initial shaping. Then, using progressively finer grades of wet-and-dry paper, wrapped round a sanding block, and copious amounts of clean water, rub down the filler until glass smooth. 'Feather' the edges of adjoining paintwork.

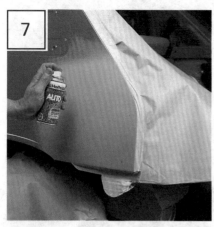

7

Protect adjoining areas before spraying the whole repair area and at least one inch of the surrounding sound paintwork with Holts Dupli-Color primer.

8

Fill any imperfections in the filler surface with a small amount of Holts Body Plus Knifing Putty. Using plenty of clean water, rub down the surface with a fine grade wet-and-dry paper – 400 grade is recommended – until it is really smooth.

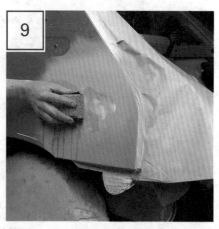

9

Carefully fill any remaining imperfections with knifing putty before applying the last coat of primer. Then rub down the surface with Holts Body Plus Rubbing Compound to ensure a really smooth surface.

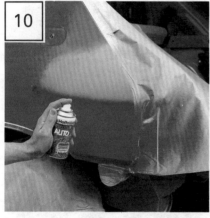

10

Protect surrounding areas from overspray before applying the topcoat in several thin layers. Agitate Holts Dupli-Color aerosol thoroughly. Start at the repair centre, spraying outwards with a side-to-side motion.

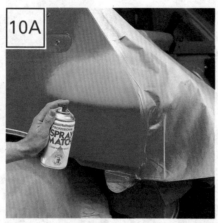

10A

If the exact colour is not available off the shelf, local Holts Professional Spraymatch Centres will custom fill an aerosol to match perfectly.

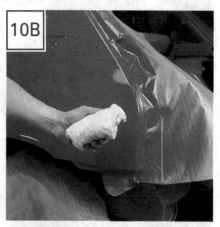

10B

To identify whether a lacquer finish is required, rub a painted unrepaired part of the body with wax and a clean cloth.

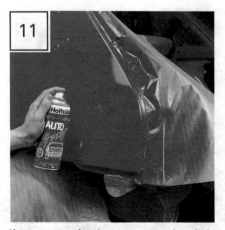

11

If *no* traces of paint appear on the cloth, spray Holts Dupli-Color clear lacquer over the repaired area to achieve the correct gloss level.

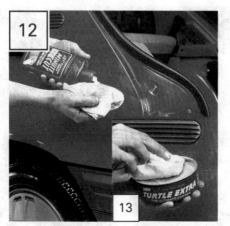

12

13

The paint will take about two weeks to harden fully. After this time it can be 'cut' with a mild cutting compound such as Turtle Wax Minute Cut prior to polishing with a final coating of Turtle Wax Extra.

14

When carrying out bodywork repairs, remember that the quality of the finished job is proportional to the time and effort expended.

12.3 The tailgate lock assembly

12.7 Lift the moulding away to gain access to the striker retaining bolts

14.3 Removing the window regulator handle retaining screw

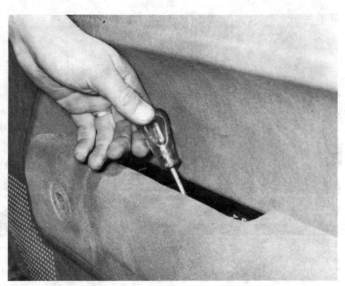

14.4 Removing the single screw from the upper part of the door pull

14.5 Removing the ashtray housing retaining screw

14.7 Lift away the door trim panel

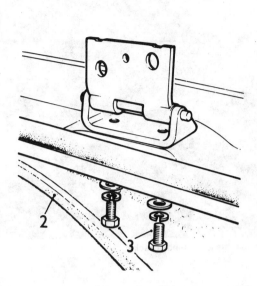

Fig. 12.9 Tailgate hinge

2 'Velcro' retaining strip
3 Bolts

2   Ease the rear edge of the headlining away from the 'Velcro' retaining strips.
3   Mark around the hinge with a pencil then remove the two retaining bolts, spring washers and plain washers.
4   Refitting is the reverse of the removal procedure. The door alignment can be adjusted by loosening the hinge retaining bolts, and moving the tailgate as necessary.

12 Rear tailgate lock and striker – removal, refitting and adjustment

Tailgate lock
1   Remove the four screws retaining the number plate lamps and the screws retaining the plastic moulding.
2   Pull the moulding away and detach the spade connectors at the rear of the number plate lamps.
3   From the recesses under the door remove the two long screws, spring washers and shakeproof washers which retain the lock (photo).
4   Withdraw the lock, after detaching the three wiring connectors inside the door on the right-hand side.
5   Refitting is the reverse of the removal procedure.

Tailgate lock striker
6   Remove the self-tapping screws which secure the luggage compartment right-hand sill moulding.
7   Lift the moulding away to gain access to the three bolts, plain and shakeproof washers which retain the stiker unit (photo).
8   Refitting is the reverse of the removal procedure, but before fully tightening the striker retaining screws, check that the latching operations and body alignment are satisfactory. Where adjustment is necessary, loosen the striker retaining screws and move the striker within the limits of the vertical slots. Temporarily tighten the screws and check the adjustment.
9   On completion secure the striker retaining screws.

13 Door rattles – tracing and rectification

1   The most common cause of door rattles is a misaligned, loose or worn striker plate, but other causes may be:

(a) Loose door handles, window winder handles or door hinges
(b) Loose, worn or misaligned door lock components
(c) Loose or worn remote control mechanism

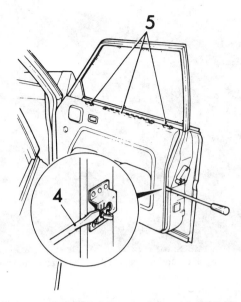

Fig. 12.10 Removal procedure for door trim panel

4 Releasing the spring retainer clips with a screwdriver
5 Window sill channel retainer

or a combination of these.
2   If the striker catch is worn, renew and adjust, as described later in this Chapter.
3   Should the hinges be badly worn then it may become necessary for new ones to be fitted.

14 Doors – removal and refitting

Front doors
1   Disconnect the battery earth lead.
2   Release the window regulator handle plastic cover which is clipped into position. Pivot the cover to one side in order to gain access to the retaining screw.
3   Remove the retaining screw and withdraw the regulator handle (with plastic cover) and bezel (photo).
4   Remove a single self-tapping screw from the upper part of the door pull moulding. On the driver's door this screw also retains the door lock switch protection ramp (photo).
5   Remove the ashtray as for normal emptying. Locate and remove the single screw securing the ashtray housing to the inner door panel (photo) and withdraw the housing.
6   The door trim panel is retained to the door frame by conventional spring clips along its sides and bottom. To release the clips insert a large flat blade screwdriver between the inner door panel and the trim pad. Position the blade over the spring clip retaining bridge as shown in Fig. 12.10 and prise out the clip. Repeat this operation for the remaining eight clips.
7   After releasing the nine spring clips, lift the trim panel up and off the window sill retaining channel (photo).
8   Carefully peel off the adhesive tape and protective sheet from the door panel.
9   Separate the wiring connectors which are located at the lower edge of the door.
10 If the passenger's door is being removed then it will be necessary to remove the radio speaker and rubber shroud. Two snap-connectors are provided to enable the speaker wires to be easily disconnected.
11 Support the door then remove the six nuts, spring washers, plain washers and the clamping plates from inside the door frame.
12 Now the door can be lifted away.
13 Refitting is the reverse of the removal procedure, but after 'hanging' the door check that it opens and closes satisfactorily and that it is also correctly aligned with the body shell. Adjustments can be made, if necessary, by loosening the hinge fixings and moving the

15.3 Window regulator and retaining bolts (one already removed)

16.2 Remove the lock steady bracket

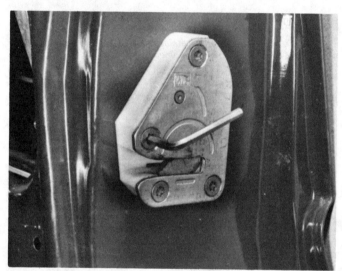

16.3 Use an Allen key to remove the latch torque screws

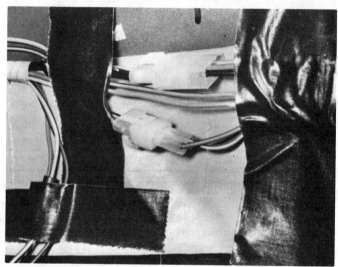

16.8 Separate the two wiring plug connectors

17.4 The rear door latch and control knob for childproof lock

door. Temporarily tighten the door fixings, after each adjustment, and make them secure when a satisfactory door fit is obtained.

Rear doors

14   The removal and refitting procedure for the rear doors is basically identical to that of the front doors (paragraphs 1 to 12). Points which refer specifically to either of the front doors should, however, be ignored.

15   Manual window regulator – removal and refitting

1   Wind the window glass fully upwards to the closed position then tape or wedge the glass in position.
2   Remove the door trim pad as described in Section 14, paragraphs 2 to 8. Ignore the details relating to other doors.
3   Remove the four bolts which secure the regulator unit to the door frame (photo).
4   Disengage the scissor linkage and lifting studs, from the horizontal glass support and the support plate channels, by sliding it forwards or backwards as necessary.
5   Withdraw the window regulator assembly through the large aperture in the door inner panel.
6   Refitting is the reverse of the removal operation.

16 Door lock (front doors) – removal and refitting

1 Remove the window regulator assembly as described in Section 15.
2 Remove the steady bracket retaining the lock to the inner door panel – two screws, plain and shakeproof washers (photo).
3 Using a Torx tool, remove the four screws retaining the outer latch assembly to the door shut face. Lift the latch assembly away (photo).
4 Disconnect the latch release and lock relay rods from the outer handle by releasing the retaining clips.
5 Release the interior lock control from the inner door panel by removing the two retaining screws, plain and shakeproof washers. Note that the coloured dot on the assembly is facing towards the front.
6 Withdraw the interior locking control through the large aperture in the door frame after disconnecting the release operating rod retaining clip.
7 Disconnect the forward end of the operating rod at the remote control release unit.
8 At the lower edge of the door separate the two wiring plug connectors (photo).
9 Withdraw the lock unit together with its four operating rods and solenoid wiring, through the large aperture in the inner door panel. The door exterior handle may be removed after unscrewing the two retaining nuts.
10 Refitting is the reverse of the removal procedure. When refitting the interior lock control ensure that the coloured dot is facing towards the front.

17 Door lock (rear doors) – removal and refitting

1 Wind the window glass upwards to the fully closed position then tape or wedge the glass in position.
2 Remove the door trim pad as described in Section 14, paragraphs 2 to 8. Ignore the details which relate to other doors.
3 Remove the steady bracket retaining the lock to the inner door panel. The steady bracket is held in position by two screws, plain washers and shakeproof washers.
4 Using a Torx tool, remove the four screws retaining the latch assembly to the door shut face. Lift the latch assembly away (photo).
5 Carefully pull the rubber moulding out of the rear channel and hold it back out of the way using a strip of sticky tape.
6 Remove the door rear cheater channel, located at the rear edge of the door frame. This is retained from inside the car by a screw and a bolt, spring washer and plain washer, and a bracket.
7 Release the operating rod from the outside door handle by removing the retainer clip.
8 Release the interior lock control from the interior door panel by removing the two retaining screws, plain and shakeproof washers. Note that the coloured dot on the assembly is facing towards the front.
9 Withdraw the interior lock control after disconnecting the clip and operating rod.
10 Disconnect the clip which retains the locking control rod to the lock lever. The control rod can be withdrawn from the aperture next to the lock.
11 Disconnect the operating rod at the remote control release, after removing the spring retainer clip.
12 At the door shut face, remove the children's safety lock knob, which is simply a screwed on fixture.
13 Pull out the wiring block connector. Remove the lock unit, together with the operating rods and attached wiring loom. The door exterior handle may be removed after unscrewing the two retaining nuts.
14 Refitting is the reverse of the removal procedure. When refitting the interior lock control, ensure that the coloured dot is facing towards the front.

18 Door lock striker (side doors) – removal, refitting and adjustment

1 Remove the two special Torx screws which secure the striker assembly to a tapped plate, located inside the door frame. An impact type screwdriver may be needed to undo these screws.

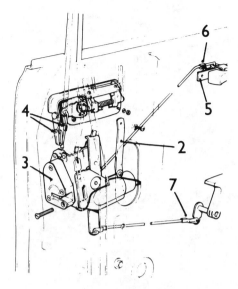

Fig. 12.11 Front door lock components

2 *Steady bracket*	5 *Interior lock control*
3 *Latch*	6 *Operating rod*
4 *Latch release and lock relay rods*	7 *Operating rod*

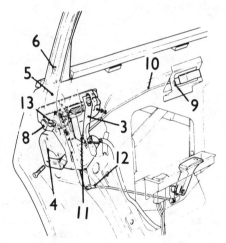

Fig. 12.12 The rear door lock assembly

3 *Steady bracket*	9 *Interior lock control*
4 *Latch*	10 *Operating rod*
5 *Rubber mounting*	11 *Locking control rod*
6 *'Cheater' channel retaining screw*	12 *Operating rod clip*
8 *Latch release operating rod*	13 *Childrens safety lock*

2 Lift away the outer cover, rubber seal, striker plate, rubber gasket and backplate.
3 Refitting is the reverse of the removal procedure. Before fully tightening the Torx screws, check that the latching action and door alignment are correct. Where adjustments are necessary loosen the Torx screws and move the striker in the horizontal or vertical planes as necessary.
4 When correctly adjusted, it should be possible after closing the door, to press it in against its seals by a small amount. This measure ensures that the striker is not set in too far.
5 After correct adjustment has been made, it will be necessary to tighten the Torx screws using a similar method as used for their removal.

19 Lock remote control – removal and refitting

1 Wind up the window to its fully closed position.

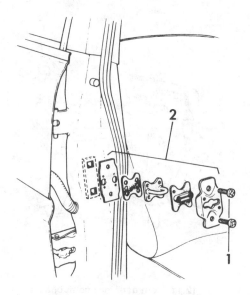

Fig. 12.13 Side door lock striker

1 Retaining screws
2 Striker components

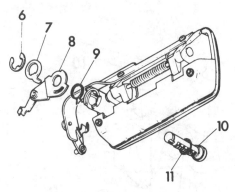

Fig. 12.15 Front door lock barrel and outer door handle

6 Circlip	*9 Indexing spring*
7 Indexing plate	*10 Lock barrel*
8 Lock operating lever	*11 O-ring*

19.7 The three screws which retain the remote control unit to the inner door panel

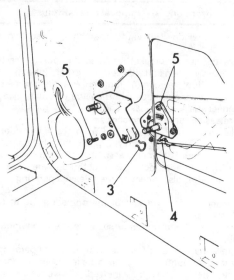

Fig. 12.14 Lock remote control assembly

3 Horseshoe retainer clip
4 Operating rod retaining clip
5 Remote control unit retaining screws

2   Remove the door trim pad as described in Section 14, paragraphs 2 to 8. Ignore any instructions referring to other doors.
3   Where work is being carried out on the driver's door, unplug the wiring plug connector at the locking control switch.
4   Remove the door pull which is retained by two bolts, plain and shakeproof washers.
5   Pull out the horse shoe shaped spring clip, retaining the remote control handle spindle, and withdraw the handle.
6   Disconnect the operating rod from the remote control release, by releasing the spring retainer clip (photo).
7   Remove the three screws with their plain and shakeproof washers which retain the remote control unit to the inner door panel. Withdraw the remote control unit through the large aperture in the door (photo).
8   Refitting is the reverse of the removal process, but in order to prevent tension or compression being exerted on the lock release mechanism it is advisable to tighten the remote control retaining screws, after refitting the operating rod.

20 Front door lock barrel – removal and refitting

1   Remove the window regulator unit as described in Section 15.
2   Remove the steady bracket, retaining the lock to the inner door panel (two screws, plain and shakeproof washers).
3   Remove the bolt, plain and shakeproof washers, which locate the bottom of the rear glass guide channel.
4   Pull the rubber moulding strip to one side and restrain it using a piece of sticky tape.
5   Withdraw the guide channel from the door.
6   Prise off the circlip at the rear of the outside handle. Access to the circlip can be gained by using the rectangular shaped hole in the door panel.
7   Withdraw the indexing plate, lock operating lever and release lock indexing spring in that order.
8   The lock barrel can now be pressed out, together with its rubber O-ring.
9   Refitting is the reverse of the removal procedure, but ensure that the rubber O-ring is located under the head of the lock barrel before inserting it.

21 Outer door handle (front door) – removal and refitting

1   Remove the window regulator unit as described in Section 15.
2   Remove the steady bracket retaining the lock to the inner door panel (two screws, plain and shakeproof washers).

3   Remove the bolt, plain and shakeproof washers which locate the bottom of the rear glass guide channel.
4   Pull the rubber moulding strip to one side and restrain it with a piece of sticky tape.
5   Withdraw the guide channel from the door.
6   Disconnect the latch release and lock operating rods from the outside door handle, after releasing the retaining clips.
7   Remove the two handle retaining nuts, plain and shakeproof washers, in order to release the inner clamping plate.
8   Withdraw the handle from the door, noting the gasket between the two parts.
9   Refitting is the reverse of the removal procedure.

22 Outer door handle (rear door) – removal and refitting

1   Remove the window regulator unit as described in Section 15.
2   Remove the steady bracket retaining the lock to the inner door panel (two screws, plain and shakeproof washers).
3   Locate and remove a screw at the rear edge of the door frame, which retains the upper cheater section of the rear glass guide channel.
4   Remove a bolt, plain and shakeproof washers, which locate the bottom of the rear glass guide channel.
5   Withdraw the glass guide channel from the door.
6   Disconnect the latch release operating rod from the door handle.
7   Remove the two handle retaining nut, plain and shakeproof washers, in order to release the inner clamping plate.
8   Withdraw the handle from the door noting the gasket positioned between the two components.
9   Refitting is the reverse of the removal procedure. When relocating the bolt, securing the bottom of the rear guide channel, it will be found necessary to use a pair of long-nosed pliers.

23 Centre console (manual transmission models) – removal and refitting

1   Disconnect the battery earth lead.
2   Apply the handbrake and pull off the handbrake lever grip.
3   Using a flat blade screwdriver, prise out the rear cover panel which is retained by four spigots.
4   At the front end of the assembly remove the two screws which secure it to the heater bracket.
5   Remove a further four screws which secure the console to the transmission tunnel. The exact location of these screws is shown in Fig. 12.16 at either end of the assembly.
6   Carefully prise out the cigar lighter and housing from the console. Disconnect the single snap connector and pull off the two spade connectors from the cigar lighter.
7   Unscrew and remove the gear lever knob.
8   Lift up the choke control lever. Remove the spring clip retaining the choke inner cable to the control lever.
9   Raise the rear of the console and guide the choke cable through the console.
10 Pull off the two spade connectors from the choke warning light switch.
11 On models with electrically operated windows pull out the four harness plugs from the operating switches.
12 Lift the console up and withdraw it from the car.
13 Refitting is the reverse of the removal procedure.

24 Centre console (automatic transmission models) – removal and refitting

1   Disconnect the battery earth lead.
2   Using a small pin punch drive out the roll pin retaining the plastic selector lever sleeve.
3   Apply the handbrake and pull off the handbrake lever grip.
4   Remove the two retaining screws and withdraw the selector lever shroud. The selector indicator panel can be lowered into the recess of the console.
5   Using a flat blade screwdriver prise out the rear cover panel, which is retained by four spigots.
6   At the forward end of the console remove the two screws which

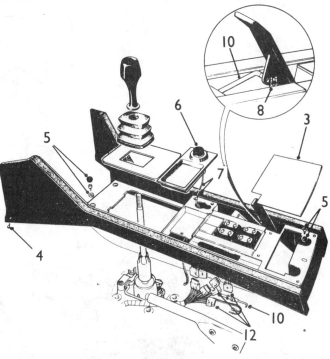

Fig. 12.16 Centre console (manual transmission models)

3   Rear cover panel
4   Console to heater bracket screw
5   Console to transmission tunnel screw
6   Cigar lighter
7   Wiring connectors – cigar

lighter
8   Fixing clip – choke cable
10 Choke control cable
12 Harness plugs (four shown are for electric windows)

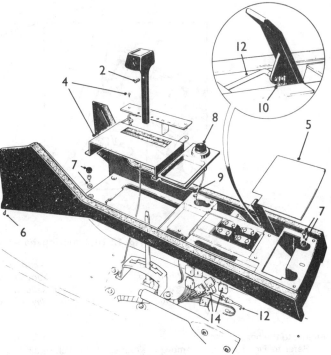

Fig. 12.17 Centre console (automatic transmission models)

2   Roll pin
4   Gear shift lever shroud
5   Rear cover panel
6   Console to heater bracket screw
7   Console to transmission tunnel screw

8   Cigar lighter
9   Wiring connectors – cigar lighter
10 Fixing clip – choke cable
12 Choke cable
14 Harness plugs (four shown are for electric windows)

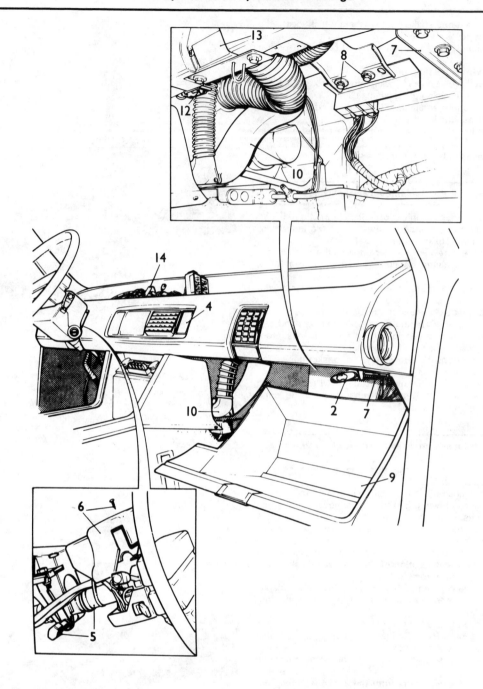

Fig. 12.18 Removing the fascia (left-hand drive model shown)

2	*Bonnet release control*	7	*Bolts securing fascia to*
5	*Steering column and*		*outer body brackets*
	column rake angle adjuster	8	*Bolts securing fascia*
6	*Nacelle half and retaining*		*and relay bracket to*
	screw		*bulkhead*

9	*Glovebox*
10	*Demister vent*
12	*Glovebox lamp*
13	*Map light*

14	*Wiring harness and*
	speedometer cable
	assembly

retain it to the heater bracket.

7   Refer to Fig. 12.17 and remove the four screws which retain the console to the transmission tunnel (two screws at either end).

8   Prise out the cigar lighter and housing. Disconnect the single snap connector and the two spade connectors. Lift the housing away from the console.

9   Raise the choke control lever and remove the clip retaining the choke inner cable.

10 Raise the rear of the console and guide the choke cable through the console.

11 Pull off the two spade connectors at the choke warning light

switch.

12 On models fitted with electrically operated windows pull out the four harness plugs at the operating switches.

13 Lift the console up and withdraw it from the car.

14 Refitting is the reverse of the removal procedure.

---

25 Glovebox – removal and refitting

1   Open the glovebox and disconnect the support straps from it.

2   Remove the two screws at the rear of the glovebox, which secure

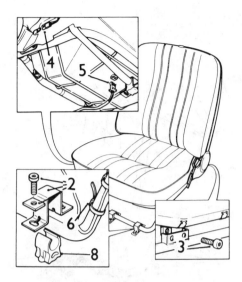

Fig. 12.19 Front seat fixings

2 *Screw and clamping plate*
3 *Screw cushion frame to seat runner bracket*
4 *Harness plug*

5 *Harness plug*
6 *Harness retaining clip*
8 *Bearing block*

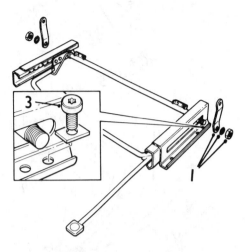

Fig. 12.20 Front seat runner assembly

1 *Seat belt bracket, washer and nut*
3 *Screw seat runner to floor*

it to the pivot brackets.
3   Lift the glovebox away after detaching it from the spigots on the pivot brackets.
4   Refitting is the reverse of the removal procedure.

26 Fascia – removal and refitting

1   Disconnect the battery earth lead.
2   Remove both the gloveboxes as described in Section 25.
3   Unscrew the nut securing the bonnet release cable to the bracket and detach the cable from the bracket.
4   Remove the instrument housing and the time clock as described in Chapter 10.
5   Remove the steering wheel as described in Chapter 11.
6   Remove the steering column upper nacelle, which is retained by a single screw.
7   Remove the six bolts and washers which secure the fascia to the outer body brackets (three bolts at either side of the car).
8   Remove two bolts and washers which secure both the fascia and the relay bracket to the bulkhead.
9   Pull the two demister vents away from the heater unit.
10   Disconnect the right-hand side vent hose from the demister vent and move it away from the steering column.
11   Disconnect the wiring connectors to each of the glovebox lamps, and the map light.
12   Lift the fascia away, and at the same time, guide the wiring harness and the speedometer cable through the apertures in the top part of the fascia.
13   Refitting is the reverse of the removal procedure.

27 Front seats and runners – removal and refitting

1   Release the seat belt brackets from their fixing studs at the seat runners.
2   Using a suitable size Torx tool or Rover service tool 18G 1256A, remove the screws, clamping plate and rectangular washers that secure the seat pivot tube to the floor panel.
3   Using either of the tools mentioned in paragraph 2, remove the two screws retaining the cushion frame to the bracket fitted to the seat runners.
4   Separate the wiring harness plug located between the seat and

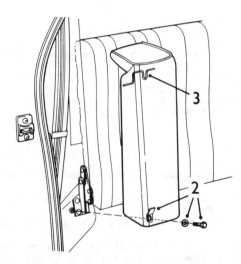

Fig. 12.21 Rear seat squab wing fixing

2 *Squab wing bracket, bolt and washer*
3 *Retainer*

the console.
5   Lift out the seat sufficiently to disconnect the harness plug from its underside.
6   Remove the two plastic straps which retain the harness to the seat frame.
7   The seat can now be lifted from the car.
8   To remove the seat runners simply remove the six screws and rectangular washers which secure the assembly to the floor.
9   Refitting is the reverse of the removal procedure.

28 Rear seat cushion, squab wings and squab – removal and refitting

1   The reat seat cushion is secured to the floor panel by two clips

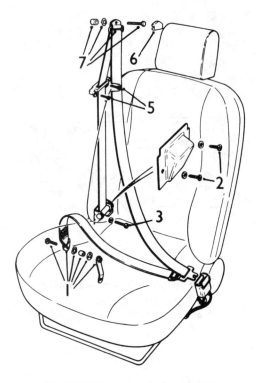

Fig. 12.22 Front seat belt assembly

1 *Swivel bracket, wavy washers, spacer, seat runner bracket and bolt*
2 *Reel cover plate screws*
3 *Reel retaining screw*
5 *Seat belt guide piece screws*
6 *Upper swivel bracket cover*
7 *Swivel bracket, bolt, wavy washer and spacer*

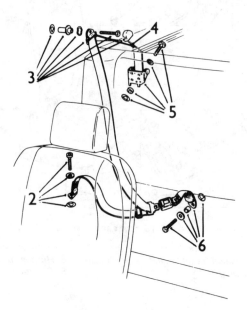

Fig. 12.23 Rear seat belt assembly

2 *Seat belt anchorage to floor*
3 *Swivel bracket components*
4 *Cut-out in rear parcel tray extension panel*
5 *Reel assembly*
6 *Floor mounted swivel bracket components*

beneath the forward edge. Release the cushion from these clips and lift it out.
2   Tilt the seat squab forward and remove the bolts and washers (one either side) which retain the squab wing brackets to the body frame.
3   Raise the squab wings sufficiently to disengage the retainers from the body bracket.
4   Having removed the left and right-hand squab wings remove the four bolts and washers (two either side), which secure the seat squab brackets to the body.
5   The seat squab can now be lifted away from the car.
6   Refitting is the reverse of the removal procedure.

29 Seat belt (front) – removal and refitting

1   Disconnect the swivel bracket from the bracket which is attached to the seat runner by removing the retaining bolt. Note the positions of the spacer, wave washers and plastic washer.
2   Pull the carpet away to expose the reel cover plate and remove the two cover plate retaining screws.
3   Lift the cover plate away. Remove the single screw and washer securing the reel assembly to the base of the 'B' post.
4   Remove the 'B' post lower trim panel (two screws), after prising off the five front and three rear carpet retainer clips.
5   Remove the two screws which secure the 'B' post seat belt guide piece.
6   Carefully prise off the plastic swivel bracket cover. Remove the bolt, wave washer and spacer securing the swivel bracket to the 'B' post.
7   Where necessary the seat belt switch can be removed as described in Chapter 10, Section 35.

30 Seat belt (rear) – removal and refitting

1   Remove the rear seat cushion as described in Section 28.
2   Remove the bolt, shakeproof washer, bracket, and plastic washer which anchor the seat belt to the floor panel.
3   Carefully prise off the plastic swivel bracket cover. Remove the bolt, swivel bracket, wave washer, spacer and plastic washer anchoring the seat belt to the 'D' post.
4   Guide the belt, and its attached brackets, through the cut out in the rear parcel tray extension panel.
5   Pull the carpet away to expose the reel assembly. Remove the screw and spring washer securing it to the body.
6   The remaining section of the seat belt is anchored to the floor panel by a bolt, swivel bracket, spacer and plastic washer.
7   Refitting is the reverse of the removal procedure.

31 Door glass (front) – removal and refitting

1   Remove the window regulator assembly as described in Section 15.
2   Release the interior sealing strip which is retained by five clips to the window sill.
3   Release the interior waist rail moulding, which is retained by four clips.
4   Remove the sticky tape or wedge, securing the glass to the door frame.
5   Withdraw the glass, by raising it and tilting it upwards, from the outside of the door. Take care when removing the glass as it is easily scratched if it comes into direct contact with the door frame.

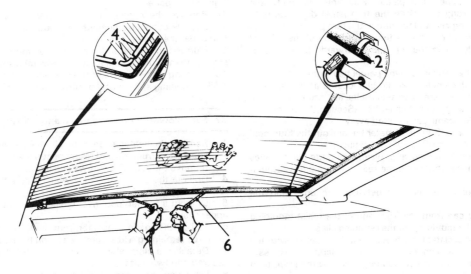

Fig. 12.24 Installing a heated rear window

2 *Wiring connector for heater element*
4 *Weatherstrip finisher*
6 *Draw-cord*

6   Refitting is the reverse of the removal procedure.

32 Door glass (rear) – removal and refitting

1   Remove the window regulator unit as described in Section 15.
2   Release the interior sealing strip, which is retained to the window sill by five clips.
3   Release the interior waist rail moulding, which is retained by four clips.
4   At the rear edge of the door frame, remove the screw which retains the upper cheater section of the rear glass guide channel.
5   Remove the locating bolt, plain and shakeproof washer from the bottom part of the rearmost glass guide channel.
6   Withdraw the guide channel, after pulling out and taping the rubber moulding to one side.
7   Remove the tape or wedge, securing the glass to the top door frame.
8   Withdraw the glass from the outside of the door by tilting the glass upwards at the front. Take care when carrying out this operation, because the glass can easily be scratched if allowed to come into contact with the door frame.
9   Refitting is the reverse of the removal procedure.

33 Windscreen – removal and fitting

The windscreen is retained in the aperture by a neoprene based material, which is supplied in round strip form. It contains a resistance wire core which is heated by electric current to cure the sealing strip after it is installed. Fitting of the windscreen requires special techniques and equipment. This should never be attempted by the do-it-yourself owner. This is definitely a job for the Rover dealer or a windscreen specialist.

34 Heated rear window – removal and refitting

1   Using a blunt tool, break the existing seal.
2   Disconnect the two wiring harness plugs at the rear window connection.
3   With help from an assistant, push out the glass taking care that it is not scratched.
4   Remove the weatherstrip and finishers from the glass.
5   When refitting, ensure that the edges of the glass and body

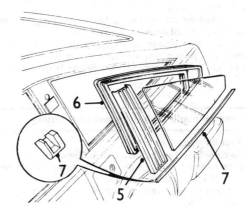

Fig. 12.25 Quarter light components

5 *'D' post capping*
6 *Weatherstrip*
7 *End cap and waist moulding*

aperture are clean and dry. Apply a metallic sealing compound to the glass channel, then fit the weatherstrip and finishers around the windscreen.
6   Insert a strong draw-cord into the weatherstrip inner channel, allowing the ends to protrude from the lower edge.
7   With an assistant holding the glass centrally in the aperture, apply steady pressure and pull the cord ends so that the lip of the weatherstrip is pulled over the body flange.
8   Seal the outer channel to the body flange using the mastic sealer.
9   Reconnect the two wiring harness plugs.

35 Quarter light glass – removal and refitting

1   Remove the appropriate seat squab wing as described in Section 28.
2   On cars fitted with rear seat belts, prise off the plastic swivel bracket cover. Remove the bolt, spring washer and spacer securing the

swivel bracket to the 'D' post.
3   Pull the 'D' post upper trim panel away from the body and disengage the upper fixing clip. Slide the trim panel downwards to disengage the lower fixing clip and to remove the trim panel.
4   Remove the screw which secures the forward end of the 'E' post trim panel to the body. Slide the trim panel forwards to release its lower fixing clip.
5   Lift out the parcel tray and loosen the parcel tray stops.
6   Carefully prise off the single retaining clip located at the rear end of the extension panel. Where rear seat belts are fitted it will be necessary to remove the appropriate seat belt (Section 30) before the rear parcel tray extension panel can be lifted away.
7   Using a drill with a $\frac{1}{8}$ in (3 mm) diameter bit, drill out the four 'pop' rivets retaining the front edge of the 'D' post capping.
8   Withdraw the 'D' post capping, after disengaging the two tongues on the rear edge, from the channel in the rear quarter light weatherstrip.
9   Using a blunt tool break the seal between the body and the weatherstrip.
10 Withdraw the end cap from the front end of the waist moulding and prise each end of the moulding off the retaining clips.
11 With the help of an assistant, push out the glass together with the weatherstrip and waist moulding, taking care not to scratch the glass.
12 Note the positions of the waist moulding and weatherstrip, then remove them from the glass.
13 When refitting, ensure that the edges of the glass and the body aperture are clean and dry. Apply a mastic sealing compound to the glass channel, and fit the weatherstrip to the glass. The waist moulding can now be slid into position, in the weatherstrip outer channel.
14 Insert a strong draw-cord into the weatherstrip inner channel, allowing the ends to protrude from the lower edge.
15 With an assistant holding the glass centrally in the aperture, apply steady pressure. Pull the cord ends so that the lip of the weatherstrip is pulled over the body flange.
16 Press the waist moulding down onto the retaining clips and refit the end cap to the forward edge of the moulding.
17 Refit the 'D' post capping by engaging the two tongues in the channel. Use a 'pop' rivet gun to relocate the front edge.
18 The remainder of the reassembly procedure is the reverse of the removal.

36 Heater and ventilation unit – removal and refitting

1   Disconnect the battery earth lead.
2   Drain the cooling system as described in Chapter 2.
3   Loosen the heater hose clips and pull the hoses off the bulkhead connections. Note their exact locations for refitting.
4   Remove the two heater rear fixing nuts, plain and spring washers as shown in Fig. 12.26.
5   From within the car, remove the screws retaining the triangular shaped air dust covers, located either side of the transmission tunnel. Note that these dust covers are fitted with their open side upwards, facing the front of the car.
6   Release the rectangular shaped air duct covers from each side of the transmission tunnel by pressing the centres of the special Rokut plastic rivets. Note that the vanes of these covers are inclined rearwards to deflect the air in the required direction.
7   Remove the centre console (Section 23 manual transmission models or Section 24 automatic transmission models). Remove the fascia panel as described in Section 26.
8   Remove the two large bolts, plain and spring washers from the heater support bracket which secures the lower side of the heater. When removed, these console front mounting brackets will also be released.
9   Loosen the two bolts, plain and shakeproof washers which secure the slotted heater bracket to the floor. This will enable the bracket to be released and lifted, with the heater, to clear the angle piece on the floor.
10 Remove the four bolts, plain and shakeproof washers which secure the glovebox mounting brackets and fibre optic master bulb unit. These are located at each side of the heater base plate. Remove the heater top fixing screw (12) Fig. 12.26.
11 Lift the heater in a rearwards direction allowing the fixing studs, at its rear, to clear the front bulkhead.
12 Disconnect the radio aerial from the radio.

13 Pull off the five wiring spade connectors from the heater control illumination panel.
14 Remove the heater motor end cover. Disconnect the red feed cable spade connector beneath the motor and the earth wire connection under the heater.
15 Plug the inlet and outlet water pipes to prevent the coolant from spilling, then lift the complete heater assembly away.
16 Refitting is the reverse of the removal procedure. After completion refill the cooling system as described in Chapter 2.

37 Fan (blower) motor – removal and refitting

1   Remove the heater as described in the previous Section.
2   Loosen the trunnion and disconnect the air intake control rod.
3   Remove the retaining screws and lift off the air inlet box.
4   Drill out the three 'pop' rivets which secure the upper casing to the lower casing.
5   Drill out a further 'pop' rivet which secures the pipe bracket to the upper casing.
6   Pull off the spade connector from the top of the motor and release the three remaining wires from the clip on the heater base.
7   Detach the clips which secure the two halves of the casing and separate the two parts.
8   Lift away the motor assembly and pull the rotor unit from the motor shaft.
9   Remove the rubber mounting strips carefully from the motor housing and locating tab.
10 When refitting the motor, apply adhesive to the rubber mounting strips, and stick them to the motor housing.
11 Press the rotor onto the motor shaft, exerting even pressure to prevent possible distortion. The rotor should be pressed on until $\frac{3}{16}$ (5 mm) of the shaft protrudes through the rotor hub.
12 Fit the motor assembly so that its locating tang is correctly positioned in the lower half of the heater casing.
13 Reposition the foam sealing strips. Lower the upper casing onto the lower casing, whilst ensuring that the flap pivot shafts are correctly relocated.
14 Secure the upper and lower casings together using the retaining clips. The locking sprags, of the retaining clips, locate under the thicker parts of the lower casing.
15 Secure the pipe bracket to the upper casing using a 'pop' rivet.
16 Fit three further 'pop' rivets to secure the upper casing to the lower casing.
17 Refit the air inlet box and reconnect the air inlet control rod. Ensure that the trunnion is positioned to permit full movement of the air intake control lever and flap.
18 Refit the heater unit as described in the previous Section.

38 Fan (blower) motor resistor unit – removal and refitting

1   Disconnect the battery earth lead.
2   Remove the fascia panel as described in Section 26.
3   Disconnect the wiring connection at the fan (blower) motor.
4   Remove the radio as described in Chapter 10.
5   Note the colours and positions of the wires connected to the blower switch. The switch is attached to the remote control lever assembly.
6   Push the edge of the spring clip, securing the resistor, into the heater casing and withdraw the resistor and spring clip.
7   Remove the spring clip from the resistor unit.
8   Refitting is the reverse of the removal procedure.

39 Heater matrix – removal and refitting

1   Remove the heater unit as described in Section 36.
2   Separate the upper and lower casings as described in Section 36, paragraphs 2 to 7.
3   Lift off the face level flap.
4   Lift the air blend flap upwards and disconnect the operating link from the lever.
5   Extract the thick packing seal from the matrix casing and withdraw the matrix by holding the pipe bracket and pipes. Push the pipes up through the heater casing.
6   Hold the pipes and pull the matrix off.

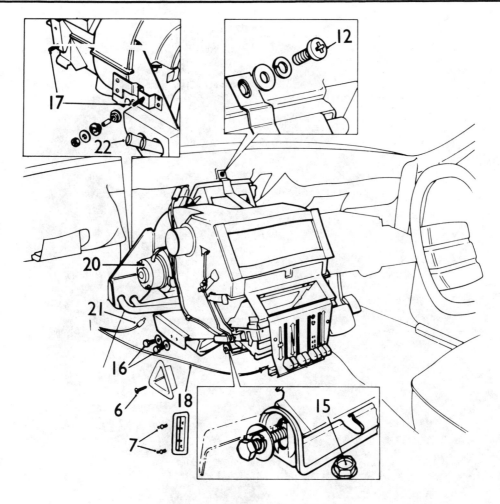

Fig. 12.26 Heater fixing detail

6 Triangular air duct fixing screw
7 'Rokut' plastic rivet for retaining rectangular air duct
12 Heater top fixing screw

15 bracket
Heater support bracket to floor bolt
16 Fibre optic lamp and glovebox

mounting bracket retaining bolts
17 Rear fixing studs
18 Radio aerial lead

20 Heater motor cover
21 Earth wire
22 Heater water pipes

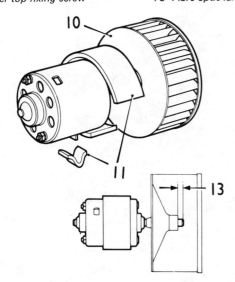

Fig. 12.27 Fan (blower) motor components and installation diagram

10 Rotor unit
11 Rubber mounting strips
13 Protrusion ($\frac{3}{16}$ in/5 mm) of shaft through rotor hub

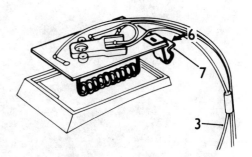

Fig. 12.28 Fan (blower) motor resistor unit

3 Wiring connector
6 Press spring clip at point arrowed to release the resistor unit
7 Spring retainer clip

7   Where a matrix is leaking, repair is best entrusted to a radiator repair specialist. Seldom does a do-it-yourself repair prove satisfactory.
8   Refitting is the reverse of the removal procedure. When fitting the matrix pipes always fit new pipe seals. Lubricate both the seals and pipes, with an antifreeze solution, to facilitate fitment.

Rover 3500 Vitesse

Chapter 13 Supplement:
Revisions and information on later models

Contents

1 Introduction

This Supplement contains information which is additional to, or a revision of, material in the first twelve Chapters. Although most of the material relates to additions to the various systems employed in this range of vehicles, some items apply retrospectively to the appropriate models from the start of production.

The Sections in the Supplement follow the same order as the Chapters to which they relate. The Specifications are all grouped together for convenience, but they follow Chapter order.

It is recommended that before any particular operation is undertaken, reference be made to the appropriate Section(s) of the Supplement. In this way any changes to procedure or components can be noted before referring to the main Chapters.

2 Specifications

The specifications below are supplementary to, or revisions of, those at the beginning of the preceding Chapters.

Engine (1982 on)
General
Compression ratio:

Vitesse and Vanden Plas EFI	9.75 : 1
US fuel injection models	8.15 : 1

Crankshaft and bearings

Main journal diameter	2.2996 to 2.3000 in (58.41 to 58.42 mm)
Main bearing diametrical clearance	0.0005 to 0.0022 in (0.013 to 0.056 mm)
Main and big-end bearing undersizes available	0.010 and 0.020 in (0.254 and 0.508 mm)

Valves

Valve stem diameter (exhaust)	0.3149 to 0.3405 in (8.00 to 8.65 mm)
Valve stem-to-guide clearance (exhaust)	0.0015 to 0.0031 in (0.038 to 0.079 mm)

Lubrication system

Oil pressure (hot, at 2400 rpm)	35 lbf/in² (2.5 kg/cm²) approx
Oil capacity:	
Drain and refill, sump only	8.5 pints (4.8 litres) approx
Drain and refill, including filter	9.7 pints (5.5 litres) approx
Oil filter type:	
SU carburettor models (1985 to 1986)	Champion C105
Fuel injection models (1982 to 1986)	Champion C105

Engine (all models)
Flywheel

Minimum thickness after refinishing	1.155 in (29.33 mm)

Cooling system (1982 on)
Thermostat
Opening temperature .... 190°F (88°C)

Fan belt adjustment .... 0.276 to 0.748 in (7.0 to 19.0 mm) deflection midway between pulleys under load of 10.0 lbf (4.5 kgf)

Fuel system – Zenith carburettors (1982 to 1984)
General
Make and type .... Twin Zenith 175 CDEF with fully automatic starting device (FASD)
Specification number 4027
Piston spring colour .... Blue
Jet size .... 0.100 in
Needle B1FB
Initial needle setting .... Shoulder flush with piston

Adjustment data
Idle speed .... 750 to 800 rpm
CO emission at idle .... 1.5 to 2.5%

Fuel system – SU carburettors (1985 on)
General
Make and type .... Twin SU HIF 44E with electronic fuel management
Piston spring colour .... Yellow
Jet size .... 0.100 in
Needle .... BFW
Air cleaner element .... Champion W185

Adjustment data
Idle speed .... 700 to 800 rpm
Fast idle speed .... 900 to 1000 rpm

Fuel system – fuel injection
General
System type .... Lucas 'L' electronically controlled fuel injection
Fuel pressure:
    UK models .... 26 to 36 lbf/in² (1.83 to 2.5 kgf/cm²)
    US models .... 36 lbf/in² (2.5 kgf/cm²)

Adjustment data
Idle speed:
    US models .... 750 to 900 rpm
    UK models .... 800 to 850 rpm
CO emission at idle:
    US models .... 0.3 to 0.7%
    UK models .... 1.5 to 2.5%

Torque wrench settings

	lbf ft	Nm
Air cleaner bracket to body	15	20
Air cleaner to bracket	7	10
Airflow meter to bracket	15	20
Cold start injector	7	10
Decel valve	8	11
Exhaust manifold sampling plug	20	27
Extra air valve	8	11
Injector clamp plates	8	11
Plenum chamber to inlet manifold	8	11
Potentiometer (throttle switch) to plenum chamber	8	11
Pressure regulator to inlet manifold	8	11
Pressure regulator to bracket	22	30

Ignition system
Distributor
Type:
    Except 1985 on carburettor and Vitesse models .... Lucas 35 DM 8
    1985 on carburettor and Vitesse models .... Lucas 35 DLM 8
Air gap .... 0.006 in (0.15 mm) minimum

Module
Type .... Lucas 32 C 5

Spark plugs (1982 on)
Type:
    Carburettor models .... Champion N9YCC or N9YC
    Fuel injection models .... Champion RN9YCC or RN9YC

Ignition timing
US models:
    Static or idle (vacuum disconnected) .... TDC
UK models:
    Carburettor models .... 6° BTDC at 600 rpm*
    Fuel injection models .... 8° BTDC at 600 rpm**
*With vacuum connected, or 2 to 6° BTDC at 1200 rpm with vacuum disconnected
**with vacuum connected, or 8 to 10° BTDC at 1000 rpm with vacuum disconnected

Manual gearbox (1982 on)
Ratios
5th	0.792 : 1
4th	1.000 : 1
3rd	1.396 : 1
2nd	2.087 : 1
1st	3.321 : 1
Reverse	3.428 : 1

Automatic transmission (1981 on)
Make and type .... Borg Warner 66 or GM 180

Fluid type
Borg Warner .... Type 'G' ATF to M2C 33F or M2C 33G (Duckhams Q-Matic)
GM 180 .... Dexron IID type ATF (Duckhams D-Matic)

Rear axle
Final drive ratio
Vitesse (manual and automatic) .... 2.85 : 1

Braking system (Vitesse and Vanden Plas EFI)
Front brakes
Disc type	Ventilated
Disc diameter (nominal)	10.16 in (258 mm)
Disc thickness (new)	0.94 in (23.8 mm)
Pad lining minimum thickness	0.12 in (3 mm)

Electrical system (1982 on)
Battery
Make	Chloride, Lucas or Unipart
Capacity (20-hour rate)	36 or 44 Ah

Alternator
Type	Lucas A133
Output at 6000 rpm	65 A
Rotor resistance at 68°F (20°C)	3.2 ohms ± 5%
Output voltage	13.6 to 14.4 V
Brush length:	
New	0.8 in (20 mm)
Minimum (protrusion from brush box)	0.4 in (10 mm)
Brush spring tension (brush face flush with brush box)	4.7 to 9.8 ozf (1.3 to 2.7 N)

Starter motor (August 1983 on)
Type	Lucas 9M90 pre-engaged
Minimum brush length	0.32 in (8.0 mm)

Fuse ratings (1982 on)
Main fusebox:
A1* (5 amp)	Side/tail number plate lamps and panel illumination
A2 (10 amp)	Front foglamps
A3 (3 amp)	Radio
A4 (7.5 amp)	Electric aerial
A5 (7.5 amp)	Rear foglamps
B1 (25 amp)	Heater blower motor
B2 (7.5 amp)	Blower motor control
B3 (10 amp)	Trip computer, electric mirrors, reversing lights, electric windows, gauges and warning lights
B4 (15 amp)	Windscreen wash/wipe
B5* (7.5 or 10 amp)	Direction indicators and stop-lamps
C1 (7.5 amp)	Air conditioning compressor clutch
C2 (10 amp)	Horns
C3 (20 amp)	Cigarette lighter(s), interior light, under-bonnet light, map light, clock
C4 (10 amp)	Hazard warning flasher
C5 (7.5 amp or as marked)	Spare or air conditioning condenser fans

Auxiliary fusebox:
No 1 (25 amp)	Heated rear window
No 2 (5 amp)	Luggage area light, reading light
No 3 (10 or 15 amp)	Rear wash/wipe

| No 4 (25 amp) .... | Sliding roof |
| No 5 (25 amp) or in-line (30 amp) .... | Central door locking system |

Increase rating to 10 amp (A1) and 15 amp (B5) when a towing socket is fitted

Bulbs
	Wattage
Interior lamp	5
Glovebox	5
Number plate lamp	5
Map light	10

Suspension and steering
Steering (1982 on)
Pump drivebelt tension	0.28 to 0.47 in (7 to 12 mm) deflection under 10 lbf (4.5 kgf) pressure
Steering geometry:	
Camber	0° 30' negative ± 1°
Castor	2° positive ± 1°
Kingpin inclination	11° 15' ± 1°

Wheels (1982 on)
Type	Cast alloy
Size:	
Vitesse and Vanden Plas EFI	6^1/2J x 15
Other models	6J x 14

Tyres (1982 on)
	Front	Rear
Size:		
6J x 14 wheels	195/70 HR 14	
6^1/2 x 15 wheels	205/60 VR 15	
Pressures in lbf/in² (kgf/cm²)	**Front**	**Rear**
195/70, normal load	26 (1.8)	26 (1.8)
195/70, full load	27 (1.9)	30 (2.1)
205/60, normal load	26 (1.8)	28 (2.0)
205/60, full load	28 (2.0)	30 (2.1)

Torque wrench settings
	lbf ft	Nm
Tie-rod locknuts	22	30

Bodywork and fittings
Torque wrench settings – air conditioning
	lbf ft	Nm
Condenser outlet	11 to 13	15 to 18
Condenser inlet	15 to 20	20 to 27
VIR inlet from condenser	11 to 13	15 to 18
VIR outlet to evaporator	15 to 20	20 to 27
VIR inlet from evaporator	28 to 33	38 to 45
VIR outlet to compressor	28 to 33	38 to 45
Evaporator inlet	28 to 33	38 to 45
Evaporator outlet	15 to 20	20 to 27
Compressor hose retaining plate	21	29
Pressure switch capillary union	6 to 9	8 to 12
VIR plug	5 to 7	7 to 10

Dimensions and weights
Dimensions
Overall length:	
Except Vitesse	185.0 in (4698 mm)
Vitesse	186.1 in (4728 mm)
Overall width (including mirrors)	78.5 in (1994 mm)
Overall height	54.5 in (1385 mm)
Wheelbase	110.8 in (2815 mm)
Track (front and rear) – all models	59.3 in (1506 mm)

Weights
Kerb weight:	
Vitesse (manual)	3820 lb (1488 kg)
Vitesse and Vanden Plas EFi (automatic)	3258 lb (1478 kg)
All other models	3214 lb (1458 kg)
Maximum towing weight	3360 lb (1524 kg)
Maximum roof rack load	110 lb (50 kg)

---

3 Routine maintenance

Maintenance intervals

1 The operations described for the 3000-mile maintenance schedule at the beginning of the manual have since been deemed necessary only at 6000-mile or six-monthly intervals. This applies to all models.

2 1982 and later models are supposed to require maintenance only annually or every 12 000 miles. The schedule incorporates the items in the old 3000-mile and 6000-mile schedules.

3 The DIY mechanic, who does not have to consider labour costs for maintenance tasks, may well prefer to continue using the old

Under bonnet view of a Rover 3500 Vitesse

1	Radiator filler plug	10	Crankcase ventilation flame trap	19	Power resistor unit
2	Headlamp washer filler	11	Cold start injector	20	Air cleaner
3	Headlamp washer jet	12	Fuel pressure regulator	21	Distributor
4	Battery	13	Throttle linkage	22	Bonnet light switch
5	Expansion tank filler cap	14	Idle speed adjustment screw	23	Radiator top hose
6	Windscreen washer reservoir	15	Fuel filter	24	Alternator
7	Brake hydraulic fluid reservoir	16	Dipstick (engine oil)		
8	Dipstick/filler tube (automatic transmission)	17	Engine oil filler cap		
9	Brake servo vacuum hose	18	Airflow meter		

maintenance intervals. This is particularly desirable with older or high-mileage vehicles.

Maintenance tasks (additional) – all models

4   The following maintenance tasks are additional to those specified at the beginning of the book. They apply to all models with the appropriate equipment.

5   These tasks are due every 12 000 miles (20 000 km) or annually:

(a)   *Check operation of brake fluid level warning switch*
(b)   *Check operation of brake pad wear warning system*
(c)   *Clean and lightly grease the roadwheel locating spigots*
(d)   *Lubricate the sliding roof mechanism*
(e)   *Inspect bodywork and paintwork for damage and corrosion*
(f)   *Check that underbody sealant or wax coating is intact*
(g)   *Check engagement of automatic transmission parking pawl*
(h)   *Check roadwheels for damage*
(i)   *Check suspension self-levelling units for leaks*
(j)   *Check antifreeze strength and adjust if necessary*
(k)   *Clean distributor cap and coil tower*

6   These tasks are due every 24 000 miles (40 000 km) or two years:

(a)   *Renew automatic transmission fluid and (on GM 180) renew the pick-up filter*
(b)   *Adjust automatic transmission brake band(s)*
(c)   *Renew air cleaner elements*
(d)   *Renew the spark plugs*
(e)   *Renew crankcase ventilation filter.*

7   The following task is due every 48 000 miles (80 000 km) or four years:

(a)   *Renew fuel filter (fuel injection models).*

8   Most of these tasks are self-explanatory, or are described in the appropriate Section of this Chapter.

9   To check the brake fluid level switch, withdraw the reservoir cap (ignition on) and check that the warning light illuminates.

10   To check the pad wear warning system, disconnect the plug at one caliper, join the terminals together and earth them. With the ignition on, the warning lamp should light.

4   Engine

Engine oil level – checking

1   The engine oil level is best checked when the engine is cold. If this is not possible, wait at least ten minutes after switching off.

2   Withdraw the dipstick, wipe it clean, re-insert it fully, remove it for the second time and read off the oil level. This should be between the 'high' and 'low' marks.

3   Top up if necessary by pouring in oil of the specified grade through the filler on the rocker cover.

Engine oil and filter – renewal

4   At the intervals specified in *'Routine Maintenance'*, drain the engine oil hot, immediately after a run. Unscrew the sump drain plug and catch the oil in a suitably sized container.

5   While the oil is draining, do not attempt to remove the oil filter, as this will cause the oil pump to drain and could cause lack of lubrication on re-starting.

6   Refit and tighten the sump drain plug, and fill the engine with the correct grade and quantity of oil.

7   Now the filter can be removed and discarded. An oil filter removal tool will probably be required to unscrew it.

8   Smear the rubber sealing ring of a new filter cartridge with engine oil and screw it into position using hand pressure only.

9   Start the engine, run for a few minutes and then check, and if necessary top up, the oil level as previously described.

Low oil level warning system – later models

10   From 1982, an electronically controlled low oil level warning system is fitted. Oil level is registered by a sensor which screws into the side of the sump (photo).

11   When the ignition is first switched on, the low oil level warning will light will flash up to three times by way of a bulb check. Should the light continue to flash, a low oil level is indicated and the driver should check the oil level in the traditional manner.

12   After the warning light has been flashing for between 10 and 20 seconds, it will extinguish until the next time the ignition is switched on. The system does not monitor the oil level in a running engine.

High oil pressure gauge reading – all models

13   On some models it is possible for indicated oil pressure to exceed the maximum marking on the gauge scale, especially when cold, and for the hot oil pressure to exceed the specified value. This is not in itself a fault.

14   The type of oil pressure gauge fitted to this engine is not necessarily accurate, and it may be that changing the oil pressure gauge sender will result in more moderate gauge readings.

Engine removal and refitting – fuel injection models

15   Removal of an engine equipped with fuel injection is essentially as described in Chapter 1 for carburettor models. The differences are largely self-evident, but the following points should be noted:

(a)   *Depresssurize the fuel system (Section 7) before disconnecting the battery*
(b)   *Disconnect the fuel pipe on the engine side of the filter. Plug both openings, taking great care to avoid the introduction of dirt*
(c)   *Disconnect and plug the return line from the fuel pressure regulator*
(d)   *Remove delicate items, such as the airflow meter and the plenum chamber, before attempting engine removal*
(e)   *Label wiring harness connectors when removing them if there is any possibility of subsequent confusion.*

16   On models with evaporative emission control, remember to label and disconnect the hoses running to and from the charcoal canisters.

17   On refitting, adjust the throttle linkage so that there is a small amount of slack when the pedal is released.

Other major operations – fuel injection models

18   The notes above concerning engine removal will apply, in whole or in part, to work undertaken with the engine *in situ*.

19   Details of removal and refitting procedures for the various components of the fuel injection system will be found in Section 7.

Crankshaft main bearing bolts – checking

20   The crankshaft main bearing bolts should be examined after removal for signs of touching the bottom of the holes in the crankcase. If evident, the bolts should be discarded, as it is possible for the bearing cap to be loose even with the bolts correctly torqued. The correct genuine bolts will have the letters 'BH' or 'UNC' stamped on their heads, and these alone should be used as replacements.

4.10 Oil level sensor on side of sump pan

5 Cooling system

Fan blades/viscous coupling (Vitesse and Vanden Plas EFI) – removal and refitting

1 Disconnect the battery earth lead.
2 Unscrew the central nut which secures the viscous coupling to the water pump spindle. This nut has a *left-hand thread*, ie it is undone in a clockwise direction. Release the nut and pull the viscous coupling off the water pump spindle.
3 Separate the fan blades from the viscous coupling by removing the bolts which hold them together.
4 Refitting is a reversal of the removal procedure.

Low coolant level warning system – description and testing

5 Most later models are equipped with a low coolant level warning system. Two sensors, one in the radiator and one in the expansion tank, are connected to a low coolant warning module situated inside the instrument housing. The module normally causes the low coolant warning lamp to illuminate for up to eight seconds when the ignition is first turned on, thus showing the driver that the lamp is working. Should the lamp remain on indefinitely, or come on whilst driving, the coolant level should be checked and topped up if necessary. *Take adequate precautions against scalding* if you wish to add coolant to a hot engine. **Do not** add cold water to a seriously overheated engine, or damage may result.
6 If the low coolant level warning system is suspected of giving false alarms, make sure first that the correct filling procedure has been adopted. Refer to Chapter 2, Section 4 for details, and note that a *full expansion tank does not guarantee a full cooling system.*
7 If the cooling system is known to be full, but the low level warning lamp remains on, the system may be tested as follows.
8 With the ignition off, disconnect the wires from the expansion tank sensor. Join the two wiring connectors together and earth them (connect them to the battery negative terminal or to engine metal) by means of a suitable test lead.
9 Switch on the ignition, observing the low coolant level warning light. The light should illuminate for a few seconds and then go out. If it remains on, either the low coolant warning module or the lead from the module to the expansion tank is defective. Access to the module is gained by removing the instrument housing top cover.
10 If the test just described is satisfactory, leave the ignition on and disconnect and separate the expansion tank sensor connectors. This action (producing an open-circuit at the sensor connection point) mimics a 'low level' signal and should cause the warning light to illuminate within eight seconds.
11 If the above test is satisfactory, proceed to the radiator level sensor. With the expansion tank sensor reconnected, repeat the earthing and open-circuit tests described in paragraphs 8 to 10. (There is only a single lead to the radiator sensor.) Similar results should be obtained, ie short-circuiting the lead to earth should give an 'OK' result, and producing an open-circuit should give a low level warning. Failure to obtain an 'OK' result means either that the lead from the expansion tank to the radiator sensor is defective, or that the expansion tank sensor is defective.
12 Assuming that all the above tests have had satisfactory results, if a false low level warning is obtained when the radiator sensor is reconnected, then that sensor is defective and must be renewed.
13 Always renew the grommet or seal at the same time when renewing a sensor.

Automatic transmission oil cooler – later models

14 On later models with automatic transmission it may be found that there is an oil cooler tank on each side of the radiator. The two tanks are connected in series.
15 Remember to disconnect and plug the oil cooler lines before attempting to remove the radiator (photo). Take care not to damage the pipe connecting the cooler tanks.

6 Fuel system – carburettors

Part A: Zenith carburettors

Description

1 Models from 1982 to 1984 may be fitted with Zenith/Stromberg/Solex 175 CDEF carburettors instead of the SU carburettors described in Chapter 3.
2 The Zenith carburettor operates in a fashion almost identical to the SU. The main difference is that a diaphragm separates the top cover and the carburettor body; the piston rises and falls by virtue of the flexibility of the diaphragm.
3 Cold starting is achieved with the aid of a unit known as a fully automatic starting device (FASD). This is effectively a small auxiliary carburettor which feeds extra mixture to the engine when it is cold. A very rich mixture is provided during cranking and in the first few seconds after a cold start; with increasing coolant temperature the mixture supply from the FASD is reduced, until at normal operating temperature it is shut off completely.
4 Other fuel system components are essentially the same as those described in Chapter 3, to which reference should be made.

Carburettor adjustments – general

5 Refer to Chapter 3, Section 8, and note the remarks made there.
6 If it is necessary to remove tamperproof plugs in the course of adjustment, satisfy yourself that you are not in breach of local, national or international regulations by so doing. Fit new tamperproof caps on completion where this is required by law. In some EEC countries (though not yet in the UK) it is an offence to drive a vehicle on the road whose tamperproof caps are missing.
7 To carry out idle speed, mixture and balance adjustments, the following equipment will be needed:

> (a) An accurate tachometer
> (b) A balancing device or flow meter
> (c) An exhaust gas analyser (CO meter) or equivalent mixture checking device
> (d) Special mixture setting tool No S 353.

8 Before commencing adjustment, remove the air intake elbows and the carburettor dampers. Raise each piston in turn and release it. The piston should rise and fall smoothly and hit the bridge with a distinct click – if not, overhaul is required. If the mixture is to be adjusted, both needles should first be set with their shoulders flush with the piston faces, using the mixture setting tool as described in paragraphs 18 and 19.

5.15 Automatic transmission oil cooler pipe union at radiator

Idle speed adjustment

9   Have the engine at normal operating temperature.

10 Disconnect the throttle interconnecting rod (Fig. 13.1).

11 Connect an independent tachometer to the engine. Start the engine.

12 Act on the throttle levers by hand and raise the engine speed to 2500 rpm. Hold this speed for 30 seconds, then allow the engine to idle. Repeat this procedure every three minutes when idle adjustments are being carried out.

13 Turn each idle speed adjuster equally to bring the idle speed within the specified limits.

14 Connect a balancing device or airflow meter in accordance with its maker's instructions. Act further on the idle speed adjusters until the carburettors are in balance and the idle speed is still within the specified limits.

15 Proceed to adjust the idle mixture if wished, then stop the engine and disconnect the test equipment. Reconnect the throttle interconnecting rod.

Idle mixture adjustment

16 Check the idle speed and carburettor balance as described above.

17 Connect the exhaust gas analyser to the vehicle in accordance with its maker's instructions. Measure the exhaust CO content and compare it with the value given in the Specifications. If adjustment is necessary, proceed as follows.

18 Remove the damper from each carburettor, and into one dashpot insert tool S 353. Engage the hexagon key on the tool in the needle adjuster, and the pin on the outer tool with the slot in the air valve.

19 Adjustment is made by rotating the hexagon key whilst holding the outer tool stationary. *If the air valve is not held still, the carburettor diaphragm may be damaged.* Rotate the key clockwise (viewed from above) to enrich the mixture, anti-clockwise to weaken.

20 Adjust each carburettor by an equal amount and in the same direction.

21 If a proprietary mixture checking device is being used, follow the maker's instructions.

22 When the CO emission is within limits, recheck the idle speed and adjust if necessary, then recheck the CO emission.

23 On completion, top up the carburettor dampers if necessary and refit the damper caps.

Carburettor(s) – removal and refitting

24 Disconnect the battery earth lead.

25 Remove the air cleaner assembly, as described in Chapter 3.

26 Remove the air intake adaptor(s), noting the fuel filter bracket secured to the left-hand adaptor.

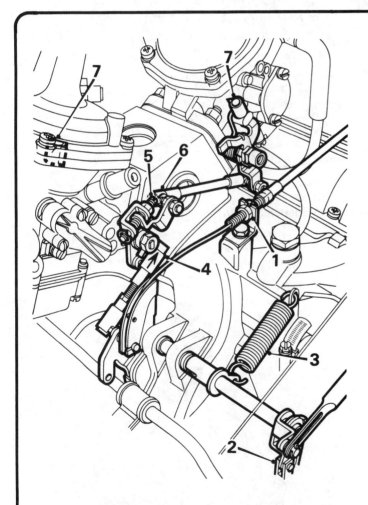

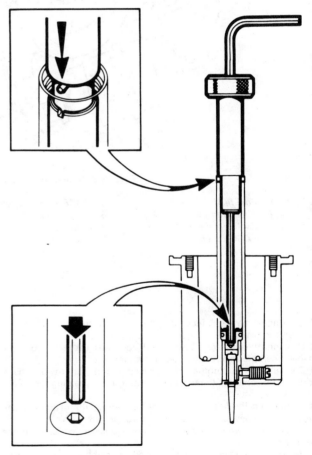

Fig. 13.1 Throttle linkage – Zenith carburettor (Sec 6A)

1 Cable adjuster	4 Operating rod
2 Downshift cable (automatic transmission)	5 Lever adjuster
	6 Interconnecting rod
3 Return spring	7 Idle speed adjusters

Fig. 13.2 Mixture adjusting tool (S 353) for Zenith carburettor – for details see text (Sec 6A)

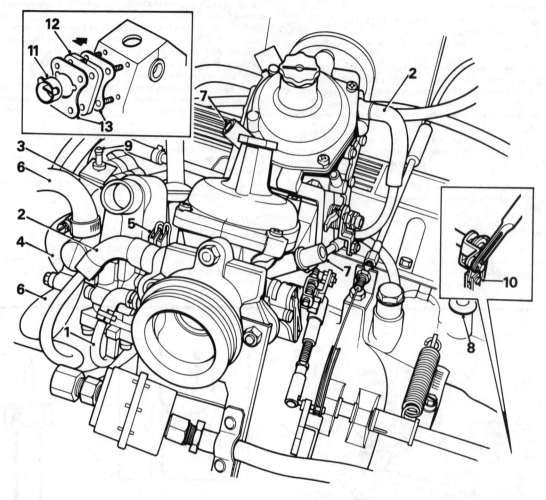

Fig. 13.3 Zenith twin carburettor installation (Sec 6A)

1	Fuel feed	5	FASD delay switch
2	Fuel overflow	6	FASD coolant hoses
3	FASD intake	7	Breathers
4	FASD outlet	8	Air cleaner peg

9	ATC peg	11	Intake liner
10	Kickdown linkage	12	Insulator
	(automatic transmission)	13	Gaskets

27 Disconnect the fuel feed and return hoses and plug them. Be prepared for some fuel spillage.

28 Disconnect the crankcase ventilation hose(s) and (on the left-hand carburettor) the distributor vacuum pipe.

29 Disconnect the throttle interconnecting rod. On the left-hand carburettor disconnect the throttle operating rod by sliding the sleeve outwards.

30 If removing the left-hand carburettor, remove the distributor cap and place it to one side. Unscrew the through-bolts which retain the FASD and delay switch to the carburettor and separate them from the carburettor.

31 Remove the retaining nuts and lift off the carburettor(s). Some of the retaining nuts are not easy to get at, and a short or sawn-off spanner may be useful.

32 Retrieve the intake liner, insulator and gaskets from the inlet manifold. Note that the arrow on the insulator points to the manifold.

33 Refitting is a reversal of removal. Synchronise the throttle levers by means of the throttle lever adjuster so that both throttles begin to open simultaneously when the slack in the cable is taken up. There must be some free play in the linkage when adjustment is complete.

34 Top up the carburettor dampers with clean engine oil (Fig. 13.4).

35 Check the idle speed and mixture and adjust if necessary.

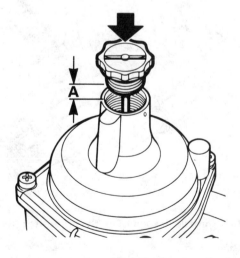

Fig. 13.4 Zenith carburettor damper – resistance should be felt at point A when cap (arrowed) is pressed down (Sec 6A)

A = 0.25 in (6.0 mm) approx

Carburettor – overhaul

36 With the carburettor removed from the vehicle, remove the damper cap with float chamber plug and empty out the oil and fuel.

37 Remove the four screws which secure the top cover. Note the alignment of the cover relative to the carburettor body, then remove the cover and the piston return spring.

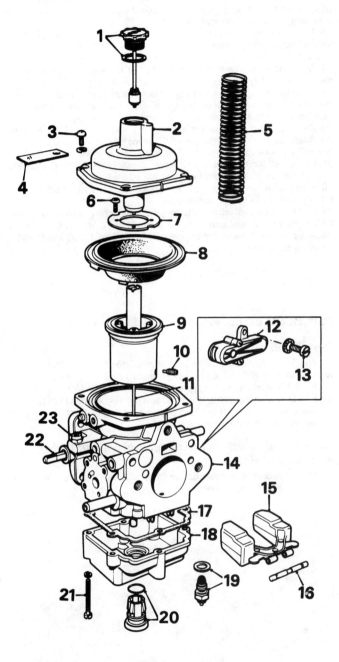

38 Lift out the piston complete with diaphragm. Take care not to damage the diaphragm if it is to be re-used.

39 Separate the diaphragm from the piston by removing the four retaining screws and taking off the retaining ring. Note the locating tabs on the diaphragm.

40 Slacken the grub screw which retains the needle, then insert mixture adjusting tool S 353 into the needle adjuster. Turn the needle adjuster three full turns anti-clockwise (viewed from the top of the piston) to release the needle. **Do not** attempt to remove the needle adjuster itself.

41 Undo the float chamber securing screws and remove the float chamber. Recover the gasket.

42 Withdraw the float pivot pin and remove the float.

43 Unscrew and remove the needle valve. Recover its washer.

44 Undo its securing screw and remove the temperature compensator unit. Extract the seal from the carburettor body.

45 Remove the throttle lever and its spring from the throttle spindle.

46 Undo the throttle disc securing screws – they may be tight – and remove the throttle disc. The throttle spindle can now be withdrawn.

47 Clean all parts (except the diaphragm) in solvent and blow them dry. Blow through jets and other orifices with compressed air. (If an air line is not available, a foot pump with a suitable adaptor may be used.)

48 Renew worn parts as necessary. The needle valve and the diaphragm should be renewed as a matter of course unless they are known to be in perfect condition.

49 Commence reassembly by fitting the throttle spindle and offering the throttle disc to it. (If there is a poppet valve in the disc, this should go at the bottom. The top edge of the disc goes towards the piston.) Fit the throttle disc retaining screws, but leave them loose.

50 Operate the throttle a few times so that the disc takes up its correct position, then tighten the retaining screws. Spread the ends of the screws to stop them coming undone.

51 Refit the throttle lever and its spring.

52 Fit a new seal into its housing, then refit and secure the temperature compensator unit.

53 Refit the needle valve and the float, then measure the float height as shown (Fig. 13.6). Adjust either by bending the float contact tab or by using a different thickness of washer under the needle valve seat. It is desirable that when adjustment is complete, the float contact tab and the needle valve are at right-angles.

54 Fit the needle to the piston. Use tool S 353 to turn the adjuster fully clockwise to raise the needle, then lower the needle until its shoulder is flush with the piston face.

55 Fit the diaphragm, engaging the locating tabs, and secure with the retaining ring and the screws.

56 Refit the piston assembly to the carburettor body.

57 Refit the spring, top cover and damper. Have the cover in correct alignment when refitting to avoid winding up the spring. Secure the cover with the retaining screws.

Fig. 13.5 Exploded view of Zenith carburettor (Sec 6A)

1	Piston damper and washer	13	Screw
2	Top cover	14	Body
3	Screw	15	Float
4	Identity tag	16	Pivot pin
5	Spring	17	Gasket
6	Screw	18	Float chamber
7	Retaining ring	19	Needle valve and washer
8	Diaphragm	20	Sealing plug and O-ring
9	Piston	21	Screw
10	Needle retaining screw	22	Throttle spindle
11	Needle	23	Idle speed adjusting screw
12	Temperature compensator		

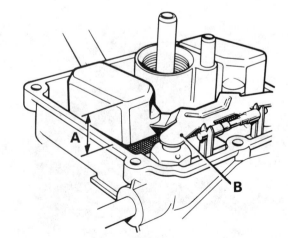

Fig. 13.6 Float setting diagram – Zenith carburettor (Sec 6A)

A = 0.63 to 0.67 in (16.0 to 17.0 mm)
B = Float contact tab

FASD – removal and refitting

58 Disconnect the battery earth lead.
59 Remove the air temperature control valve by disconnecting its hoses and lifting it off its locating pegs.
60 Disconnect the FASD air intake hose.
61 Disconnect and plug the fuel feed and return pipes from the left-hand carburettor. Be prepared for some fuel spillage.
62 Release any pressure in the cooling system by removing the expansion tank filler cap. Take precautions against scalding if the engine is hot.
63 Disconnect and plug the FASD coolant hoses. Be prepared for some coolant spillage.
64 Disconnect the wires from the delay switch.
65 Loosen the clip which secures the FASD outlet hose to the intake manifold adaptor.
66 Unclip the distributor cap and place it to one side.
67 Remove the through-bolts and withdraw the FASD and delay switch from the carburettor, freeing the outlet hose at the same time.
68 Refit in the reverse order to removal. Do not overtighten the FASD securing bolts, and remember to check the coolant level after the engine is next run.

FASD – fault finding and adjustment

69 Before looking for a fault in the FASD, make sure that all other engine systems are in good order and that the correct starting procedure is being followed.
70 It is possible for a fault in the FASD module (located behind the minor instruments) to stop the delay valve opening. In such a case the engine will start well from cold and will run well when hot, but in the intervening period will show symptoms of excessive richness (eg lumpiness and black exhaust smoke). This condition is confirmed if battery voltage is not present across the cables supplying the delay valve when the engine is running.
71 If starting and initial running are satisfactory, but the FASD seems to stay on too long, check that with the engine hot coolant is circulating past the FASD capsule.
72 Reluctance to start and run when cold may be due to fuel starvation. Remove the FASD adaptor (accessible after removing the float chamber cover) and check particularly that the non-return valve ball is not dislodged.
73 If the above points are all in order, but it is still felt that the FASD is not functioning correctly, adjustments may be attempted. To carry out adjustment it will be necessary to possess a means of determining when airflow through the FASD has ceased – a paper or cardboard disc with a hole in the centre may suffice – and a means of measuring accurately the temperature of the FASD water jacket. Temperature-sensitive labels are available from Rover dealers or carburettor specialists. If the reader can judge correctly a temperature of 65°C (150°F) with the hand, there will be no need for temperature-sensitive labels. One further item is required for adjustment, namely a 1.5 mm Allen key.
74 Remove the air intake hose from the FASD.
75 With the engine cold, remove the rubber plug from the end of the adjustment tube. Insert the Allen key into the tube, long end first, until it engages with the adjuster (photos).
76 If a temperature-sensitive label is being used, degrease the water jacket and attach the label so that it can be seen. Do not put it on the jacket flange, or inaccurate readings may result.
77 Start the engine and allow it to idle. (If the engine will not start, turn the Allen key two full turns clockwise and try again.)
78 With the engine idling and cold, place the airflow detector over the FASD air intake so that the passage of air holds it in place. Shield the cooling fan with a suitable piece of cardboard.
79 As soon as the water jacket temperature reaches 65°C (150°F), turn the Allen key clockwise until the FASD stops taking in air (indicated by the airflow detector falling off). *This must be done within 30 seconds of the desired temperature being reached;* otherwise, allow the engine to cool for not less than an hour and start again.
80 When adjustment is complete, remove the Allen key and refit the rubber plug. Refit the air intake hose.
81 If the above procedure fails to give satisfactory operation of the FASD, renewal would appear to be the only solution. No provision is made for overhaul. Note that the delay valve and the FASD itself can be renewed separately.

Part B: SU carburettors

Description

1   The 1985 3500 SE and Vanden Plas carburettor models are fitted with twin SU HIF 44 carburettors incorporating an electronically controlled fuel management system; the function of which is similar to the FASD unit on the Zenith carburettor. The computerised control unit for this system is located beneath the passenger glovebox. There is no choke control on these models.

Idling speed adjustment (later models without fuel management system)

2   The procedure is as described in Chapter 3, but the idle adjustment screws are fitted with tamperproof caps.

6A.75A FASD adjustment tube rubber plug

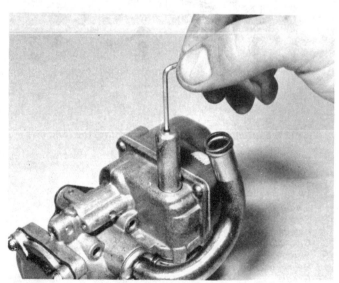

6A.75B Allen key in FASD adjuster

Idling speed and mixture adjustment (1985 models with fuel management system)

3 Run the engine to normal operating temperature. Remove the air cleaner.

4 Disconnect the coolant thermistor multi-plug and bridge the two terminals. Switch the ignition on, then off, to ensure that the mixture control is fully off.

5 Check that the throttle operates correctly and that the cable has 1.0 mm (0.04 in) free movement.

6 Disconnect the throttle interconnecting rod.

7 Unscrew the idle adjusting screws until they are just clear of the lever. Turn them clockwise until they are just touching the lever, and then give a further 1^1/2 turns.

8 Remove the suction chamber and withdraw the damper. Check that the needle guide is flush with the piston face. Turn the mixture adjusting screw to bring the jet flush with the bridge, and then turn the screw two turns clockwise.

9 Refit the suction chamber without the damper. Avoid winding up the piston spring, then lift the piston and check that it falls freely onto the bridge.

10 Top up the damper oil level and fit the damper.

11 Remove the bridge from the thermistor multi-plug and then connect the plug to the engine.

12 Start the engine, turn the idle speed screws equally until the engine is running at 1500 rpm. Make sure that the engine runs for a further five minutes at normal operating temperature.

13 It is essential that during the tuning operation, a clearance of 'B' is maintained between the fast idle screw and the stepper motor pin. Also, a clearance 'A' must be maintained at the lost motion link. Adjust the clearance if necessary by turning screw (2) (Fig. 13.7).

14 Adjust the idle speed screws on both carburettors by equal amounts in the same direction until the engine is running at the specified idle speed. When adjusting the idle speed, achieve the specified value by speed reduction, not increase. Do not allow the idle speed to fall more than 100 rpm below the specified value during the adjustment process, otherwise throttle jacking (anti-stall action by ECU) may occur. Should this happen, wait two minutes for conditions to stabilise before further adjustment.

15 Increase the engine speed to 2500 rpm for 30 seconds.

16 Using an air flow balance meter, check the synchronisation of the carburettors and adjust if necessary by turning the idle mixture screws.

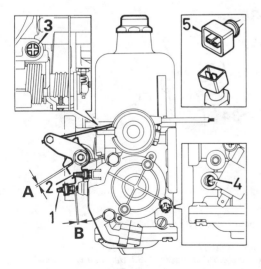

Fig. 13.7 SU carburettor adjustment screws – 1985 on models (Sec 6B)

1 Fast idle adjustment screw
2 Lost motion link adjustment
3 Idle speed screw
4 Mixture screw
5 Coolant thermistor multi-plug

A Lost motion link clearance – 0.07 ± 0.01 in (1.8 ± 0.25 mm)
B Fast idle lever clearance – not critical

17 Working on each carburettor in turn, first turn the mixture screw until the fastest engine idle speed is obtained. Turn the screw anti-clockwise until the speed just starts to fall, then clockwise again to just obtain the highest idle speed.

18 Re-adjust the idle speed screws so that the engine idle speed is as specified.

19 Using a suitable exhaust gas analyser, connected in accordance with the manufacturer's instructions, check the CO level. Where necessary, turn the mixture screws equally, in ^{1}/8th of a turn increments, to bring the CO level within the specified limits.

Carburettor (SU HIF 44E) – removal and refitting

20 Disconnect the battery and remove the air cleaner.

21 Disconnect the fuel and vacuum hoses, control cables and electrical leads. **Note:** On 1985 on Vanden Plas models fitted with the electronically controlled fuel management system and cruise control, the carburettor fuel shut-off solenoids, though fitted, are not operational. The solenoid wiring is taped to the harness and **must not** under any circumstances be connected to the solenoids.

22 Unscrew the fixing nuts and remove the carburettor.

23 Refitting is a reversal of removal, use new joint gaskets.

Carburettor (SU HIF 44E) – overhaul

24 With the carburettor removed from the car, clean away external dirt from the carburettor body.

25 Unscrew the damper and drain the oil.

26 Extract the screws and take off the suction chamber.

27 Lift the piston and extract the C-clip from the top of the piston rod. Remove the piston assembly and spring.

28 Remove the needle guide lock screw and withdraw the needle, guide and spring.

29 Unscrew the jet bearing nut and remove the bearing.

30 Remove the bottom cover plate and sealing ring, then the jet adjusting screw, spring and lever retaining screw. Withdraw the jet complete with adjusting lever. Disengage the lever.

31 Remove the float pivot pin, needle valve and seat.

32 Extract the screws and remove the fuel cut-off valve and solenoid.

33 Do not disturb the mixture control unit.

34 Disconnect the vacuum pipe and prise the vacuum unit from its bracket. Note the sealing washer on the shorter pipe.

35 If the throttle spindles are worn, it is not recommended that the spindles or valve plates are dismantled, but consideration should be given to the purchase of a new or reconditioned unit.

36 Obtain a repair kit which will contain all necessary renewable items.

37 Commence reassembly by locating the piston in the suction chamber, but without the damper and spring. Hold the assembly horizontally and spin the piston. It should spin freely without sticking.

38 If the mixture control unit or stepper motor are faulty, renew them. The stepper motor is of low voltage type – **do not** connect it to a 12V supply for testing.

39 Use a new seal when fitting the vacuum switch.

40 Fit the jet bearing nut and the jet assembly. Check that the jet head moves freely in the bi-metal cut-out.

41 Secure the adjusting lever so that the small diameter of the jet adjusting screw engages in the slot in the adjusting lever. Set the jet flush with the bridge of the body. Use a new sealing ring and refit the bottom cover in its original position.

42 Fit the needle using a new screw. The needle etch mark must align with the piston transfer holes, and the base of the guide must align with the base of the piston.

43 To prevent piston spring wind-up during assembly, temporarily refit the piston and suction chamber (without the spring) to the body. Mark their relative position to each other, then remove the suction chamber and fit the spring to the piston. Hold the suction chamber above the piston, align the marks previously made, and then lower the chamber over the spring and piston. Fit the C-clip to the top of the piston rod. Secure the suction chamber and then fit the damper.

44 Fit the fuel inlet needle valve and float assembly.

45 Invert the carburettor so that the weight of the float closes the needle valve. Check that the float setting is as shown in Fig. 13.10. If adjustment is required, bend the tab on the float arm.

46 Fit the float chamber cover with a new seal.

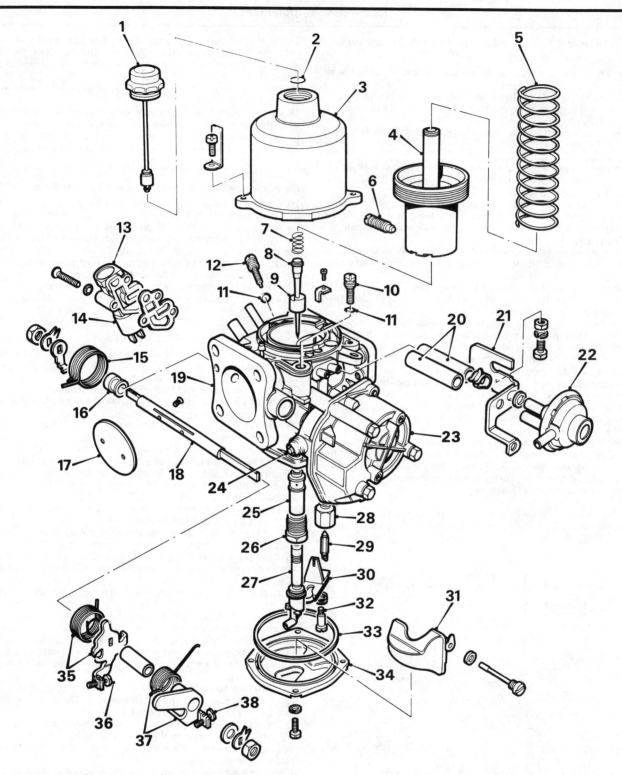

Fig. 13.8 Exploded view of SU HIF 44E carburettor (Sec 6B)

1 Damper	12 Mixture adjustment screw	22 Vacuum switch	31 Float
2 Circlip	13 Fuel cut-off valve	23 Mixture control stepper motor	32 Jet retaining screw
3 Suction chamber	14 Fuel cut-off valve solenoid		33 Float chamber cover seal
4 Piston	15 Throttle return spring	24 Fast idle pushrod	34 Float chamber cover
5 Spring	16 Seal	25 Jet bearing	35 Throttle lever and return spring
6 Needle retaining screw	17 Valve plate (butterfly)	26 Jet bearing nut	
7 Needle bias spring	18 Throttle spindle	27 Jet assembly	36 Fast idle adjusting screw
8 Jet needle	19 Carburettor body	28 Fuel inlet needle seat	37 Lost motion link and return spring
9 Needle guide	20 Pipe stubs	29 Fuel inlet needle	
10 Idle adjustment screw	21 Bracket	30 Bi-metal jet lever	38 Lost motion adjusting screw
11 Adjustment screw seal			

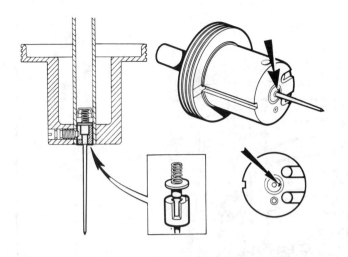

Fig. 13.9 Needle correctly set in piston (Sec 6B)

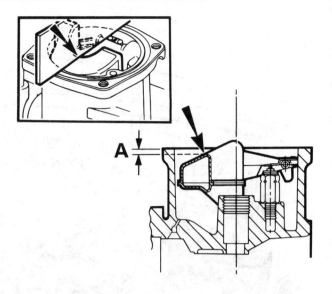

Fig. 13.10 SU carburettor float setting diagram (Sec 6B)

A = 0.039 to 0.059 in (1.0 to 1.5 mm)
Arrows indicate centre point of float

7 Fuel system – electronic fuel injection

General description

1   The electronic fuel injection (EFI) system fitted to certain models may for descriptive purposes be divided into two parts: the injection system itself, and the electronic control system.

2   Fuel is drawn from the tank by an electric pump located under the floor of the car. Filtered fuel under pressure is fed to the eight injectors via a pressure regulator. Excess fuel is returned from the pressure regulator to the fuel tank.

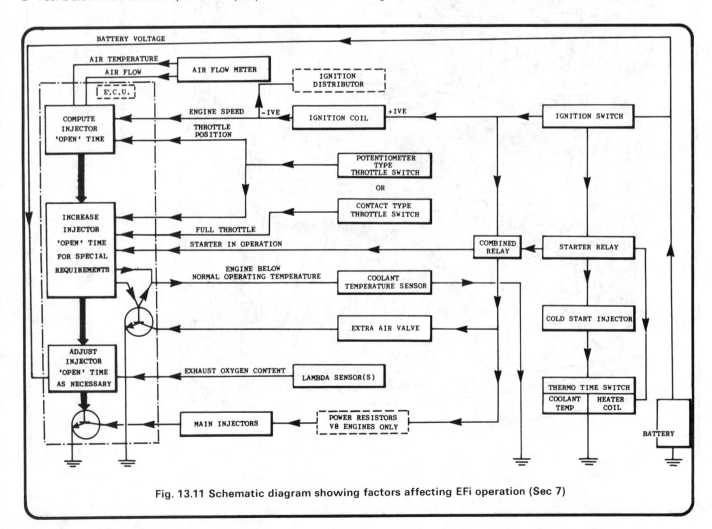

Fig. 13.11 Schematic diagram showing factors affecting EFi operation (Sec 7)

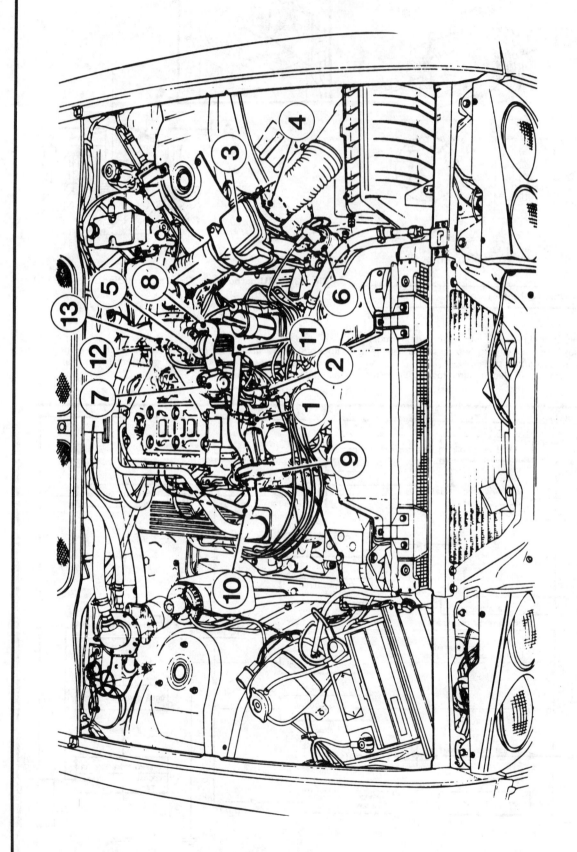

Fig. 13.12 Fuel injection system components – US models (Sec 7)

1 Coolant temperature sensor
2 Thermotime switch
3 Airflow meter
4 Air temperature sensor
5 Throttle switch
6 Ignition coil
7 Overrun valve
8 Pipe – overrun valve to constant depression region
9 Extra air valve
10 Pipe – plenum chamber to extra air valve
11 Pipe – extra air valve constant depression region
12 Throttle spindle
13 Throttle disc

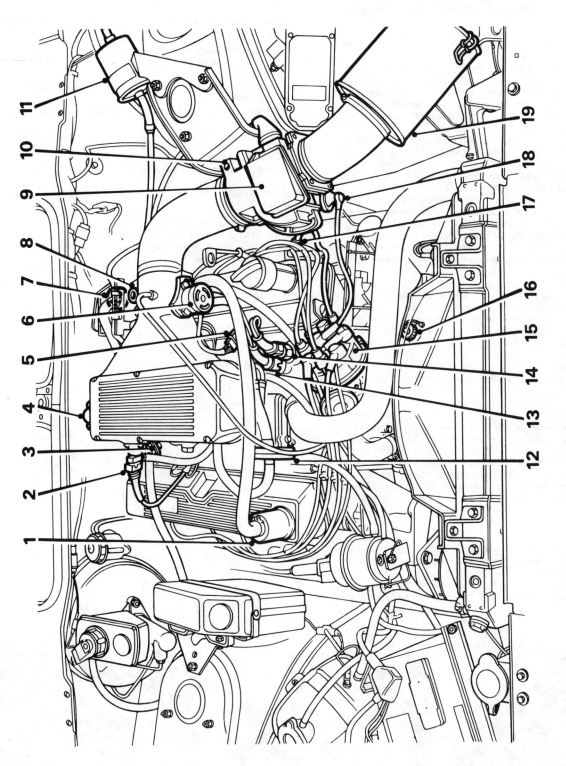

Fig. 13.13 Fuel injection system components – UK models (Sec 7)

1 Crankcase ventilation flame
   trap
2 Cold start injector
3 Fuel pressure regulator
4 Overrun valve

5 No 1 injector
6 Throttle switch
7 Crankcase ventilation
   breather filter
8 Idle speed adjusting screw

9 Airflow meter
10 Idle mixture adjustment
    screw
11 Fuel filter

12 Extra air valve
13 Coolant temperature sensor
14 Thermotime switch
15 Distributor

16 Diagnostic plug
17 No 1 HT lead
18 Ignition coil
19 Air cleaner

3   The injectors are opened electrically. Their state is either fully open or fully closed, the amount of fuel delivered being controlled by the time for which they are open. On the Rover V8 engine the injectors are controlled in two groups of four; the groups opening alternately. There is no direct relationship between any one injector and one cylinder, and thus no need for injection timing to relate directly to ignition timing or valve timing.

4   A separate cold start injector, controlled by a temperature-sensitive switch, supplies extra fuel for cold starting enrichment when the engine is cranking.

5   The control system must be considered to include the fuel pump. The pump is wired in such a way that it is only energised when the ignition is switched on and the engine is running, or when the starter motor is cranking. An inertia switch, in series with the pump, stops the pump operating in the event of an accident involving impact.

6   The injectors are controlled by an electronic control unit (ECU) which receives information relating to engine speed, airflow into the engine, throttle position and coolant temperature. Injector output is thus matched very closely to engine and driver requirements.

7   Engine speed information is supplied to the ECU in the form of pulses from the LT side of the ignition system.

8   Airflow into the engine is measured by the deflection of a flap in the airflow meter which alters the position of a potentiometer (variable resistance) to which it is connected. Because the mass as well as the volume of air is significant, the air temperature is also measured. A bypass channel, the size of which can be varied by an adjustment screw, allows fine adjustment of the quantity of air passing at idle speed.

9   Throttle position information is supplied to the ECU by a simple potentiometer, confusingly referred to as the throttle switch. The ECU can 'read' throttle position from the voltage at the potentiometer, and can determine the rate of change of throttle position by the rate of change of the voltage. A sudden 'foot down' signal will cause the ECU to pulse all the injectors once, so delivering extra fuel for acceleration.

10 The coolant temperature sensor is located between the cylinder heads. A 'cold' signal to the ECU causes the injection pulses to be lengthened slightly, and activates the heater element in the extra air valve.

11 The extra air valve opens, and so provides the additional air needed for smooth idling when the engine is cold. The valve is closed by increasing coolant temperature and by the heat generated by its own heater element, which is under the control of the ECU.

12 Models intended for territories with strict emission control regulations have a Lambda sensor in each exhaust pipe, upstream of the catalytic converter, to monitor the oxygen content of the exhaust gas. These sensors provide another input to the ECU and enable toxic emissions to be kept to a minimum; they are considered more fully in Section 8.

Maintenance

13 Maintenance of the fuel injection system consists of inspecting and renewing the air cleaner element at the specified intervals. At the same time the fuel line filter(s) should be renewed.

14 If suitable equipment is available, the idle speed and mixture may be checked and adjusted, if necessary. In the absence of the correct equipment, the task should be left to a competent specialist.

15 Apart from the above, regular inspection should be made to verify the security and good condition of all pipes, hoses, unions, connectors, injectors etc. Remember that the EFI system supplies fuel under considerable pressure and that even a small leak may be most dangerous.

Air cleaner (US models) – removal, element renewal and refitting

16 Disconnect the hoses from the air cleaner housing.

17 Undo the single wing nut which holds the air cleaner to its bracket.

18 Lift away the air cleaner.

19 Remove the eight screws which hold the two halves of the air cleaner case together.

20 Lift off the top half of the case and note the correct fitted position of the element.

21 Discard the old element and wipe clean the inside of the case.

22 Fit the new element, observing its correct position, then reassemble the air cleaner case and secure with the screws.

23 Refit the air cleaner in the reverse order to removal.

Air cleaner (UK models) – removal, element renewal and refitting

24 Disconnect the hose from the air cleaner.

25 Remove the air cleaner from its mounting studs.

26 Release the endplate retaining clips and remove the endplate (photo). (It may be a very firm fit.)

27 Unscrew the nut which secures the element retaining plate. Remove the plate and extract the element (photo). Note the spacer which fits over the retaining plate stud (photo).

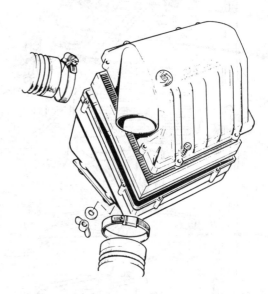

Fig. 13.14 Air cleaner – US models (Sec 7)

7.26 Removing air cleaner endplate

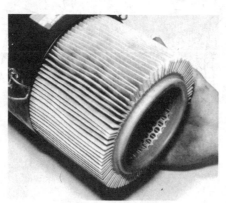

7.27A Withdrawing air cleaner element

7.27B Air cleaner endplate stud spacer

7.28 Air cleaner endplate washer and self-locking nut

7.33 Releasing fuel hose clip from filter

28 Wipe clean inside the case and fit a new element. Secure with the retaining plate, washer and nut (photo).
29 Clip the endplate on and refit the air cleaner to its studs.
30 Reconnect the hose to the air cleaner.

Fuel filter(s) – renewal

31 One or two filters may be fitted, according to year and model, located on the left-hand side of the engine bay.
32 Depressurize the fuel system as described in paragraphs 42 to 45.
33 Disconnect the fuel pipes from the filter(s) (photo). Be prepared for some fuel spillage.
34 Slacken the clamp nut and remove and discard the filter(s).
35 Fit a new filter in the reverse order to removal, observing any direction-of-flow markings on the new filter.
36 Pressurize the system and check for leaks on completion.

Idle speed and mixture adjustment

37 Refer to Chapter 3, Section 8. Disregarding specific references to carburettors, the rest of the information is applicable.
38 Idle speed adjustment is carried out by turning an adjustment

screw or bolt at the throttle housing (Fig. 13.15). On UK models the screw may be covered by a tamperproof cap; on US models the bolt is secured by a locknut. Remove the cap or release the locknut and turn the adjuster clockwise to decrease the idle speed, anti-clockwise to increase it.
39 If mixture adjustment is to be attempted, connect an exhaust gas analyser in accordance with its maker's instructions. Note that on US models the analyser probe must be inserted upstream of the catalyst, using the plug provided (Fig. 13.16).
40 Idle mixture adjustment is carried out at the airflow meter bypass screw. The screw is protected by a tamperproof cap. Remove the cap and turn the screw as necessary to bring the CO level within the specified limits (photos). Readjust the idle speed on completion if necessary.
41 Disconnect the test gear and restore any tamperproof caps to their locations. Note that in some territories it is an offence to drive a car with tamperproof caps missing.

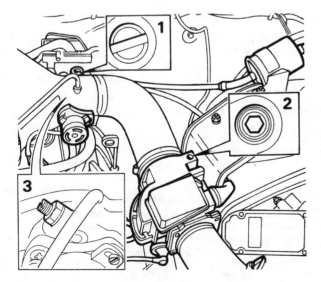

Fig. 13.15 Fuel injection system adjustment screws (Sec 7)

1 Idle speed screw (UK models)
2 Mixture screw
3 Idle speed screw (US models)

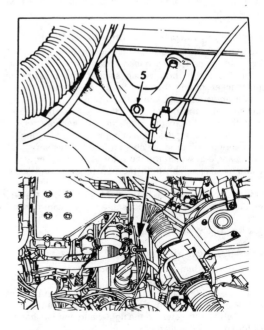

Fig. 13.16 Exhaust gas sampling plug (5) on US models (Sec 7)

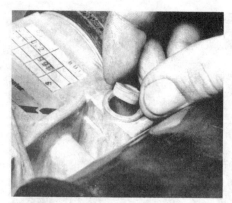
7.40A Idle mixture screw tamperproof cap

7.40B Using an Allen key to adjust idle mixture screw

7.43 Disconnecting multi-plug from airflow meter

Fuel system – depressurizing

42 Before any fuel line or union is disconnected, the EFI system must be depressurized.

43 On UK models, disconnect the multi-plug from the airflow meter (photo) or remove the fuel pump relay, then crank the engine for a few seconds using the starter motor.

44 On US models, disconnect the fuel pump earth lead or unplug the inertia switch, then crank the engine for a few seconds using the starter motor.

45 Remember to restore the original connections before attempting to run the engine again.

Fuel pump – removal and refitting

46 Depressurize the fuel system, as previously described.

47 For ease of access, raise and securely support the rear of the car. (The pump is located centrally in front of the rear axle). Disconnect the battery earth lead.

48 Remove the screws, nuts and washers which secure the fuel pump cover. Move the cover out of the way of the pump.

49 Disconnect and plug the pump outlet hose. Be prepared for some fuel spillage.

50 Similarly disconnect and plug the pump inlet hose.

51 Disconnect the electrical leads from the fuel pump.

52 Remove the two mounting bolts and extract the pump from its location.

53 Refit in the reverse order to removal. Check for leaks when the engine is next run.

Fuel pressure regulator – removal and refitting

54 Depressurize the fuel system, as previously described.

55 Disconnect the battery earth lead.

56 Remove the single bolt which secures the pressure regulator mounting bracket, noting the location of the washers. Carefully pull the regulator upwards, complete with bracket.

57 Clamp the inlet and outlet pipes, then release the pipe clips and disconnect the pipes from the regulator. Be prepared for some fuel spillage. If clamps are not available and it is decided to plug the pipes, take great care not to introduce any dirt into the system.

58 Note the angle at which the regulator fits its bracket, then remove the nut and washer which hold the two together and separate the regulator from the bracket.

59 Refit in the reverse order to removal. Make sure that the orientation of the regulator in its bracket is correct, and take care not to twist or kink the fuel pipes.

60 Check for leaks when the engine is next run.

Fuel rails – removal and refitting

61 Depressurize the fuel system, as previously described.

62 Disconnect the battery earth lead.

63 Remove the plenum chamber, as described later in this Section.

64 Disconnect the fuel input pipe from the right-hand rail, and the feed pipe(s) which run between the right-hand and left-hand rails. Be prepared for some fuel spillage.

65 Disconnect the injectors from the rails.

66 Remove the fuel rails from the car.

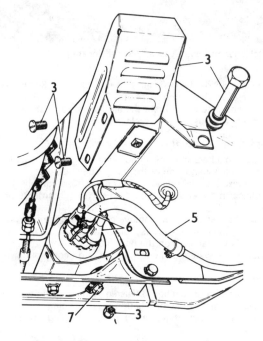

Fig. 13.17 Fuel pump mounting details (Sec 7)

3   Cover fastenings   6   Electrical connectors
5   Fuel inlet hose   7   Mounting bolt

67 Refit in the reverse order of removal. Check for leaks when the engine is next run.

Fuel injector(s) – removal and refitting

68 Remove the fuel rail on the side concerned, as described above.

69 Disconnect the electrical leads from the injector(s).

70 Unscrew the injector(s) from the manifold.

71 Refit in the reverse order to removal, using a new seal on each injector.

Cold start injector – removal and refitting

72 Depressurize the fuel system, as previously described.

73 Disconnect the electrical leads from the cold start injector (photo).

74 Unscrew the injector securing screws and remove the injector from the plenum chamber (photo). If it is wished to remove the injector completely, disconnect the fuel line from the injector; otherwise, just move it out of the way.

75 Refit in the reverse order to removal.

Plenum chamber (single throttle type – removal and refitting

76 If a water-heater plenum chamber is fitted, drain the cooling

system (see Chapter 2) and disconnect the coolant pipes from the plenum chamber.

77 On all models, unclip the pipes and cables from around the plenum chamber.

78 Disconnect the crankcase ventilation hose from the plenum chamber.

79 Disconnect the airflow meter hose from the plenum chamber.

80 Disconnect the electrical leads from the cold start injector and from the throttle swtch. Release the cold start injector from the plenum chamber.

81 Disconnect the throttle lever from its linkage at the plenum chamber by undoing the single nut which secures it.

82 Remove the bolts which secure the plenum chamber.

83 Lift off the plenum chamber and take it to the bench, where any associated components can be removed.

84 Refitting is a reversal of removal. Make sure that all mating surfaces are clean; where necessary, refer to Chapter 2 for information on refilling the cooling system.

Plenum chamber (twin throttle type) – removal and refitting

85 Remove the cold start injector fixing screws and withdraw the injector and gasket.

86 Disconnect the pressure regulator hose from the plenum chamber, also the wiring harness multi-plug from the throttle potentiometer.

87 Release the air intake hoses from the plenum chamber.

88 Release the air intake locating stud from its mounting on the support bracket, and then remove the air intake from the air flow meter.

89 Slacken the throttle cable adjuster locknut, release the adjuster from the mounting bracket, and disconnect the throttle cable from the quadrant.

90 Disconnect the hoses and the wiring harness from the bracket on the plenum chamber.

91 Partially drain the cooling system and disconnect the coolant hoses from the plenum chamber.

92 Unscrew and remove the through-bolts, raise the plenum chamber, release the fuel pipes from their clips and lift the plenum chamber away.

93 Any ancillary units may now be removed from the plenum chamber, but do not disturb the throttle coupling screws as they are preset in production. Refitting is a reversal of removal.

EFI relay – removal and refitting

94 Disconnect the battery earth lead.

95 Remove the passenger side glovebox. The relay is behind it.

96 Unplug the electrical leads from the relay.

97 Extract the securing bolt and remove the relay from the car.

98 Refit in the reverse order to removal.

Throttle switch – removal and refitting

99 For ease of access, disconnect the pipes from the extra air valve.

100 Unplug the electrical connector from the throttle switch.

101 Remove the two screws which secure the throttle switch to the plenum chamber.

102 Carefully pull the switch off the throttle spindle, noting the flat on the spindle on which the switch locates.

103 Refit in the reverse order to removal.

Electronic control unit – removal and refitting

104 Disconnect the battery earth lead.

105 Roll back the carpet from the front passenger footwell and locate the ECU cover plate, or open the driver's side glovebox (as applicable).

106 Remove the screws which secure the cover plate and lift away the plate.

107 Move the ECU to one side until it is possible to release the multi-plug spring retainer. Release the retainer and disconnect the multi-plug.

108 Remove the bolts which secure the ECU to its mounting plate, then remove the ECU.

109 Refitting is a reversal of removal.

Power resistor unit – removal and refitting

110 Unplug the connector from the power resistor unit (located on the left-hand side of the engine bay, near the airflow meter).

111 Extract the two securing bolts and remove the resistor unit.

112 Refit in the reverse order to removal.

Airflow meter – removal and refitting

113 Disconnect the multi-plug from the airflow meter.

114 Disconnect the two air hoses from the airflow meter.

115 Remove the mounting bolts and separate the airflow meter from its mounting bracket.

116 Refit in the reverse order to removal, ensuring that the meter mounting surfaces are clean.

Air temperature sensor – removal and refitting

117 The air temperature sensor is part of the airflow meter; it should not be separated from it. It cannot be renewed independently of the airflow meter.

Thermotime switch – removal and refitting

118 With the engine cold, remove the cooling system expansion tank cap in order to depressurize the cooling system.

119 Disconnect the electrical leads from the switch, which is located just behind the distributor.

120 Unscrew and remove the switch; be prepared for some coolant spillage.

121 Refit in the reverse order to removal. Do not overtighten the switch. Check for leaks and top up the cooling system after the engine is next run.

Coolant temperature sensor – removal and refitting

122 Proceed as described above for the thermotime switch.

Fuel cut-off inertia switch – removal and refitting

123 Disconnect the battery earth lead.

124 On US models, open the hood and locate the switch at the rear of the engine bay on the right-hand side.

125 On UK models, remove the driver's glovebox and locate the switch mounted on a bracket next to the pedal bracket (photo).

7.73 Disconnecting the cold start injector plug

7.74 Extracting cold start injector fixing screw

7.125 Fuel cut-off inertia switch mounted next to pedal bracket

126 On all models, disconnect the multi-plug from the switch, release the switch from its retaining clip or screws and remove it.
127 Refit in the reverse order to removal.

Extra air valve – removal and refitting
128 With the engine cold, disconnect the multi-plug from the extra air valve.
129 Disconnect the two air hoses from the valve (photo).
130 Remove the two bolts which secure the valve to the inlet manifold then remove the valve.
131 Refit in the reverse order to removal.

7.129 Releasing extra air valve hose clip

Fuel injection system components – testing
132 Most fuel injection components are tested by substitution of a known good unit; those items which can also be tested by the DIY mechanic with modest equipment are listed below.
133 The reader is warned that various fuel injection control components are mechanically and/or electrically fragile. Improvised or clumsy testing procedures may cause more damage than was originally present.
134 Testing and fault diagnosis of the EFI system as a whole requires specially dedicated test equipment which will only be possessed by a Rover dealer or fuel injection specialist.
Exhaust air valve
135 Check that when the engine is being cranked on the starter motor, battery voltage is present at the extra air valve connector terminals. If not, there is a supply fault.
136 With the voltage supply verified, check the electrical resistance between the terminals of the extra air valve. A reading of 33 ohms should be obtained; a short-circuit (zero) or open-circuit (infinite) reading means that the valve must be renewed.
Coolant temperature sensor
137 Disconnect the battery earth lead.
138 Unplug the coolant temperature sensor connector and connect an ohmmeter to the sensor terminals. The resistance measured between the terminals should vary according to coolant temperature as follows:

Coolant temperature	Resistance (ohms)
−10°C (+14°F)	9200
0°C (+32°F)	5900
+20°C (+68°F)	2500
+40°C (+104°F)	1180
+60°C (+140°F)	600
+80°C (+176°F)	330

139 Measure the resistance between each sensor terminal and the body of the sensor. An infinite (open-circuit) reading should result.
140 If the sensor fails any of the above tests, renew it.
Air temperature sensor
141 Proceed as described for the coolant temperature sensor, using ambient air temperature instead of coolant temperature in the table of resistance values. (The higher temperatures are unlikely to be encountered under normal conditions.)
Thermotime switch
142 Check the rated temperature of the thermotime switch (stamped on its body).
143 Measure the coolant temperature with a thermometer of known accuracy.
144 Disconnect the battery earth lead and unplug the electrical connector from the thermotime switch.
145 Measure the resistance between switch terminal 'W' and earth. If the coolant temperature exceeds the switch rating, an infinite resistance (open-circuit) should be recorded; if the coolant temperature is lower than the switch rating, a zero or very low resistance (closed-circuit) should be recorded. Renew the switch if it fails this test.
146 If the above test is satisfactory, wait if necessary until the coolant temperature falls below the switch rating, then connect a switched 12 volt electrical supply to switch terminal 'G' and earth. Leave the ohmmeter connected as before.
147 Switch on the electrical supply and record the time taken for the thermotime switch state to change from low to high resistance. The time taken will depend on the coolant temperature as follows:

Coolant temperature	Delay time
−10°C (14°F)	8 sec
0°C (+32°F)	$4^1/2$ sec
+10°C (+50°F)	$3^1/2$ sec
+35°C (+95°F)	0 sec

148 Renew the switch if the recorded time differs widely from that specified.
Injector winding
149 The resistance of each injector winding (measured with the wiring disconnected from the injector) should be 2.4 ohms at 20°C (68°F). Such a low resistance will show up on most multi-meters as a zero reading; an infinite (open circuit) reading shows that the injector must be renewed.
150 The resistance between either terminal of an injector and the injector body should be infinite (open-circuit). If not, renew the injector.
151 Note that the injectors are designed to operate on a nominal 3 volt supply, the excess voltage being dropped across the power resistors. **Do not** apply battery voltage directly to the injector terminals, during testing or otherwise.
Fuel pressure regulator
152 Depressurize the fuel system, as previously described.
153 Disconnect the cold start injector pipe from the right-hand fuel rail and connect a suitable pressure gauge, of known accuracy, in its place.
154 Disconnect the coil LT negative lead.
155 Have an assistant crank the engine on the starter motor. Observe the pressure gauge reading; it should stabilise at the value given in the Specifications. Have the assistant stop cranking and check that the fuel pressure remains steady or declines slowly. A rapid fall is not acceptable.
156 If the above test does not produce satisfactory results, it is wise to seek specialist advice before renewing the fuel pressure regulator. It is possible for a defective fuel pump or a leaky pump non-return valve to produce the same symptoms as a defective pressure regulator. Trial by substitution in such a case becomes prohibitively expensive unless spare parts can be obtained on a 'sale or return' basis.

Fault diagnosis – fuel injection system
157 As mentioned previously, special equipment is needed for thorough fault diagnosis of the fuel injection system.
158 Before seeking professional assistance in tracing a fault, make sure that the battery is in good condition and fully charged; that the fuel tank contains clean fuel of the correct grade; that all electrical connections are clean and tight, and that the inertia switch has not tripped.
159 If the inertia switch has been tripped, it can be reset by depressing the button protruding from one face.

Fuel injection system hoses
160 Lengths of fuel hose cut from a roll should never be used on fuel injection systems.

161 Replacement hoses are supplied in correct lengths as individual parts by Rover dealers.
162 When fitting a hose to a pipe stub, take care not to fold back the inner lining.
163 Slide the hose onto the pipe so that the securing clip can be positioned as shown in Fig. 13.18.

Fuel injection system – engine speed surge

164 It is possible for engine speed surges to occur when starting from cold. If this is a regular symptom, and it is known that the engine is correctly tuned (ignition, fuel, *etc*) carry out the following modification.
165 Remove the connector plug from the coolant sensor. This is the white plug to which are connected the black/white (B) and the black/grey (C) wires (Fig. 13.19).
166 Pull back the rubber boot (D).
167 Disconnect the connectors (E) from the wires and discard them.
168 Fit new connectors to the wires with a 10 kilohm resistor (F) soldered in parallel as shown.
169 Locate the connectors in the plug (A), refit the rubber boot and push the plug onto the coolant temperature sensor.

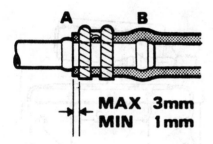

Fig. 13.18 Fuel injection system hose correctly connected (Sec 7)

A   Swage 1   B   Swage 2

8   Exhaust and emission control systems

Exhaust system (Vitesse and Vanden Plas EFI) – removal and refitting

1   Raise and securely support the vehicle, preferably on a ramp or hoist.
2   Remove the nuts and bolts from the rearmost flanged joint. Free the rubber support rings and remove the tailpipe and the rearmost silencer (resonator).
3   Similarly unbolt the intermediate flanged joint and the mounting rubbers to free the second silencer section.
4   Unbolt the front silencer flanged joint, free its mounting rubbers and remove the front silencer.
5   Release the Y-shaped intermediate pipe clamps, and remove the bolts which secure the pipe to the gearbox bracket. Remove the intermediate pipe.
6   Remove the bolts which secure the downpipe(s) to the manifold(s). Remove the downpipe(s) and retrieve the gasket(s).
7   Refit in the reverse order to removal, noting the following points:

   (a)   Use new gaskets on the manifold flanges
   (b)   Renew the olives (joint rings) where necessary
   (c)   Finally tighten all fixings and clamp bolts after the system has been warmed up and then allowed to cool down.

Evaporative emission control system (US models) – description

8   The evaporative emission control system is intended to prevent fuel fumes reaching the atmosphere. The fuel tank is vented via two charcoal canisters which can absorb fuel vapour when the engine is not running. When the engine is run, the vapour is drawn into the induction system and burnt.
9   A vapour separator, and a limited-fill device in the fuel tank, prevent neat fuel from entering the charcoal canister. A non-vented fuel filter cap is fitted to prevent vapour escaping at the filler.
10 Maintenance consists of periodically checking the hoses and connections for soundness and security. Remember that explosive gases are present in the canisters and hoses. Check occasionally that the restrictor in the canister purge hose is not blocked.

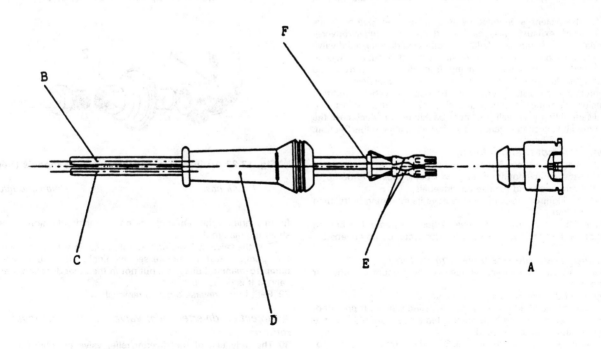

Fig. 13.19 Coolant sensor plug (Sec 7)

A   Plug   C   Black/grey wire   E   Connectors
B   Black/white wire   D   Rubber boot   F   Resistor

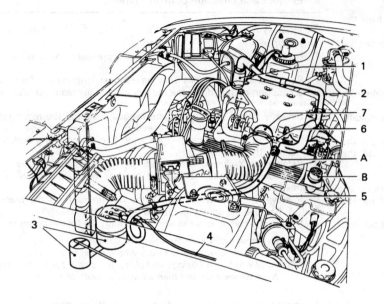

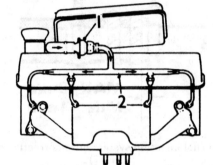

Fig. 13.20 Evaporative emission control and crankcase ventilation components – US models (Sec 8)

1 *Crankcase ventilation flame trap*
2 *Crankcase ventilation purge hose*
3 *Charcoal canisters*
4 *Fuel tank vent pipe*
5 *Canister purge hose*
6 *Throttle spindle*
7 *Throttle disc*
A *Restrictor in canister purge hose*
B *Breather filter*

Fig. 13.21 Air injection system check valve (1) and air manifold (2) – US models (Sec 8)

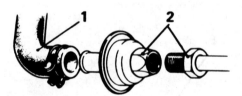

Fig. 13.22 Air injection check valve – US models (Sec 8)

1 *Air hose*   2 *Union and nut*

Evaporative emission control canister – removal and refitting

11 Remove the engine bay undersheild.
12 Disconnect and plug all hoses from the canisters, noting the fitted position of each hose if there is a possibility of confusion later.
13 Slacken the retaining clamps and remove the canisters.
14 Refit in the reverse order to removal.

Air injection system (US models) – description

15 The air injection system reduces emission levels by injecting air just downstream of each exhaust port, so promoting secondary combustion of unburned hydrocarbons and carbon monoxide in the exhaust system.
16 Air for the system is provided by an engine-driven pump. Check valves prevent exhaust gas reaching the pump under adverse conditions such as pump drive failure. A combined diverter/relief valve temporarily cuts off air injection in the event of a sudden rise in manifold vacuum (eg when changing from drive to overrun), so preventing backfiring, and also vents excess air to atmosphere.
17 Maintenance consists of checking the pump drivebelt condition and tension, and the condition and security of pipes, valves and unions. Malfunction may well present as backfiring, in which case the valves should be checked or renewed as described later in this Section.

Air pump – removal and refitting

18 Disconnect the air hose from the pump.
19 Release the pump mounting and pivot bolts, move the pump to slacken the driveshaft and remove the drivebelt.
20 Take the weight of the pump and remove its mounting bolts, then remove the pump.
21 Refit in the reverse order to removal. Adjust the pump drivebelt on completion in the same way as the alternator/water pump drivebelt.

Air injection manifold – removal and refitting

22 If necessary to improve access, remove the plenum chamber air intake hose.
23 Disconnect the manifold at the check valve.
24 Unscrew the manifold unions from the cylinder head. If preferred, the two centre branches can be disconnected at the manifold, and the branches left attached to the head.
25 Refit in the reverse order to removal. Start the engine and check for air leaks on completion.

Air injection check valve – removal, testing and refitting

26 Disconnect the air hose from the check valve.
27 Unscrew the check valve from the air manifold. Use two spanners

for this, one on the vent and one on the manifold union, so as not to strain the manifold.
28 Test the valve by blowing through it with low air pressure (lungs or foot-pump – **not** a compressed air line). Air should pass in the pump-to-manifold direction, but not in the other direction. Renew the valve if it is defective.
29 Refit in the reverse order to removal.

Air injection diverter/relief valve – testing, removal and refitting

30 The only test of the diverter/relief valve possible for the home mechanic is a functional one. If the diverter function of the valve is not operational, backfiring on the overrun will be evident. If the air and vacuum connections to the valve are sound and backfiring continues, the valve should be renewed.
31 Commence removal by disconnecting the battery earth lead.

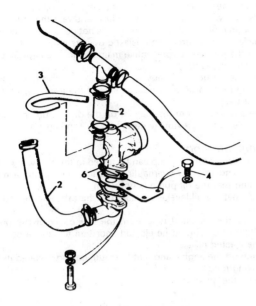

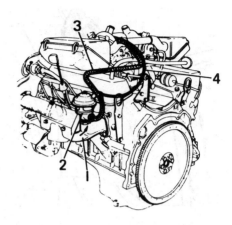

Fig. 13.24 EGR system components – US models (Sec 8)

1 *Exhaust manifold*	3 *EGR pipe*
2 *EGR valve*	4 *Vacuum pipe*

Fig. 13.23 Air injection diverter/relief valve – US models (Sec 8)

2 *Air hoses*	4 *Securing bolt*
3 *Vacuum pipe*	6 *Gaskets*

32 Disconnect the air and vacuum hoses from the valve.
33 Remove the two bolts which secure the valve mounting plate and lift away the valve.
34 Refit in the reverse order to removal, using new gaskets where necessary.

EGR system (US models) – description
35 The EGR (exhaust gas recirculation) system reduces the emission of nitrogen oxides (NOx) by returning a metered amount of exhaust gas to the induction side of the combustion cycle.
36 The amount of exhaust gas which is recycled is determined by the EGR valve. The valve is connected to the intake manifold vacuum in such a way that it inhibits recirculation at idle and at full load, but allows recirculation under part throttle conditions.
37 If the EGR valve sticks open, rough idling and loss of top end power will result. A valve which is sticking due to carbon deposits can be cleaned in an abrasive blasting spark plug cleaner.

EGR valve – testing, removal and refitting
38 To test the EGR valve, bring the engine to normal operating temperature.
39 With the engine running, open and close the throttle several times while an assistant feels the EGR valve. (Warn the assistant that the valve is liable to be hot.) It should be possible to feel the valve opening when part throttle is applied, and closing when it is released.
40 To remove the EGR valve, first disconnect the vacuum pipe from it.
41 Disconnect the lagged pipe from the valve. Take care not to damage the lagging, which is asbestos-based.
42 Unscrew the EGR valve from the exhaust manifold.
43 Refit in the reverse order of removal. Use a little anti-seize compound on the manifold union, and check for exhaust leaks on completion.

Lambda sensors (US models) – description
44 The Lambda sensors, one in each branch, supply a voltage signal to the EFI ECU. The signal varies according to the oxygen content of the exhaust gas; the ECU compares the signal with a reference value and alters the open time of the fuel injectors as necessary to maintain ideal combustion conditions.
45 Very low emission levels can be achieved when this system is working properly. Should the Lambda sensors fail, the vehicle will still

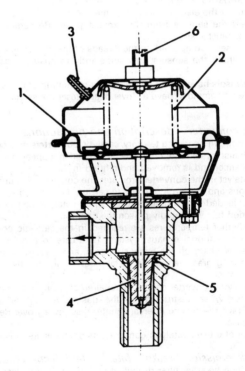

Fig. 13.25 Sectional view of EGR valve (Sec 8)

1 *Diaphragm*	5 *Valve seat*
2 *Spring*	6 *Production adjustment*
3 *Vacuum connection*	*facility (sealed after setting)*
4 *Pintle*	

be driveable, but engine efficiency will be reduced and emissions increased.
46 Air leaks in the exhaust system upstream of the Lambda sensors will mislead the ECU into supplying an excessively rich mixture.
47 Only unleaded fuel must be used when Lambda sensors are fitted; leaded fuel will poison the catalytic layer on which the action of the sensor depends. The sensors should in any case by renewed every 30 000 miles (48 000 km).

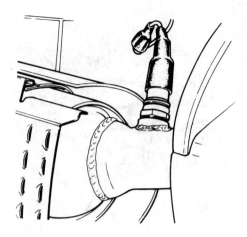

Fig. 13.26 Lambda sensor location in exhaust branch – US models (Sec 8)

Lambda sensors – removal and refitting

48 Disconnect the electrical lead from the sensors.
49 Unscrew the sensors from the exhaust pipes. Be careful not to strain the exhaust system.
50 Use anti-seize compound on the threads of the new sensors when refitting. Tighten the sensors only sufficiently to ensure a gas-tight seal.
51 If the sensors have been renewed at the prompting of a dashboard service interval reminder, have a Rover dealer reset the service interval counter.

Catalytic converter – description and precautions

52 Depending on operating territory, catalytic converters may be fitted in the exhaust system. A converter is similar in appearance to an ordinary silencer and is removed and refitted in the same way.
53 The catalyst in the converter promotes the conversion of unburned hydrocarbons and carbon monoxide to carbon dioxide and water.
54 Only unleaded fuel should be used when catalytic converters are fitted. Leaded fuel will rapidly poison the catalyst.
55 Much higher temperatures are reached in the catalytic converter than in a conventional exhaust system. Take care to avoid personal injury when working on the exhaust system, and exercise care when parking on long grass, leaves, etc, which can be ignited by the heat from the catalyst.
56 The catalytic converter cannot be repaired and must be renewed if defective, or when instructed by the dashboard service interval reminder. Have the service interval counter reset by a Rover dealer in the latter case.
57 Dispose of a used catalytic converter: its contents are poisonous.

Crankcase emission breather filter – fuel injection models

58 The in-line breather filter described in Chapter 3 is replaced by a filter pressed directly into the left-hand rocker cover on fuel injection models.
59 The filter is removed by prising it upwards until it is released from the cover. Fit a new filter by pressing it into position until it snaps home.

9　Manual gearbox

Oil level checking and oil changing

1 The gearbox oil level should be checked at the specified intervals. Have the car standing on level ground with the gearbox cold, preferably first thing in the morning. If this is not possible, allow at least ten minutes to elapse after the vehicle has been used.
2 Unscrew the oil level/filler plug. The oil level should be level with the bottom of the plug hole.

3 Top up if necessary with the specified grade of oil until it just starts to trickle out, wipe clean around the hole and refit the plug.
4 Although renewal of the gearbox oil is not considered necessary by the vehicle manufacturers, enthusiastic owners may decide to change the oil in the interests of preventive maintenance at (say) 30 000 mile (48 000 km) intervals.
5 Drain the oil hot by removing the level/filler and drain plugs, the latter being located on the opposite side of the transmission from the level/filler plug.
6 Wipe any swarf from the magnet on the drain plug and refit it. Fill the transmission as previously described for topping-up.

Oil pump – testing

7 The transmission oil pump can be tested in the following way. This is worth doing prior to overhauling the transmission as a means of establishing that the oil pump is not worn or faulty.
8 Check that the oil level is correct, then start the engine and allow it to idle.
9 Remove the threaded plug from the rear cover of the pump – a steady flow of oil should be ejected (position a suitable container to catch the ejected oil).
10 Switch off the engine and refit the plug, having smeared its threads with locking fluid.
11 Top up the oil level.

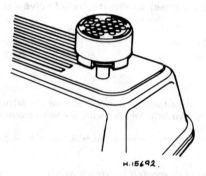

H.15692.

Fig. 13.27 Crankcase breather filter in left-hand rocker cover – fuel injection models (Sec 8)

10　Automatic transmission

GM 180 transmission – description

1 During 1982, the Borg Warner 66 automatic transmission was superseded by the GM 180. This transmission functions in a similar manner to the Borg Warner version described in Chapter 6, but procedures peculiar to it are given in the following sub-sections.

GM 180 transmission – maintenance

2 Every 6000 miles (10 000 km), or at the first sign of any malfunction, check the automatic transmission fluid level as follows.
3 Drive the car for at least 15 miles (25 km) to bring the transmission fluid to operating temperature. Park on level ground, and with the engine running and the footbrake applied, move the selector lever through all positions three times, finishing in position 'P'.
4 With the engine still running, 'P' selected and the handbrake applied, open the bonnet and locate the automatic transmission dipstick (on the left-hand side of the engine bay, towards the rear). Withdraw the dipstick, wipe it with a clean non-fluffy rag, reinsert it and withdraw it again. If the level is at or below the minimum mark, top up with fresh fluid of the specified type (photo). *Take great care not to introduce foreign matter into the filler/dipstick tube.*
5 Every 24 000 miles (40 000 km) the transmission should be drained by removing the sump. The filter and gasket should be renewed, the sump refitted with a new gasket and the transmission refilled with fresh fluid. Where the car is operated under arduous conditions this work should be carried out every 12 000 miles (20 000 km).
6 Only about 4 pints (2.3 litres) of ATF will be needed to refill the

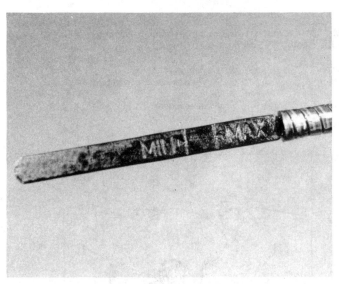

10.4 Automatic transmission dipstick markings (GM 180)

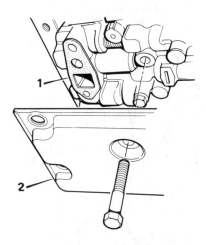

Fig. 13.28 GM 180 automatic transmission filter (2) and gasket (1) (Sec 10)

transmission after draining as described – the remainder of the fluid is retained in the torque converter. Refill a cold transmission to the level of the triangle on the dipstick (below the minimum mark). Recheck the level when the transmission has reached operating temperature.
7   Every 24 000 miles (40 000 km) the brake band should be adjusted (see paragraphs 28 to 34).

GM 180 transmission – removal and refitting
8   Position the car on ramps or jack it up and support on axle stands. Select 'N' and disconnect the battery.
9   Disconnect the downshift cable at the carburettor.
10 Remove both front exhaust pipes (Chapter 3).
11 Disconnect and unclip the vacuum pipe from the transmission modulator valve.
12 Unbolt and remove the dipstick tube and remove the seal. Plug the vacant hole.
13 Unclip the selector rod.
14 Disconnect the wiring from the speed transducer and inhibitor switch.
15 Remove the propeller shaft (Chapter 7).
16 Remove the engine sump stiffening plate bolts and the driveplate cover. Remove the starter motor bottom bolt and disconnect the earth strap.
17 Unscrew the driveplate bolts; turning the engine as necessary.
18 Support the rear of the engine and take the weight of the transmission on a trolley jack.
19 Unbolt the mounting bracket from the underbody and detach the oil cooler pipe bracket.
20 Lower the transmission sufficiently far to disconnect and plug the oil cooler pipes. Tie the pipes to one side.
21 Unscrew the remaining transmission-to-engine bolts and recover the dipstick tube support bracket.
22 Withdraw the transmission until the torque converter clears the crankshaft spigot then lower it to the ground.
23 Refitting is a reversal of removal with reference to Chapter 6, Section 10. Finally adjust the downshift cable.

Downshift cable (GM 180) – checking and adjustment
24 Hold the accelerator pedal fully depressed with a block of wood or similar.
25 Check that both throttles are fully open with the levers touching the stops, and the downshift cable fully withdrawn from the transmission.
26 Loosen the cable locknuts at the bracket then position the cable as necessary to eliminate any free play keeping the throttle fully open. Tighten the locknuts with the cable in this position.
27 Release the accelerator pedal, then check again that both throttles are fully open and the downshift cable fully withdrawn with the pedal fully depressed. The downshift cable must not act as a throttle stop.

Low brake band (GM 180) – adjustment
28 Position the car on ramps and jack it up and support on axle stands.
29 Place a suitable container beneath the transmission then unbolt the sump pan and drain the fluid.
30 Unbolt the brake band servo cover and remove the gasket.
31 Loosen the locknut then tighten the adjustment screw to 3.3 lbf ft (4.5 Nm) using an Allen key.
32 Hold the piston sleeve stationary with a spanner, then back off the adjustment screw exactly five turns and tighten the locknut.
33 Refit the servo cover and sump pan using new gaskets and tighten the bolts.
34 Refill the transmission with fluid.
35 Apply the handbrake and footbrake then start the engine and move the selector lever three times through all the gears.
36 Check and if necessary top up the fluid level, as described earlier.

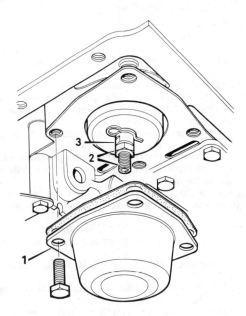

Fig. 13.29 GM 180 automatic transmission low brake band adjustment (Sec 10)

1   Servo cover and gasket   3   Piston sleeve
2   Adjuster screw and locknut

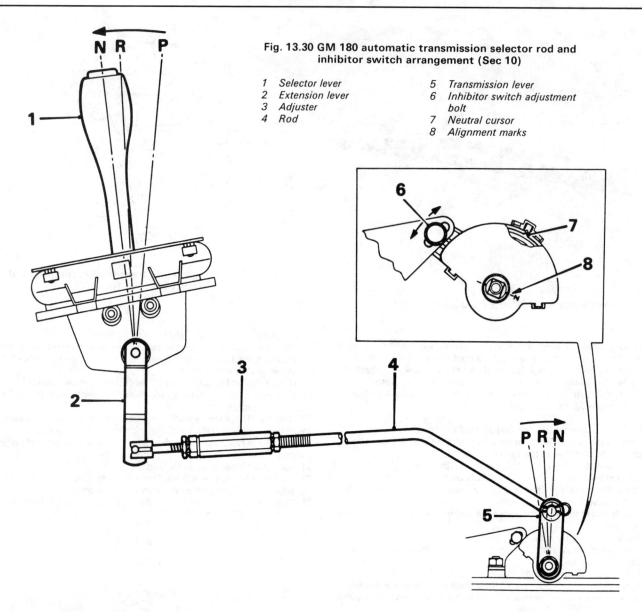

Fig. 13.30 GM 180 automatic transmission selector rod and inhibitor switch arrangement (Sec 10)

1 Selector lever
2 Extension lever
3 Adjuster
4 Rod
5 Transmission lever
6 Inhibitor switch adjustment bolt
7 Neutral cursor
8 Alignment marks

Selector rod (GM 180) – adjustment

37 Position the car on ramps or jack it up and support on axle stands.
38 Select 'N' then detach the selector rod at the transmission lever by extracting the clip.
39 Check that the transmission lever is in position 'N' by turning it fully anti-clockwise, then two detents clockwise.
40 With the selector lever in 'N', adjust the length of the selector rod so that it enters the transmission lever hole freely. Tighten the locknuts.
41 Fit the clip to the end of the selector rod.
42 Check that the starter motor can only be operated with 'P' or 'N' selected. If necessary adjust the inhibitor switch as follows.

Starter inhibitor switch (GM 180) – adjustment

43 Jack up the front of the car and support on axle stands. Apply the handbrake.
44 Select 'N' then loosen the adjustment bolt and turn the switch fully anti-clockwise.
45 Turn the switch clockwise slowly until a click is heard – the switch and shaft marks should now be in alignment.
46 Turn the switch clockwise a further 0.060 in (1.5 mm), measured at the adjustment bolt, then tighten the bolt.
47 Lower the car to the ground.

Speed transducer (GM 180) – removal and refitting

48 Chock the front wheels then jack up the rear of the car and support on axle stands.

49 Disconnect the wiring from the speed transducer.
50 Unscrew the bolt and remove the transducer from the extension housing. Be prepared for some loss of fluid.
51 Renew and then lubricate the O-ring seal.
52 Push the transducer into position, making sure that the gear engages correctly.
53 Insert and tighten the bolt, then reconnect the wiring; routing it over the extension housing away from the exhaust system.
54 Lower the car to the ground.

---

11 Rear axle

Halfshaft bearing and oil seals – addition of circlip (later models)

1   From 1981 a circlip has been fitted to the halfshaft between the bearing retainer and the inner oil seal (see Fig. 13.31). The purpose of the circlip is to stop the halfshaft parting company with the axle in the event of bearing failure.
2   Since the modification is to the halfshaft itself and not to the axle casing, later pattern halfshafts may be fitted to early pattern axles.
3   If a bearing and/or oil seal kit is purchased, the circlip which it contains may be discarded if the components are to be fitted to an early pattern halfshaft.

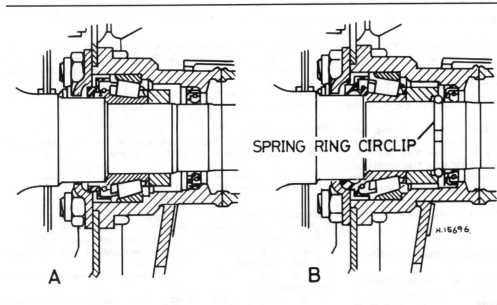

SPRING RING CIRCLIP

H.15696.

A   B

Fig. 13.31 Early (A) and later
(B) halfshaft details
(Sec 11)

Pinion extension housing – removal and refitting
4   Wear between the pinion extension shaft and the differential pinion splines can result in transmission knock when changing from drive to overrun and *vice versa*. It is therefore recommended that locking fluid is applied to the splines before refitting the extension housing. The splines should be thoroughly cleaned before application of the locking fluid, and the fluid should be allowed to cure for a minimum of 12 hours.

Oil draining and refilling
5   The vehicle manufacturers do not specify changing the rear axle lubricant, only topping-up.
6   If the oil must be drained for any reason, remove the rear cover from the differential housing to allow the oil to run out.
7   Always use a new gasket when refitting.
8   Refill through the filler/level plug hole.

12 Braking system

Brake servo knock (all models)
1   If a knocking noise is heard from the brake servo, proceed as follows.
2   With the engine not running, press the brake pedal several times to dissipate any residual vacuum.
3   Extract the non-return valve and its seal, leaving the valve attached to the vacuum hose.
4   Have an assistant depress the brake pedal as far as it will go. With the pedal depressed, stick a finger in through the non-return valve hole and rotate the metal plate inside through approximately 10°. The assistant may then release the pedal.

5   Refit the non-return valve and its seal.
6   Road test the car. If servo knock is still present, repeat the above procedure until it is cured. If no cure is forthcoming, renewal of the servo may be the only solution.

Brake pad wear warning system (1982 on) – description
7   The brake pad wear warning light should illuminate every time the starter motor is operated. If it illuminates when the brakes are applied the brake pads must be renewed without delay.
8   Operation of the warning light is controlled by wires embedded in the brake pad friction lining. When the lining has worn so far that the wires touch the disc, an electrical circuit is completed and the warning light is activated. Note that it is the inboard brake pad on each side which is equipped with the wires (photo).
9   It is necessary to disconnect the wires at the caliper when removing the pads, and to reconnect them on completion.
10 The conscientious owner will wish to inspect the brake pads at regular intervals, even when not prompted by the warning light.

Ventilated disc brakes (Vitesse and Vanden Plas EFI) – description
11 The brake discs on these models are ventilated, to improve heat dissipation under heavy braking.
12 Pad renewal is basically as described in Chapter 9. Note that the pad retaining pins are not of the split variety, but must be knocked out with a drift or punch (photo). The anti-rattle clips are easily damaged during this operation, new clips are supplied by the makers only with brake pad sets.
13 Observe the correct orientation of the holes in the anti-rattle clips (photo).

12.8 Inboard disc brake pad with wear sensor leads and plug

12.12 Disc pad retaining pin – Vitesse and Vanden Plas EFi

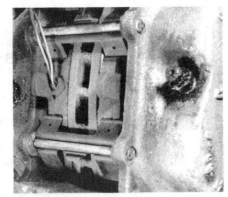

12.13 Note orientation of holes in anti-rattle clips

Hydraulic system bleeding (all models) – alternative methods

14 Various 'one-man' brake bleeding kits are now available from motor accessory shops. The use of such a kit greatly simplifies the bleeding procedure and dispenses with the need for an assistant.
15 The simplest kits comprise a non-return valve which is attached to some bleeding tube. The tubing must be routed so that it is visible to the operator, in order that the operator may know when the expelled fluid is free of air.
16 Somewhat more expensive, but extremely simple in use, are pressure bleeding kits. These kits use low air pressure, usually from the spare tyre, to pressurise a large reservoir of brake fluid which is connected to the master cylinder. The system is then bled simply by opening the bleed screws unti air-free fluid comes out. This method is particularly suitable when renewing the hydraulic fluid as specified in the maintenance schedule.
17 Use any proprietary brake bleeding kit in accordance with its maker's instructions.

Hydraulic system bleeding (Vitesse and Vanden Plas EFI) – special notes

18 The primary hydraulic circuit supplies both rear brakes and two of the four pistons on each front caliper. The secondary circuit supplies the other two pistons on each front caliper.
19 Provided that the level of hydraulic fluid in the brake master cylinder reservoir has been maintained, if only the primary circuit has been disconnected there is no need to bleed the secondary circuit, and *vice versa*.
20 On each front caliper there are three bleed screws. The two rearward facing screws bleed the primary circuit. Bleeding must take place from the two screws simultaneously. The single inward facing bleed screw serves the secondary circuit.
21 Follow the alphabetical sequence shown in Fig. 13.32 when bleeding the hydraulic system, ignoring the intact circuit's bleed screws if only one circuit is being bled.
22 The Vitesse examined during the preparation of this Chapter had no bleed screw at position 'A'; instead there was a cross-pipe feeding the right-hand rear wheel cylinder. In this case bleeding would start at position 'B'.

Brake caliper (Vitesse and Vanden Plas EFI)– overhaul

23 Overhaul procedures are essentially as described in Chapter 9, Section 5. There are, however, four pistons per caliper instead of two.

Brake master cylinder (Vitesse and Vanden Plas EFI) – overhaul

24 The brake master cylinder shown in Chapter 9 has been modified slightly for Vitesse and Vanden Plas EFI models. As will be seen from Fig. 13.34 the pressure differential switch is no longer built into the master cylinder.
25 Making due allowance for the reduced number of components, overhaul is as described in Chapter 9, Section 12.

Rear brake assembly

26 The accompanying Fig. 13.35 is included for clarification of the individual components of the rear brake assembly.

13 Electrical system

Alternator type A133 – description and brush renewal

1   The type A133 alternator may be found on later models. It is a more compact version of the ACR series alternator fitted previously.
2   To renew the brushes, first remove the alternator from the vehicle (Chapter 10, Section 8).
3   Disconnect and remove the interference suppression capacitor from the end cover.
4   Undo the screws or nuts which secure the end cover. Remove the cover.
5   Unscrew the surge protection diode securing screw. Either move the diode carefully out of the way, or disconnect it from the rectifier board and remove it.
6   Make a careful note of the regulator lead colours and fitting arrangements, then disconnect the regulator leads from the rectifier board and the brushbox.
7   Remove the regulator screw and withdraw the regulator. Note that the regulator securing screw also holds one of the brush mounting plates in position.
8   Remove the two securing screws and withdraw the brushbox. Extract the free brush, then undo the securing screw to release the other brush. Remove the sealing pad.
9   Renew the brushes if they are at or approaching the minimum specified length. Check the brush spring pressure with the brush ends flush with the end of the brushbox; renew the springs if they have become weak.
10 Reassemble the alternator in the reverse sequence to dismantling. Refit the alternator and tension the drivebelt as described in Chapter 10.

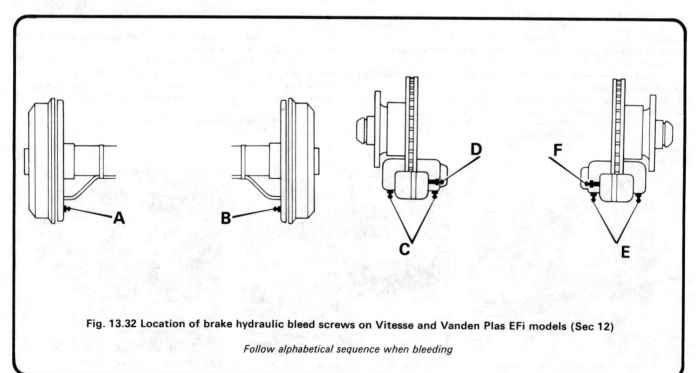

Fig. 13.32 Location of brake hydraulic bleed screws on Vitesse and Vanden Plas EFi models (Sec 12)

Follow alphabetical sequence when bleeding

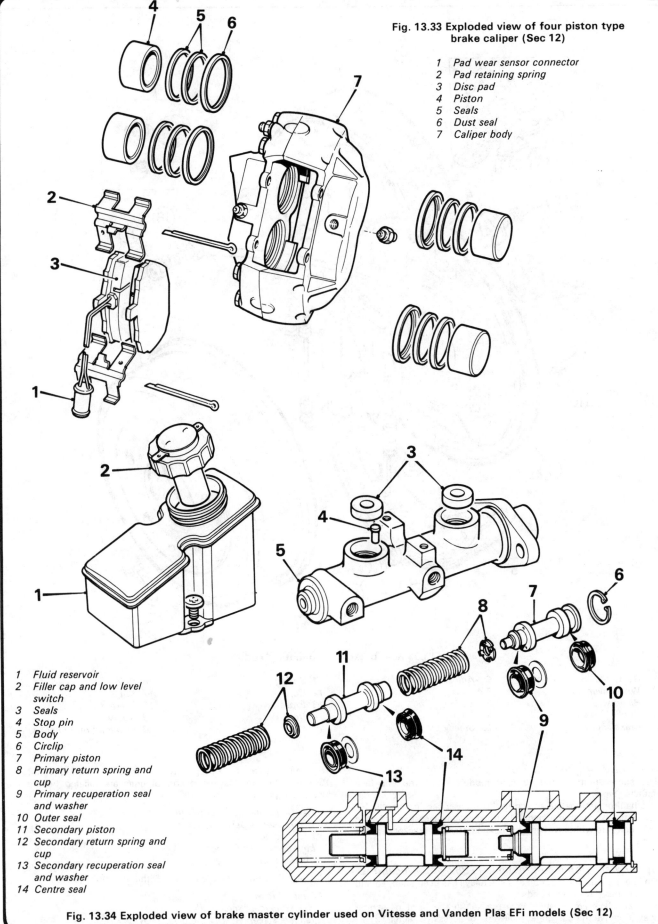

Fig. 13.33 Exploded view of four piston type brake caliper (Sec 12)

1 Pad wear sensor connector
2 Pad retaining spring
3 Disc pad
4 Piston
5 Seals
6 Dust seal
7 Caliper body

1 Fluid reservoir
2 Filler cap and low level switch
3 Seals
4 Stop pin
5 Body
6 Circlip
7 Primary piston
8 Primary return spring and cup
9 Primary recuperation seal and washer
10 Outer seal
11 Secondary piston
12 Secondary return spring and cup
13 Secondary recuperation seal and washer
14 Centre seal

Fig. 13.34 Exploded view of brake master cylinder used on Vitesse and Vanden Plas EFi models (Sec 12)

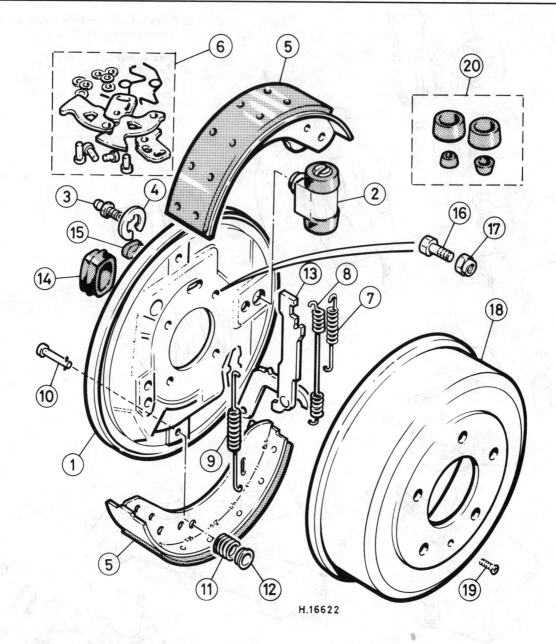

Fig. 13.35 Rear brake components (Sec 12)

1	Backplate	6	Adjuster components	11	Spring	16	Bolt
2	Wheel cylinder	7	Spring	12	Cup	17	Nut
3	Bleed screw	8	Spring	13	Cross-lever	18	Brake drum
4	Circlip	9	Spring	14	Boot	19	Screw
5	Brake shoes	10	Steady pin	15	Plug	20	Repair kit of rubber seals

Starter motor (August 1983 on)

11 The starter motor fitted to later models is of the end-face commutator type.

12 Overhaul operations are similar to those described in Chapter 10, except for the brush arrangement. The brushes are accessible once the through-bolts are withdrawn and the commutator and bracket partially removed.

Relays and electronic control units (1982 on) – locations

13 On later models, the location of some relays has been changed and additional ones have been fitted.

14 Several relays are located on a bracket in the front passenger footwell. Remove the passenger glovebox for access (Chapter 12).

15 The relays are of the plug-in type – for details, see Fig. 13.38.

16 The following relays and control units are located behind the instrument panel.

FASD (carburettor) control unit
Windscreen wiper delay relay
Low engine oil level unit
Low coolant level unit
Interface unit

17 The following relays are located within the luggage area.

Sunroof relay
Heated tailgate screen relay
Tailgate screen wash/wipe delay relay

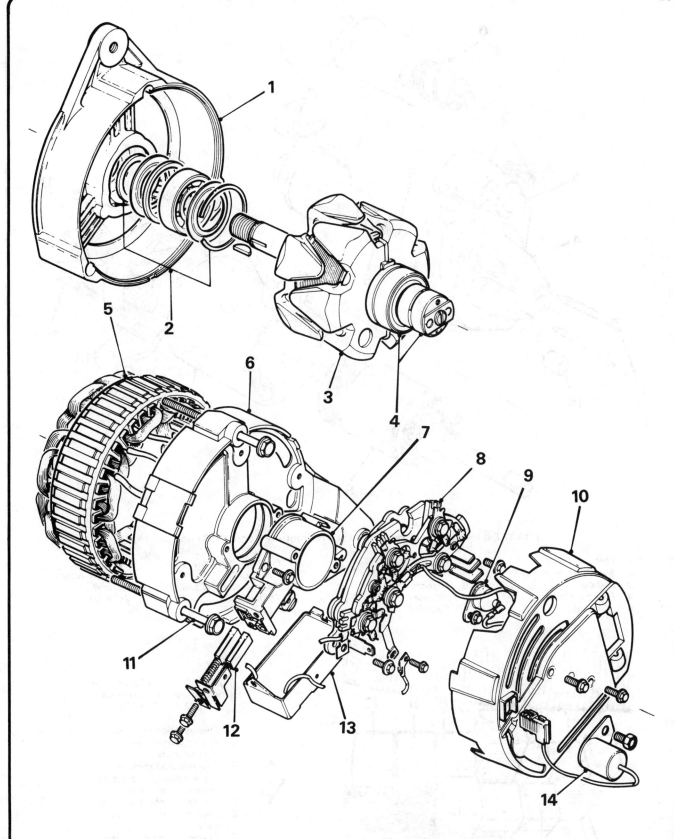

Fig. 13.36 Exploded view of type A133 alternator (Sec 13)

1	Drive end bracket	5	Stator	9	Surge protection diode	13	Voltage regulator
2	Bearing pack	6	Slip ring end bracket	10	Cover	14	Interference suppression
3	Rotor	7	Brushbox	11	Fixing bolt		capacitor
4	Slip rings and bearing	8	Rectifier (diode) pack	12	Brushes		

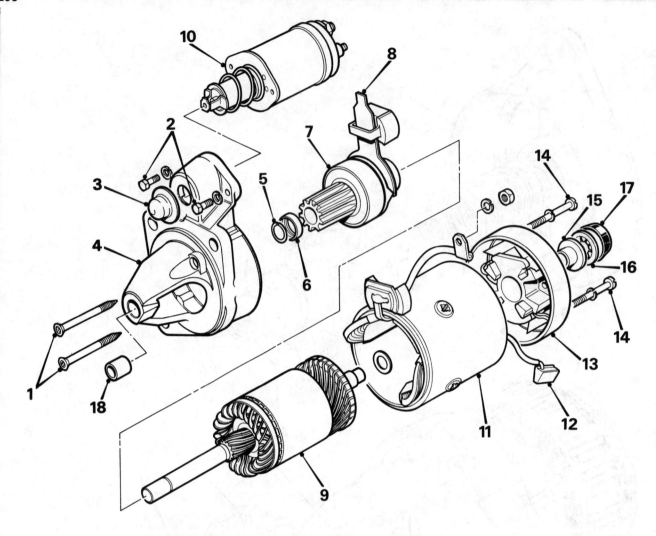

Fig. 13.37 Exploded view of type 9M90 starter motor – August 1983 on (Sec 13)

1	Through-bolts	6	Thrust collar
2	Solenoid screws	7	Drive assembly
3	End cap	8	Engagement lever
4	Fixing bracket	9	Armature
5	Jump ring	10	Solenoid

11	Field coil assembly	15	Bush
12	Field brush	16	Spire washer
13	Commutator end bracket	17	End cap
14	Through-bolt	18	Bush

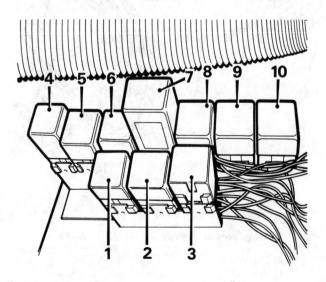

Fig. 13.38 Relays located in front passenger footwell – 1982 on (Sec 13)

1 Fuel injection pump relay
2 Fuel injection 'steering module' relay
3 Fuel injection main relay
4 Brake warning and dipped beam relay diode unit
5 Headlamp main beam relay
6 Headlamp dipped beam relay
7 Courtesy lamp delay unit
8 Air conditioner compressor clutch relay
9 Rear foglamp relay
10 Electric aerial relay

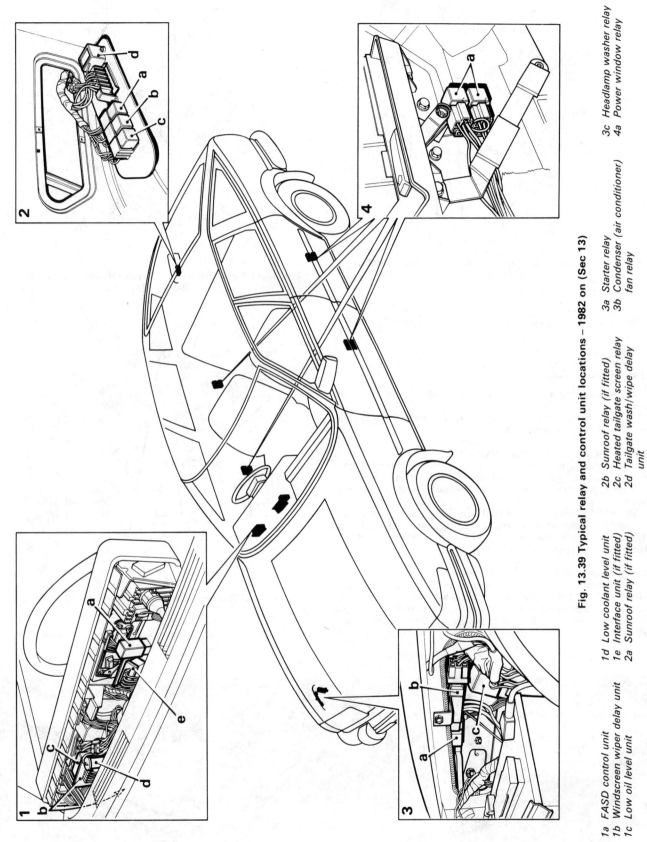

Fig. 13.39 Typical relay and control unit locations – 1982 on (Sec 13)

1a FASD control unit
1b Windscreen wiper delay unit
1c Low oil level unit

1d Low coolant level unit
1e Interface unit (if fitted)
2a Sunroof relay (if fitted)

2b Sunroof relay (if fitted)
2c Heated tailgate screen relay
2d Tailgate wash/wipe delay
    unit

3a Starter relay
3b Condenser (air conditioner)
    fan relay

3c Headlamp washer relay
4a Power window relay

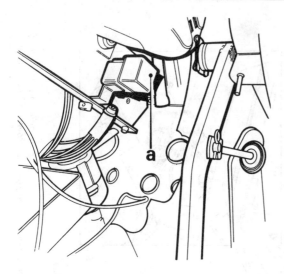

Fig. 13.40 Heater relay (a) in driver's footwell – 1982 on (Sec 13)

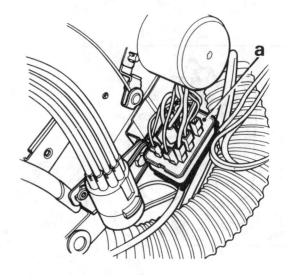

Fig. 13.41 Air conditioner relay (a) in driver's footwell – 1982 on (Sec 13)

18 The following relays are located inside the right-hand front wing valance.

Starter solenoid relay
Condenser (air conditioner) fan relay
Headlamp wash relay

19 The power-operated window relays are located within the door cavities.
20 The heater relay, the air conditioner relay (if fitted) and the flasher units are located in the driver's footwell.

Fusebox locations and fuse ratings (1982 on)
21 On later models, the main fusebox is located beneath the mat in the passenger's front tray. An auxiliary fusebox is fitted at the rear of the car, behind the carpet at the rear of the right-hand wheel arch (photos).
22 The manufacturer's recommended fuse ratings are given in the Specifications. Note that the ratings of the fuses serving the rear lights and the direction indicators (A1 and B5 respectively) must be increased when a towing socket is fitted.

Towing socket wiring and flasher unit location
23 To avoid damage to the bulb failure indicator unit, note that if a towing socket is fitted, the wiring for the trailer lights must be taken from the input side of the bulb failure indicator unit (BFIU) and **not** from the rear lamp unit itself. The cables providing the inputs to the BFIU are coloured red/orange (for side and tail lights) and

Fig. 13.42 Flasher units in driver's footwell – 1982 on (Sec 13)

a   Direction indicator unit   *b   Hazard*

13.21A Main fusebox beneath front passenger's tray mat

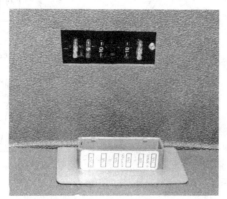

13.21B Auxiliary fusebox located behind right-hand wheel arch

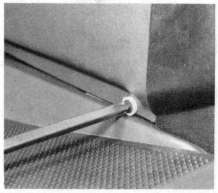

13.27 Extracting instrument panel top cover screw

green/purple (for stop-lights). The other cables of interest are coloured green/white (RH indicator), green/red (LH indicator) and red (rear foglamp).

24 On models already fitted with a dashboard warning light to show when the trailer direction indicators are operational, a green/light green cable will be found next to the flasher unit. This lead should be connected to the trailer warning light terminal of the heavy duty flasher unit or relay which will have to be fitted in conjunction with the towing socket. The warning light will then be operational.

25 As from VIN 298524 a combined electronic hazard and flasher unit is fitted inside the instrument housing. When fitting a towing socket this unit can be replaced with a heavy duty version providing a warning facility without the need for additional wiring at the facia. However, 10 amp fuses should be fitted for the side/tail lamps and boost lamp, and a 15 amp fuse for the combined electronic hazard and flasher unit.

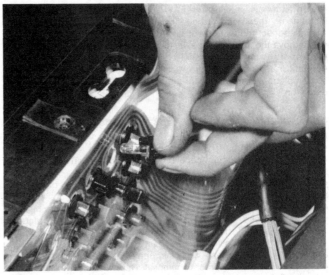

13.29 Removing an instrument panel bulb

Instrument panel lamps (1982 on) – renewal

26 To renew an instrument illumination or warning lamp on later models, first disconnect the battery earth lead.
27 Remove the screw which secures the instrument panel top cover (photo).
28 Remove the cover by sliding it to the passenger's side to release the studs.
29 Extract the appropriate bulbholder by twisting it anti-clockwise and pulling it (photo). Remove the capless bulb from its holder and push in a new one.
30 Refit in the reverse order to removal.

Instrument panel switches (1982 on) – removal and refitting

31 Disconnect the battery earth lead.
32 Remove the instrument panel top cover, as described above.
33 Disconnect the wiring multi-plug from the appropriate switch.
34 Ease the switch and its wiring out from the front of the instrument panel.
35 Refit in the reverse order to removal.

Minor instruments (1982 on) – removal and refitting

36 Disconnect the battery earth lead.
37 Remove the instrument panel top cover, as described in paragraphs 27 and 28.
38 Disconnect the multi-plug from the digital clock (if fitted).
39 If a trip computer is fitted, remove the instrument panel front cover, then disconnect the multi-plugs and the blade connector from the computer.

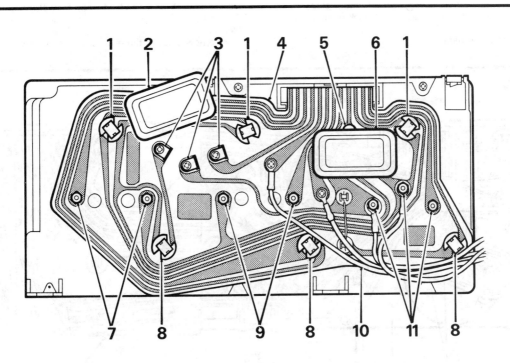

Fig. 13.43 Rear view of minor instrument pack – 1982 on (Sec 13)

1 Illumination lamps	5 Plastic retainer	9 Temperature gauge retaining nuts
2 Thermal delay unit	6 Instrument voltage stabiliser	10 Digital clock leads
3 Blade connectors	7 Fuel gauge retaining nuts	11 Oil pressure gauge retaining nuts
4 Printed circuit board	8 Warning lamps	

40 On all models, release the FASD ECU from its bracket behind the instruments, then remove the bracket.
41 Disconnect the instrument wiring multi-plug.
42 Remove the retaining screws, then extract the instruments through the rear of the instrument panel.
43 Refit in the reverse order to removal. Reset the clock or computer on completion, when applicable, and check the instruments for correct operation.

Speedometer/tachometer (1982 on) removal and refitting

44 Disconnect the battery earth lead.
45 Remove the instrument panel top cover, as described in paragraphs 27 and 28.
46 Disconnect the multi-plugs from the speedometer and tachometer and remove their securing screws.
47 Slacken the screws which secure the plate carrying the low oil level warning unit and the wash/wipe programme unit. (This plate is immediately behind the speedometer and tachometer.)
48 Move the plates aside, then extract the speedometer/tachometer assembly through the rear of the instrument panel.
49 Refit in the reverse order to removal. Reset the clock or computer on completion, where applicable, and check the speedometer and tachometer for correct operation.

Instrument panel (1982 on) – removal and refitting (complete)

50 Disconnect the battery earth lead.
51 Remove the glovebox on the driver's side.
52 Remove the instrument panel top cover, as described in paragraphs 27 and 28.
53 Remove the instrument panel front cover.
54 Remove the instrument panel mounting nuts and bolts.
55 Ease the instrument panel away from the facia so that the wiring connectors are accessible.
56 Label or sketch the various connectors if there is any possibility of confusion on reassembly, then disconnect all multi-plugs, blade connectors etc from the instruments, switches, clock or computer (as applicable).
57 Remove the instrument panel.

58 Refit in the reverse order to removal. Reset the clock or computer on completion and check the instruments for correct operation.

Instrument panel (1982 on) – dismantling

59 With the instrument panel or the appropriate instrument pack removed as described above, individual instruments or components may be removed and refitted as follows.
Minor instruments
60 Remove the lens from the instrument pack.
61 Remove the shroud and faceplate, taking care not to strain the connections to the digital clock (where applicable).
62 Remove the retaining screws or nuts from the appropriate gauge and extract the gauge from its housing. Note that when a digital clock is fitted, two of its leads are normally secured by the oil pressure gauge retaining nuts.
63 Reassemble in the reverse order to dismantling, making sure to relocate the clock leads correctly (where applicable).
Speedometer or tachometer
64 From the front of the instrument pack remove the lens, the shroud and the warning lamp symbol plate.
65 Remove the retaining screws or nuts and extract the tachometer or speedometer.
66 Reassemble in the reverse order to dismantling, making sure in the case of the speedometer that the trip meter reset control is located correctly.
Printed circuit
67 Remove the instruments from the printed circuit board, as already described.
68 Remove all bulbholders from the printed circuit board. Also remove all nuts, bolts, screws, leads and hardware such as the instrument voltage stabilizer, the thermal delay unit and any blade connectors.
69 Release the plastic retainers and remove the printed circuit.
70 Transfer all the hardware, bulbs and gauges to the new printed circuit when it is fitted.
Digital clock
71 With the minor instrument pack removed, disconnect the clock leads from the printed circuit. Note their locations for use when reassembling. Release the leads from their securing tape.
72 Undo and remove the clock securing screws, then remove the clock.
73 Fit a new clock in the reverse order to removal.

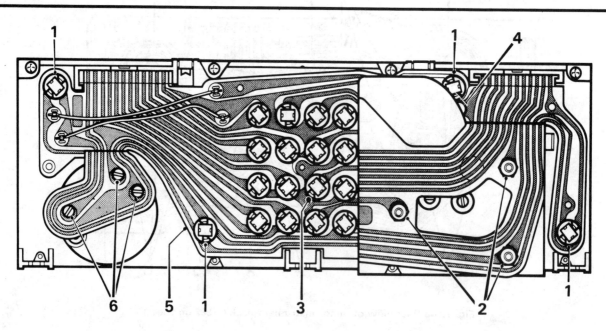

Fig. 13.44 Rear view of speedometer/tachometer pack – 1982 on (Sec 13)

1	Illumination lamps	3	Warning lamp cluster	5	Printed circuit board
2	Speedometer retaining nuts	4	Plastic retainer	6	Tachometer retaining screws

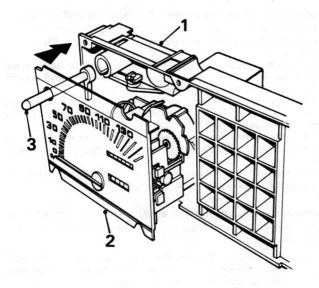

Fig. 13.45 Refitting the speedometer – 1982 on (Sec 13)

1   Instrument panel   *3   Trip meter reset control*
2   Speedometer

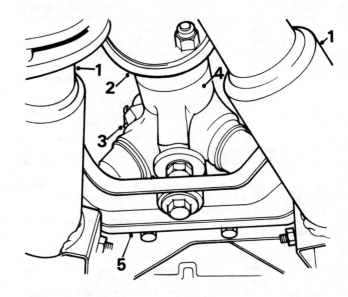

Fig. 13.46 Speedometer transducer – 1982 on (Sec 13)

1   Exhaust pipes   *4   Gearbox*
2   Propeller shaft   *5   Crossmember*
3   Speedometer transducer

Electronic speedometer (1982 on) – description and fault diagnosis

74 All later models are fitted with an electronic speedometer. This instrument operates in the same way as the familiar electronic tachometer. The input in the speedometer consists of electrical impulses operated by a transducer which is fitted to the gearbox in the same place as the old mechanical cable take-off. Inside the speedometer, a stepper motor drives the mileage recorders.

75 In the event of malfunction, the first check must be of the wiring between the transducer and the instrument panel, not forgetting the printed circuit.

76 If the wiring is in order, subsequent checking consists of substituting a known good transducer or speedometer head. The following points may assist in determining which unit is defective:

(a) When a trip computer is fitted, if its distance-related functions are satisfactory, the speedometer transducer is almost certainly OK

(b) If the speedometer needle returns to zero with the ignition off, but stays above zero with the ignition on, the transducer is probably defective

(c) If the speedometer needle stays above zero with the ignition off, the instrument itself is defective

(d) An absence of speed or mileage reading when cold, followed by inaccurate readings after a few miles, denotes a faulty transducer.

77 On vehicles not equipped with a trip computer, the spare plug and socket in the instrument wiring harness which would feed distance information to this trip computer **must not** be connected together; this can lead to transducer failure.

78 Note that the number of gear teeth on the speedometer transducer varies according to final drive ratio, so a transducer taken from another car will not necessarily give satisfactory results. The transducers are colour-coded: black (20 teeth, 3.08:1 final drive), orange (23 teeth, 3.45 : 1 final drive) or red (22 teeth, 3.90 : 1 final drive).

Central door locking system (all models) – precaution

79 When the battery has been disconnected on models with a central door locking system, make sure before reconnecting it that both front door interior locking buttons are in the unlocked (raised) position.

80 Failure to observe the above point can cause damage to the central door locking control unit as a result of a current surge when the battery is reconnected.

Heated rear window – inhibition of operation

81 On models equipped with air conditioning, wiring of the heated rear window relay is such that the relay is de-energised whenever the condenser cooling fans are operating. This arrangement is designed to prevent overloading of the car's electrical system. No attempt should be made to bypass it.

Electric window safety switch – description

82 If the windows are jammed when being opened or closed, the increased current drawn by the motor will cause the safety switch to trip. The safety switch is located behind the front passenger's glovebox (Fig. 13.47). It may be reset, once the obstruction has been cleared, by pressing the red button.

Electric window lift motors – removal and refitting

83 Disconnect the battery earth lead

84 Remove the door trim panel, referring to Chapter 12, Section 14, if necessary.

85 Remove the door-mounted speaker, where applicable, then disconnect the motor wires at the multi-plug.

H.15692.

Fig. 13.47 Electric window safety switch (Sec 13)

86 If suspected motor failure is being investigated, apply battery voltage at the motor multi-plug. If the motor now operates where it did not before, the fault is in the wiring or control circuitry.

87 If the motor does not operate, it must be renewed. Remove the anti-vibration bracket, the interior door catch and plastic moulding and the insulating sheet.

88 Disconnect the door catch operating rod. Unhook the lower lifting stud (front doors only) and remove the abutment plate.

89 Remove the motor mounting bolts, then raise the motor and glass so that the window is fully closed. Wedge the glass in this position.

90 On front doors, remove the front channel securing bolt.

91 Slide the linkage backwards and forwards to release the lifting studs from their channels and withdraw the assembly from the door. If difficulty is experienced on rear doors, drill out the rivet securing the secondary link to the quadrant.

92 Commence refitting by applying battery voltage to the motor multi-plug to position the linkage in the fully closed position.

93 Apply grease to the lifting studs and pivots.

94 Fit the assembly to the door, engaging the upper lifting studs in the glass horizontal support channel.

Front doors

95 Screw in one of the motor mounting bolts.

96 Connect the multi-plug and operate the motor until the other mounting holes are aligned, then fit and tighten the bolts.

97 Refit the front channel securing bolt. Position the lower lifting stud in the abutment plate and refit the abutment plate to the door.

Rear doors

98 Engage the lower lifting stud in its support plate.

99 Connect the multi-plug and operate the motor until the mounting holes are aligned, then fit and tighten the bolts.

All doors

100 Remove the wedge, temporarily reconnect the battery and check the window for correct operation.

101 The remainder of the refitting procedure is a reversal of removal.

Headlamp washer system – description

102 The headlamp washer system, when fitted, is fully automatic in operation. If the driver operates the windscreen washer and the headlamps are switched on, a short burst is delivered by the headlamp washer jets.

103 The headlamp washer reservoir is located at the front of the engine bay on the right-hand side. The filler orifice is accessible from above (photo); the reservoir and the pump are accessible from below after removing the undertray.

104 The headlamp washer jets are integral with the bumper overriders. Section 15 deals with their removal and refitting.

13.103 Headlamp washer reservoir filler

Radio aerial (manually operated) – removal and refitting

105 Remove the radio, as described in Chapter 10, Section 44.

106 Remove the passenger side glovebox, as described in Chapter 12, Section 25.

107 Lift up the carpet in the passenger footwell and carefully free the large grommet from the left-hand panel. Feed the aerial lead through the grommet from the inside of the car.

108 Slacken, but do not remove, the aerial mounting nut so that the aerial is free to move. Swivel the aerial so that its base can be grasped through the grommet hole.

109 Have an assistant remove the aerial mounting nut and retrieve the dome, spacer and seal. Pull the aerial into the car through the grommet hole.

110 Refit in the reverse order to removal. Extend the aerial to make sure it is properly positioned before tightening the mounting nut.

Radio aerial (electrically operated) – removal and refitting

111 Refer to the procedure above for the manually operated aerial, and in addition note the following points:

   (a) Tie a 10 foot (3 metre) length of strong string to the aerial wiring harness (located in the LH wing valance aperture), then separate the harness multi-plug

   (b) Remove the motor mounting screw (above the large grommet hole) before attempting to draw the aerial and motor into the car

   (c) Untie the string when the aerial has entered the car, and use it to draw the harness back into position when refitting.

Radio aerial (electrically operated) – mast renewal

112 If the aerial mast only is damaged, it may be possible to renew it independently of the rest of the aerial. If the mast is available from your Rover dealer, proceed as follows.

113 Extend the aerial by a foot (300 mm) or so, then grip the top section with one pair of pliers and unscrew the tip of the aerial with another pair.

114 Unscrew the wing outer mounting nut and withdraw the mast assembly from the aerial body in an upwards direction.

115 Separate the wire rod section of the mast from the Delrin drive wire by breaking the joint as shown Fig. 13.51.

116 Fit the new mast in the reverse order to removal. **Do not** lubricate the mast now or in service, the only maintenance which should be attempted is the cleaning of the mast with alcohol and wiping with a soft cloth in an upwards direction.

Radio interference (later models)

117 On some later models (1985 on) interference may be caused by the carbon brush in the distributor cap.

118 If a suitable test meter is available, check that the resistance between the coil lead socket on the distributor cap and the tip of the carbon brush does not exceed 30 ohms. If necessary, change the carbon brush or the complete cap.

Electric door mirrors – general

119 Electrically adjustable door mirrors, with built-in heating elements for defrosting purposes, are fitted to some models.

120 Refer to Figs. 13.68 and 13.78 for wiring details.

121 The mirror glass is available separately for renewal.

Cruise control – description

122 Cruise control, when fitted, enables the vehicle to maintain a constant speed without the need for the driver to touch the throttle pedal. It is particularly useful on motorways and similar roads. Two types of control switch may be encountered.

123 With the steering column stalk switch in the 'ON' position, selecting the 'SET' function momentarily will cause the vehicle to hold the speed at which the control was released, provided that the speed is in excess of 30 mph (48 km/h).

124 Operation of the brake or clutch pedals will cause the cruise control to disengage, but the set speed will be held in its memory and may be regained by moving the switch to the 'RESUME' position momentarily. Again, vehicle speed must be in excess of 30 mph (48 km/h).

125 If the ignition is switched off, or the control moved to the 'OFF'

Fig. 13.48 Manually operated radio aerial fitting details (Sec 13)

3   Large grommet

7   Mounting components

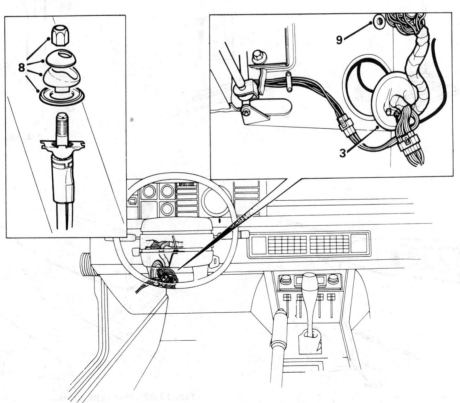

Fig. 13.49 Electrically operated radio aerial fitting details – LHD shown, RHD similar (Sec 13)

3   Large grommet

8   Mounting components

9   Mounting screw

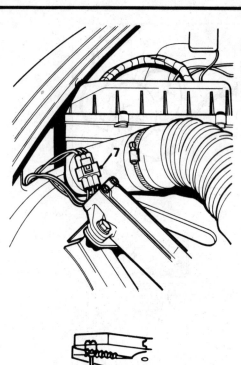

Fig. 13.50 Electrically operated aerial wiring harness multi-plug (7) (Sec 13)

Fig. 13.51 Electrically operated radio aerial mast renewal sequence (Sec 13)

1 Unscrewing tip
2 Withdrawing mast
3 Breaking the joint
A Delrin drive wire

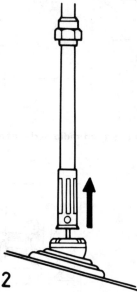

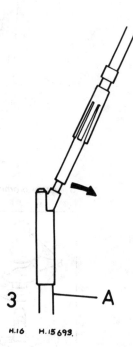

H.16   H.15693.

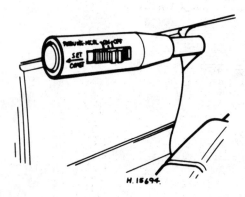

H. 15694.

Fig. 13.52 Early type cruise control switch (Sec 13)

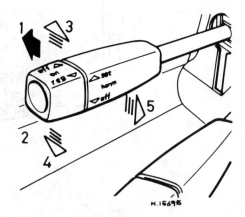

H.15695

Fig. 13.53 Later type cruise control switch (Sec 13)

1 Off (memory lost)
2 On (rest position)
3 Set
4 Off (memory held)
5 Resume

position, the cruise control will disengage and its memory will be lost. (The later type control also has an 'OFF' position whereby memory is retained.)

126 An inertia (deceleration) switch will cause the cruise control to disengage if the vehicle is subject to sudden deceleration, eg as a result of impact.

127 One of two makes of cruise control system may be fitted – Dana or Hella.

Cruise control – test procedure

128 Drive the car at a speed in excess of 30 mph (48 km/h). Move the cruise control switch to the 'ON' position (early type). Select the 'SET' function momentarily and release the throttle; the car should hold the speed at which the control was released.

129 Move the switch to the 'RESUME' position and hold it there; the car should accelerate until the switch is released. Release the switch and check that the car returns to the speed previously selected.

130 Accelerate (using the throttle pedal) to approximately 40 mph (63 km/h). Select and hold the 'SET' function and release the throttle; the car should decelerate as long as the control is held. Release the control at a speed above 30 mph (48 km/h) and check that the cruise control holds the vehicle at that speed.

131 Accelerate again and set a cruise speed around 45 mph (71 km/h). Press the brake pedal lightly and check that the control disengages; when speed has dropped to 40 mph (63 km/h), move the switch momentarily to the 'RESUME' position and check that the previously selected speed is regained and held.

132 On manual transmission models, repeat the above test, this time applying light pressure to the clutch pedal to disengage the cruise control.

133 Cruising at 45 mph (71 km/h), move the cruise control switch to the 'OFF' position. (On later type controls within a slide switch, select the 'OFF' position which cancels the memory). The vehicle must decelerate. Move the switch back to the 'ON' position: the control must not re-engage (ie deceleration must continue).

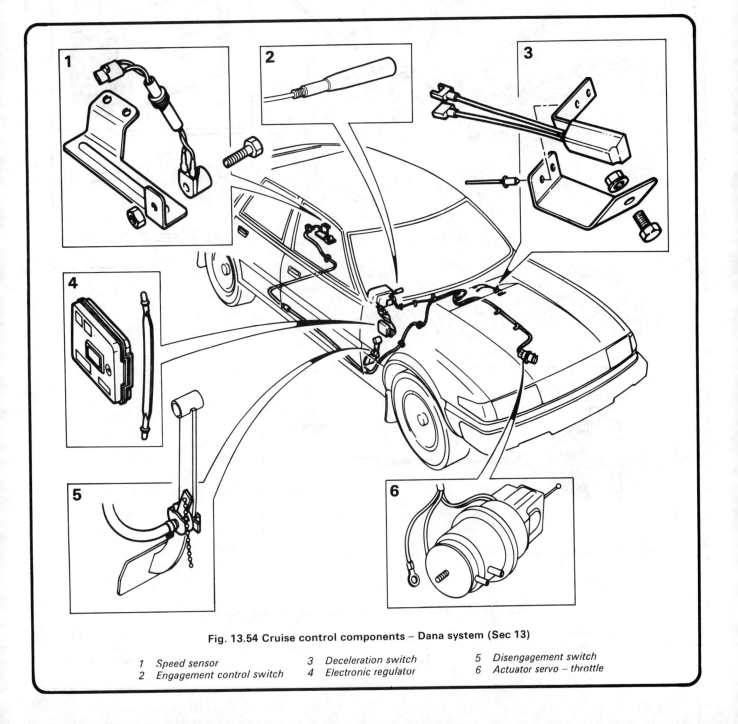

Fig. 13.54 Cruise control components – Dana system (Sec 13)

1 Speed sensor	3 Deceleration switch	5 Disengagement switch
2 Engagement control switch	4 Electronic regulator	6 Actuator servo – throttle

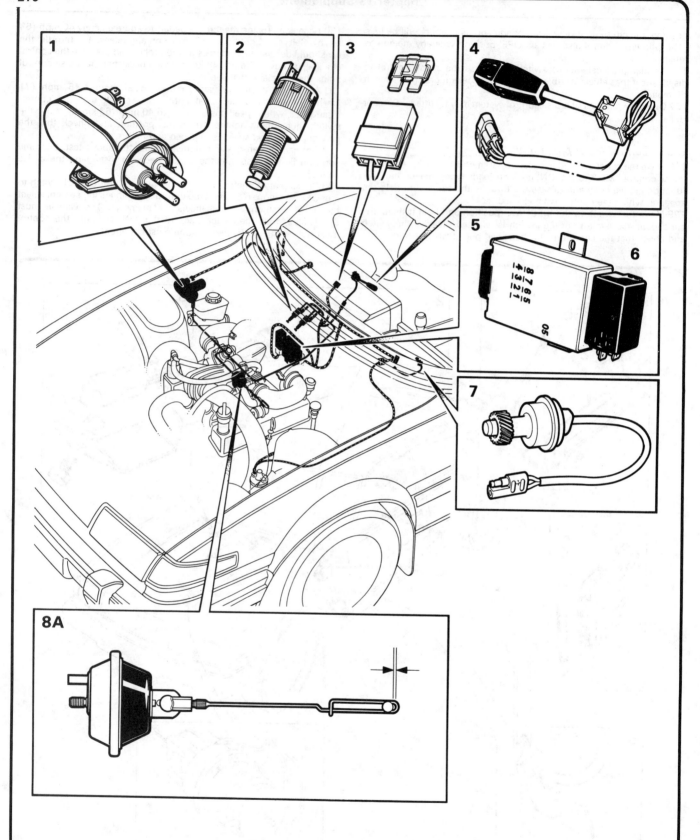

Fig. 13.55 Cruise control components – Hella system (Sec 13)

1	Vacuum control unit	3	Line fuse	5	ECU	7	Speed transducer –
2	Switch and vent valve	4	Control switch	6	Overspeed relay		speedometer
						8A	Pneumatic actuator

Cruise control – component renewal

134 Excepting the adjustment of the regulator, described below, there is little that the DIY mechanic can do to rectify cruise control malfunction apart from renewing components. Mechanical faults such as cable breakage or detachment should be obvious on inspection. The following paragraphs will enable the reader to renew a defective component or to check that the existing item is properly installed.

Servo unit

135 Disconnect the battery earth lead.

136 Remove the air cleaner (not necessary on fuel injection models).

137 Disconnect the operating cable from the servo as follows.

138 Disconnect the vacuum lines from the servo.

139 Disconnect the wiring multi-plugs to release the cruise control harness. Undo the harness securing straps.

140 Unscrew the nut which secures the servo and remove the servo.

141 Refitting is a reversal of removal. Make sure that the earth lead is fitted to the mounting stud, and adjust the operating cable on completion as described further on.

Operating cable

142 On carburettor models, remove the air cleaner.

143 Disconnect the cable from the throttle linkage and free it from the adjustment bracket.

144 At the servo end of the cable, pull back the rubber boot and disconnect the inner cable link.

145 Remove the screws which secure the outer cable to the servo. The cable can now be removed.

146 Refitting is a reversal of removal. Adjust the cable so that there is a clearance of 0.08 in (2 mm) between the throttle pin and the end of the sliding link, then tighten the adjuster locknut.

Disengagement switch

147 Remove the driver's glovebox.

148 Undo the switch harness straps and disconnect the multi-plug.

149 Disconnect the vacuum hose from the switch.

150 Undo the screw which secures the switch. Remove the screw and release the switch from the brake pedal.

151 Detach the bead chain from the actuating lever and remove the switch.

152 When refitting, secure the switch to the brake pedal, then push the actuating lever forwards as far as possible, pull the chain tight and fit the split pin.

153 Make sure that the brake and (if applicable) clutch pedals return to their stops when released. Operate the pedal(s) a couple of times to make sure.

154 The remainder of the refitting procedure is a reversal of removal.

Speed sensor – Dana

155 Raise and securely support the rear of the car.

156 Inside the car, lift the rear carpet and disconnect the speed sensor harness multi-plug.

157 Push the sensor harness and its grommet through the heel board.

158 Working under the car, unclip the harness and remove the sensor retaining bolt. Remove the sensor and wiring harness.

159 Refitting is a reversal of removal, but note the following points:

(a) *Fit the sensor retaining bolt with the head of the bolt nearest the magnet*

(b) *Adjust the mounting bracket to give a clearance of 0.75 to 1.25 in (19 to 32 mm) between the sensor and the magnet*

(c) *Use sealant on the wiring harness grommet*

(d) *Secure the wiring harness under the rear carpet with sticky tape, in a position where it will not be disturbed by fidgety feet.*

Speed sensor magnet – Dana

160 Raise and securely support the rear of the car.

161 Remove the nuts which secure the magnet to the propeller shaft flange.

162 Slide the propeller shaft forwards and extract the bolts and magnet.

163 Refitting is a reversal of removal, but check the magnet-to-sensor clearance as described in paragraph 159 and adjust if necessary.

Electronic regulator – Dana

164 Disconnect the battery earth lead.

165 Open the driver's glovebox and free the regulator (inside the glovebox) from its securing strap.

166 Disconnect the multi-plug and remove the regulator.

167 Refitting is a reversal of removal. Adjust a new regulator, as described in paragraph 186 on, before securing it.

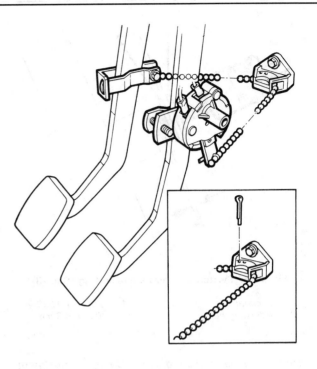

Fig. 13.56 Cruise control disengagement switch (Sec 13)

Inset – automatic transmission chain with pin

Inertia (deceleration) switch – Dana

168 This switch is mounted on the left-hand front suspension tower. Removal and refitting procedures should be self-evident, but note that when refitting, the switch body must be positioned so that it inclines upwards towards the front of the car at an angle of 16°.

ECU and overspeed relay – Hella

169 Disconnect the battery earth lead, and remove the driver's glovebox.

170 Release the mounting bracket, disconnect the multi-plug and remove the overspeed relay with the mounting bracket.

171 Disconnect the multi-plug, extract the fixing screws and remove the ECU from its bracket.

172 Refitting is a reversal of removal.

Control switch – Hella

173 Remove the upper section of the steering column shroud.

174 Disconnect the wiring multi-plug, and release the mounting bracket and the control switch.

175 Refitting is a reversal of removal.

Switch and vent valve – Hella

176 Remove the driver's glovebox.

177 Disconnect the foot pedal switch multi-plug and the hose from the valve.

178 Unscrew the adjusting nut and withdraw the switch and vent valve.

179 Refitting is a reversal of removal, but adjust the valve after loosening the locknuts to give a clearance (A) as shown in Fig. 13.57 between the valve body and the contact button.

Vacuum control unit – Hella

180 Disconnect the wiring multi-plug and the vacuum pipe elbow.

181 Extract the fixing screws and remove the unit.

182 Refitting is a reversal of removal.

Pneumatic actuator – Hella

183 Release the connecting rod from the throttle cam and disconnect the vacuum hose from the actuator.

184 Remove the actuator from its mounting bracket, and at the same time, release the connecting rod balljoint.

185 Refitting is a reversal of removal, but adjust the connecting rod so that there is a clearance of between 0.004 and 0.012 in (0.10 and 0.31 mm) between the end of the rod and the throttle pin.

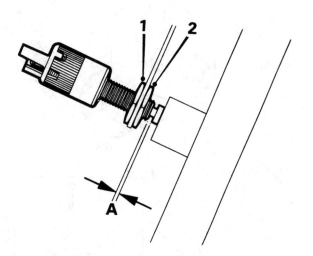

Fig. 13.57 Switch and vent valve setting (Sec 13)

| 1 | Locknut | A | 0.012 to 0.035 in |
| 2 | Adjusting nut | | (0.3 to 0.9 mm) |

Cruise control electronic regulator (Dana) – adjustment

186 The procedure which follows can only be carried out safely by two people. Road conditions must also be suitable for sustained steady speed driving.

187 Connect the regulator multi-plug, but do not stow it in the driver's glovebox. The regulator should be accessible to the person who is going to make the adjustments.

Low speed switch adjustment

188 Start the car and accelerate gently, holding the control switch in the 'RESUME' position. The cruise control should engage (noticeable by the throttle pedal moving away from the driver's foot) at a road speed between 27 and 33 mph (43 and 53 km/h).

189 If adjustment is necessary, turn the low speed adjusting screw clockwise to raise the engagement speed or anti-clockwise to lower it.

Centering adjustment

190 Drive at 40 mph (64 km/h) on a level road and engage the cruise control. Speed should be maintained within ± 2mph (3 km/h). If speed falls off, turn the centering adjustment screw clockwise; turn the screw anti-clockwise if speed increases.

Sensitivity adjustment

191 The sensitivity adjusting screw determines the rate at which the cruise control cycles between 'drive' and 'coast' conditions. To a large extent its adjustment is a matter of personal preference. Turn the adjusting screw clockwise to increase the sensitivity and anti-clockwise to decrease it.

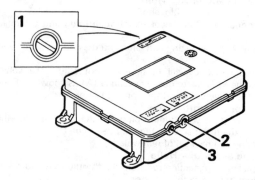

Fig. 13.58 Regulator adjustment screws (Sec 13)

| 1 | Sensitivity screw | 3 | Centring screw |
| 2 | Low speed screw | | |

192 Repeat the centering adjustment check after making any adjustment to the sensitivity.

193 Secure the regulator in the driver's glovebox when adjustments are complete.

Trip computer – description

194 A trip computer is available as an optional extra on certain models. The computer displays time and date information; it can also process and display information relating to fuel consumption (both instantaneous and average) and speed. If the driver enters the length of the journey proposed, the computer will count down the distance to destination and will display an estimated time of arrival. A stopwatch function is also available.

195 Full operating instructions for the trip computer are provided in the operator's handbook supplied with the car. The information given below is intended to assist the owner in tracing possible faults.

Trip computer – checking procedure

196 Disconnect the battery for at least two minutes, then reconnect it. (See paragraph 79 for vehicles with central door locking.)

197 Switch on the ignition and watch the computer display. The 'AV SPEED' LED should light and the alpha-numeric display should show a sequence of five figure eights, from left to right, finishing with a colon in the centre position. The other LEDs should then illuminate in sequence from left to right. After the 'ARR DIST' LED has been illuminated, the 'EL TIME' LED will illuminate once more and the display will start to record elapsed time.

198 Any deviation from the above sequence indicates a fault, either in the keyboard or in the cable and connectors which link the keyboard to the display unit.

199 If the test is satisfactory so far, press the 'CLEAR' button until the display disappears, then release it. Elapsed time will again be displayed, starting from the time when the 'CLEAR' button was pressed.

200 Set the clock as follows. Press the 'TIME' button once, then press the 'SET' button: the word 'SET' will be displayed. Press the correct buttons to enter the time in 24-hour format, then press the 'SET' button again. The clock should now start.

201 To set the date, press the 'TIME' button once (if time is already being displayed) or twice (if any other information is being displayed), then press the 'SET' button. Push the correct buttons to enter the date in numerical form, day first, prefixing single digits with a zero. Thus the 1st May would be entered as 01 05, the 14th day of July as 14 07, and so on. Press the 'SET' button again: the calendar is now operational. The computer display will revert to showing clock time, but the date can be recalled by pressing the 'TIME' button once or twice (as above).

202 To set the stop watch to zero, press the 'STP START' button once; the figures displayed should be the same as for elapsed time. Press the 'STP START' button again and the colon should stop flashing. Press 'CLEAR' to zero the display; the stop watch will start counting when the 'STP START' button is pressed for a third time. The stopwatch will continue to count, first in minutes and seconds, then in hours and minutes, while other computer functions are in use.

203 Any road test of the computer must be over a distance of at least 1.5 miles (or 2.5 kilometres, if metric units are preferred). To set an arrival distance of 1.5 miles, press 'ARR DIST', '1', '5' and 'SET'. (Note that the last digit entered is always preceded by the decimal point when displayed).

204 Drive the car on the chosen test route, trying (so far as road safety and speed limits allow) to drive at a steady 50mph (80 km/h). After one mile press the 'AV CONS' button: the fuel consumption displayed should be roughly 15 to 25 mpg (11 to 19 litres/100km). Press the 'INST CONS' button and note the reading; if a steady speed is maintained, the 'AV CONS' reading should approach the 'INST CONS' reading.

205 Press the 'ARR DIST' button and check that the display is counting downwards in tenths of a mile (or kilometre); similarly pressing the 'DIST' button should show the display counting upwards in tenths.

206 Press the 'ETA' button and check that the display shows a sensible time of arrival, given the distance left to cover and the speed of the vehicle.

207 This completes the road test of the computer. Faults may be due to

the computer itself; its wiring or a faulty transducer. The following points may be of interest when tracing a fault:

(a) *If speed and distance-related information is unsatisfactory and the speedometer is also malfunctioning, the speedometer transducer is faulty, or disconnected.*

(b) *If the fuel consumption (instantaneous or average) is falsely claimed to be 0.0 mpg (or 0.0 litre/00 km), the fuel flow sensor is faulty or disconnected. Similar conclusions may be drawn from an 'INST CONS' reading of 6553.5.*

208 When tracing computer wiring, note that many wire colours change across multi-plugs. This does not necessarily mean that the wiring is incorrect.

209 If the computer 'locks up', ie it will neither accept commands nor display information, disconnect the battery for at least two minutes, then set the computer up as previously described. 'Lock-up' can be caused by incorrect operation, voltage irregularities or strong eletro-magnetic fields.

Trip computer – removal and refitting

210 Disconnect the battery earth lead.

211 Remove the minor instrument pack.

212 Remove the screws which secure the trip computer to the instrument shroud and lens, then remove the computer.

213 Refit in the reverse order to removal. Reset the computer on completion.

Printed circuit board edge connector – renewal

214 Where one connector in a printed circuit board multiple edge connector is defective, there is no need to renew the whole multi-block. Individual connectors are available from a Rover dealer.

215 To remove a connector, unplug the multi-block and insert a thin rod or stiff wire from the circuit board side of the connector. Release the connector with the rod, as shown in Fig. 13.59.

216 Cut the old connector off its wire, strip the insulation on the end of the wire and crimp or solder the new connector in place.

217 Press the connector into place in the multi-block until the tag clicks home.

Horns – removal and refitting

218 The horns are located ahead of the radiator.

219 Before removing a horn, disconnect the battery and pull off the Lucar type connectors.

220 Unscrew the horn mounting nut, take off the lock washer and withdraw the horn downward through the upper air intake slot. Refitting is a reversal of removal

Tailgate wash/wipe system

221 The pushbutton type switch operates the tailgate wiper and washer simultaneously. Once the switch button is released, the wipe and wash action stops automatically after a predetermined period.

222 The wiper arm and blade are removed in a similar way to that described for the windscreen wiper in Chapter 10.

223 To remove the tailgate wiper motor, remove the wiper arm and blade, and the drive spindle seal.

224 Open the tailgate fully, remove the wiper motor cover and unscrew the wiper motor mountings.

225 Disconnect the wiring plug and withdraw the motor.

226 Refitting is a reversal of removal, but make sure that the motor has been run, and then switched off, to ensure it is in its parked position before fitting the wiper arm and blade.

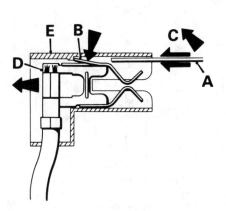
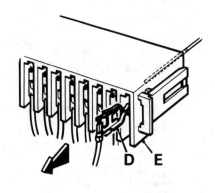

Fig. 13.59 Renewing a printed circuit board edge connector (Sec 13)

A *Stiff wire* C *Lift rod to release tag* E *Multi-block*
B *Tag* D *Connector*

Wiring diagrams commence overleaf

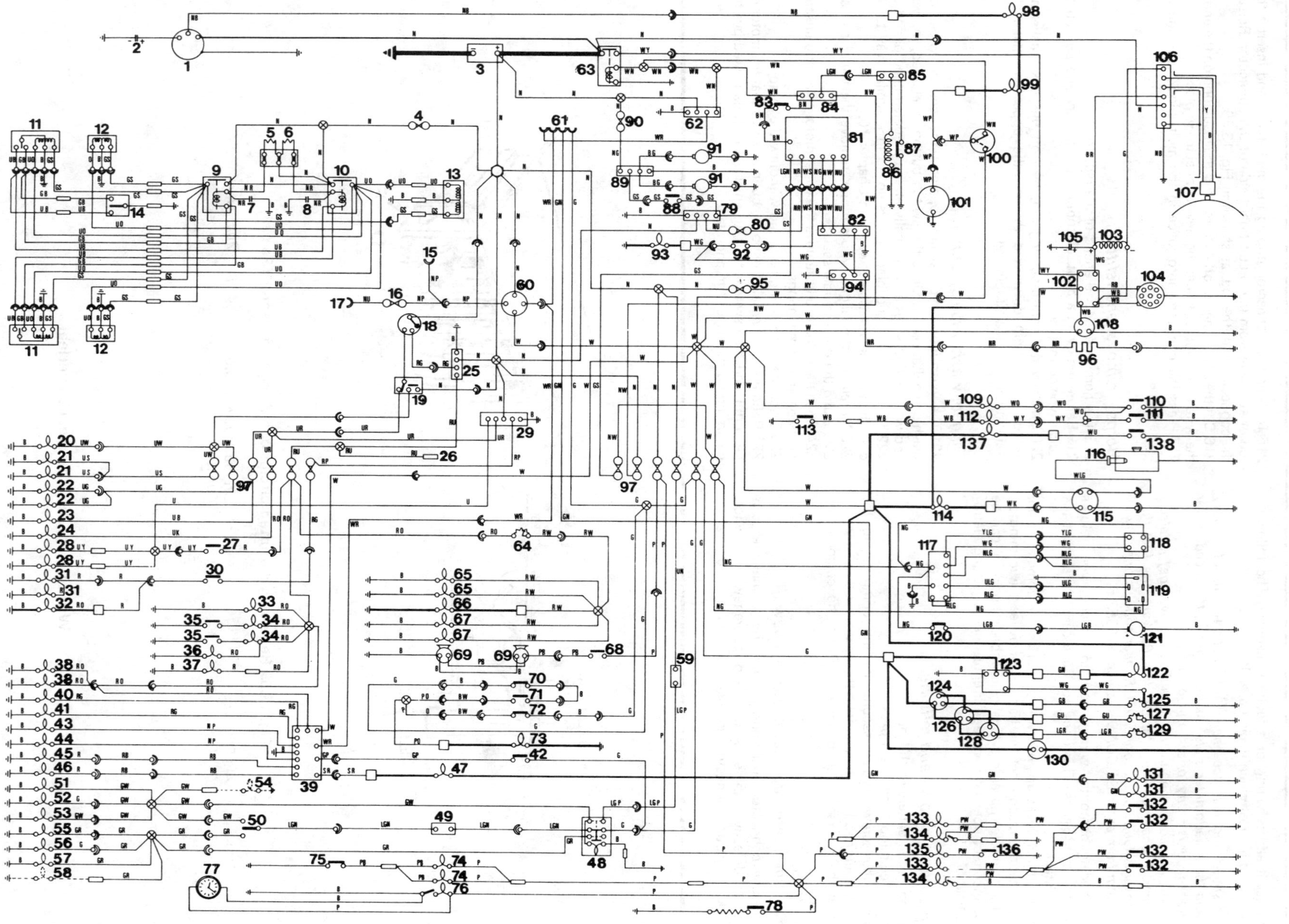

Fig. 13.60 Wiring diagram for V8 S models

Key to Fig. 13.60

No	Description	No	Description	No	Description
1	Alternator	47	Bulb failure warning lamp	93	Heated rear window warning light
2	Radio capacitor	48	Hazard switch	94	Heated rear window relay
3	Battery	49	Turn signal lamp flasher unit	95	Heated rear window in-line fuse
4	Door lock fuse	50	Turn signal switch	96	Heated rear window
5	Resistor – lock	51	RH flasher warning light	97	Fusebox
6	Resistor – unlock	52	RH front flasher lamp	98	Ignition warning light
7	Capacitor – lock	53	RH rear flasher lamp	99	Oil pressure warning light
8	Capacitor – unlock	54	RH flasher repeater lamp	100	Oil pressure switch
9	Relay – lock	55	LH rear flasher lamp	101	Fuel pump
10	Relay – unlock	56	LH front flasher lamp	102	Ballast resistor
11	Front door lock solenoid and key switch	57	LH flasher warning lamp	103	Ignition coil
12	Rear door lock solenoid	58	LH flasher repeater lamp	104	Ignition distributor
13	Tailgate lock solenoid	59	Hazard flasher unit	105	Radio capacitor
14	Door lock interior switch	60	Ignition/starter switch	106	Engine diagnosis socket
15	Window lift circuit pick-up	61	Starter inhibitor switch and reverse lamp switch pick-up	107	Engine diagnosis timing reference transducer
16	Radio fuse	62	Starter relay	108	Tachometer
17	Radio pick-up	63	Starter motor solenoid	109	Brake warning light
18	Master light switch	64	Panel rheostat	110	Brake fluid level switch
19	Main/dip/flash switch	65	Tachometer illumination	111	Brake pressure differential switch
20	Main beam warning light	66	Instrument illumination	112	Handbrake warning light
21	RH main beam	68	Horn-push	113	Handbrake switch
22	LH main beam	69	Horn	114	Coolant low warning light
23	RH dip beam	70	Passenger's belt switch	115	Coolant low indicator unit
24	LH dip beam	71	Passenger's seat switch	116	Coolant low sensor
25	Lighting supply line relay	72	Driver's belt switch	117	Windscreen wiper switch
26	Headlamp wash/wipe pick-up	73	Seat belt warning lamp	118	Windscreen wiper delay unit
27	Front foglamp switch	74	Engine bay lamp	119	Windscreen wiper motor
28	Front foglamp	75	Engine bay lamp switch	120	Windscreen washer switch
29	Rear foglamp relay	76	Map lamp	121	Windscreen washer pump
30	Rear foglamp switch	77	Clock	122	Low fuel warning light
31	Rear foglamp	78	Cigarette lighter	123	Low fuel delay unit
32	Rear foglamp warning light	79	Blower motor supply relay	124	Fuel indicator
33	Fibre optic lamp	80	Blower motor in-line fuse	125	Fuel tank unit
34	Glovebox lamp	81	Air conditioning unit	126	Temperature indicator
35	Glovebox lamp switch	82	Blower motor speed control relay	127	Temperature transmitter
36	Clock illumination	83	Plenum chamber ambient temperature switch	128	Oil pressure indicator
37	Cigarette lighter illumination	84	Clutch relay	129	Oil pressure transmitter
38	Number plate illumination lamp	85	Thermal fuse	130	Battery condition indicator
39	Bulb failure indicator	86	Clutch	131	Reverse lamp
40	RH tail lamp	87	Superheat switch	132	Door switch
41	LH tail lamp	88	Ranco valve high pressure cut-in	133	Front door guard lamp
42	Stop-lamp switch	89	Condenser fan relay	134	Interior lamp
43	RH stop-lamp	90	Condenser fan in-line fuse	135	Luggage area lamp
44	LH stop-lamp	91	Condenser fan	136	Luggage area lamp switch
45	RH front parking lamp	92	Heated rear window switch	137	Choke warning light
46	LH front parking lamp			138	Choke warning light switch

Colour code

B	Black	LG	Light green	P	Purple	U	Blue
G	Green	N	Brown	R	Red	W	White
K	Pink	O	Orange	S	Slate	Y	Yellow

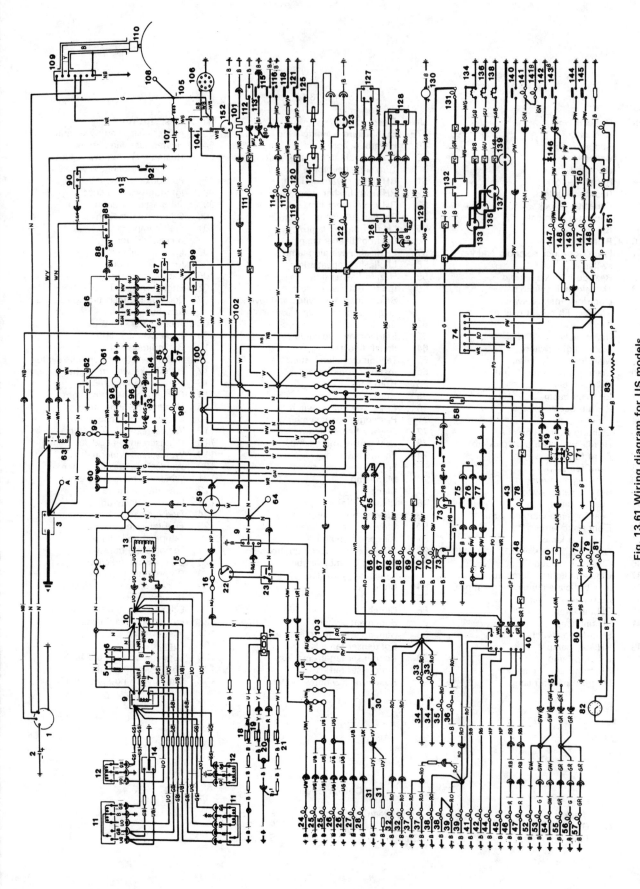

Fig. 13.61 Wiring diagram for US models

Key to Fig. 13.61

No	Description	No	Description	No	Description
1	Alternator	53	Front flasher lamp – LH	104	Ballast resistor
2	Radio capacitor	54	Rear flasher lamp – RH	105	Ignition coil
3	Battery	55	Rear flasher lamp – LH	106	Ignition distributor
4	Door lock fuse	56	Front flasher lamp – LH	107	Radio capacitor
5	Resistor – lock	57	Flasher warning lamp – LH	108	Fuel injection pick-up
6	Resistor – unlock	58	Hazard flasher unit	109	Engine diagnosis socket
7	Capacitor – lock	59	Ignition/starter switch	110	Engine diagnosis timing reference transducer
8	Capacitor – unlock	60	Starter inhibitor switch and reverse lamp switch pick-up	111	Oxygen sensor warning light
9	Relay – lock	61	Fuel injection pick-up	112	Service interval counter
10	Relay – unlock	62	Starter relay	113	Ignition switch
11	Front door lock solenoid and key switch	63	Starter motor solenoid	114	Brake warning light
12	Rear door lock solenoid	64	Fuel injection pick-up	115	Brake pressure differential switch
13	Tailgate lock solenoid	65	Panel rheostat	116	Brake fluid level switch
14	Door lock interior switch	66	Radio illumination	117	Handbrake warning light
15	Window lift circuit pick-up	67	Fibre optic lamp	118	Handbrake switch
16	Radio fuse	68	Tachometer illumination	119	Ignition warning light
17	Radio and stereo cassette	69	Instrument illumination	120	Oil pressure warning light
18	Speaker – RH front	70	Speedometer illumination	121	Oil pressure switch
19	Speaker – RH rear	71	Hazard switch illumination	122	Coolant low warning light
20	Speaker – LH rear	72	Horn-push	123	Coolant low indicator unit
21	Speaker – LH front	73	Horn	124	Coolant low sensor – expansion tank
22	Master light switch	74	Seat belt timer/buzzer unit	125	Coolant low sensor – radiator
23	Main/dip/flash switch	75	Passenger's belt switch	126	Windscreen wiper switch
24	Main beam warning light	76	Passenger's seat switch	127	Windscreen wiper delay unit
25	Main beam – RH	77	Driver's belt switch	128	Windscreen wiper motor
26	Main beam – LH	78	Seat belt warning lamp	129	Windscreen washer switch
27	Dip beam – RH	79	Engine bay lamp	130	Windscreen washer pump
28	Dip beam – LH	80	Engine bay lamp switch	131	Low fuel warning light
29	Lighting supply line relay	81	Map lamp	132	Low fuel delay unit
30	Front foglamp switch	82	Clock	133	Fuel indicator
31	Front foglamp pick-up	83	Cigarette lighter	134	Fuel tank unit
32	Front marker lamp	84	Blower motor supply relay	135	Temperature indicator
33	Glovebox lamp	85	Blower motor line fuse	136	Temperature transmitter
34	Glovebox lamp switch	86	Air conditioning unit	137	Oil pressure indicator
35	Clock illumination	87	Blower motor speed control relay	138	Oil pressure transmitter
36	Cigarette lighter illumination	88	Plenum chamber ambient temperature switch	139	Battery condition indicator
37	Licence plate illumination lamp	89	Clutch relay	140	Key switch
38	Rear marker lamp	90	Thermal fuse	141	Reverse lamp
39	Tail lamp	91	Clutch	142	Door switch – LH front
40	Bulb failure indicator	92	Superheat switch	143	Door switch – LH rear
41	Tail lamp – RH	93	Ranco valve high pressure cut-in	144	Door switch – RH front
42	Tail lamp – LH	94	Condenser fan relay	145	Door switch – RH rear
43	Stop-lamp switch	95	Condenser fan in-line fuse	146	Diode
44	Stop-lamp – RH	96	Condenser fan	147	Front door guard lamp
45	Stop-lamp – LH	97	Heated backlight switch	148	Interior lamp
46	Front parking lamp – RH	98	Heated backlight warning light	149	Luggage boot lamp
47	Front parking lamp – LH	99	Heated backlight relay	150	Luggage boot lamp switch
48	Bulb failure warning light	100	Heated backlight in-line fuse	151	Sun visor illumination circuit
49	Hazard switch	101	Heated backlight	152	Tachometer
50	Turn signal lamp flasher unit	102	Fuel injection pick-up		
51	Turn signal switch	103	Fusebox		
52	Flasher warning light – RH				

Wiring colour code as Fig. 13.60

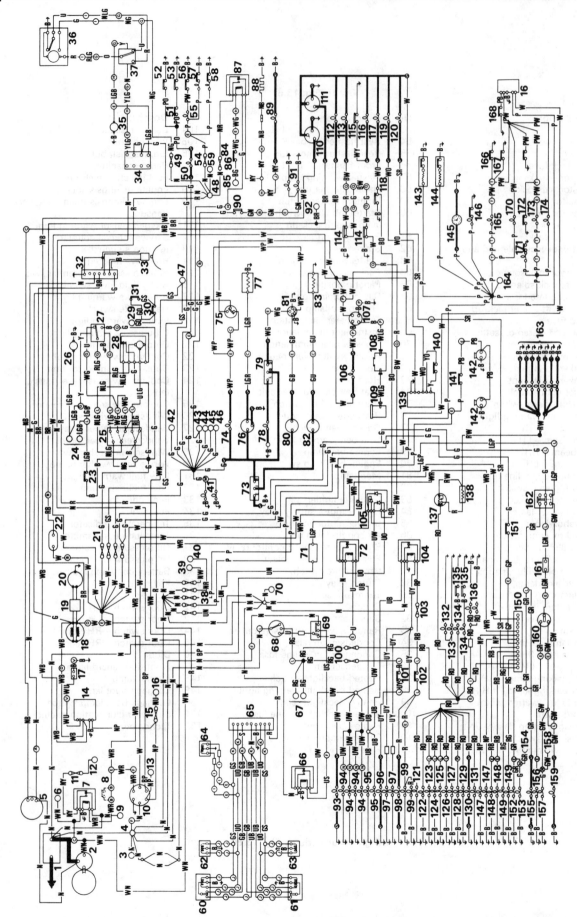

Fig. 13.62 Wiring diagram for 1982 and 1983 UK models

Key to Fig. 13.62

No	Description	No	Description	No	Description
1	Battery	54	Fuse (rear fusebox)	114	Brake pad wear sensor
2	Starter motor and solenoid	55	Boot lamp	115	Handbrake switch
3	Thermal cut-out (window lift) pick-up point	56	Boot lamp switch	116	Handbrake warning light
4	Terminal stud	57	RH reading lamp and switch	117	Brake failure warning light
5	Alternator	58	LH reading lamp and switch	118	Brake fluid level indicator
6	Magnetic clutch relay (air conditioning) pick-up point	59	Sunroof pick-up point	119	Low oil level warning light
		60	Front RH door key switch and solenoid	120	Bulb failure warning light
7	Starter relay	61	Front LH door key switch and solenoid	121	Rear foglamp switch illumination
8	Starter inhibitor switch (automatic)	62	Rear RH door solenoid	122	Front foglamp switch illumination
9	Headlamp washer connection	63	Rear LH door solenoid	123	Interior light switch illumination
10	Ignition switch	64	Tailgate solenoid	124	Hazard switch illumination
11	Fuse (main fusebox)	65	Central door locking control unit	125	Heated rear screen switch illumination
12	Aerial pick-up point	66	Main beam relay	126	Window lift isolation switch illumination
13	Sunroof switch pick-up point	67	Headlamp washer connection	
14	FASD (fully automatic starting device) module unit	68	Master lighting switch	127	Fibre optic light source
		69	Headlamp dip and flash switch	128	Trip computer illumination
15	Fuse (main fusebox)	70	Headlamp washer connection	129	Sunroof switch illumination
16	Radio pick-up point	71	Hazard unit	130	Clock illumination
17	FASD unit	72	Dip beam relay	131	Rear wash/wipe switch illumination
18	Coil	73	Voltage stabilizer	132	Rear cigar lighter illumination
19	Amplifier	74	Oil pressure warning light	133	Front cigar lighter illumination
20	Distributor	75	Oil pressure switch	134	Glovebox illumination
21	Fuses (main fusebox)	76	Oil pressure gauge	135	Glovebox switch
22	Speed transducer	77	Oil pressure transmitter	136	Number plate illumination
23	Screen washer switch	78	Low fuel warning light	137	Illumination rheostat
24	Headlamp washer connection	79	Thermal delay switch	138	Ballast
25	Front wash/wipe switch	80	Fuel gauge	139	Low oil level unit
26	Screen washer pump	81	Fuel tank and pump unit	140	Low oil level switch
27	Front wiper programme unit	82	Temperature gauge	141	Horn push
28	Wiper motor	83	Temperature transmitter	142	Horn
29	Cooling fan relay (air conditioning) pick-up point	84	Fuse (rear fusebox)	143	Rear cigar lighter
		85	Cooling fan (air conditioning) connection	144	Front cigar lighter
30	Pressure switch (air conditioning)			145	Clock
31	Temperature switch (air conditioning)	86	Heated rear screen switch	146	Map light and switch
		87	Heated rear screen relay	147	Stop-lamp
32	Engine sensing socket	88	Heated rear screen	148	Side lamp
33	Transducer	89	Heated rear screen warning light	149	Tail lamp
34	Rear wash/wipe switch	90	Reversing lamp switch	150	Bulb failure monitor unit
35	Screen washer pump	91	Reversing lamp	151	Stop-lamp switch
36	Wiper motor	92	Trip computer connection	152	LH rear flasher lamp
37	Rear wiper programme unit	93	Main beam warning light	153	LH front flasher lamp
38	Fuses (main fusebox)	94	Headlamp main beam	154	LH repeater lamp facility
39	Magnetic clutch (air conditioning) pick-up point	95	Headlamp dip beam	155	LH flasher warning light
		96	Front foglamp warning light	156	RH rear flasher lamp
40	Blower motor (air conditioning) pick-up point	97	Front foglamp	157	RH front flasher lamp
		98	Rear foglamp warning light	158	RH repeater lamp facility
41	Automatic transmission selector level illumination	99	Rear foglamp	159	RH flasher warning light
		100	Fuses (main fusebox)	160	Direction indicator switch
42	Trip computer connection	101	Front foglamp switch	161	Flasher unit
43	Window lift circuit pick-up point	102	Rear foglamp switch	162	Hazard switch
44	Door mirror switch pick-up point	103	Fuse (main fusebox)	163	Panel illumination
45	Window isolation switch pick-up point	104	Rear foglamp relay	164	Trip computer connection
		105	Diode unit	165	RH door open lamp
46	Window lift circuit pick-up point	106	Low coolant warning light	166	RH front door switch
47	Fan speed switch (air conditioning) pick-up point	107	Low coolant level indicator	167	RH rear door switch
		108	Expansion tank probes	168	Interior light switch
48	Terminal stud	109	Radiator probe	169	Courtesy light delay unit
49	Fuse (rear fusebox)	110	Tachometer	170	RH interior light
50	Seat belt warning light	111	Speedometer	171	Underbonnet lamp and switch
51	Sensor switch	112	Ignition warning light	172	LH front door switch
52	Driver's seat belt buckle switch	113	Brake pad wear warning light	173	LH door open lamp
53	Passenger's seat belt buckle switch			174	LH interior light

Wiring harness identification

A	Engine sensing connection	I	Tailgate harness connection	R	Trip computer connection
B	Gearbox harness connection	J	Central door locking connection	S	Printed circuit connection
C	Engine harness connection	K	Door locking unit connection	T	Door harness connection
D	Constant energy coil connection	L	Facia harness connection	U	Heater/air conditioning harness connection
E	Body harness connection	M	Automatic transmission selector lever connection	
F	Column switch connection			V	Fuel flow harness connection
G	Wiper programme unit connection	N	Low coolant sensor connection	W	Throttle potentiometer connection
H	Boot harness connection	Q	Brake pad wear harness connection	

Wiring colour code as Fig. 13.60

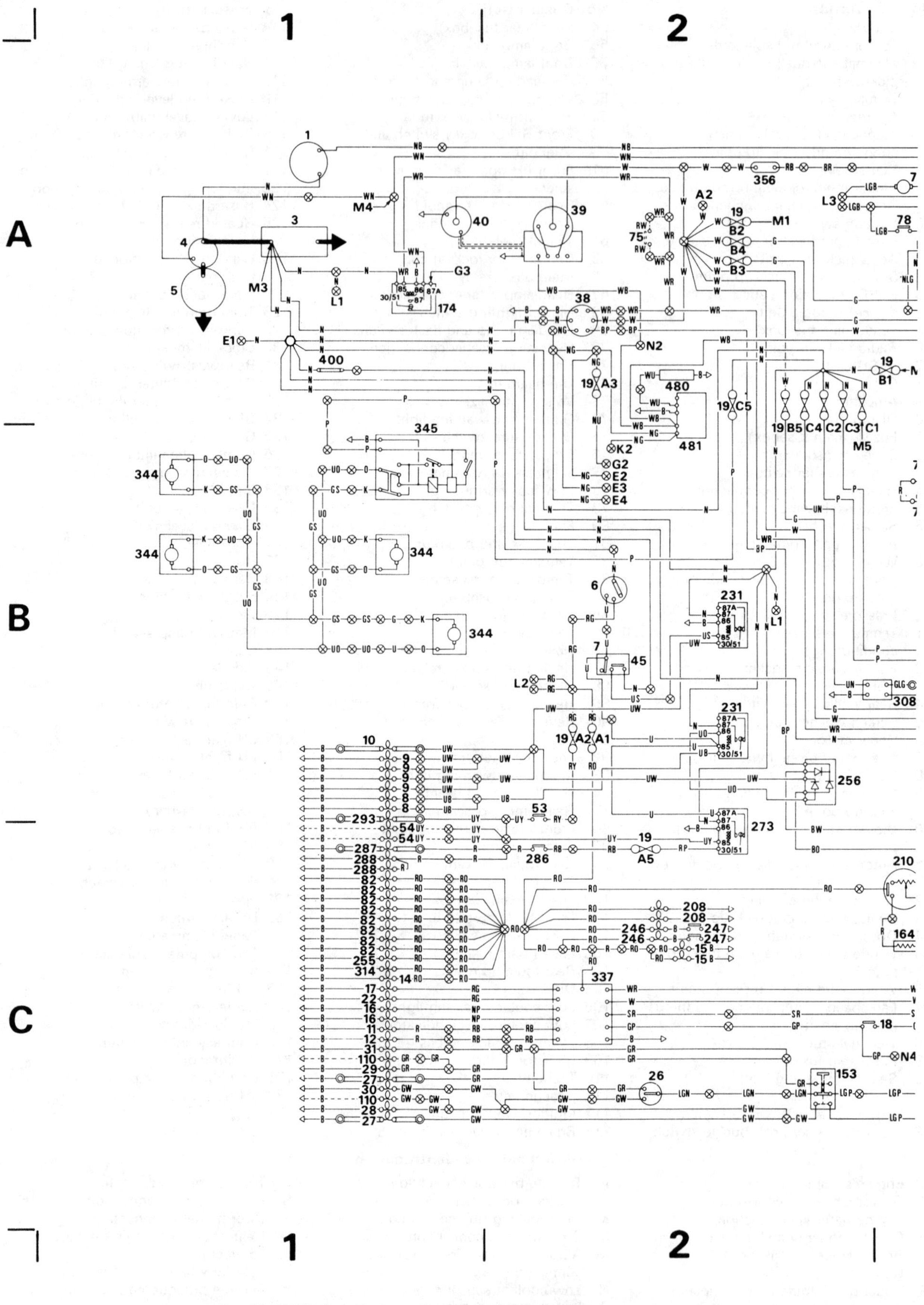

Fig. 13.63 Wiring diagram for SE and Vanden Plas models – 1984

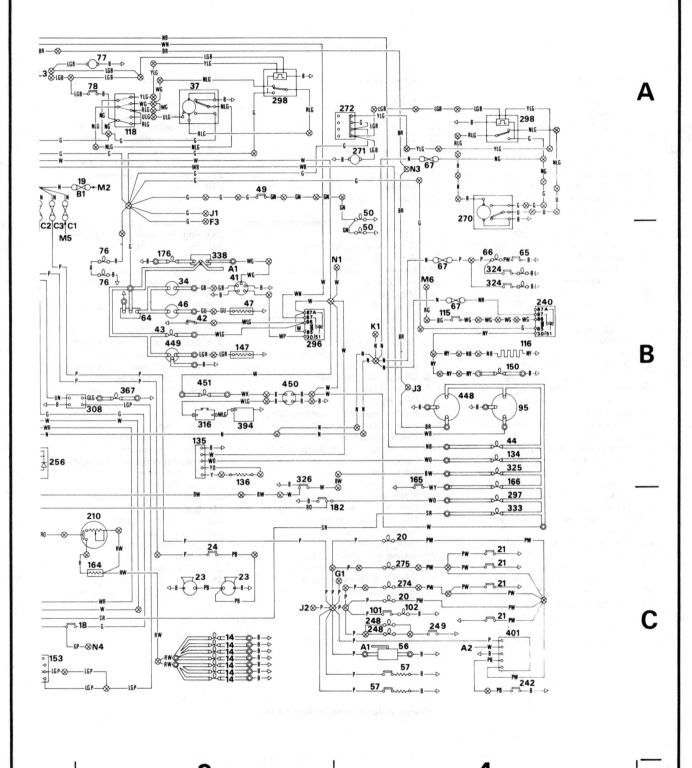

Fig. 13.63 Wiring diagram for SE and Vanden Plas models – 1984 (continued)

Key to Fig. 13.63

No	Description
1	Alternator
3	Battery
4	Starter motor solenoid
5	Starter motor
6	Lighting switch
7	Headlamp dip switch
8	Headlamp dip beam
9	Headlamp main beam
10	Main beam warning lamp
11	RH side lamp
12	LH side lamp
14	Panel illumination lamp(s)
15	Number plate illumination lamps(s)
16	Stop lamp(s)
17	RH tail lamp
18	Stop lamp switch
19	Fusebox
20	Interior lamp(s)
21	Interior lamp door switch
22	LH tail lamp
23	Horn(s)
24	Horn push
26	Direction indicator switch
27	Direction indicator warning lamp(s)
28	RH front direction indicator lamp
29	LH front direction indicator lamp
30	RH rear direction indicator lamp
31	LH rear direction indicator lamp
34	Fuel level indicator
37	Windscreen wiper motor
38	Ignition/starter switch
39	Ignition coil
40	Distributor
41	Fuel pump/tank unit
42	Oil pressure switch
43	Oil pressure warning lamp or indicator
44	Ignition or no charge warning lamp
45	Headlamp flash switch
46	Water temperature indicator
47	Washer temperature transducer
49	Reverse lamp switch
50	Reverse lamp(s)

No	Description
53	Fog lamp switch
54	Fog lamp(s)
56	Clock
57	Cigar lighter
64	Voltage stabiliser
65	Boot lamp switch
66	Boot lamp
67	Line fuse
75	Automatic gearbox ignition inhibitor switch
76	Automatic gearbox selector indicator lamp
77	Windscreen washer motor
78	Windscreen washer switch
82	Switch illumination lamp(s)
95	Tachometer
101	Map light switch
102	Map light
110	Direction indicator repeater lamps
115	Heated rear screen switch
116	Heated rear screen
118	Windscreen washer/wiper switch
134	Oil level indicator
135	Oil level indicator switch
136	Oil level sump unit
147	Oil pressure transducer
150	Heated rear screen warning lamp
153	Hazard warning switch
164	Ballast resistor or resistive cable
165	Handbrake warning lamp switch
166	Handbrake warning lamp
174	Starter solenoid relay
176	Fuel level warning lamp
182	Brake fluid level switch
208	Cigar lighter illumination lamp
210	Panel illumination lamp rheostat/resistor
231	Headlamp relay
240	Heated rear screen relay
242	Two way interior lamp switch
246	Glove box illumination lamp
247	Glove box illumination switch

No	Description
248	Bonnet lamp
249	Bonnet lamp switch
255	Fibre optics illumination bulb
256	Brake warning blocking diode
270	Rear screen wiper motor
271	Rear screen washer motor
272	Rear screen wipe wash switch
273	Front fog lamp(s) relay
274	LH door lamp
275	RH door lamp
286	Fog rearguard lamp switch
287	Fog rearguard warning lamp
288	Fog rearguard lamp(s)
293	Foglamp warning lamp
296	Fuel pump protection relay
297	Brake failure warning lamp
298	Windscreen wiper delay unit
308	Direction indicator/hazard flasher unit
314	Clock illumination lamp (console)
316	Coolant level sensor/switch
324	Parcel shelf/map lamp
325	Brake pad wear warning lamp
326	Brake pad wear sensor
333	Bulb failure warning lamp
337	Bulb fail unit(s)
338	Low fuel warning light delay unit
344	Door lock motor
345	Door lock motor control unit
356	Speed transducer
367	Trailer towing warning light
394	Radiator switch
400	Fusible link
401	Interior lamp delay unit
448	Speedometer
449	Oil pressure gauge
450	Low coolant level indicator
451	Low coolant warning lamp
480	FASD
481	FASD Control unit
A1	Digital clock pick-up point
A2	Ignition feed pick-up point

Wiring colour code as Fig. 13.60

Key to Fig. 13.64

No	Description
1	Alternator
3	Battery
4	Starter motor solenoid
5	Starter motor
6	Lighting switch
7	Headlamp dip switch
8	Headlamp dip beam
9	Headlamp main beam
10	Main beam warning lamp
11	RH side lamp
12	LH side lamp
14	Panel illumination lamp(s)
15	Number plate illumination lamp(s)
16	Stop lamp(s)
17	RH tail lamp
18	Stop lamp switch
19	Fuse box
20	Interior lamp(s)
21	Interior lamp door switch
22	LH tail lamp
23	Horn(s)
24	Horn push
26	Direction indicator switch
27	Direction indictor warning lamp(s)
28	RH front direction indicator lamp
29	LH front direction indicator lamp
30	RH rear direction indicator lamp
31	LH rear direction indicator lamp
34	Fuel level indicator
35	Fuel level indicator tank unit
37	Windscreen wiper motor
38	Ignition/starter switch
39	Ignition coil
40	Distributor
42	Oil pressure switch
43	Oil pressure warning lamp or indicator
44	Ignition or no charge warning lamp
45	Headlamp flash switch
46	Water temperature indicator
47	Water temperature transducer
49	Reverse lamp switch

No	Description
50	Reverse lamp(s)
53	Fog lamp switch
54	Fog lamp(s)
56	Clock
57	Cigar lighter
64	Voltage stabiliser
65	Boot lamp switch
66	Boot lamp
67	Line fuse
75	Automatic gearbox ignition inhibitor switch
76	Automatic gearbox selector indicator lamp
77	Windscren washer motor
78	Windscreen washer switch
82	Switch illumination lamp(s)
95	Tachometer
101	Map light switch
102	Map light
110	Direction indicator repeater lamps
115	Heated rear screen switch
116	Heated rear screen
118	Windscreen washer/wiper switch
134	Oil level indicator
135	Oil level indicator switch
136	Oil level sump unit
147	Oil pressure transducer
150	Heated rear screen warning lamp
153	Hazard warning switch
164	Ballast resistor or resistive cable
165	Handbrake warning lamp switch
166	Handbrake warning lamp
174	Starter solenoid relay
176	Fuel level warning lamp
182	Brake fluid level switch
208	Cigar lighter illumination lamp
210	Panel illumination lamp rheostat/resistor
231	Headlamp relay
240	Heated rear screen relay
242	Two way interior lamp switch

No	Description
246	Glove box illumination lamp
247	Glove box illumination switch
248	Bonnet lamp
249	Bonnet lamp switch
255	Fibre optics illumination bulb
256	Brake warning blocking diode
270	Rear screen wiper motor
271	Rear screen washer motor
272	Rear screen wipe wash switch
273	Front fog lamp(s) relay
274	LH door lamp
275	RH door lamp
286	Fog rearguard lamp switch
287	Fog rearguard warning lamp
288	Fog rearguard lamp(s)
293	Foglamp warning lamp
297	Brake failure warning lamp
298	Windscreen wiper delay unit
308	Direction indicator/hazard flasher unit
314	Clock illumination lamp (console)
316	Coolant level sensor/switch
324	Parcel shelf/map lamp
325	Brake pad wear warning lamp
326	Brake pad wear sensor
333	Bulb failure warning lamp
337	Bulb fail unit(s)
338	Low fuel warning light delay unit
344	Door lock motor
345	Door lock motor control unit
356	Speed transducer
367	Trailer towing warning light
394	Radiator switch
400	Fusible link
401	Interior lamp delay unit
448	Speedometer
449	Oil pressure gauge
450	Low coolant level indicator
451	Low coolant warning lamp
A	Digital clock pick-up point
A2	Ignition feed pick-up point

Wiring colour code as Fig. 13.60

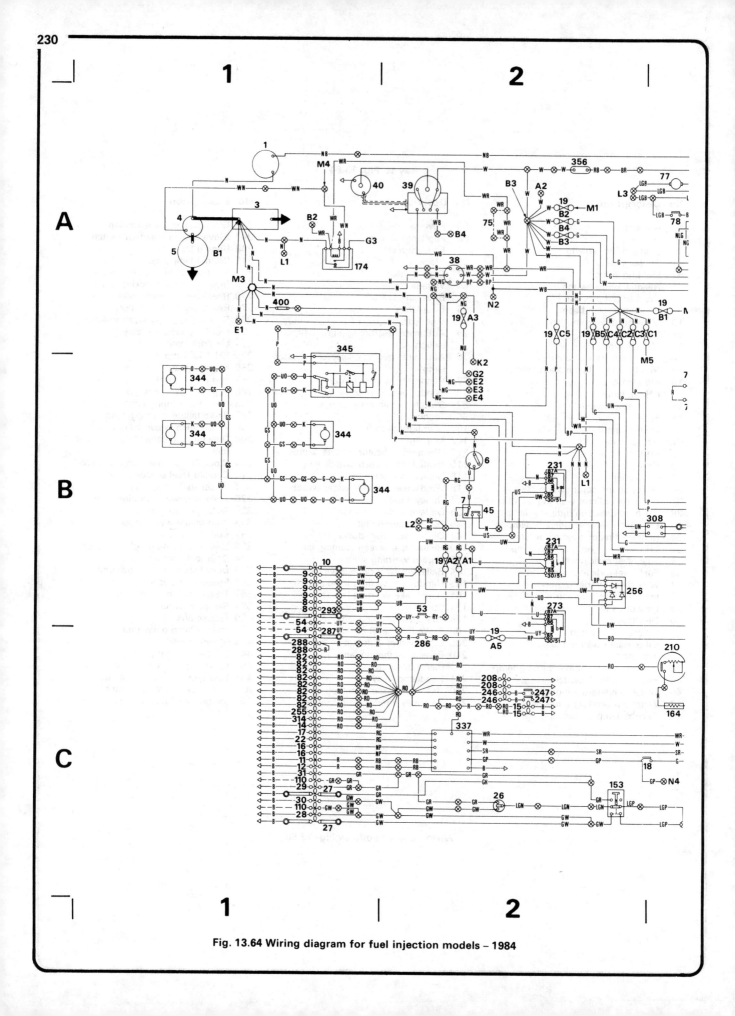

Fig. 13.64 Wiring diagram for fuel injection models – 1984

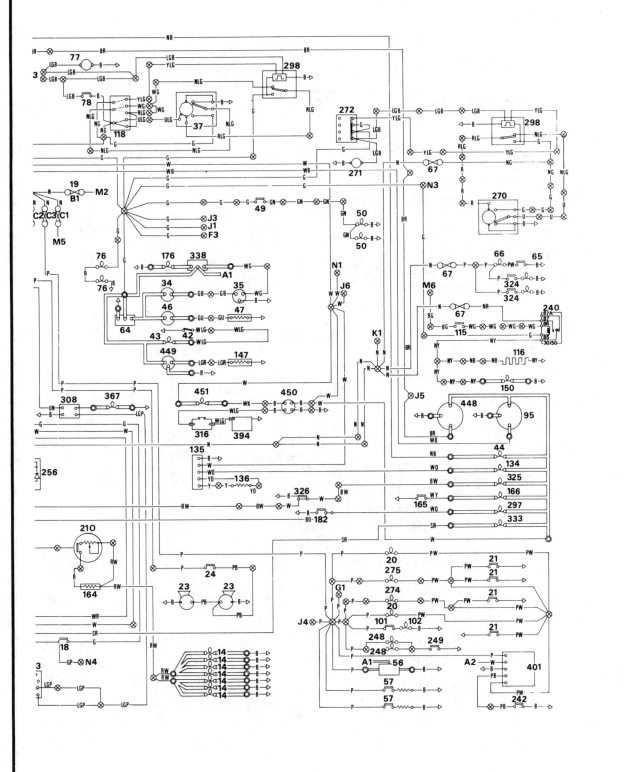

Fig. 13.64 Wiring diagram for fuel injection models – 1984 (continued)

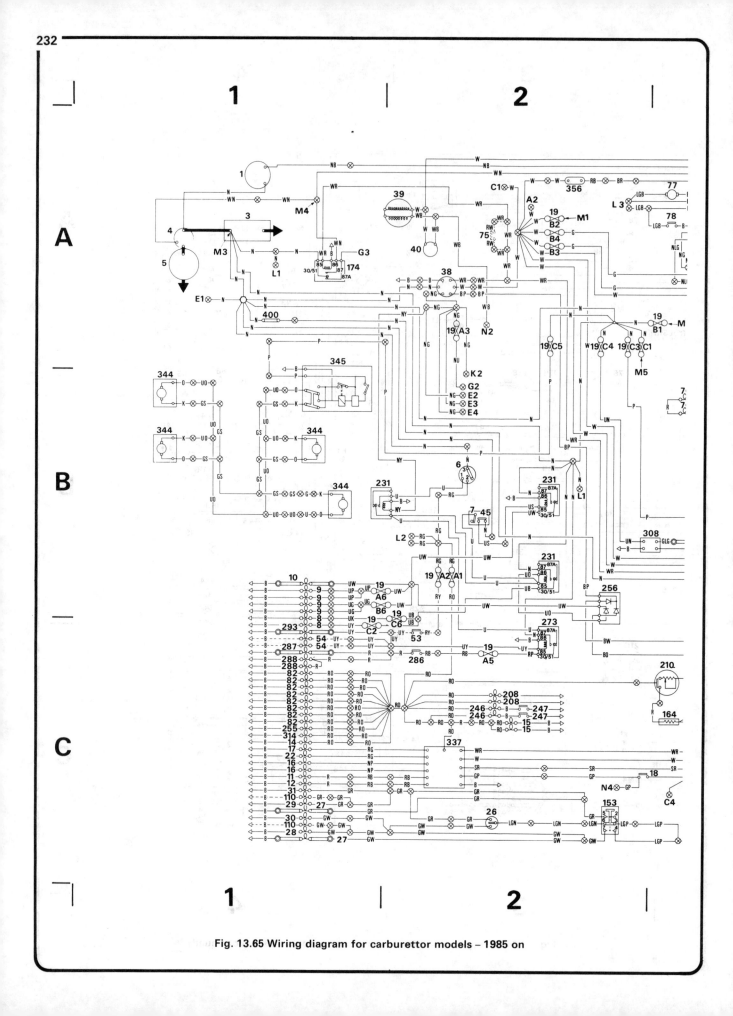

Fig. 13.65 Wiring diagram for carburettor models – 1985 on

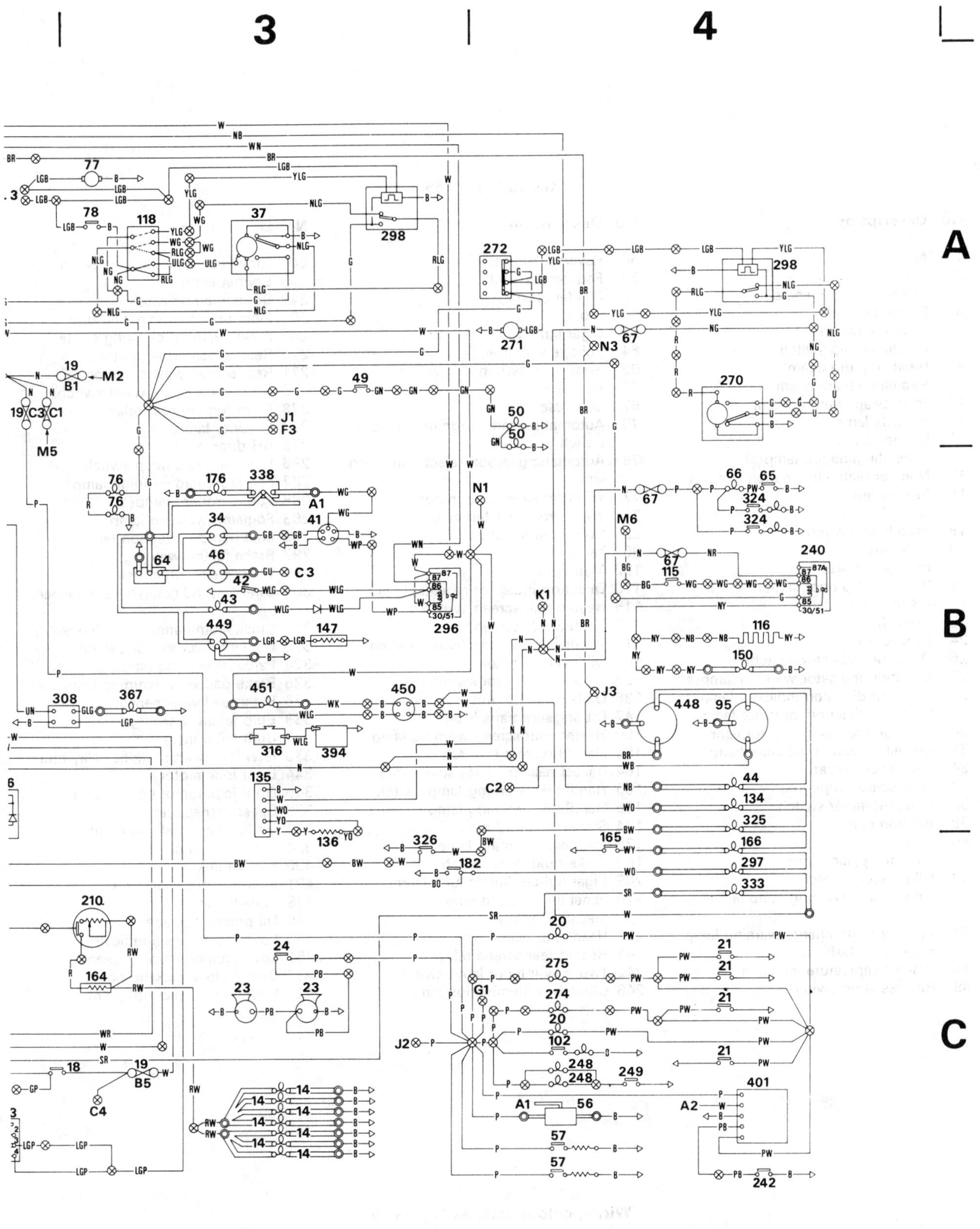

Fig. 13.65 Wiring diagram for carburettor models – 1985 on (continued)

Key to Fig. 13.65

No	Description
1	Alternator
3	Battery
4	Starter motor solenoid
5	Starter motor
6	Lighting switch
7	Headlamp dip switch
8	Headlamp dip beam
9	Headlamp main beam
10	Main beam warning lamp
11	RH side lamp
12	LH side lamp
14	Panel illumination lamp(s)
15	Number plate illumination lamp(s)
16	Stop lamp(s)
17	RH tail lamp
18	Stop lamp switch
19	Fuse box
20	Interior lamp(s)
21	Interior lamp door switch
22	LH tail lamp
23	Horn(s)
24	Horn push
26	Direction indicator switch
27	Direction indicator warning lamp(s)
28	RH front direction indicator lamp
29	LH front direction indicator lamp
30	RH rear direction indicator lamp
31	LH rear direction indicator lamp
34	Fuel level indicator
37	Windscreen wiper motor
38	Ignition/starter switch
39	Ignition coil
40	Distributor
41	Fuel pump/tank unit
42	Oil pressure switch
43	Oil pressure warning lamp or indicator
44	Ignition or no charge warning lamp
45	Headlamp flash switch
46	Water temperature indicator
49	Reverse lamp switch

No	Description
50	Reverse lamp(s)
53	Fog lamp switch
54	Fog lamp(s)
56	Clock
57	Cigar lighter
64	Voltage stabiliser
65	Boot lamp switch
66	Boot lamp
67	Line fuse
75	Automatic gearbox ignition inhibitor switch
76	Automatic gearbox selector indicator lamp
77	Windscreen washer motor
78	Windscreen washer switch
82	Switch illumination lamp(s)
95	Tachometer
102	Map light
110	Direction indicator repeater lamps
115	Heated rear screen switch
116	Heated rear screen
118	Windscreen washer/wiper switch
134	Oil level indicator
135	Oil level indicator switch
136	Oil level sump unit
147	Oil pressure transducer
150	Heated rear screen warning lamp
153	Hazard warning switch
164	Ballast resistor or resistive cable
165	Handbrake warning lamp switch
166	Handbrake warning lamp
174	Starter solenoid relay
176	Fuel level warning lamp
182	Brake fluid level switch
208	Cigar lighter illumination lamp
210	Panel illumination lamp rheostat/resistor
231	Headlamp relay
240	Heated rear screen relay
242	Two way interior lamp switch
246	Glove box illumination lamp

No	Description
247	Glove box illumination switch
248	Bonnet lamp
249	Bonnet lamp switch
255	Fibre optics illumination bulb
256	Brake warning blocking diode
270	Rear soreen wiper motor
271	Rear screen washer motor
272	Rear screen wipe wash switch
273	Front fog lamp(s) relay
274	LH door lamp
275	RH door lamp
286	Fog rearguard lamp switch
287	Fog rearguard warning lamp
288	Fog rearguard lamp(s)
293	Foglamp warning lamp
296	Fuel pump protection relay
297	Brake failure warning lamp
298	Windscreen wiper delay unit
308	Direction indicator/hazard flasher unit
314	Clock illumination lamp (console)
316	Coolant level sensor/switch
324	Parcel shelf/map lamp
325	Brake pad wear warning lamp
326	Brake pad wear sensor
333	Bulb failure warning lamp
337	Bulb fail unit(s)
338	Low fuel warning light delay unit
344	Door lock motor
345	Door lock motor control unit
356	Speed transducer
367	Trailer towing warning light
394	Radiator switch
400	Fusible link
401	Interior lamp delay unit
448	Speedometer
449	Oil pressure gauge
450	Low coolant level indicator
451	Low coolant warning lamp
A1	Digital clock pick-up point
A2	Ignition feed pick-up point

Wiring colour code as Fig. 13.60

Key to Fig. 13.66

No	Description
1	Alternator
3	Battery
4	Starter motor solenoid
5	Starter motor
6	Lighting switch
7	Headlamp dip switch
8	Headlamp dip beam
9	Headlamp main beam
10	Main beam warning lamp
11	RH side lamp
12	LH side lamp
14	Panel illumination lamp(s)
15	Number plate illumination lamp(s)
16	Stop lamp(s)
17	RH tail lamp
18	Stop lamp switch
19	Fuse box
20	Interior lamp(s)
21	Interior lamp door switch
22	LH tail lamp
23	Horn(s)
24	Horn push
26	Direction indicator switch
27	Direction indicator warning lamps(s)
28	RH front direction indicator lamp
29	LH front direction indicator lamp
30	RH rear direction indicator lamp
31	LH rear direction indicator lamp
34	Fuel level indicator
35	Fuel level indicator tank unit
37	Windscreen wiper motor
38	Ignition/starter switch
39	Ignition coil
40	Distributor
42	Oil pressure switch
43	Oil pressure warning lamp
44	Ignition or no charge warning lamp
45	Headlamp flash switch
46	Water temperature indicator
47	Water temperature transducer
49	Reverse lamp switch
50	Reverse lamp(s)

No	Description
53	Fog lamp switch
54	Fog lamp(s)
56	Clock
57	Cigar lighter
64	Voltage stabiliser
65	Boot lamp switch
66	Boot lamp
67	Line fuse
75	Automatic gearbox ignition inhibitor switch
76	Automatic gearbox selector indicator lamp
77	Windscreen washer motor
78	Windscreen washer switch
82	Switch illumination lamp(s)
95	Tachometer
101	Map light switch
102	Map light
110	Direction indicator repeater lamps
115	Heated rear screen switch
116	Heated rear screen
118	Windscreen washer/wiper switch
134	Oil level indicator
135	Oil level indicator switch
136	Oil level sump unit
147	Oil pressure transducer
150	Heated rear screen warning lamp
153	Hazard warning switch
164	Ballast resistor or resistive cable
165	Handbrake warning lamp switch
166	Handbrake warning lamp
174	Starter solenoid relay
176	Fuel level warning lamp
182	Brake fluid level switch
208	Cigar lighter illumination lamp
210	Panel illumination lamp rheostat/resistor
231	Headlamp relay
240	Heated rear screen relay
242	Two way interior lamp switch
246	Glove box illumination lamp

No	Description
247	Glove box illumination switch
248	Bonnet lamp
249	Bonnet lamp switch
255	Fibre optics illumination bulb
256	Brake warning blocking diode
270	Rear screen wiper motor
271	Rear screen washer motor
272	Rear screen wipe wash switch
273	Front fog lamp(s) relay
274	LH door lamp
275	RH door lamp
286	Fog rearguard lamp switch
287	Fog rearguard warning lamp
288	Fog rearguard lamp(s)
293	Foglamp warning lamp
297	Brake failure warning lamp
298	Windscreen wiper delay unit
308	Direction indicator/hazard flasher unit
314	Clock illumination lamp (console)
316	Coolant level sensor/switch
324	Parcel shelf/map lamp
325	Brake pad wear warning lamp
326	Brake pad wear sensor
333	Bulb failure warning lamp
337	Bulb fail unit(s)
338	Low fuel warning light delay unit
344	Door lock motor
345	Door lock motor control unit
356	Speed transducer
367	Trailer towing warning light
394	Radiator switch
400	Fusible link
401	Interior lamp delay unit
448	Speedometer
449	Oil pressure gauge
450	Low coolant level indicator
451	Low coolant warning lamp
452	Fuel injection trigger
A1	Digital clock pick-up point
A2	Ignition feed pick-up point

Wiring colour code as Fig. 13.60

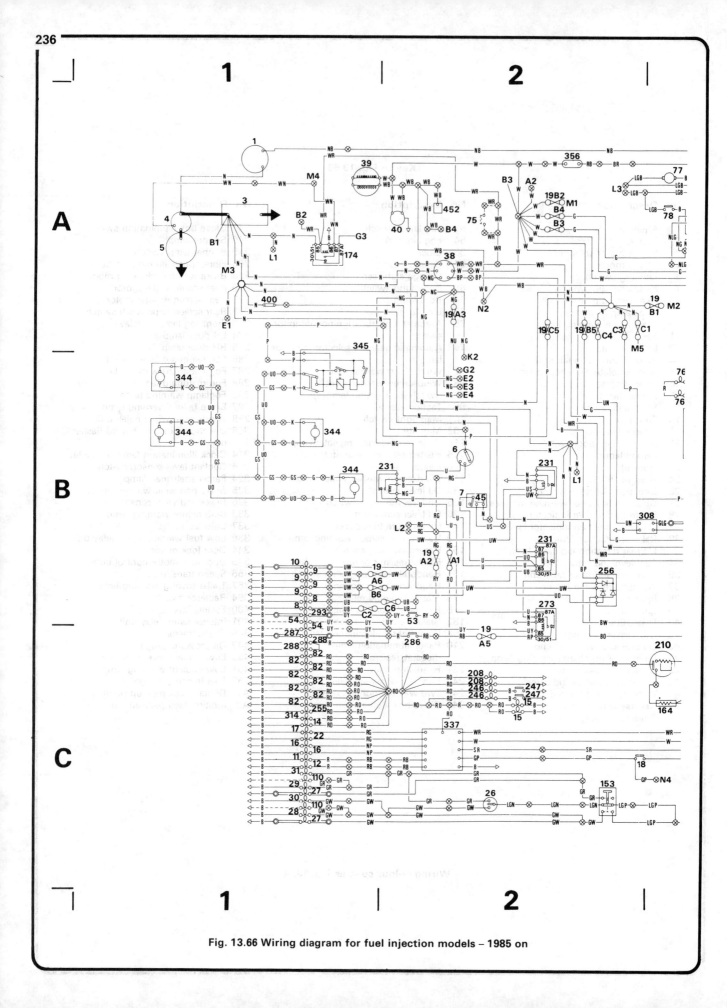

Fig. 13.66 Wiring diagram for fuel injection models – 1985 on

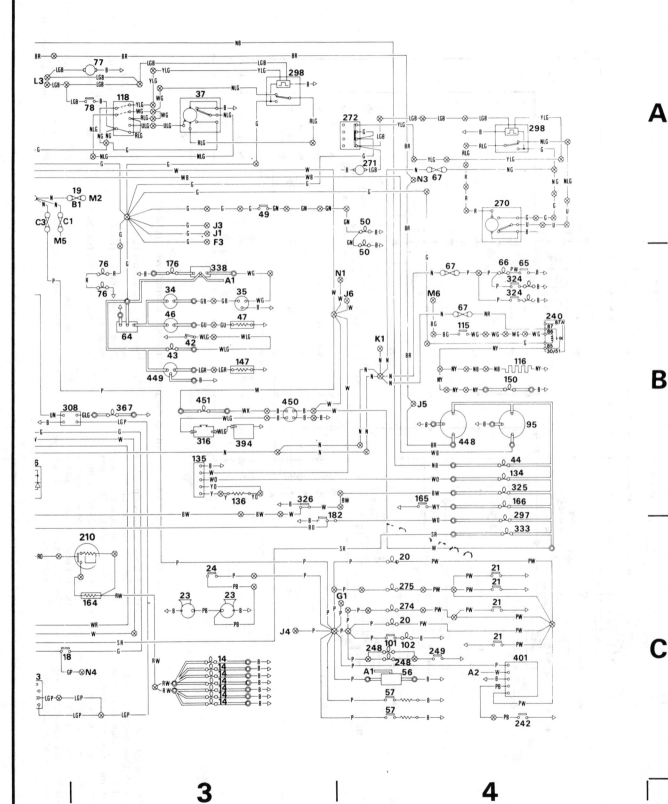

Fig. 13.66 Wiring diagram for fuel injection models – 1985 on (continued)

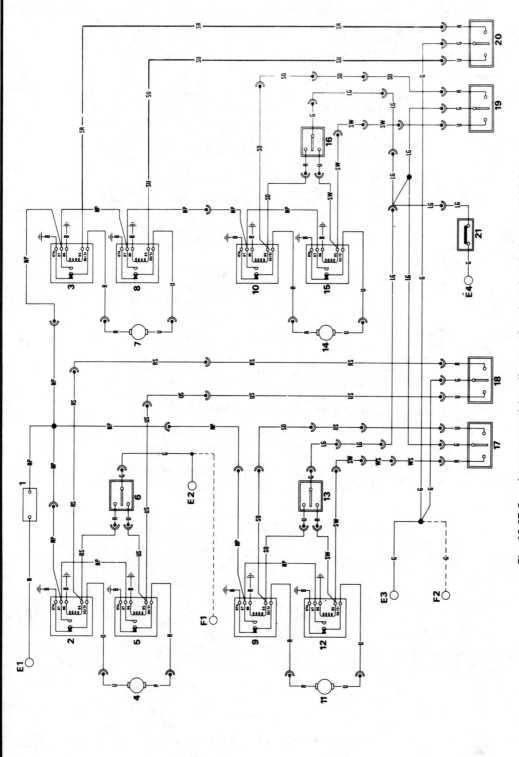

Fig. 13.67 Supplementary wiring diagram for electric windows – 1982-84

1   Thermal cut-out
2   LH front window open relay
3   RH front window open relay
4   LH front window lift motor
5   LH front window close relay
6   LH front window lift switch
7   RH front window lift motor
8   RH front window close relay
9   LH rear window open relay

10   RH rear window open relay
11   LH rear window lift motor
12   LH rear window close relay
13   LH rear window lift switch
14   RH rear window lift motor
15   RH rear window close relay
16   RH rear window lift switch
17   Driver's master switch (LH rear window)

18   Driver's master switch (LH front window)
19   Driver's master switch (RH rear window)
20   Driver's master switch (RH front window)
21   Isolation switch
E1   Thermal cut-out pick-up point

E2   Passenger front window lift switch pick-up point
E3   Driver's front window master switch pick-up point
E4   Window isolation switch pick-up point
F1   Passenger's electric door mirror pick-up point
F2   Driver's electric door mirror pick-up point

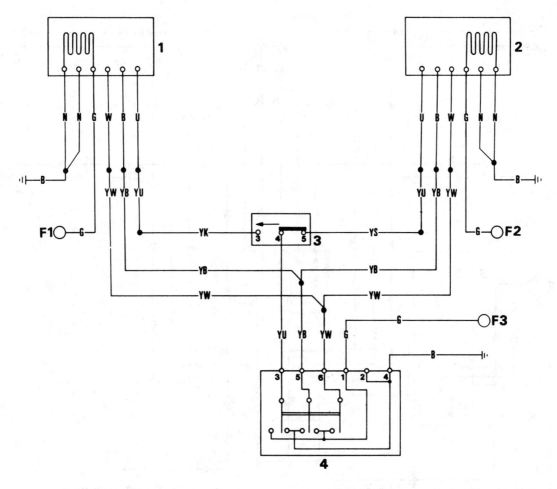

Fig. 13.68 Supplementary wiring diagram for electric door mirrors – 1982–84

1   LH door mirror and demist element
2   RH door mirror and demist element
3   Door mirror changeover switch
4   Door mirror control switch

F1   Passenger's door mirrors demist element pick-up point
F2   Driver's door mirror demist element pick-up point
F3   Door mirror control switch pick-up point

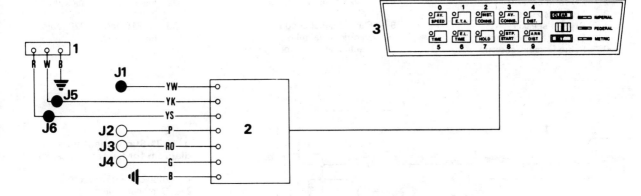

Fig. 13.69 Supplementary wiring diagram for trip computer – 1982–1984

1   Fuel transducer
2   Trip computer
3   Keyboard
J1   Speed transducer pick-up point

J2   Trip computer pick-up point
J3   Trip computer illumination
J4   Trip computer pick-up point
J5   Fuel injection only

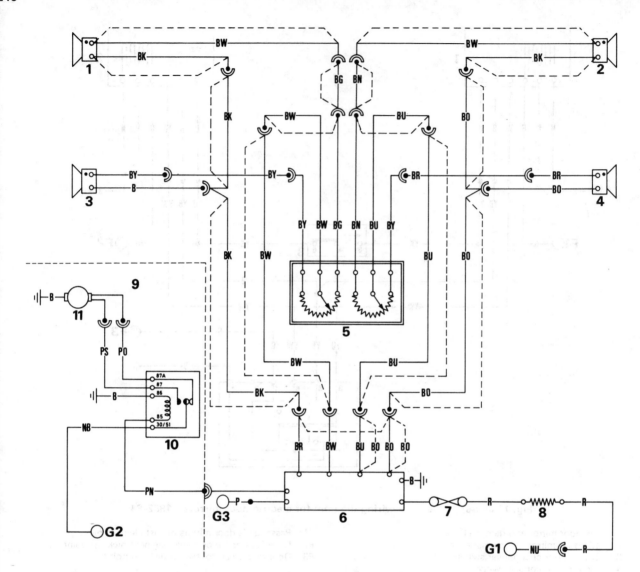

Fig. 13.70 Supplementary wiring diagram for radio/cassette unit – 1982–84

1	LH front speaker	7	In-line fuse – 3 Amp
2	RH front speaker	8	Choke – radio/cassette only
3	LH rear speaker	9	Electric aerial circuit
4	RH rear speaker	10	Electric aerial relay
5	Speaker balance control	11	Electric aerial motor
6	Radio or radio/cassette		

G1	Radio pick-up point
G2	Electrical aerial pick-up point
G3	AC810 and AC820 radio battery feed

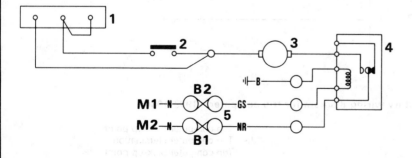

Fig. 13.71 Supplementary wiring diagram for heater – 1982–84

1	Blower motor switch
2	Overheat switch
3	Heater motor
4	Heater relay
5	Fuses
M1	Heater pick-up point
M2	Blower motor pick-up point

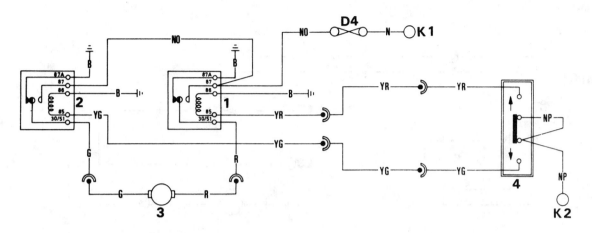

Fig. 13.72 Supplementary wiring diagram for electrically operated sunroof – 1982–84

1	Sun roof relay	3	Sun roof motor	K1	Sunroof pick-up point
2	Sun roof relay	4	Sun roof switch	K2	FASD module unit pick-up point

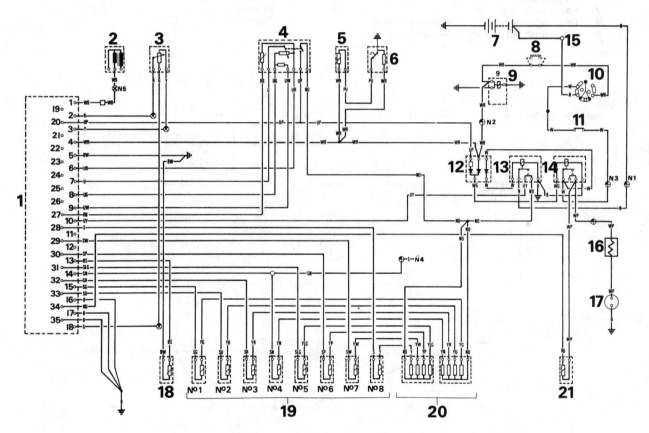

Fig. 13.73 Supplementary wiring diagram for fuel injection system – 1982–84

1	Electronic control unit	10	Ignition switch	19	Injectors
2	Ignition coil	11	Inertia switch	20	Power resistors
3	Throttle potentiometer	12	Fuel injection relay	21	Extra air valve
4	Air flow meter	13	Main relay	N1	Pick-up point
5	Cold start injector	14	Pump relay	N2	Pick-up point
6	Thermo time switch	15	Terminal stud	N3	Pick-up point
7	Battery	16	Fuel pump resistor	N4	Trip computer interface unit
8	Starter inhibitor switch – automatic	17	Fuel pump	N5	Control unit pick-up point
9	Starter relay	18	Coolant temperature sensor		

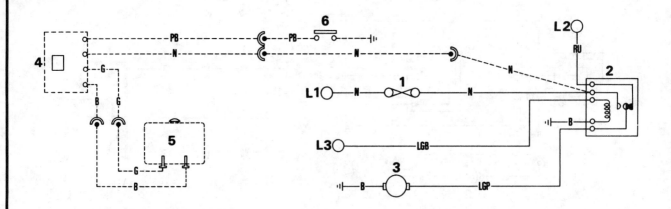

Fig. 13.74 Supplementary wiring diagram for headlamp washer system – 1982–84

1	In-line fuse – 25 amp	6	Underbonnet lamp switch (German market only)
2	Powerwash relay	L1	Powerwash pick-up point
3	Powerwash pump	L2	Powerwash pump
4	Level indicator module (German market only)	L3	Powerwash pick-up point
5	Powerwash bottle probes (German market only)		

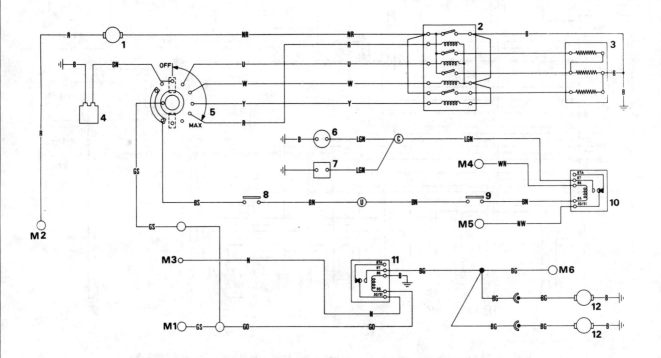

Fig. 13.75 Supplementary wiring diagram for air conditioning system – 1982–84

1	Blower motor	7	Fast idle solenoid	M1	Cooling fan relay pick-up point
2	Air conditioning relay	8	Mode micro switch	M2	Blower motor pick-up point
3	Resistor assembly	9	Ambient temperature switch	M3	Cooling fan pick-up point
4	Vacuum solenoid	10	Magnetic clutch relay	M4	Magnetic clutch pick-up point
5	Blower speed switch	11	Cooling fan relay	M5	Magnetic clutch pick-up point
6	Compressor	12	Cooling fan	M6	Heated rear screen connection

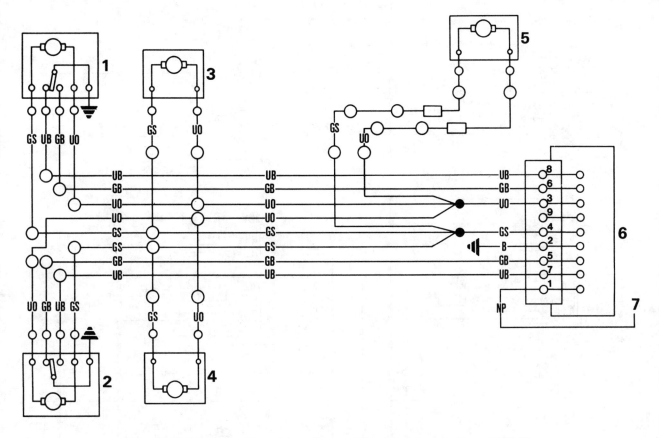

Fig. 13.76 Supplementary wiring diagram for central door locking – 1982–84

1	Front door switch/motor – R.H	5	Taildoor motor
2	Front door switch/motor – L.H.	6	Control unit
3	Rear door motor – R.H.	7	Feed from fuse No. 5 in the Supplementary fusebox
4	Rear door motor – L.H.		

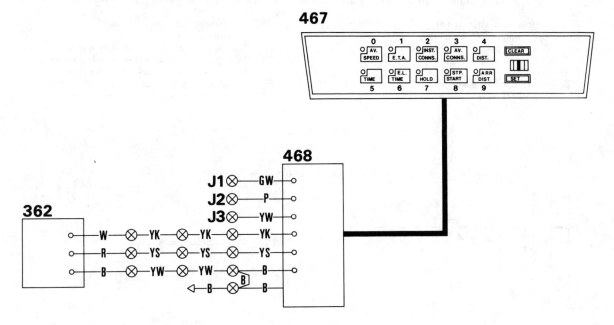

Fig. 13.77 Supplementary diagram for trip computer – carburettor models 1984 on

362 Fuel flow transducer
467 Trip computer keyboard
468 Trip computer/interface unit

J1 Ignition feed to trip computer
J2 Battery feed to computer pick-up point
J3 Speed transducer to electronic control unit pick-up point

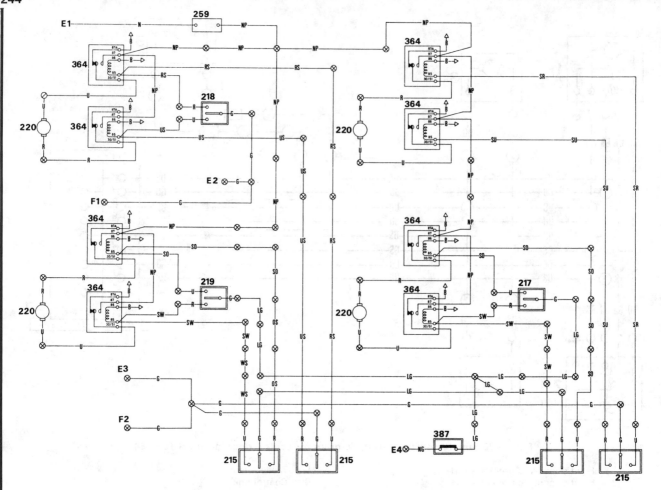

Fig. 13.78 Supplementary wiring diagram for electrically operated windows – 1984 on

215 Window lift master switch
217 Window lift switch – R.H. rear
218 Window lift switch – Passenger, front
219 Window lift switch – L.H. rear
220 Window lift motor
259 Thermal circuit breaker
364 Window lift relay

387 Rear window lift isolator switch
E1 Thermal cut out
E2 Passenger front window lift switch pick-up point
E3 Driver front window master switch pick-up point
E4 Window isolation switch pick-up point
F1 Passenger's electric door mirror pick-up point
F2 Driver's electric door mirror pick-up point

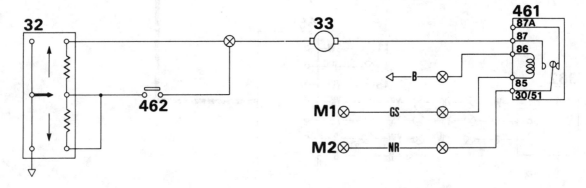

Fig. 13.79 Supplementary wiring diagram for heater – 1984 on

32 Three speed heater and blower switch
33 Heater motor
461 Heater relay

462 Overheat switch
M1 Heater pick-up point
M2 Heater motor pick-up point

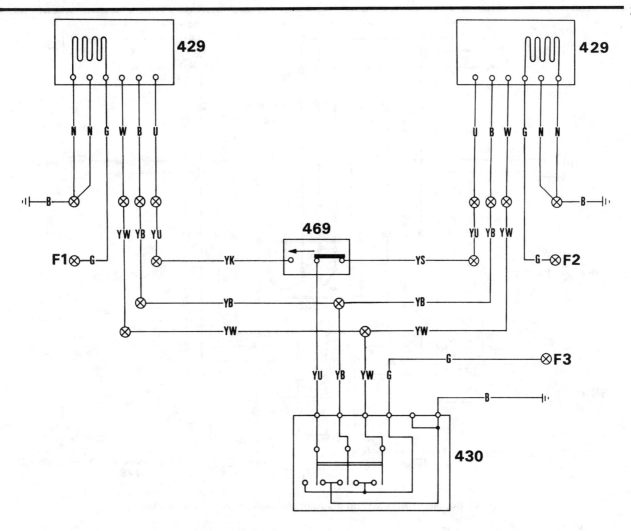

Fig. 13.80 Supplementary wiring diagram for electric door mirrors – 1984 on

429 Electric door mirror motor/heater
430 Door mirror control switch
469 Door mirror changeover switch

F1 Passenger's door mirror demist element pick-up point
F2 Driver's door mirror demist element pick-up point
F3 Door mirror control switch pick-up point

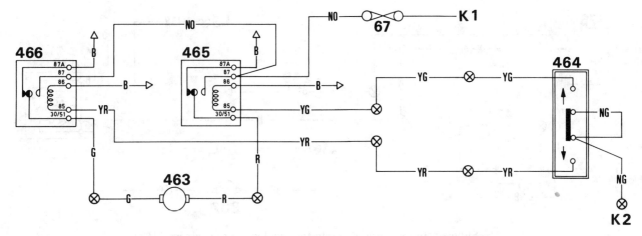

Fig. 13.81 Supplementary wiring diagram for electric sunroof – 1984 on

67 Line fuse
463 Sunroof motor
464 Sunroof motor switch
465 Sunroof open relay

466 Sunroof close relay
K1 Sunroof fuse pick-up point
K2 Sunroof switch pick-up point

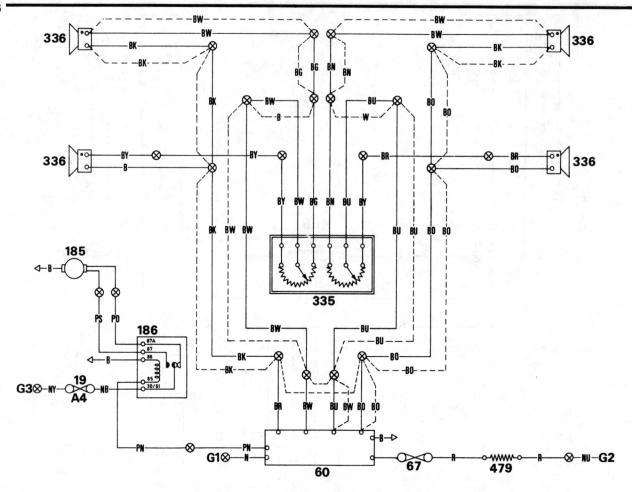

Fig. 13.82 Supplementary wiring diagram for radio/cassette unit – 1984 on

19	Fuse	336	Speakers
60	Radio/radio cassette unit	479	Choke
67	Line fuse	G1	Battery feed pick-up point
185	Electric aerial motor	G2	Auxiliary ignition feed pick-up point
186	Electric aerial relay	G3	Starter relay/electric aerial relay pick-up point
335	Balance control		

Note: *Dotted lines indicate mono system*

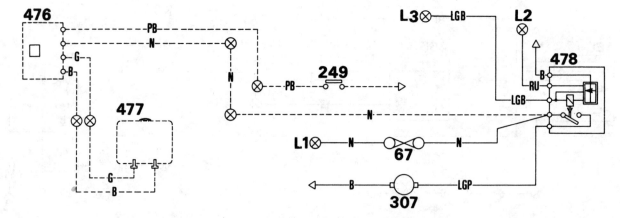

Fig. 13.83 Supplementary wiring diagram for headlamp wash system – 1984 on

67	Line fuse	478	Headlamp wash timer delay relay
249	Bonnet lamp switch	L1	Headlamp wash pick-up point
476	Headlamp wash level indicator module	L2	Timer delay relay pick-up point
477	Headlamp wash bottle	L3	Headlamp wash pump pick-up point

Note: *Dotted lines indicate circuit for German market only*

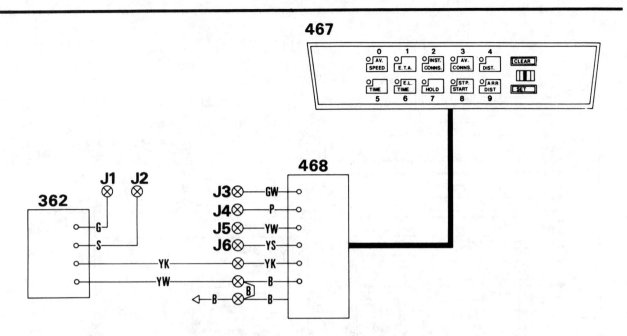

Fig. 13.84 Supplementary wiring diagram for trip computer – fuel injection models 1984 on

362	Fuel flow transducer
467	Trip computer keyboard
468	Trip computer/interface unit
J1	Ignition feed to interface unit
J2	No. 8 Cylinder pick-up point

J3	Ignition feed to trip computer
J4	Battery feed to computer pick-up point
J5	Speed transducer to computer pick-up point
J6	Ignition feed to trip computer

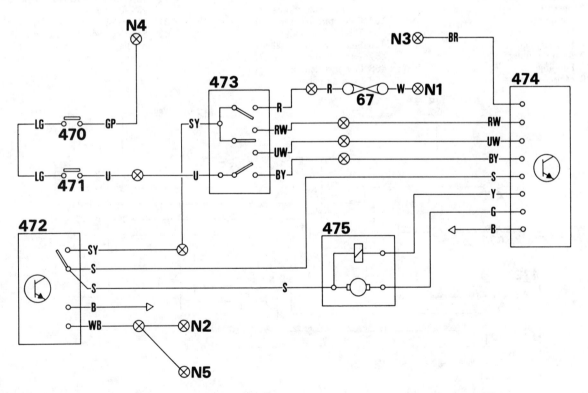

Fig. 13.85 Supplementary wiring diagram for cruise control system – 1984

67	Line fuse
470	Cruise control brake switch
471	Cruise control clutch switch
472	Cruise control overspeed relay
473	Cruise control switch
474	Cruise control ECU

475	Cruise control pneumatic control unit
N1	In line fuse pick-up point
N2	Overspeed relay pick-up point
N3	Speed transducer to electronic control unit pick-up point
N4	Brake switch pick-up point

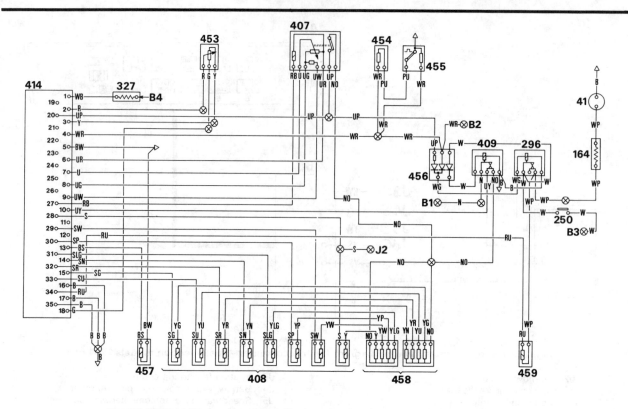

Fig. 13.86 Supplementary wiring diagram for fuel injection system – 1984 on

41	Fuel pump	414	ECU	J2	Trip computer to No. 8 cylinder pick-up point
164	Resistor	453	Throttle potentiometer		
250	Inertia switch	454	Cold start injector	B1	Main relay pick-up point
296	Fuel pump relay	455	Thermotime switch	B2	Steering module pick-up point
327	Line resistor	456	Steering module relay	B3	Inertia switch pick-up point
407	Air flow meter	457	Temperature sensor	B4	In line resistor/ECU pick-up point
408	Fuel injectors	458	Power resistors		
409	Main relay	459	Extra air valve		

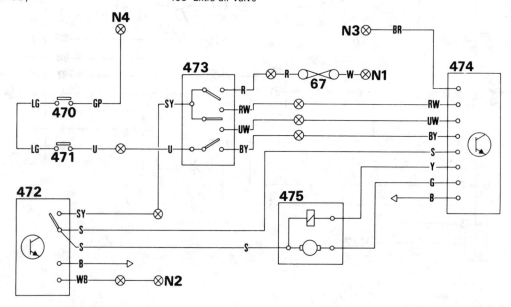

Fig. 13.87 Supplementary wiring diagram for cruise control system – fuel injection models 1985 on

67	Line fuse	475	Cruise control pneumatic control unit
470	Cruise control brake switch	N1	In line fuse pick-up point
471	Cruise control clutch switch	N2	Overspeed relay pick-up point
472	Cruise control overspeed relay	N3	Speed transducer to electronic control unit pick-up point
473	Cruise control switch		
474	Cruise control ECU	N4	Brake switch pick-up point

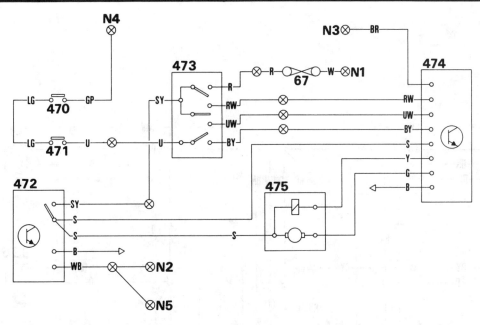

Fig. 13.88 Supplementary wiring diagram for cruise control system – carburettor models 1985 on

67	Line fuse	
470	Cruise control brake switch	
471	Cruise control clutch switch	
472	Cruise control overspeed relay	
473	Cruise control switch	

474	Cruise control ECU
475	Cruise control pneumatic control unit
N1	In line fuse pick-up point
N2	Overspeed relay pick-up point

N3	Speed transducer to electronic control unit pick-up point
N4	Brake switch pick-up point
N5	ECU pick-up point from ECU control unit circuit

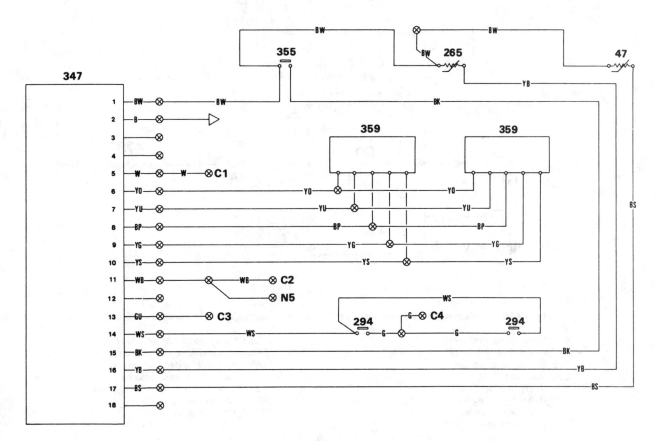

Fig. 13.89 Supplementary wiring diagram for electronic mixture control unit – carburettor models 1985 on

47	Water temperature sensor
265	Ambient sensor
294	Fuel cut-off solenoids
347	ECU

355	Throttle switch
359	Stepper motor
C1	Crimp joint
C2	Tachometer pick-up point

C3	Temperature gauge pick-up point
C4	Feed from fuse B5
N5	Cruise control pick-up point – cruise control circuit

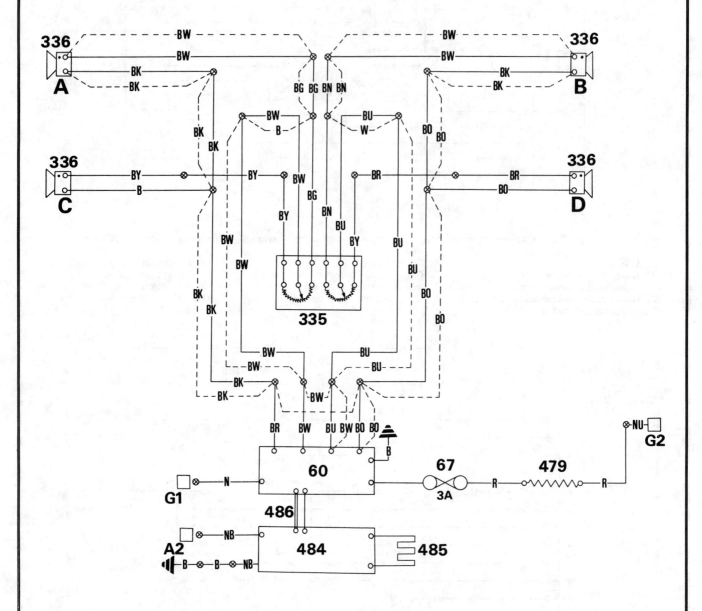

Fig. 13.90 Supplementary wiring diagram for radio/cassette/electric aerial – 1985 on

60	Radio or radio/cassette
67	In-line fuse – 3 Amp
335	Speaker balance control
336	Speakers
	A LH front speaker
	B RH front speaker
	C LH rear speaker
	D RH rear speaker

479	Choke – radio/cassette only
484	Aerial amplifier and isolator unit
485	Aerial and heated rear screen
486	Coaxial cable and radio feed
A2	Heated rear screen pick-up point
G1	Radio pick-up point
G2	Ignition pick-up point

Note: *Dotted lines indicate mono reproduction system*

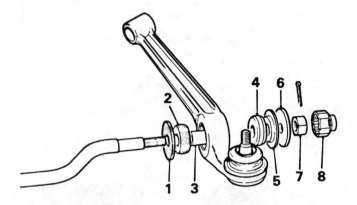

Fig. 13.91 Later type anti-roll bar bushes (Sec 14)

1	Washer (black steel)	5	Plastic washer
2	Rubber bush	6	Washer
3	Tubular spacer	7	Nut
4	Bush (white)	8	Plastic cap

14 Suspension and steering

Anti-roll bar bushes

1 As from VIN 299418 improved bushes were fitted between the anti-roll bar and front suspension lower link arms (Fig. 13.91). The new bushes can be fitted as replacements on earlier models.

2 When fitting the bushes, tighten the end nut to the specified torque, then fit the plastic cap so that the holes are aligned and insert a split pin to lock. Where a spring clip locks the original nut, this must be fitted instead of the plastic cap.

Self-levelling suspension unit – checking procedure

3 On models equipped with self-levelling rear suspension it may be found that the rear of the car settles somewhat when the luggage area is laden and the vehicle is parked for some time (eg overnight). This is not in itself a fault, provided that normal suspension height is restored when the vehicle is driven.

4 If some other malfunction of the self-levelling unit is suspected, proceed as follows.

5 Inspect the self-levelling units for oil leakage. Traces of seepage are permissible; dripping, gushing or other major leaks are not. A unit which is leaking significanrly must be renewed.

6 With the luggage area unladen and the underside of the vehicle free of heavy mud deposits, measure and record the distance from the centre of each rear wheel to the point on the wing vertically above the wheel centre. The distances should be between 15.75 and 17.75 in (400 and 450 mm); if not, renew the self-levelling unit(s) on the side(s) concerned.

7 Load the rear seat and luggage area with 440 to 550 lb (200 to 250 kg). Human ballast of known weight is probably most convenient for the DIY operator, paticularly as it should not need to be lifted into the car.

8 Have an assistant (of roughly the driver's weight) sit in the driving seat, then measure and record the distances described in paragraph 6 again.

9 Drive the car over at least 3 miles (5 km) of undulating road. Bring the car to rest by light brake application, and do not allow the ballast to move. With the driver's seat still occupied, measure and record the distances described in paragraph 6 again. The ballast may now be unloaded.

10 Subtract the initial loaded height (paragraph 8) from the final loaded height (paragraph 9). If the difference is at least one inch (25 mm) the self-levelling unit is operating correctly. A difference of less than one inch (25 mm) indicates that the self-levelling unit on that side should be renewed.

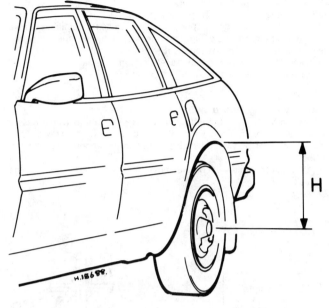

Fig. 13.92 Rear suspension height measurement (H) (Sec 14)

Rear suspension trailing link mounting – later models

11 To reduce noise coming from the trailing link and the rear axle bracket, an additional washer is fitted to each mounting on later models.

12 Earlier models can be fitted with such a washer if so wished. Suitable washers should be available from a Rover dealer.

Rear suspension crossmember-to-body mounting (all models)

13 If a problem is experienced with the rear suspension crossmember hitting the body, this can be rectified by fitting an additional washer to the mounting (Fig. 13.94).

Front hub – adjustment

14 The front hub adjustment procedure has been altered from that given in Chapter 11. Before fitting the retaining cap and hub grease cap, carry out the following.

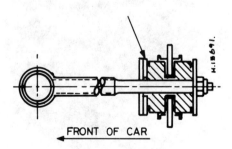

Fig. 13.93 Additional washer (arrowed) fitted to trailing link mounting – later models (Sec 14)

15 Tighten the nut to 18.0 lbf ft (25.0 Nm), whilst turning the hub by hand.

16 Fully loosen the nut then retighten it to 5.0 lbf ft (6.0 Nm) again whilst turning the hub by hand.

17 Back off the nut one complete flat, then locate the retaining cap so that the split pin holes are aligned. If necessary, tighten the nut to the nearest alignment, **do not** loosen it to align the holes.

18 Insert the split pin and lock its legs circumferentially.

19 Fit the hub grease cap.

Power steering pump with integral reservoir

20 Later models are fitted with a power steering pump which has its own fluid reservoir. The level of fluid is checked by unscrewing the filler cap and reading the dipstick attached to the underside of the cap (photo).

21 Maintain the fluid level between the 'MIN' and 'MAX' marks on the dipstick.

22 Keep the breather hole in the filler cap clear (photo).

Power steering hose routing

23 On some models which are fitted with a power steering fluid cooler, the high pressure hose is routed close to the exhaust manifold, and may suffer heat damage.

24 The hose should be clipped out of the way as shown in Fig. 13.95.

Wheels and tyres – general care and maintenance

25 Wheels and tyres should give no real problems in use provided that a close eye is kept on them with regard to excessive wear or damage. To this end, the following points should be noted.

26 Ensure that tyre pressures are checked regularly and maintained correctly. Checking should be carried out with the tyres cold and not immediately after the vehicle has been in use. If the pressures are checked with the tyres hot, an apparently high reading will be obtained

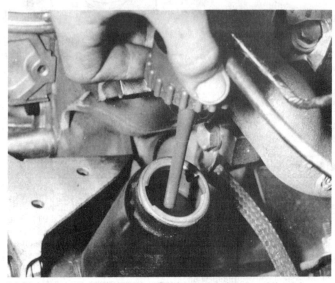

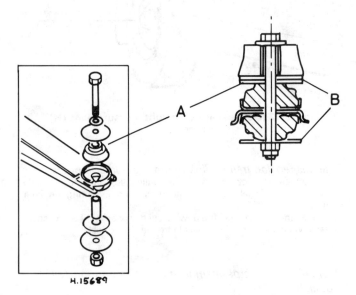

H.15689

Fig. 13.94 Rear suspension crossmember mounting (Sec 14)

A   Additional washer   B   Original washers

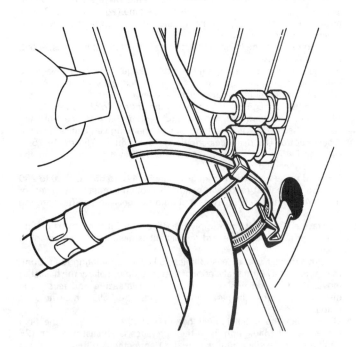

14.20 Later type power steering fluid reservoir filler cap/dipstick

14.22 Power steering fluid reservoir filler cap breather hole (arrowed)

Fig. 13.95 Power steering hose retaining strap (Sec 14)

owing to heat expansion. Under no circumstances should an attempt be made to reduce the pressures to the quoted cold reading in this instance, or effective underinflation will result.

27 Underinflation will cause overheating of the tyre owing to excessive flexing of the casing, and the tread will not sit correctly on the road surface. This will cause a consequent loss of adhesion and excessive wear, not to mention the danger of sudden tyre failure due to heat build-up.

28 Overinflation will cause rapid wear of the centre part of the tyre tread coupled with reduced adhesion, harsher ride, and the danger of shock damage occurring in the tyre casing.

29 Regularly check the tyres for damage in the form of cuts or bulges, especially in the sidewalls. Remove any nails or stones embedded in the tread before they penetrate the tyre to cause deflation. If removal of a nail *does* reveal that the tyre has been punctured, refit the nail so that its point of penetration is marked. Then immediately change the wheel and have the tyre repaired by a tyre dealer. Do *not* drive on a tyre in such a condition. In many cases a puncture can be simply repaired by the use of an inner tube of the correct size and type. If in any doubt as to the possible consequences of any damage found, consult your local tyre dealer for advice.

30 Periodically remove the wheels and clean any dirt or mud from the inside and outside surfaces. Examine the wheel rims for signs of rusting, corrosion or other damage. Light alloy wheels are easily damaged by 'kerbing' whilst parking, and similarly steel wheels may become dented or buckled. Renewal of the wheel is very often the only course of remedial action possible.

31 The balance of each wheel and tyre assembly should be maintained to avoid excessive wear, not only to the tyres but also to the steering and suspension components. Wheel imbalance is normally signified by vibration through the vehicle's bodyshell, although in many cases it is particularly noticeable through the steering wheel. Conversely, it should be noted that wear or damage in suspension or steering components may cause excessive tyre wear. Out-of-round or out-of-true tyres, damaged wheels and wheel bearing wear/maladjustment also fall into this category. Balancing will not usually cure vibration caused by such wear.

32 Wheel balancing may be carried out with the wheel either on or off the vehicle. If balanced on the vehicle, ensure that the wheel-to-hub relationship is marked in some way prior to subsequent wheel removal so that it may be refitted in its original position.

33 General tyre wear is influenced to a large degree by driving style – harsh braking and acceleration or fast cornering will all produce more rapid tyre wear. Interchanging of tyres may result in more even wear, but this should only be carried out where there is no mix of tyre types on the vehicle. However, it is worth bearing in mind that if this is completely effective, the added expense of replacing a complete set of tyres simultaneously is incurred, which may prove financially restrictive for many owners.

34 Front tyres may wear unevenly as a result of wheel misalignment. The front wheels should always be correctly aligned according to the settings specified by the vehicle manufacturer.

35 Legal restrictions apply to the mixing of tyre types on a vehicle. Basically this means that a vehicle must not have tyres of differing construction on the same axle. Although it is not recommended to mix tyre types between front axle and rear axle, the only legally permissible combination is crossply at the front and radial at the rear. When mixing radial ply tyres, textile braced radials must always go on the front axle, with steel braced radials at the rear. An obvious disadvantage of such mixing is the necessity to carry two spare tyres to avoid contravening the law in the event of a puncture.

36 In the UK, the Motor Vehicles Construction and Use Regulations apply to many aspects of tyre fitting and usage. It is suggested that a copy of these regulations is obtained from your local police if in doubt as to the current legal requirements with regard to tyre condition, minimum tread depth, etc.

15 Bodywork and fittings

Front spoiler – removal and refitting

1 Remove the blanking plugs, then undo the nuts and bolts which secure the spoiler to the under-panel and the wing flange.
2 Remove the spoiler.
3 Refitting is a reversal of removal.

Rear spoiler (Vitesse) – removal and refitting

4 Open the tailgate, remove the number plate lamps and the tailgate finisher. The finisher is secured by 6 screws (photo).
5 Remove the spoiler securing nuts and lift away the spoiler. One of the nuts is hidden by the electric lock unit.
6 Refit by reversing the removal procedure.

15.4 Tailgate finisher screw (arrowed) concealed by number plate lamp

Front bumper overrider – removal and refitting

7 When fitted, disconnect the headlight washer by prising out the elbow connector.
8 Undo the nut which secures the overrider and remove the overrider.
9 Refitting is a reversal of removal.

Rear parcel shelf extension panel – removal and refitting

10 Lift out the parcel shelf.
11 Slacken the parcel shelf stops and free the rear end of the extension panel from the body by pulling it towards the centre of the car.
12 Lift the extension panel from the stops and free it from under the seat squab.
13 If a rear seat belt is fitted, remove the floor bracket and the swivel bracket, as described in Chapter 12, Section 30. Feed the belt through the extension panel.
14 The extension panel may now be removed.
15 Refitting is a reversal of removal.

Headlining – removal and refitting

16 Disconnect the battery earth lead.
17 Remove the trim panels from the 'A' posts (to the front of the front doors). These pads are each secured by two screws.
18 Remove the upper trim pads from the 'D' posts, as described in Chapter 12, Section 35, paragraphs 2 and 3.
19 Remove the grab handles. Their securing screws are accessible after sliding off the end caps.
20 Remove the sun visors and the sun visor hinge clips.
21 Support the headlining, then remove the interior mirror and its bracket.
22 Free the rear edge of the headlining from the Velcro strips which hold it to the roof.
23 The headlining can now be removed from the car.
24 Refitting is a reversal of removal.

Sliding roof assembly (manual) – removal and refitting

25 Remove the headlining, as described above.
26 Disconnect the four drain hoses (one at each corner).

27 Remove the six nuts and washers which secure the sliding roof frame.

28 Remove the sliding roof assembly from the car.

29 Refitting is a reversal of removal. Check for correct operation and adjust if necessary as described below.

Sliding roof (manual) – panel removal and refitting

30 Open the sliding roof as far as it will go.

31 Apply a layer of masking tape to the rear edge of the hole in the roof so that the paintwork of the sliding panel is not damaged during removal.

32 Remove the four screws from the front of the sliding panel.

33 Slide the panel forwards until it is about one inch (25 mm) short of the closed position. Lift the front of the panel, being careful not to damage the rubber seal.

34 Move the panel forwards to disengage it from the retaining springs at the rear, then lift it away from the car.

35 Refitting is a reversal of removal.

Sliding roof (manual) – adjustment

36 Remove the sliding panel, as described above.

37 Operate the catch and study the action of the locking teeth.

38 Slacken the nuts which secure the linkage and extend or retract the teeth as required.

39 Tighten the nuts and check for correct operation.

40 Refit the sliding panel.

Sliding roof assembly (electric) – removal and refitting

41 Remove the headlining, the rear parcel shelf and the parcel shelf extension panels, as described earlier in this Section.

42 Remove the right-hand section of the luggage compartment floor.

43 Remove the cover from the sliding roof motor and disconnect the wires at the multi-plug.

44 Undo the screws which secure the motor and remove the motor from behind its bracket.

45 Undo the cable clamp nuts and remove the motor.

46 Remove the spare wheel, lift back the carpets and unclip the operating cable straps.

47 Disconnect the drain hoses from the sliding roof.

48 Remove the six nuts and washers which secure the sliding roof frame. Lower the frame.

49 Secure the two halves of each outer operating cable by taping them together. Pull the cables through the 'D' posts.

50 Extract the sliding roof assembly through the rear of the car.

51 Refitting is a reversal of removal.

Heater fan switch – removal and refitting

52 Remove the radio, as described in Chapter 10, Section 44.

53 Remove the console, as described in Chapter 12, Section 23 or 24.

54 Pull off the control knobs from the heater levers.

55 Remove the radio mounting plate and extract the screws which secure the heater control front plate. Carefully withdraw the heater control front plate from the control levers, being cautious not to strain the fibre optic lines.

56 Extract the screws which secure the heater control plate. Lift out the plate.

57 The heater fan switch is now accessible. Remove its securing screws and withdraw it. Make a note of the wiring connections before disconnecting the switch.

58 Refitting is a reversal of removal. Check for correct operation on completion.

Heater (later type) – removal and refitting

59 Disconnect the battery negative lead.

60 Drain the cooling system (Chapter 2).

61 Remove the centre console, radio and facia (Chapter 12).

62 Disconnect the heater hoses in the engine compartment.

63 Disconnect the nut and washer holding the bulkhead insulation, then remove the heater mounting nuts from the bulkhead.

64 Working inside the car, remove the console bracket then pull off the heater control knobs, unbolt the control panel and unclip the fibre optic leads. Disconnect the leads and remove the control panel.

65 Remove the triangular and rectangular air duct covers then remove the air duct from under the carpets.

66 Unbolt the glovebox brackets and move them to one side. Note that the fibre optic bulb is mounted on the right-hand bracket. Recover the plates from the brackets.

67 Unbolt the heater and console brackets from the slotted mounting bracket, and remove the upper mounting bolt from the bulkhead.

68 Disconnect the heater motor and relay wiring.

69 Loosen the slotted mounting bracket bolts then lift the heater and withdraw the bracket.

70 Remove the footwell ducts then position the instrument wiring loom to one side and withdraw the heater from the car.

71 Refitting is a reversal of removal, and refill the cooling system as described in Chapter 2.

Air conditioning system – description

72 Available as an optional extra on certain models, the air conditioning system works on the same principles as a domestic refrigerator or freezer. A compressor, belt-driven from the crankshaft pulley, pumps refrigerant into a condenser unit. After cooling and drying, the refrigerant evaporates under controlled conditions in an evaporator inside the heater/air conditioning unit, so cooling the incoming air.

73 Certain precautions must be observed when dealing with the air conditioning system, both for personal safety and to avoid damaging the system. These are as follows:

(a) **Do not** *undertake any work which would require the disconnection of a refrigerant hose, unless the system has first been discharged by a reftigeration engineer or an air conditioning specialist*

(b) **Do not** *leave any part of the refrigeration circuit open to the air after it has been discharged*

(c) **Do not** *apply heat (eg welding or steam cleaning) near any air conditioning components.*

74 The refrigerant gas is not of itself poisonous, but it forms poisonous gases when exposed to flame or other combustion (eg a lighted cigarette). If spilled onto skin in its liquid form it can cause damage through rapid cooling. It is irritant if inhaled. It follows that refrigerant leaks should not be approached closely and should be repaired without delay.

75 Do not attempt to operate the air conditioning system if it is known to be short of refrigerant.

Air conditioning system – maintenance

76 Operate the air conditioning system for a few minutes at monthly intervals when it is not otherwise being used (eg in winter). This will ensure the continued distribution of lubricant and refrigerant round the system.

77 Check the tension and condition of the compressor drivebelt at regular intervals. The drivebelt is adjusted in the same fashion as the water pump/alternator and power steering pump drivebelts. Where drive is via an idler pulley, this may have its own separate adjuster.

78 A sight glass on the VIR (valves in receiver) unit (Fig. 13.100) can be inspected to provide evidence of the state of the refrigerant charge. With the air conditioning system operating, the sight glass should display a clear stream of refrigerant, perhaps with occasional bubbles. Many bubbles, or even foam, are indications that the refrigerant level is low; oil leaks on the glass show that the refrigerant charge is zero. A clouded sight glass means that dessicant has escaped from the drier, or possibly that the compressor is defective.

79 Any abnormal sight glass reading should be investigated without delay. It is wise to have the air conditioning system inspected professionally evey year.

Air conditioning system – later type

80 During 1983 the VIR (valves in receiver) air conditioning system was superseded by a system known as CCOT (clutch cycling orifice tube).

81 The CCOT system has an accumulator in place of the VIR unit, and there is a clutch cycling pressure switch which controls system operation.

82 Maintenance is as described above, but there is no sight glass.

Plastic components

83 With the use of more and more plastic body components by the vehicle manufacturers (eg bumpers, spoilers, and in some cases major

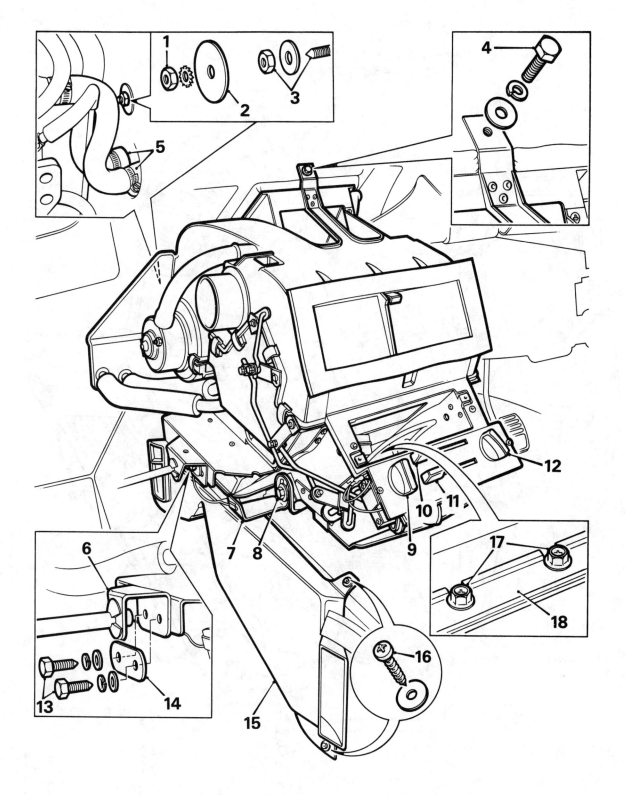

Fig. 13.96 Later type heater unit controls and fittings (Sec 15)

1	Locknut	6	Glovebox mounting rail
2	Insulation retaining washer		bracket
3	Heater mounting stud and	7	Console bracket
	nut	8	Heater lower mounting bolt
4	Heater top mounting bolt	9	Facia air vent control
5	Heater hoses	10	Air temperature control

11	Blower motor control	15	Footwell air ducts
12	Air distribution control	16	Air duct retaining screws
13	Glovebox mounting rail	17	Slotted bracket retaining
	bracket bolts		bolts
14	Retaining plates	18	Slotted bracket

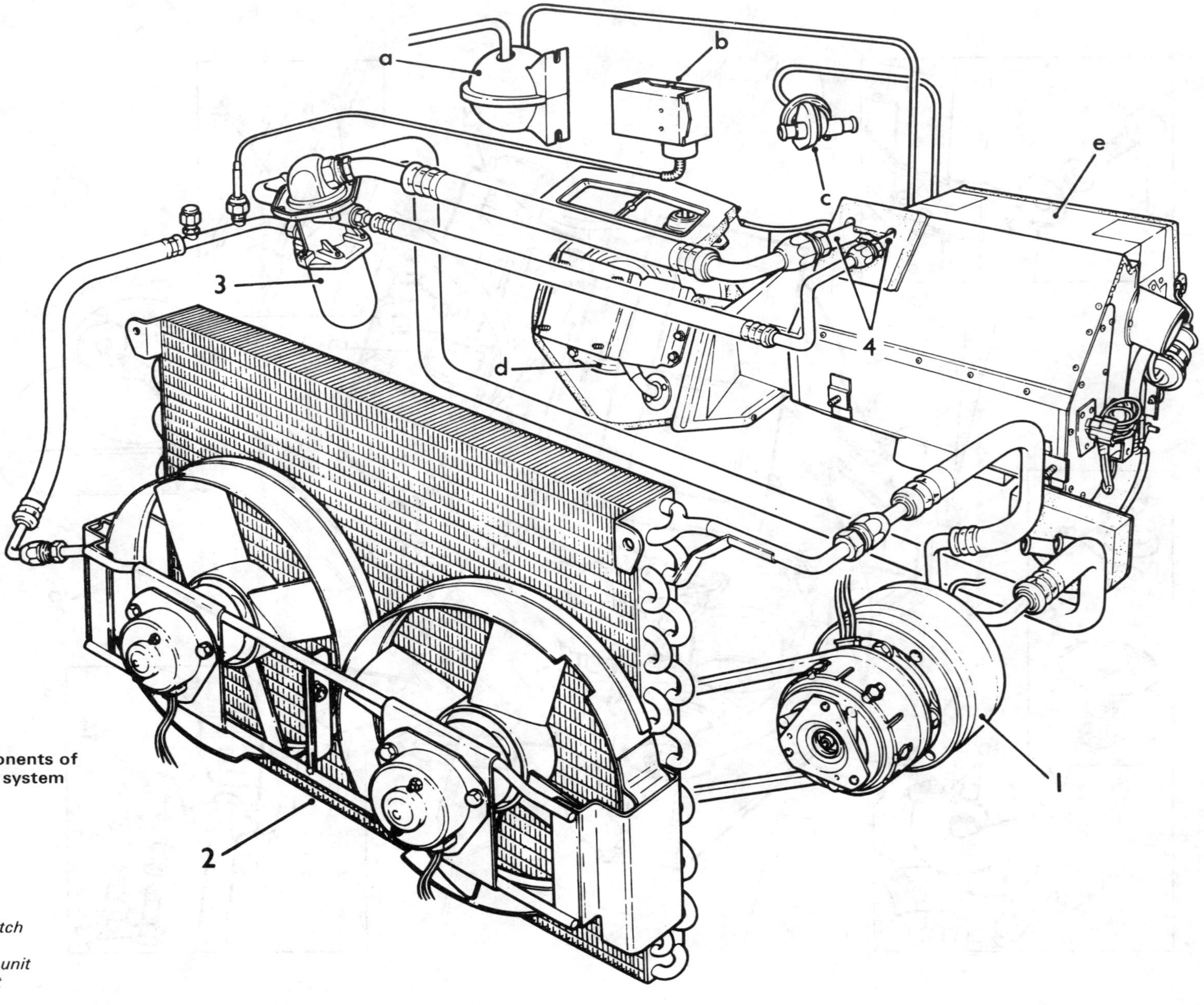

Fig. 13.97 Principal components of
the VIR air conditioning system
(Sec 15)

1   Compressor
2   Condenser
3   VIR unit
4   Evaporator
a   Vacuum reservoir
b   High pressure switch
c   Water valve
d   Air intake/blower unit
e   Heater/cooler unit

Fig. 13.98 Air conditioner compressor drivebelt tension adjustment points (Sec 15)

1 Tie-rod bolts (slacken   3 Pivot bolt
   before adjusting)   4 Compressor
2 Adjusting link

Fig. 13.99 Air conditioner compressor drivebelt idler pulley adjustment points (Sec 15)

1 Transducer bolts (remove   3 Pulley and drivebelt
   before adjusting)   4 Compressor drivebelt
2 Pulley clamp bolt

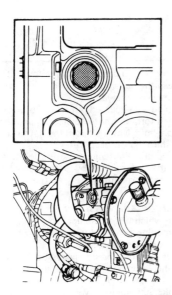

Fig. 13.100 Air conditioning sight glass – VIR unit (Sec 15)

body panels), rectification of damage to such items has become a matter of either entrusting repair work to a specialist in this field, or renewing complete components. Repair by the DIY owner is not really feasible owing to the cost of the equipment and materials required for effecting such repairs. The basic technique involves making a groove along the line of the crack in the plastic using a rotary burr in a power drill. The damaged part is then welded back together by using a hot air gun to heat up and fuse a plastic filler rod into the groove. Any excess plastic is then removed and the area rubbed down to a smooth finish. It is important that a filler rod of the correct plastic is used, as body components can be made of a variety of different types (eg polycarbonate, ABS, polypropylene).

84 If the owner is renewing a complete component himself, he will be left with the problem of finding a suitable paint for finishing which is compatible with the type of plastic used. At one time the use of a universal paint was not possible owing to the complex range of plastics encountered in body component applications. Standard paints, generally speaking, will not bond to plastic or rubber satisfactorily. However, it is now possible to obtain a plastic body parts finishing kit which consists of a pre-primer treatment, a primer and coloured top coat. Full instructions are normally supplied with a kit, but basically the method of use is to first apply the pre-primer to the component concerned and allow it to dry for up to 30 minutes. Then the primer is applied and left to dry for about an hour before finally applying the special coloured top coat. The result is a correctly coloured component where the paint will flex with the plastic or rubber, a property that standard paint does not normally possess.

General repair procedures

Whenever servicing, repair or overhaul work is carried out on the car or its components, it is necessary to observe the following procedures and instructions. This will assist in carrying out the operation efficiently and to a professional standard of workmanship.

Joint mating faces and gaskets

Where a gasket is used between the mating faces of two components, ensure that it is renewed on reassembly, and fit it dry unless otherwise stated in the repair procedure. Make sure that the mating faces are clean and dry with all traces of old gasket removed. When cleaning a joint face, use a tool which is not likely to score or damage the face, and remove any burrs or nicks with an oilstone or fine file.

Make sure that tapped holes are cleaned with a pipe cleaner, and keep them free of jointing compound if this is being used unless specifically instructed otherwise.

Ensure that all orifices, channels or pipes are clear and blow through them, preferably using compressed air.

Oil seals

Whenever an oil seal is removed from its working location, either individually or as part of an assembly, it should be renewed.

The very fine sealing lip of the seal is easily damaged and will not seal if the surface it contacts is not completely clean and free from scratches, nicks or grooves. If the original sealing surface of the component cannot be restored, the component should be renewed.

Protect the lips of the seal from any surface which may damage them in the course of fitting. Use tape or a conical sleeve where possible. Lubricate the seal lips with oil before fitting and, on dual lipped seals, fill the space between the lips with grease.

Unless otherwise stated, oil seals must be fitted with their sealing lips toward the lubricant to be sealed.

Use a tubular drift or block of wood of the appropriate size to install the seal and, if the seal housing is shouldered, drive the seal down to the shoulder. If the seal housing is unshouldered, the seal should be fitted with its face flush with the housing top face.

Screw threads and fastenings

Always ensure that a blind tapped hole is completely free from oil, grease, water or other fluid before installing the bolt or stud. Failure to do this could cause the housing to crack due to the hydraulic action of the bolt or stud as it is screwed in.

When tightening a castellated nut to accept a split pin, tighten the nut to the specified torque, where applicable, and then tighten further to the next split pin hole. Never slacken the nut to align a split pin hole unless stated in the repair procedure.

When checking or retightening a nut or bolt to a specified torque setting, slacken the nut or bolt by a quarter of a turn, and then retighten to the specified setting.

Locknuts, locktabs and washers

Any fastening which will rotate against a component or housing in the course of tightening should always have a washer between it and the relevant component or housing.

Spring or split washers should always be renewed when they are used to lock a critical component such as a big-end bearing retaining nut or bolt.

Locktabs which are folded over to retain a nut or bolt should always be renewed.

Self-locking nuts can be reused in non-critical areas, providing resistance can be felt when the locking portion passes over the bolt or stud thread.

Split pins must always be replaced with new ones of the correct size for the hole.

Special tools

Some repair procedures in this manual entail the use of special tools such as a press, two or three-legged pullers, spring compressors etc. Wherever possible, suitable readily available alternatives to the manufacturer's special tools are described, and are shown in use. In some instances, where no alternative is possible, it has been necessary to resort to the use of a manufacturer's tool and this has been done for reasons of safety as well as the efficient completion of the repair operation. Unless you are highly skilled and have a thorough understanding of the procedure described, never attempt to bypass the use of any special tool when the procedure described specifies its use. Not only is there a very great risk of personal injury, but expensive damage could be caused to the components involved.

Fault diagnosis

Introduction

The vehicle owner who does his or her own maintenance according to the recommended schedules should not have to use this section of the manual very often. Modern component reliability is such that, provided those items subject to wear or deterioration are inspected or renewed at the specified intervals, sudden failure is comparatively rare. Faults do not usually just happen as a result of sudden failure, but develop over a period of time. Major mechanical failures in particular are usually preceded by characteristic symptoms over hundreds or even thousands of miles. Those components which do occasionally fail without warning are often small and easily carried in the vehicle.

With any fault finding, the first step is to decide where to begin investigations. Sometimes this is obvious, but on other occasions a little detective work will be necessary. The owner who makes half a dozen haphazard adjustments or replacements may be successful in curing a fault (or its symptoms), but he will be none the wiser if the fault recurs and he may well have spent more time and money than was necessary. A calm and logical approach will be found to be more satisfactory in the long run. Always take into account any warning signs or abnormalities that may have been noticed in the period preceding the fault – power loss, high or low gauge readings, unusual noises or smells, etc – and remember that failure of components such as fuses or spark plugs may only be pointers to some underlying fault.

The pages which follow here are intended to help in cases of failure to start or breakdown on the road. There is also a Fault Diagnosis Section at the end of each Chapter which should be consulted if the preliminary checks prove unfruitful. Whatever the fault, certain basic principles apply. These are as follows:

Verify the fault. This is simply a matter of being sure that you know what the symptoms are before starting work. This is particularly important if you are investigating a fault for someone else who may not have described it very accurately.

Don't overlook the obvious. For example, if the vehicle won't start, is there petrol in the tank? (Don't take anyone else's word on this particular point, and don't trust the fuel gauge either!) If an electrical fault is indicated, look for loose or broken wires before digging out the test gear.

Cure the disease, not the symptom. Substituting a flat battery with a fully charged one will get you off the hard shoulder, but if the underlying cause is not attended to, the new battery will go the same way. Similarly, changing oil-fouled spark plugs for a new set will get you moving again, but remember that the reason for the fouling (if it wasn't simply an incorrect grade of plug) will have to be established and corrected.

Don't take anything for granted. Particularly, don't forget that a 'new' component may itself be defective (especially if it's been rattling round in the boot for months), and don't leave components out of a fault diagnosis sequence just because they are new or recently fitted. When you do finally diagnose a difficult fault, you'll probably realise that all the evidence was there from the start.

Electrical faults

Electrical faults can be more puzzling than straightforward mechanical failures, but they are no less susceptible to logical analysis if the basic principles of operation are understood. Vehicle electrical wiring exists in extremely unfavourable conditions – heat, vibration and chemical attack – and the first things to look for are loose or corroded connections and broken or chafed wires, especially where the wires pass through holes in the bodywork or are subject to vibration.

All metal-bodied vehicles in current production have one pole of the battery 'earthed', ie connected to the vehicle bodywork, and in nearly all modern vehicles it is the negative (–) terminal. The various electrical components – motors, bulb holders etc – are also connected to earth, either by means of a lead or directly by their mountings. Electric current flows through the component and then back to the battery via the bodywork. If the component mounting is loose or corroded, or if a good path back to the battery is not available, the circuit will be incomplete and malfunction will result. The engine and/or gearbox are also earthed by means of flexible metal straps to the body or subframe; if these straps are loose or missing, starter motor, generator and ignition trouble may result.

Assuming the earth return to be satisfactory, electrical faults will be due either to component malfunction or to defects in the current supply. Individual components are dealt with in Chapter 10. If supply wires are broken or cracked internally this results in an open-circuit,

Carrying a few spares may save you a long walk!

and the easiest way to check for this is to bypass the suspect wire temporarily with a length of wire having a crocodile clip or suitable connector at each end. Alternatively, a 12V test lamp can be used to verify the presence of supply voltage at various points along the wire and the break can be thus isolated.

If a bare portion of a live wire touches the bodywork or other earthed metal part, the electricity will take the low-resistance path thus formed back to the battery: this is known as a short-circuit. Hopefully a short-circuit will blow a fuse, but otherwise it may cause burning of the insulation (and possibly further short-circuits) or even a fire. This is why it is inadvisable to bypass persistently blowing fuses with silver foil or wire.

Spares and tool kit

Most vehicles are supplied only with sufficient tools for wheel changing; the *Maintenance and minor repair* tool kit detailed in *Tools and working facilities,* with the addition of a hammer, is probably sufficient for those repairs that most motorists would consider attempting at the roadside. In addition a few items which can be fitted without too much trouble in the event of a breakdown should be carried. Experience and available space will modify the list below, but the following may save having to call on professional assistance:

    Spark plugs, clean and correctly gapped
    HT lead and plug cap — long enough to reach the plug furthest
    from the distributor
    Distributor rotor
    Drivebelt(s) — emergency type may suffice
    Spare fuses
    Set of principal light bulbs
    Tin of radiator sealer and hose bandage
    Exhaust bandage
    Roll of insulating tape
    Length of soft iron wire
    Length of electrical flex
    Torch or inspection lamp (can double as test lamp)
    Battery jump leads
    Tow-rope
    Ignition water dispersant aerosol
    Litre of engine oil
    Sealed can of hydraulic fluid
    Emergency windscreen
    Worm drive clips

If spare fuel is carried, a can designed for the purpose should be used to minimise risks of leakage and collision damage. A first aid kit and a warning triangle, whilst not at present compulsory in the UK, are obviously sensible items to carry in addition to the above.

When touring abroad it may be advisable to carry additional spares which, even if you cannot fit them yourself, could save having to wait while parts are obtained. The items below may be worth considering:

    Throttle cables
    Cylinder head gasket
    Alternator brushes

One of the motoring organisations will be able to advise on availability of fuel etc in foreign countries.

Engine will not start

Engine fails to turn when starter operated
    Flat battery (recharge, use jump leads, or push start)
    Battery terminals loose or corroded
    Battery earth to body defective
    Engine earth strap loose or broken
    Starter motor (or solenoid) wiring loose or broken
    Automatic transmission selector in wrong position, or inhibitor
    switch faulty
    Ignition/starter switch faulty
    Major mechanical failure (seizure)
    Starter or solenoid internal fault (see Chapter 10)

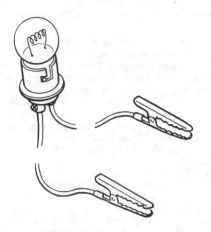

A simple test lamp is useful for investigating electrical faults

Checking for a spark at the plug — note use of insulated tool

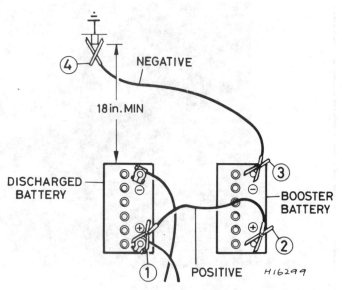

Jump start lead connections for negative earth vehicles — connect leads in order shown

Starter motor turns engine slowly

Partially discharged battery (recharge, use jump leads, or push start)
Battery terminals loose or corroded
Battery earth to body defective
Engine earth strap loose
Starter motor (or solenoid) wiring loose
Starter motor internal fault (see Chapter 10)

Starter motor spins without turning engine

Flywheel gear teeth damaged or worn
Starter motor mounting bolts loose

Engine turns normally but fails to start

Damp or dirty HT leads and distributor cap (crank engine and check for spark) (photo) – try moisture dispersant such as Holts Wet Start
No fuel in tank (check for delivery at carburettor)
Excessive choke (hot engine) or insufficient choke (cold engine)
Fouled or incorrectly gapped spark plugs (remove, clean and regap)
Other ignition system fault (see Chapter 4)
Other fuel system fault (see Chapter 3 or 13)
Poor compression (see Chapter 1)
Major mechanical failure (eg camshaft drive)

Engine fires but will not run

Insufficient choke (cold engine)
Air leaks at carburettor or inlet manifold
Fuel starvation (see Chapter 3)
Ballast resistor defective, or other ignition fault (see Chapter 4)

Engine cuts out and will not restart

Engine cuts out suddenly – ignition fault

Loose or disconnected LT wires
Wet HT leads or distributor cap (after traversing water splash)
Coil failure (check for spark)
Other ignition fault (see Chapter 4)

Engine misfires before cutting out – fuel fault

Fuel tank empty
Fuel pump defective or filter blocked (check for delivery)
Fuel tank filler vent blocked (suction will be evident on releasing cap)
Carburettor needle valve sticking
Carburettor jets blocked (fuel contaminated)
Other fuel system fault (see Chapter 3 or 13)

Engine cuts out – other causes

Serious overheating
Major mechanical failure (eg camshaft drive)

Engine overheats

Ignition (no-charge) warning light illuminated

Slack or broken drivebelt (photo) – retension or renew (Chapter 2)

Ignition warning light not illuminated

Coolant loss due to internal or external leakage (see Chapter 2)
Thermostat defective
Low oil level
Brakes binding
Radiator clogged externally or internally
Engine waterways clogged
Ignition timing incorrect or automatic advance malfunctioning
Mixture too weak

Note: *Do not add cold water to an overheated engine or damage may result*

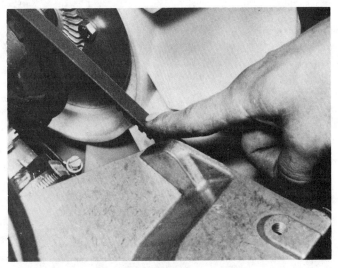

A slack drivebelt can cause battery charging and overheating problems

---

Low engine oil pressure

Gauge reads low or warning light illuminated with engine running

Oil level low or incorrect grade
Defective gauge or sender unit
Wire to sender unit earthed
Engine overheating
Oil filter clogged or bypass valve defective
Oil pressure relief valve defective
Oil pick-up strainer clogged
Oil pump worn or mountings loose
Worn main or big-end bearings

Note: *Low oil pressure in a high-mileage engine at tickover is not necessarily a cause for concern. Sudden pressure loss at speed is far more significant. In any event, check the gauge or warning light sender before condemning the engine.*

Engine noises

Pre-ignition (pinking) on acceleration

Incorrect grade of fuel
Ignition timing incorrect
Distributor faulty or worn
Worn or maladjusted carburettor
Excessive carbon build-up in engine

Whistling or wheezing noises

Leaking vacuum hose
Leaking carburettor or manifold gasket
Blowing head gasket

Tapping or rattling

Worn valve gear
Worn timing chain
Broken piston ring (ticking noise)

Knocking or thumping

Unintentional mechanical contact (eg fan blades)
Worn fanbelt
Peripheral component fault (generator, water pump etc)
Worn big-end bearings (regular heavy knocking, perhaps less under load)
Worn main bearings (rumbling and knocking, perhaps worsening under load)
Piston slap (most noticeable when cold)

Use of English

As this book has been written in England, it uses the appropriate English component names, phrases, and spelling. Some of these differ from those used in America. Normally, these cause no difficulty, but to make sure, a glossary is printed below. In ordering spare parts remember the parts list may use some of these words:

English	American	English	American
Accelerator	Gas pedal	Locks	Latches
Aerial	Antenna	Methylated spirit	Denatured alcohol
Anti-roll bar	Stabiliser or sway bar	Motorway	Freeway, turnpike etc
Big-end bearing	Rod bearing	Number plate	License plate
Bonnet (engine cover)	Hood	Paraffin	Kerosene
Boot (luggage compartment)	Trunk	Petrol	Gasoline (gas)
Bulkhead	Firewall	Petrol tank	Gas tank
Bush	Bushing	'Pinking'	'Pinging'
Cam follower or tappet	Valve lifter or tappet	Prise (force apart)	Pry
Carburettor	Carburetor	Propeller shaft	Driveshaft
Catch	Latch	Quarterlight	Quarter window
Choke/venturi	Barrel	Retread	Recap
Circlip	Snap-ring	Reverse	Back-up
Clearance	Lash	Rocker cover	Valve cover
Crownwheel	Ring gear (of differential)	Saloon	Sedan
Damper	Shock absorber, shock	Seized	Frozen
Disc (brake)	Rotor/disk	Sidelight	Parking light
Distance piece	Spacer	Silencer	Muffler
Drop arm	Pitman arm	Sill panel (beneath doors)	Rocker panel
Drop head coupe	Convertible	Small end, little end	Piston pin or wrist pin
Dynamo	Generator (DC)	Spanner	Wrench
Earth (electrical)	Ground	Split cotter (for valve spring cap)	Lock (for valve spring retainer)
Engineer's blue	Prussian blue	Split pin	Cotter pin
Estate car	Station wagon	Steering arm	Spindle arm
Exhaust manifold	Header	Sump	Oil pan
Fault finding/diagnosis	Troubleshooting	Swarf	Metal chips or debris
Float chamber	Float bowl	Tab washer	Tang or lock
Free-play	Lash	Tappet	Valve lifter
Freewheel	Coast	Thrust bearing	Throw-out bearing
Gearbox	Transmission	Top gear	High
Gearchange	Shift	Torch	Flashlight
Grub screw	Setscrew, Allen screw	Trackrod (of steering)	Tie-rod (or connecting rod)
Gudgeon pin	Piston pin or wrist pin	Trailing shoe (of brake)	Secondary shoe
Halfshaft	Axleshaft	Transmission	Whole drive line
Handbrake	Parking brake	Tyre	Tire
Hood	Soft top	Van	Panel wagon/van
Hot spot	Heat riser	Vice	Vise
Indicator	Turn signal	Wheel nut	Lug nut
Interior light	Dome lamp	Windscreen	Windshield
Layshaft (of gearbox)	Countershaft	Wing/mudguard	Fender
Leading shoe (of brake)	Primary shoe		

Conversion factors

Length (distance)

Inches (in)	X	25.4	= Millimetres (mm)	X	0.0394	= Inches (in)
Feet (ft)	X	0.305	= Metres (m)	X	3.281	= Feet (ft)
Miles	X	1.609	= Kilometres (km)	X	0.621	= Miles

Volume (capacity)

Cubic inches (cu in; in³)	X	16.387	= Cubic centimetres (cc; cm³)	X	0.061	= Cubic inches (cu in; in³)
Imperial pints (Imp pt)	X	0.568	= Litres (l)	X	1.76	= Imperial pints (Imp pt)
Imperial quarts (Imp qt)	X	1.137	= Litres (l)	X	0.88	= Imperial quarts (Imp qt)
Imperial quarts (Imp qt)	X	1.201	= US quarts (US qt)	X	0.833	= Imperial quarts (Imp qt)
US quarts (US qt)	X	0.946	= Litres (l)	X	1.057	= US quarts (US qt)
Imperial gallons (Imp gal)	X	4.546	= Litres (l)	X	0.22	= Imperial gallons (Imp gal)
Imperial gallons (Imp gal)	X	1.201	= US gallons (US gal)	X	0.833	= Imperial gallons (Imp gal)
US gallons (US gal)	X	3.785	= Litres (l)	X	0.264	= US gallons (US gal)

Mass (weight)

Ounces (oz)	X	28.35	= Grams (g)	X	0.035	= Ounces (oz)
Pounds (lb)	X	0.454	= Kilograms (kg)	X	2.205	= Pounds (lb)

Force

Ounces-force (ozf; oz)	X	0.278	= Newtons (N)	X	3.6	= Ounces-force (ozf; oz)
Pounds-force (lbf; lb)	X	4.448	= Newtons (N)	X	0.225	= Pounds-force (lbf; lb)
Newtons (N)	X	0.1	= Kilograms-force (kgf; kg)	X	9.81	= Newtons (N)

Pressure

Pounds-force per square inch (psi; lbf/in²; lb/in²)	X	0.070	= Kilograms-force per square centimetre (kgf/cm²; kg/cm²)	X	14.223	= Pounds-force per square inch (psi; lbf/in²; lb/in²)
Pounds-force per square inch (psi; lbf/in²; lb/in²)	X	0.068	= Atmospheres (atm)	X	14.696	= Pounds-force per square inch (psi; lbf/in²; lb/in²)
Pounds-force per square inch (psi; lbf/in²; lb/in²)	X	0.069	= Bars	X	14.5	= Pounds-force per square inch (psi; lbf/in²; lb/in²)
Pounds-force per square inch (psi; lbf/in²; lb/in²)	X	6.895	= Kilopascals (kPa)	X	0.145	= Pounds-force per square inch (psi; lbf/in²; lb/in²)
Kilopascals (kPa)	X	0.01	= Kilograms-force per square centimetre (kgf/cm²; kg/cm²)	X	98.1	= Kilopascals (kPa)
Millibar (mbar)	X	100	= Pascals (Pa)	X	0.01	= Millibar (mbar)
Millibar (mbar)	X	0.0145	= Pounds-force per square inch (psi; lbf/in²; lb/in²)	X	68.947	= Millibar (mbar)
Millibar (mbar)	X	0.75	= Millimetres of mercury (mmHg)	X	1.333	= Millibar (mbar)
Millibar (mbar)	X	0.401	= Inches of water (inH₂O)	X	2.491	= Millibar (mbar)
Millimetres of mercury (mmHg)	X	0.535	= Inches of water (inH₂O)	X	1.868	= Millimetres of mercury (mmHg)
Inches of water (inH₂O)	X	0.036	= Pounds-force per square inch (psi; lbf/in²; lb/in²)	X	27.68	= Inches of water (inH₂O)

Torque (moment of force)

Pounds-force inches (lbf in; lb in)	X	1.152	= Kilograms-force centimetre (kgf cm; kg cm)	X	0.868	= Pounds-force inches (lbf in; lb in)
Pounds-force inches (lbf in; lb in)	X	0.113	= Newton metres (Nm)	X	8.85	= Pounds-force inches (lbf in; lb in)
Pounds-force inches (lbf in; lb in)	X	0.083	= Pounds-force feet (lbf ft; lb ft)	X	12	= Pounds-force inches (lbf in; lb in)
Pounds-force feet (lbf ft; lb ft)	X	0.138	= Kilograms-force metres (kgf m; kg m)	X	7.233	= Pounds-force feet (lbf ft; lb ft)
Pounds-force feet (lbf ft; lb ft)	X	1.356	= Newton metres (Nm)	X	0.738	= Pounds-force feet (lbf ft; lb ft)
Newton metres (Nm)	X	0.102	= Kilograms-force metres (kgf m; kg m)	X	9.804	= Newton metres (Nm)

Power

Horsepower (hp)	X	745.7	= Watts (W)	X	0.0013	= Horsepower (hp)

Velocity (speed)

Miles per hour (miles/hr; mph)	X	1.609	= Kilometres per hour (km/hr; kph)	X	0.621	= Miles per hour (miles/hr; mph)

Fuel consumption*

Miles per gallon, Imperial (mpg)	X	0.354	= Kilometres per litre (km/l)	X	2.825	= Miles per gallon, Imperial (mpg)
Miles per gallon, US (mpg)	X	0.425	= Kilometres per litre (km/l)	X	2.352	= Miles per gallon, US (mpg)

Temperature

Degrees Fahrenheit = (°C x 1.8) + 32   Degrees Celsius (Degrees Centigrade; °C) = (°F - 32) x 0.56

*It is common practice to convert from miles per gallon (mpg) to litres/100 kilometres (l/100km), where mpg (Imperial) x l/100 km = 282 and mpg (US) x l/100 km = 235

Index